W9-CHS-587

"A little gem... A classic love triangle." —Publishers Weekly

SOMETIMES EVEN TWO'S A CROWD

Christie and Bethany are back to pimp their comic at the LAC, this time to a delightfully large crowd of loyal fans who read it online. These two will be the stars this year! But with all this confidence-boosting attention, will Christie finally have the guts to ask Matt out? And even more importantly, does she have the patience to make the relationship work?

DRAMACON

VOL 3

FOR MORE INFORMATION VISIT: WWW.T

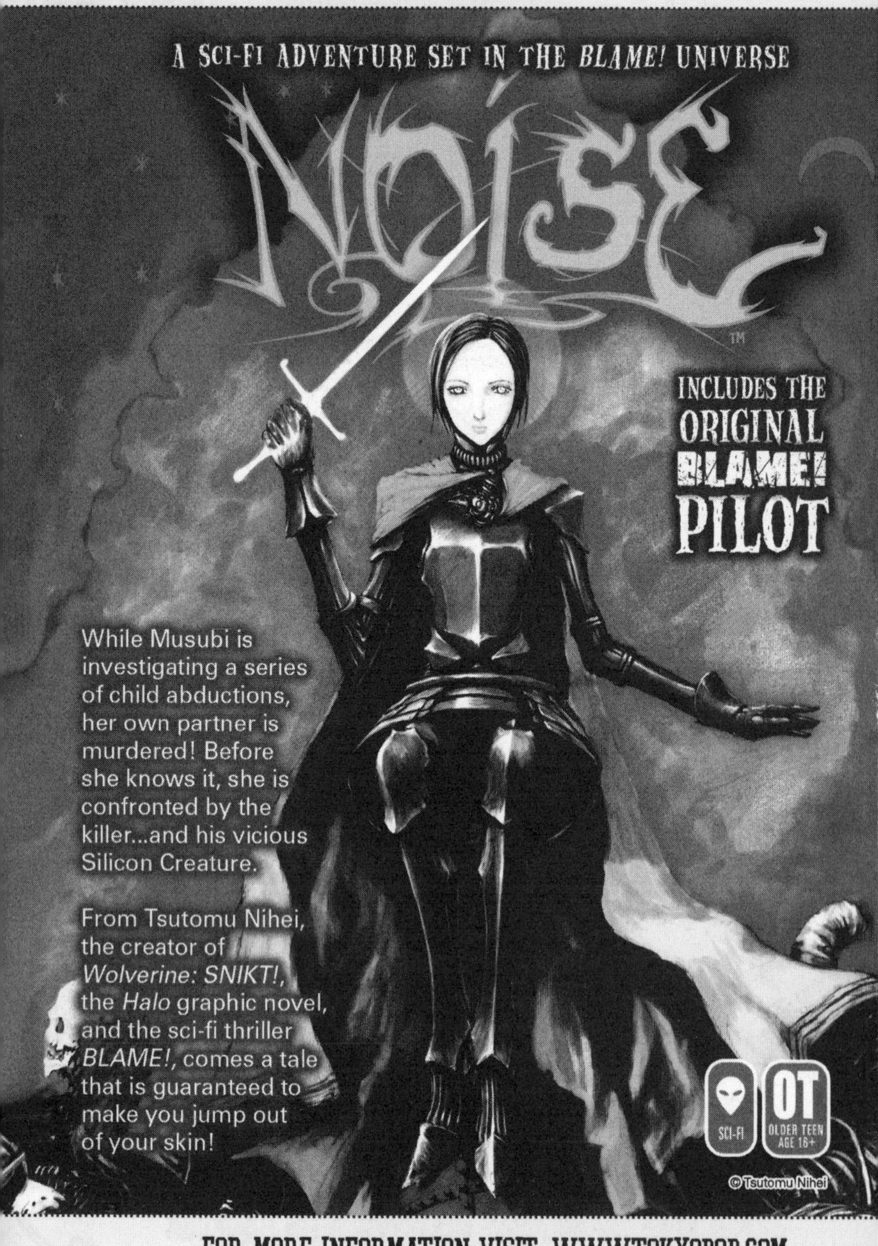
A SCI-FI ADVENTURE SET IN THE *BLAME!* UNIVERSE
NOISE™
INCLUDES THE ORIGINAL BLAME! PILOT
While Musubi is investigating a series of child abductions, her own partner is murdered! Before she knows it, she is confronted by the killer...and his vicious Silicon Creature.
From Tsutomu Nihei, the creator of *Wolverine: SNIKT!*, the *Halo* graphic novel, and the sci-fi thriller *BLAME!*, comes a tale that is guaranteed to make you jump out of your skin!
SCI-FI
OT OLDER TEEN AGE 16+
© Tsutomu Nihei

STOP!

This is the back of the book.
You wouldn't want to spoil a great ending!

This book is printed "manga-style," in the authentic Japanese right-to-left format. Since none of the artwork has been flipped or altered, readers get to experience the story just as the creator intended. You've been asking for it, so TOKYOPOP® delivered: authentic, hot-off-the-press, and far more fun!

DIRECTIONS

If this is your first time reading manga-style, here's a quick guide to help you understand how it works.

It's easy... just start in the top right panel and follow the numbers. Have fun, and look for more 100% authentic manga from TOKYOPOP®!

MISSING™

KAMIKAKUSHI NO MONOGATARI

2

ANYONE WHO MEETS *HER* DISAPPEARS

When Kyoichi, a.k.a. "His Majesty, Lord of Darkness," disappears, his friends in the Literature Club suspect he's been spirited away by a girl posing as his girlfriend. Their desperate investigation quickly spirals into a paranormal nightmare, where a fate worse than death waits on the "other side"...

© Gakuto Coda and Rei Mutsuki/Media Works

FOR MORE INFORMATION VISIT: WWW.TOKYOPOP.COM

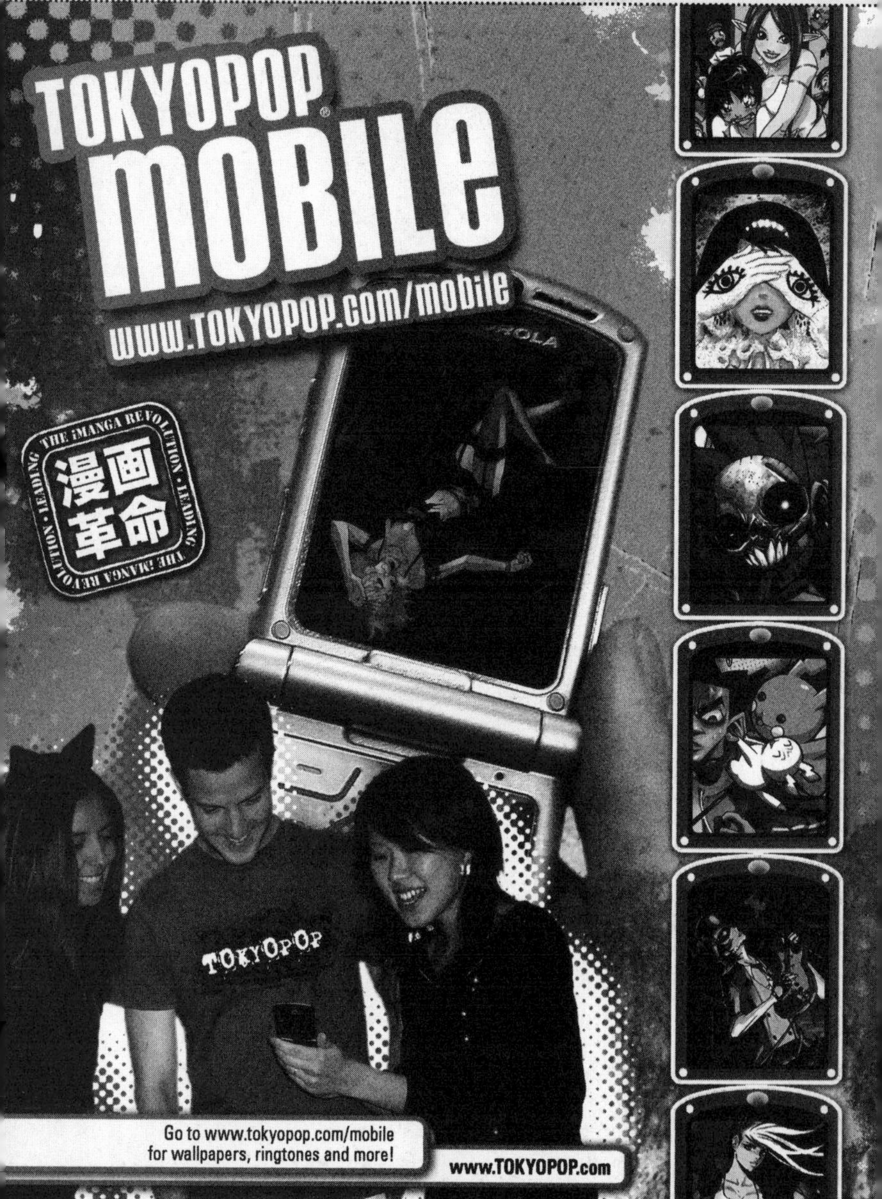
TOKYOPOP® MOBILE
www.TOKYOPOP.com/mobile
THE MANGA REVOLUTION · LEADING
漫画革命
LEADING · THE MANGA REVOLUTION
TOKYOPOP
Go to www.tokyopop.com/mobile
for wallpapers, ringtones and more!
www.TOKYOPOP.com

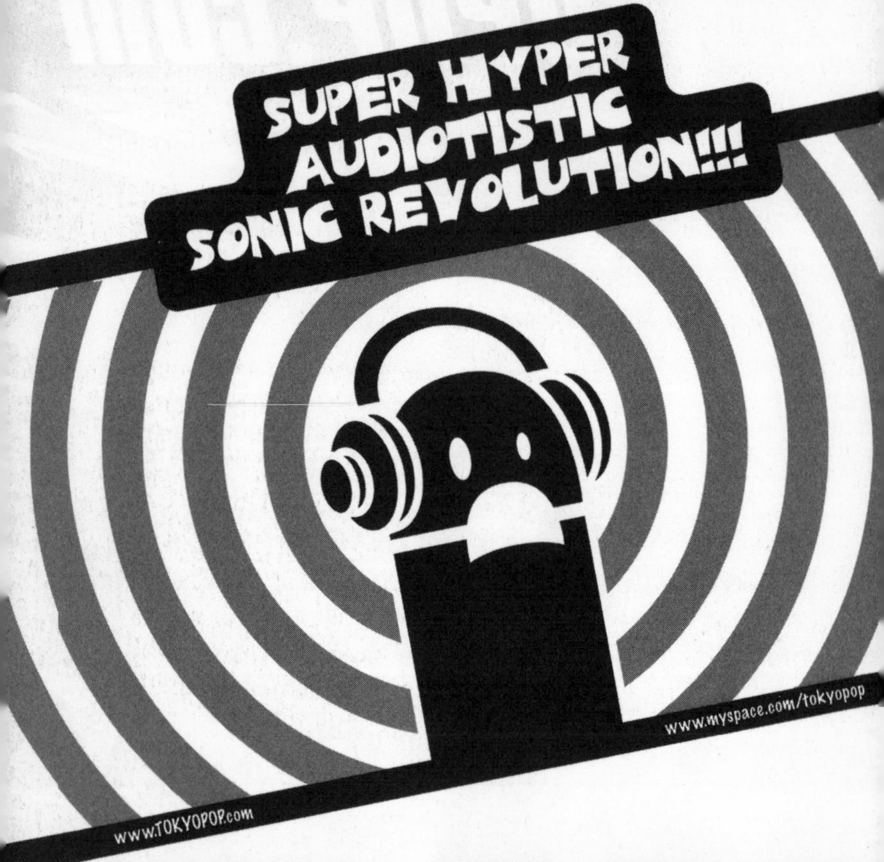
SUPER HYPER
AUDIOTISTIC
SONIC REVOLUTION!!!
www.myspace.com/tokyopop
www.TOKYOPOP.com

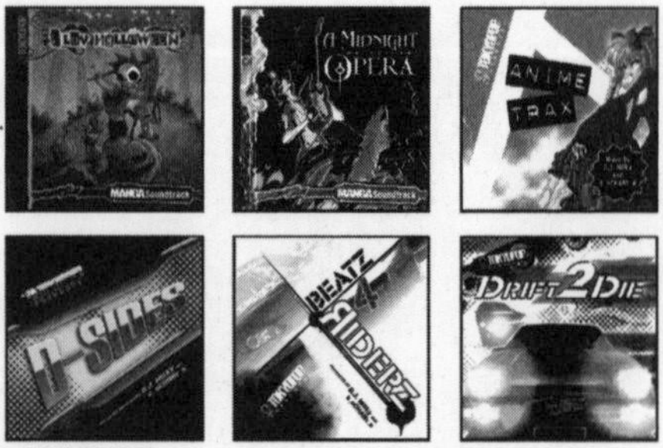
A MIDNIGHT OPERA
ANIME TRAX
DRIFT 2 DIE

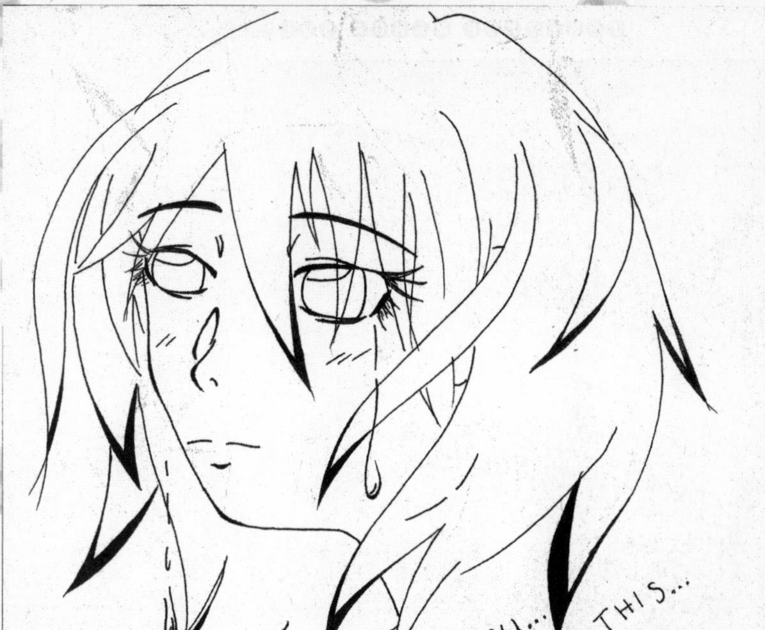
IM SORRY HARU...
I HAVE TO DO THIS...
TO SAVE THE WORLD...
TO SAVE YOU...
I LOVE YOU...
good bye...

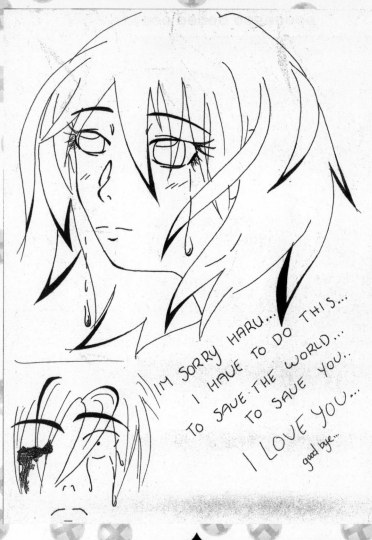

FINALLY, WE HAVE A REALLY MOVING PREDICTION OF THE FUTURE FROM LEAH. LEAH BELIEVES ELIE WILL USE HER POWER TO SAVE THE WORLD, SACRIFICING HER LIFE IN THE PROCESS. WHILE WE THINK THAT'S A VERY POWERFUL, EMOTIONAL ENDING--LET'S HOPE IT ENDS ON A HAPPIER NOTE THAN THAT! BUT ONLY TIME WILL TELL IF LEAH IS RIGHT...! GOOD JOB!

LEAH S.
AGE 16
WHARTON, NJ

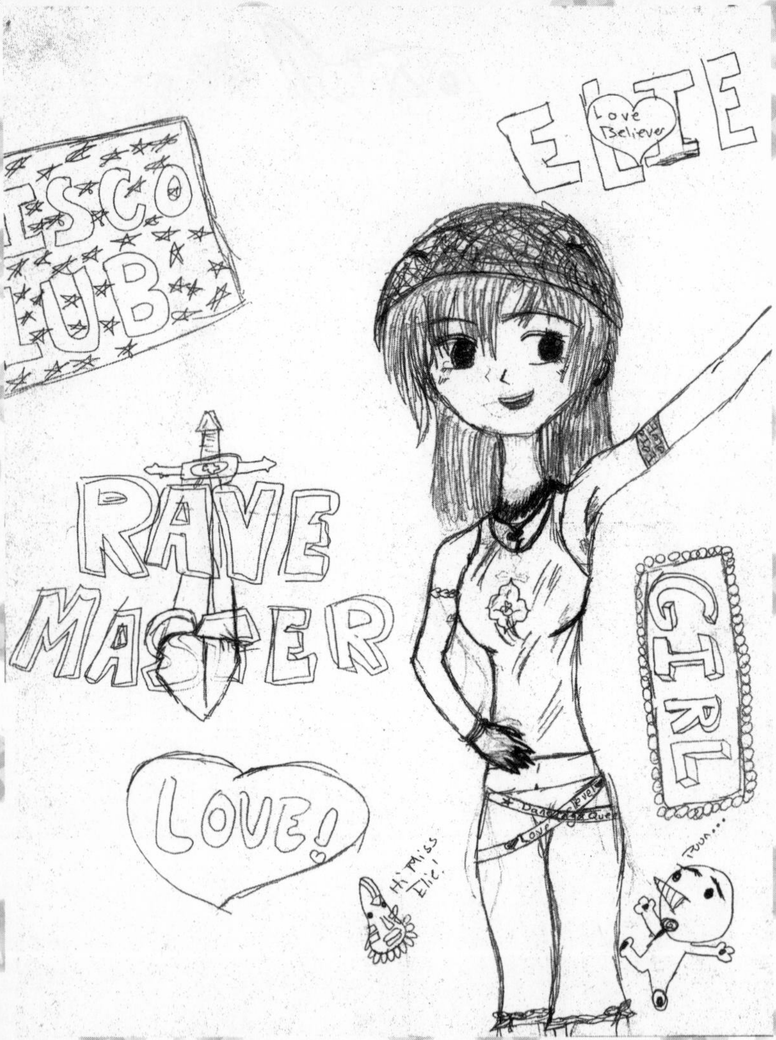
ELIE
Love Believer
SCO
UB
RAVE MASTER
GIRL
LOVE!
Hi Miss Elie!
Puuu...

HERE WE HAVE ART FROM A NEWLY CONVERTED RAVE MASTER FAN! IT'S COOL THAT YOU WANNA BE A WRITER, KAITLIN. IF YOUR WRITING IS HALF AS GOOD AS YOUR ART, YOU'RE DEFINITELY ON TRACK FOR HAVING YOUR OWN BOOK SOMEDAY! SO KEEP WORKING AT IT!

KAITLIN A.
AGE 12
CORONA, CA

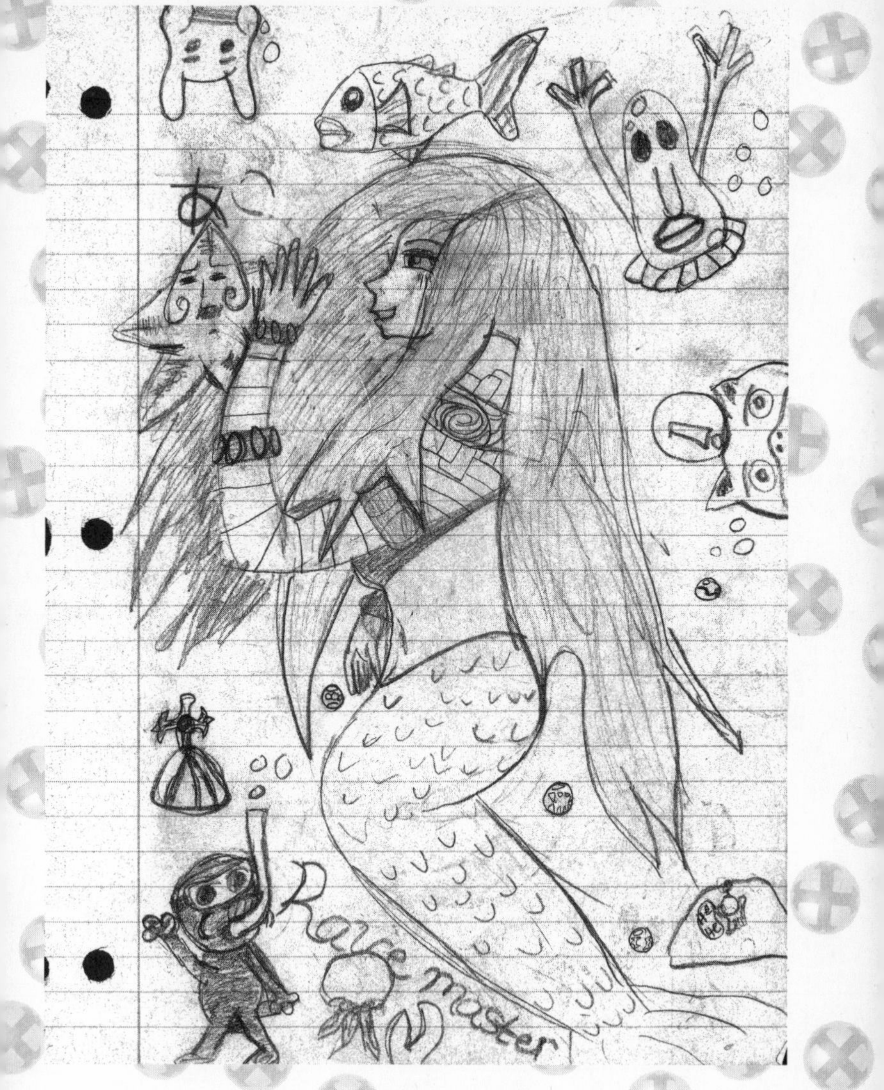
Rave master

UP NEXT WE HAVE A PICTURE OF CELIA HANGING OUT WITH HER PALS UNDER THE SEA! GOOD ONE, MIKYLA!

MIKYLA M.
AGE 12
OREGON CITY, OR

RAREGROOVE

GLORY

HERE'S A COOL PROFILE SHOT OF HARU AND SEIG. GOOD WORK, LIL!

LILIKOIFISH
AGE 12
MANHATTAN BEACH, CA

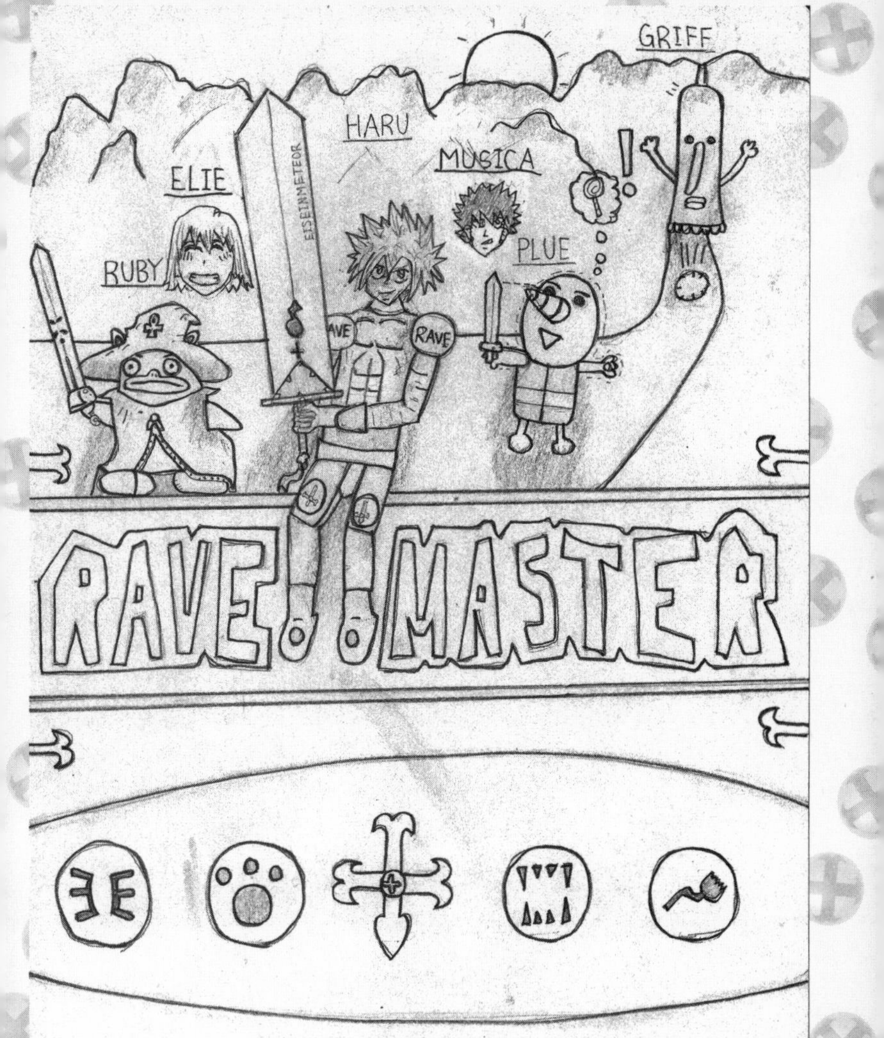
GRIFF
HARU
MUSICA
ELIE
EISEINMETEOR
RUBY
PLUE
RAVE
RAVE
RAVE MASTER

IN THIS ONE WE HAVE A COOL GROUP PICTURE. NICE LINE WORK, ELI!

ELI N.
AGE 13
BURNABY, B.C.,CAN

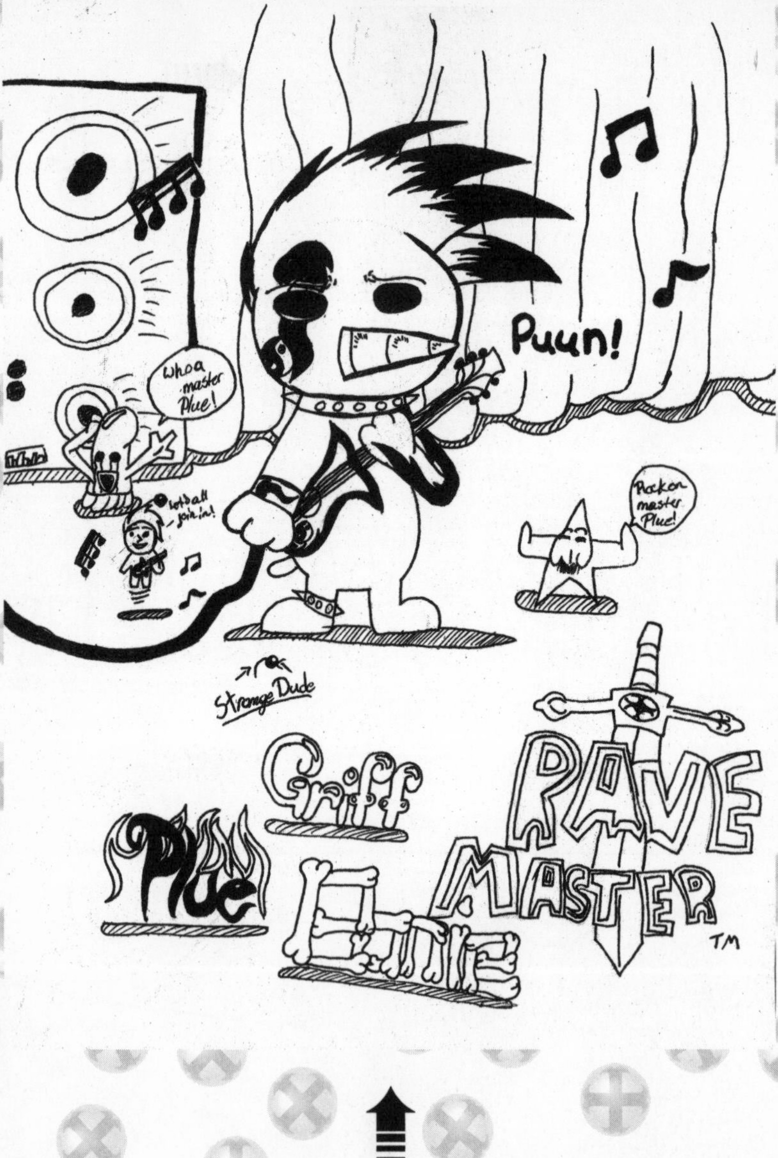
Whoa master Plue!
Let's all join in!
Puun!
Rock on master Plue!
Strange Dude
Griff
Plue
Elie
RAVE MASTER
TM

ROCK ON, PLUE!! HE'S WEARING HIS WAR PAINT, HE'S HOLDING HIS AXE--NOW LET'S BOOGIE! PLUE'S NEVER LOOKED SO STYLISH, TANAYA!

TANAYA C.
AGE 13
BOUNDARY CREEK NB, CAN

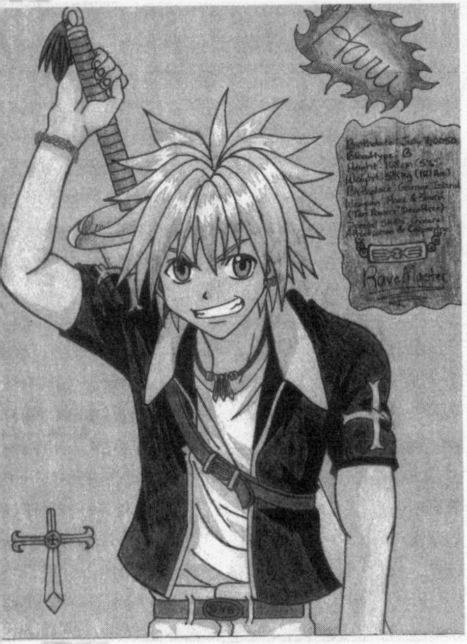
Haru
Rave Master

HERE ARE TWO FANTASTIC PICS FROM ATHENA! ONE FEATURES HARU...

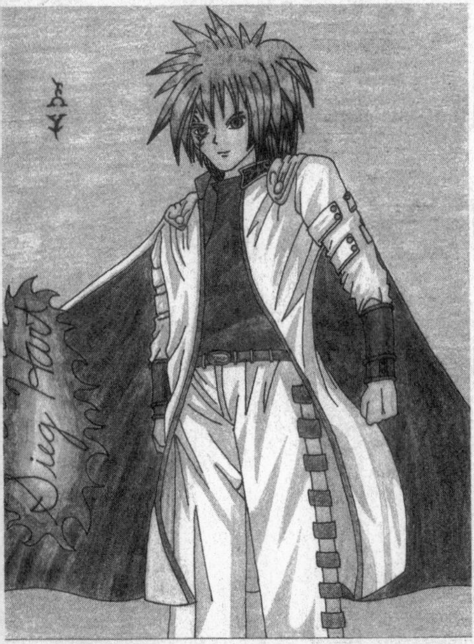
Sieg Hart

...AND THE OTHER HAS A VERY COOL-LOOKING SIEG! THESE PICTURES ARE AMAZING! GOOD JOB, ATHENA!

ATHENA A.
AGE 17
VICTORVILLE, CA

RAVE MASTER

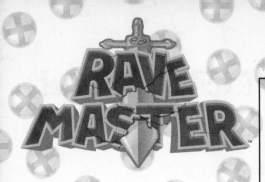

Fan Art

HEY, ASPIRING MANGA ARTIST! WANT TO SEE YOUR PICTURES IN PRINT? WELL, IF YOU THINK YOU CAN DRAW A COOL-LOOKING HARU, A SEXY ELIE OR A FUNNY PLUE, SEND 'EM THIS WAY! WHAT DO YOU HAVE TO LOSE? NOTHING!

HOW TO SUBMIT:

1) SEND YOUR WORK VIA REGULAR MAIL (NOT E-MAIL) TO:

RAVE MASTER FAN ART
C/O TOKYOPOP
5900 WILSHIRE BLVD.
SUITE 2000
LOS ANGELES, CA 90036

2) ALL WORK SUBMITTED SHOULD BE IN BLACK-AND-WHITE AND NO LARGER THAT 8.5" X 11.5". (AND TRY NOT TO FOLD IT TOO MANY TIMES)

3) ANYTHING YOU SEND WILL NOT BE RETURNED. IF YOU WANT TO KEEP YOUR ORIGINAL, IT'S FINE TO SEND US A COPY.

4) PLEASE INCLUDE YOUR FULL NAME, AGE, CITY AND STATE FOR US TO PRINT WITH YOUR WORK. IF YOU'D RATHER WE USE A PEN NAME, PLEASE INCLUDE THAT, TOO.

5) IMPORTANT: IF YOU'RE UNDER THE AGE OF 18, YOU MUST HAVE YOUR PARENT'S PERMISSION IN ORDER FOR US TO PRINT YOUR WORK. ANY SUBMISSION WITHOUT A SIGNED NOTE OR PARENTAL CONSENT CANNOT BE USED.

6) FOR FULL DETAILS, PLEASE CHECK OUT HTTP://WWW.TOKYOPOP.COM/ABOUTUS/FANART.PHP

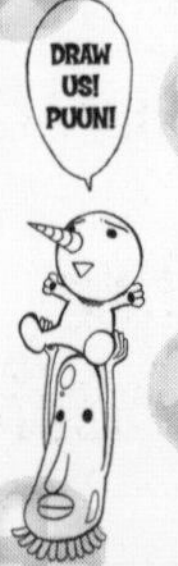
DRAW US! PUUN!

DISCLAIMER: ANYTHING YOU SEND TO US BECOMES THE PROPERTY OF TOKYOPOP INC. AND, AS WE SAID BEFORE, WILL NOT BE RETURNED TO YOU. WE WILL HAVE THE RIGHT TO PRINT, REPRODUCE, DISTRUBUTE OR MODIFY THE ARTWORK FOR USE IN FUTURE VOLUMES OF RAVE MASTER OR ON THE WEB WITHOUT PAYMENT TO YOU.

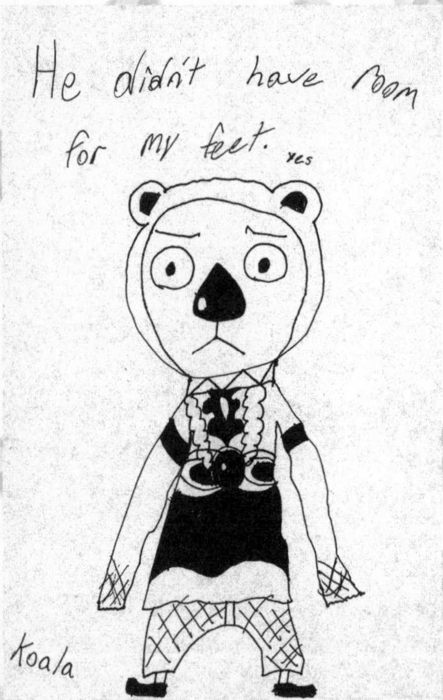
He didn't have room for my feet.
yes
Koala

FIRST UP IT'S EVERYONE'S FAVORITE FURRY BAD GUY--KOALA! HIS MIND MAY BE AS TWISTED AS A PRETZEL, BUT YOU GOTTA ADMIT HE'S NEVER LOOKED AS GOOD AS HE DOES IN THIS DRAWING. NICE ONE, DYLAN!

DYLAN S.
AGE 12
ASHBURN, VA

In the Next Exciting Volume!

RAVE MASTER

It's out of the pan and into the fire, as Belnika's latent magic powers save her and Haru from the fall, only to have them both captured by native Sentinoids! While they fight for their freedom, Julia and Let fight for their lives as they battle Hardner and his hordes of seemingly indestructible henchmen. And just when things seem their bleakest--Endless itself crashes the party! Can the Rave Master stop the Mystic Realm from being destroyed?

Rave Master Volume 27
Available March 2008

"AFTERWORDS!"
(Left-handed)

FOUR PAGES...THIS "AFTERWORDS" SECTION IS SUPPOSED TO COME WITH FOUR EXTRA PAGES! SORRY TO DISAPPOINT PEOPLE! HOPE YOU ENJOYED THE STORY.

THIS TIME, THE BATTLE HAS SHIFTED TO THE "MYSTIC REALM."

I FIGURE THERE ARE A LOT OF WAYS TO LOOK AT WHAT KIND OF PLACE IT IS, SO I WANTED T CLEAR THINGS UP A LITTLE. FIRST OF ALL, THE "GATE" IS AN INVISIBLE BORDER SEPARATIN IT FROM HARU AND FRIENDS' "HUMAN WORLD." IT'S SOME SORT OF MAGIC GATE THA ALLOWS PASSAGE INTO ANOTHER DIMENSIO (THE MYSTIC REALM) AND VICE-VERSA. HOV YOU CAN FIT ANOTHER WORLD ON THE SAM WORLD IS A LITTLE COMPLICATED.

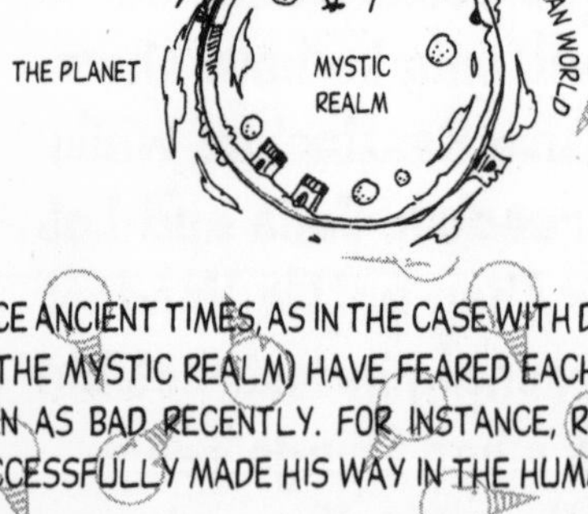
DRAMATIZATION
GATE
HUMAN WORLD
THE PLANET
MYSTIC REALM

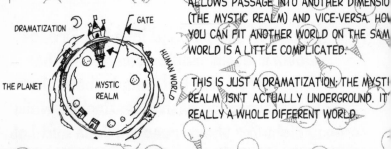

THIS IS JUST A DRAMATIZATION; THE MYSTI REALM ISN'T ACTUALLY UNDERGROUND. IT' REALLY A WHOLE DIFFERENT WORLD.

SINCE ANCIENT TIMES, AS IN THE CASE WITH DORYU, HUMANS AND SENTINOIDS (THE RESIDENT OF THE MYSTIC REALM) HAVE FEARED EACH OTHER, ALTHOUGH THOSE PROBLEMS HAVEN' BEEN AS BAD RECENTLY. FOR INSTANCE, RUBY'S FATHER, PEARL, WAS A SENTINOID WH SUCCESSFULLY MADE HIS WAY IN THE HUMAN WORLD.

THERE REALLY ARE A LOT OF TROUBLESOME LITTLE DETAILS ABOUT THIS, BUT I FEE WELL, WHATEVER. IF YOU READ ALL THIS AND END UP GOING "HMM," AND "I DON'T GET IT," IT JUST ANOTHER WORLD, AND THAT'S ALL YOU NEED TO KNOW. OKAY?

THINK OF IT LIKE THE WONDERLAND IN "ALICE IN WONDERLAND"! ONLY WITHOU HUMPTY DUMPTY.

HIRO MASHIMA

HIRO MASHIMA.

Q & A CORNER
RAVEOOQA

Q. I noticed recently that Julia's hair is longer than it used to be. It grew pretty fast.
   (Shinobu - Okahama Prefecture, and others)

A. **Yeah. Dragon Race hair grows pretty fast...actually, I hadn't noticed it was getting longer. Sorry. (^ ^;)**

Q. Tell us the origins of the BG names.
   (Sanzou Take - Aomori Prefecture)

A. **Sure. They're based on animal names in French.**
   Lunar -> Fox   Lukan -> Shark
   Giraffe -> Giraffe Leopard -> Leopard
   Koala -> Koala Reevil -> Wild Rabbit Sean -> Racoon
   All the ship names are based on birds.
   I won't spill about Hardner. It's not based on an animal, though--it's kind of special, see. (^_^)

Q. Can Leopard put on a "magic" coat with her DB?
   (Happa - Iwate Prefecture)

A. **Uh...now that you mention it...**

Q. So can you finally tell us how old Sieg Hart is? ♡ You put everything as "Unknown" in his profile.
   (Iya the Unknown - Tokyo Prefecture, and others)

A. **Actually I wrote his age and real name on a page in "Mashima-en." Why? So people who wanna know will read it.♡**
   More shameless publicity.

SPOT THE DIFFERENCES

THERE ARE TEN DIFFERENCES BETWEEN THE TOP AND BOTTOM DRAWINGS!

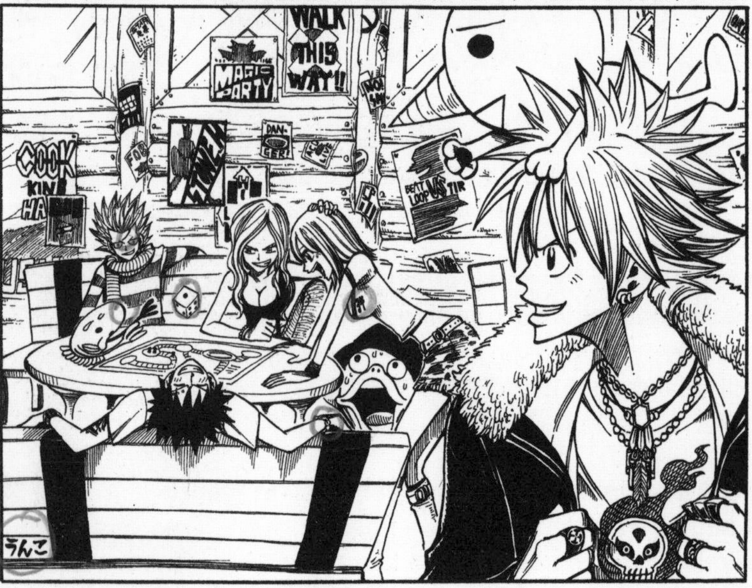
WALK THIS WAY!!
MAGIC PARTY
DAN-GER!
COOK KING HA
BEAT LOOP VS TIR
うんこ

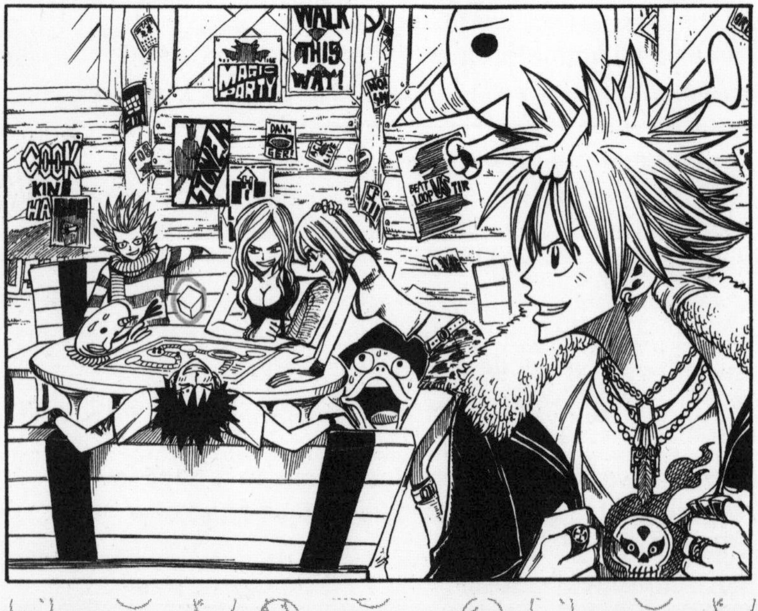
WALK THIS WAY!
MAGIC PARTY
DAN-GER!
COOK KING HA
BEAT LOOP VS TIR

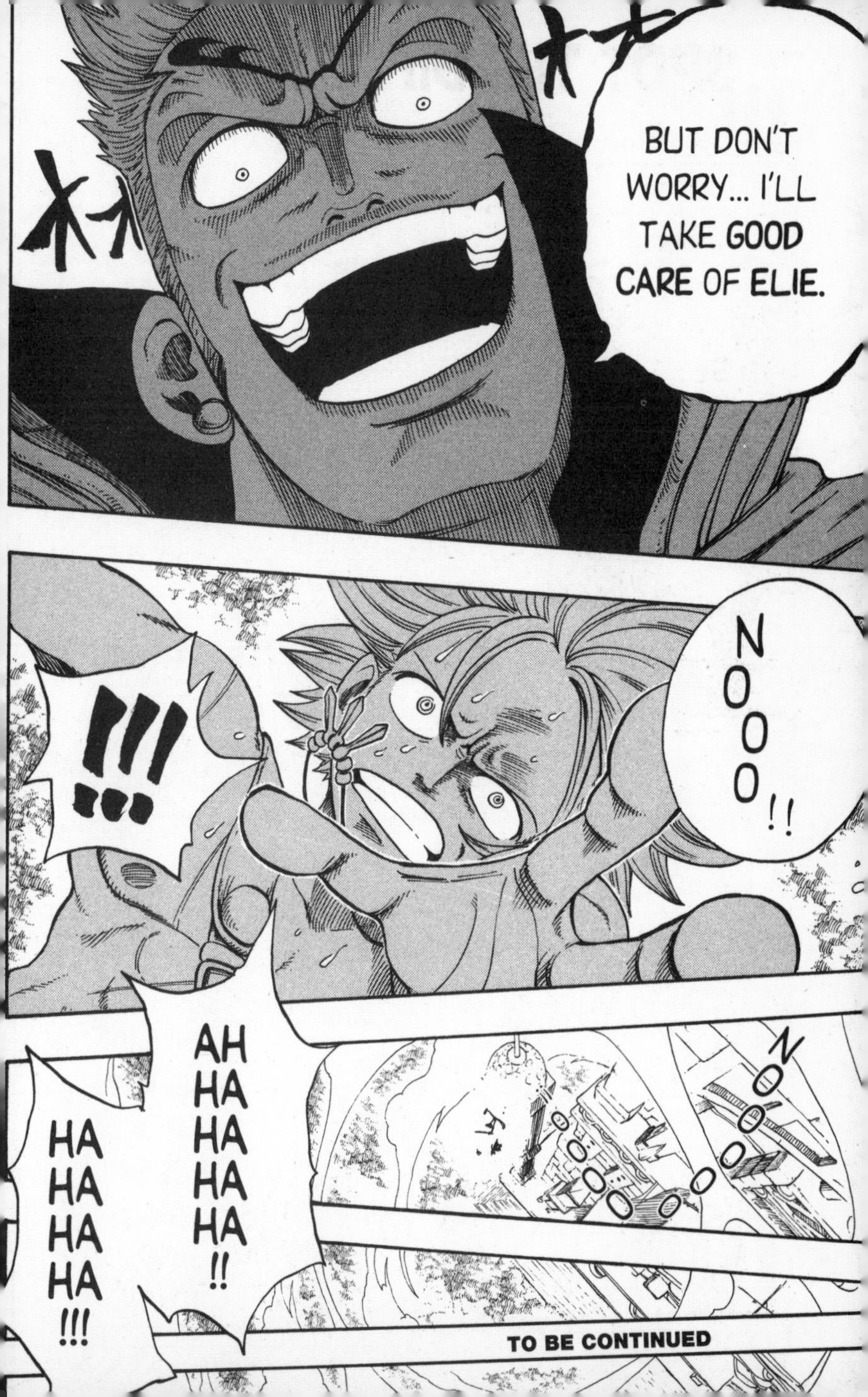
BUT DON'T WORRY... I'LL TAKE GOOD CARE OF ELIE.
NOOOO!!
!!!
NOOOOOOOOO
AH HA HA HA HA!!
HA HA HA HA!!!
TO BE CONTINUED

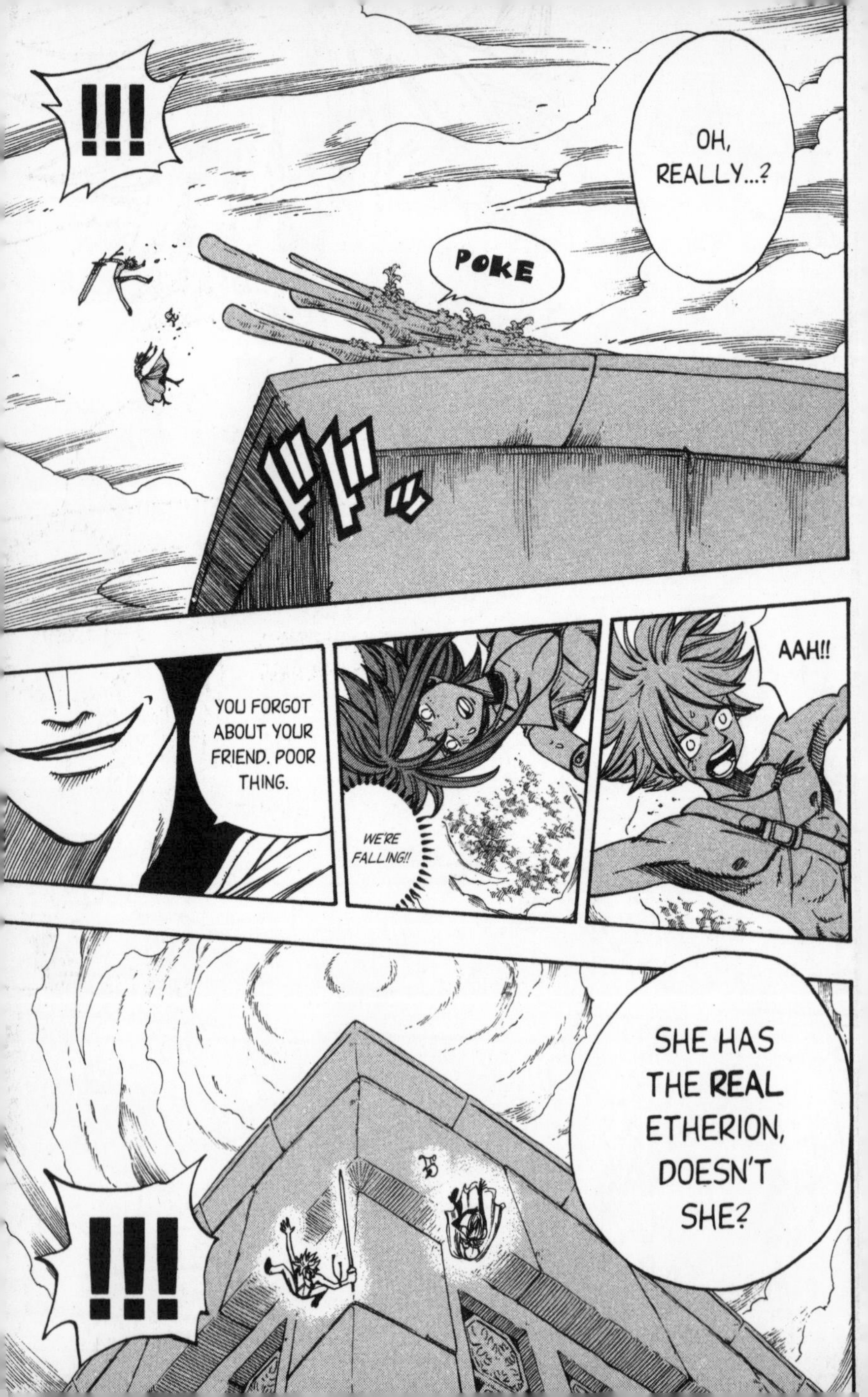
OH, REALLY...?
POKE
!!!
AAH!!
WE'RE FALLING!!
YOU FORGOT ABOUT YOUR FRIEND. POOR THING.
SHE HAS THE REAL ETHERION, DOESN'T SHE?
!!!

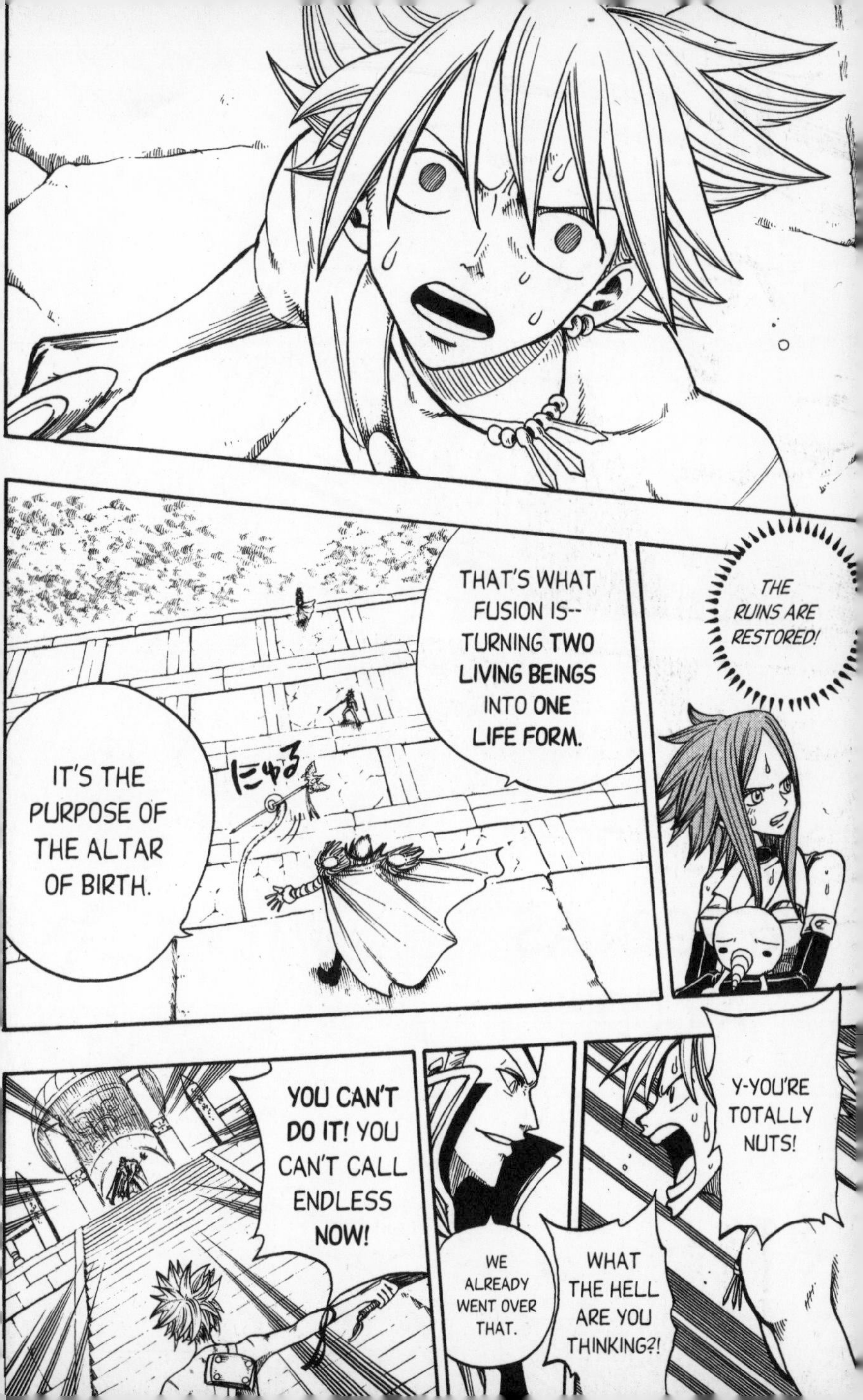
THE RUINS ARE RESTORED!
THAT'S WHAT FUSION IS-- TURNING TWO LIVING BEINGS INTO ONE LIFE FORM.
にゃる
IT'S THE PURPOSE OF THE ALTAR OF BIRTH.
Y-YOU'RE TOTALLY NUTS!
WHAT THE HELL ARE YOU THINKING?!
WE ALREADY WENT OVER THAT.
YOU CAN'T DO IT! YOU CAN'T CALL ENDLESS NOW!

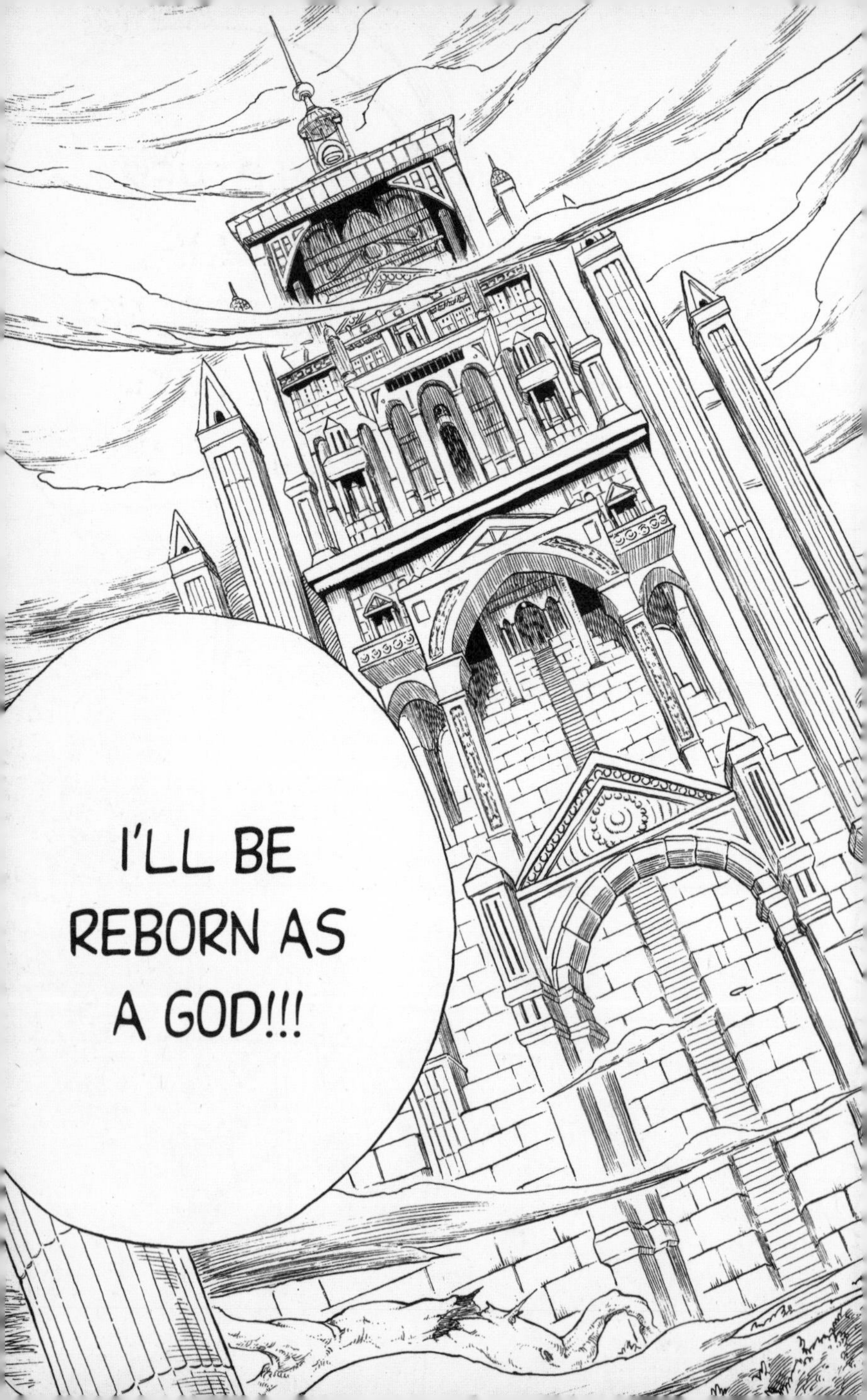
I'LL BE REBORN AS A GOD!!!

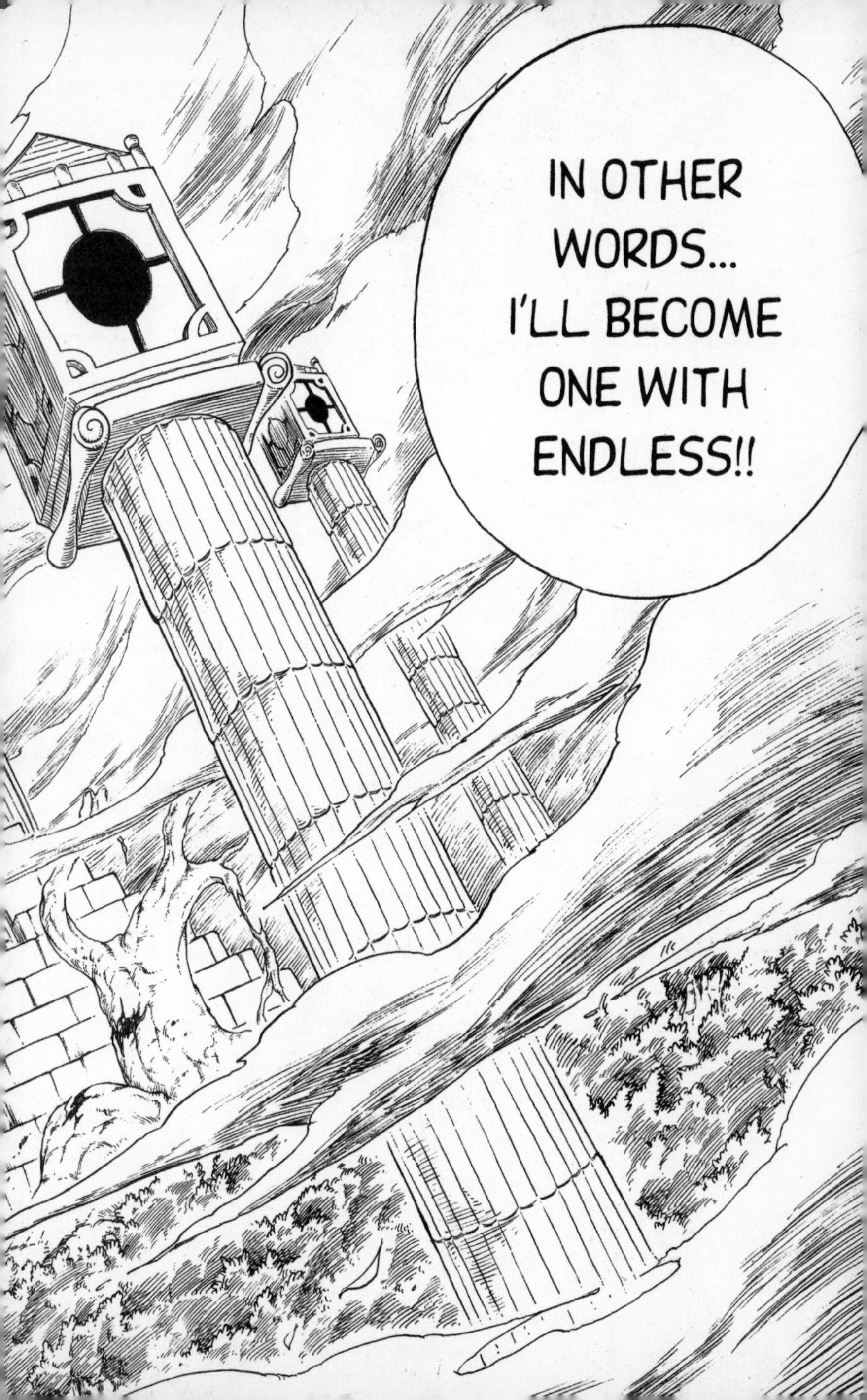
IN OTHER WORDS... I'LL BECOME ONE WITH ENDLESS!!

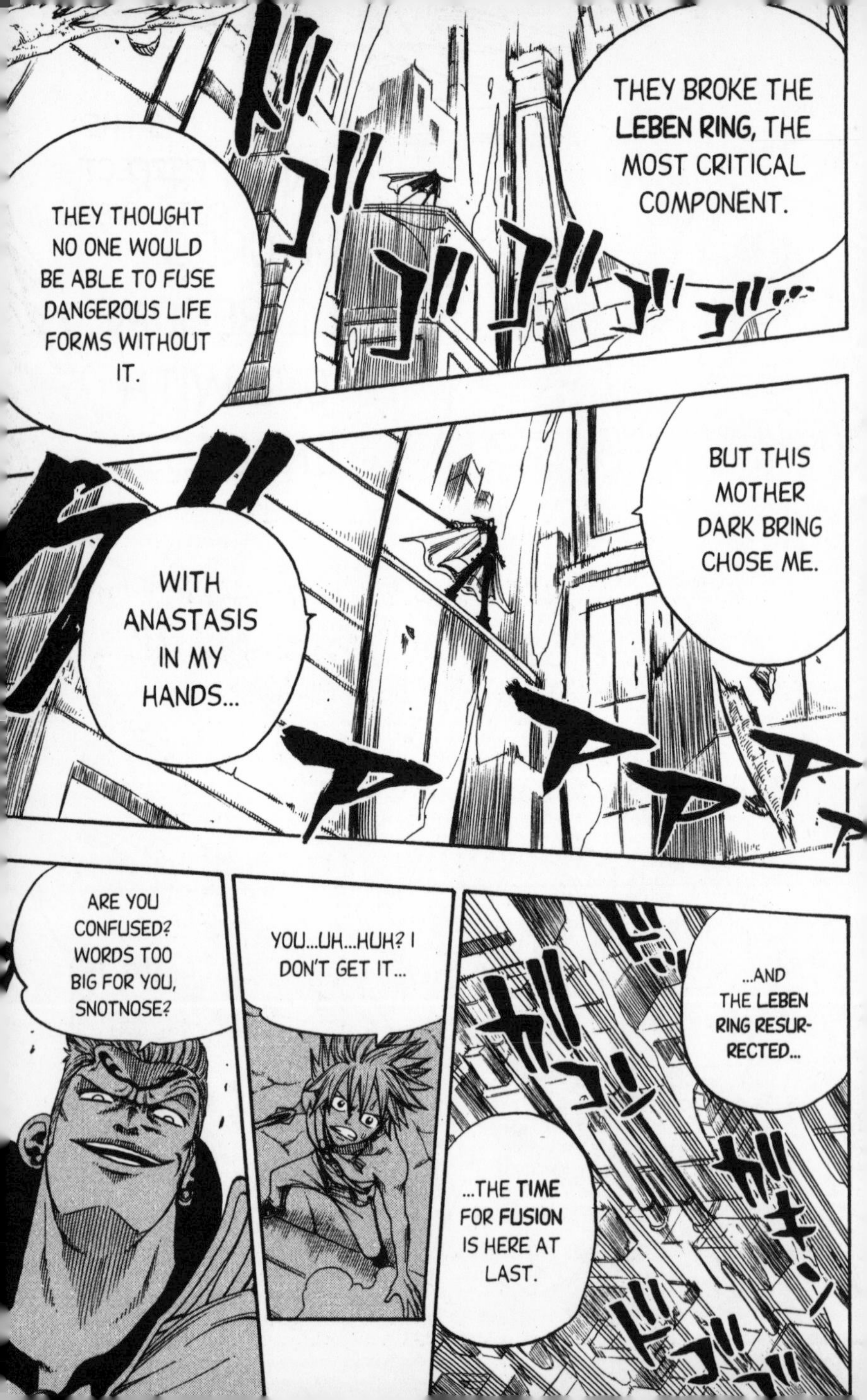
THEY BROKE THE LEBEN RING, THE MOST CRITICAL COMPONENT.
THEY THOUGHT NO ONE WOULD BE ABLE TO FUSE DANGEROUS LIFE FORMS WITHOUT IT.
BUT THIS MOTHER DARK BRING CHOSE ME.
WITH ANASTASIS IN MY HANDS...
...AND THE LEBEN RING RESURRECTED...
...THE TIME FOR FUSION IS HERE AT LAST.
YOU...UH...HUH? I DON'T GET IT...
ARE YOU CONFUSED? WORDS TOO BIG FOR YOU, SNOTNOSE?

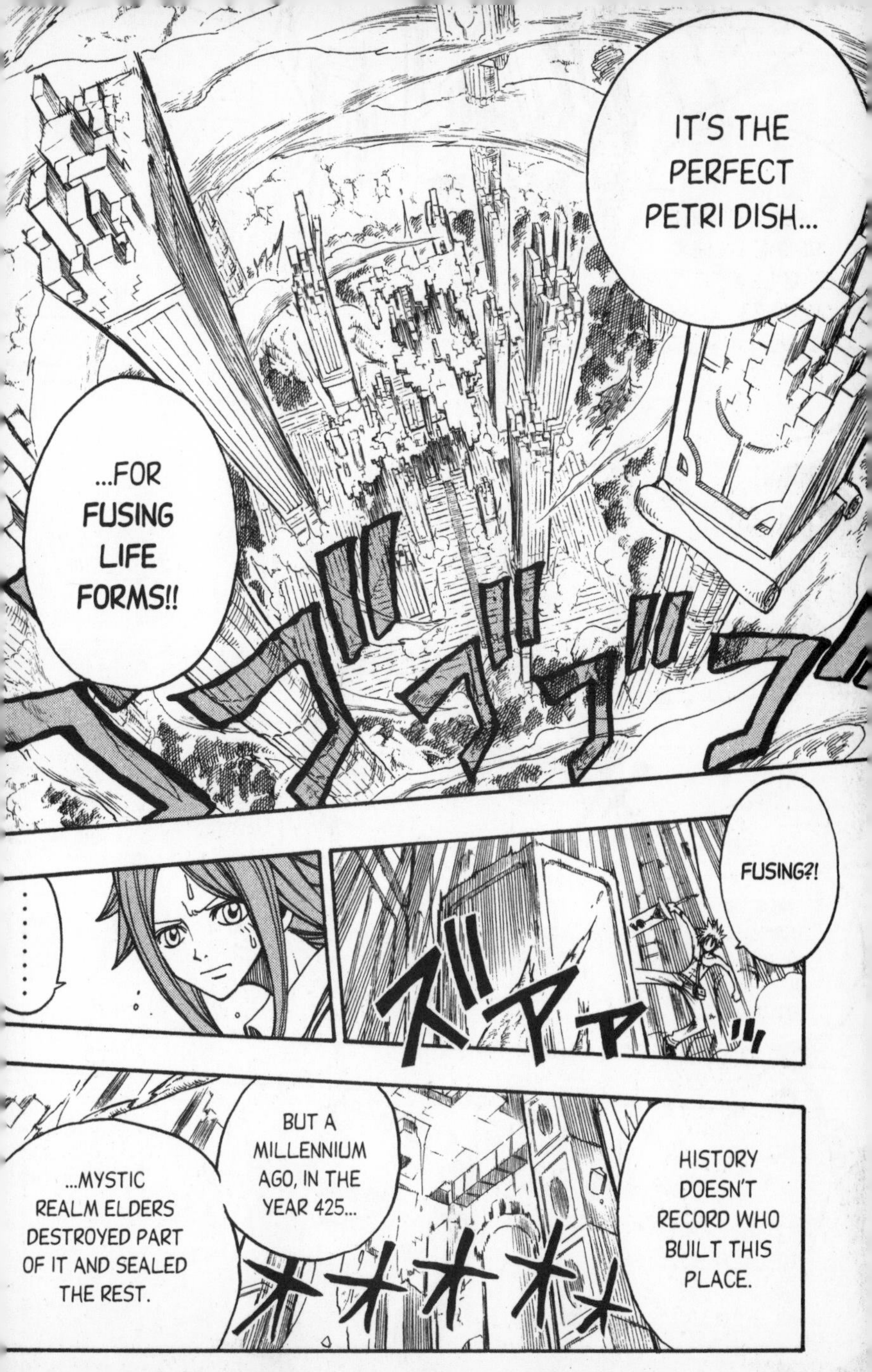
IT'S THE PERFECT PETRI DISH...
...FOR FUSING LIFE FORMS!!
FUSING?!
......
HISTORY DOESN'T RECORD WHO BUILT THIS PLACE.
BUT A MILLENNIUM AGO, IN THE YEAR 425...
...MYSTIC REALM ELDERS DESTROYED PART OF IT AND SEALED THE REST.

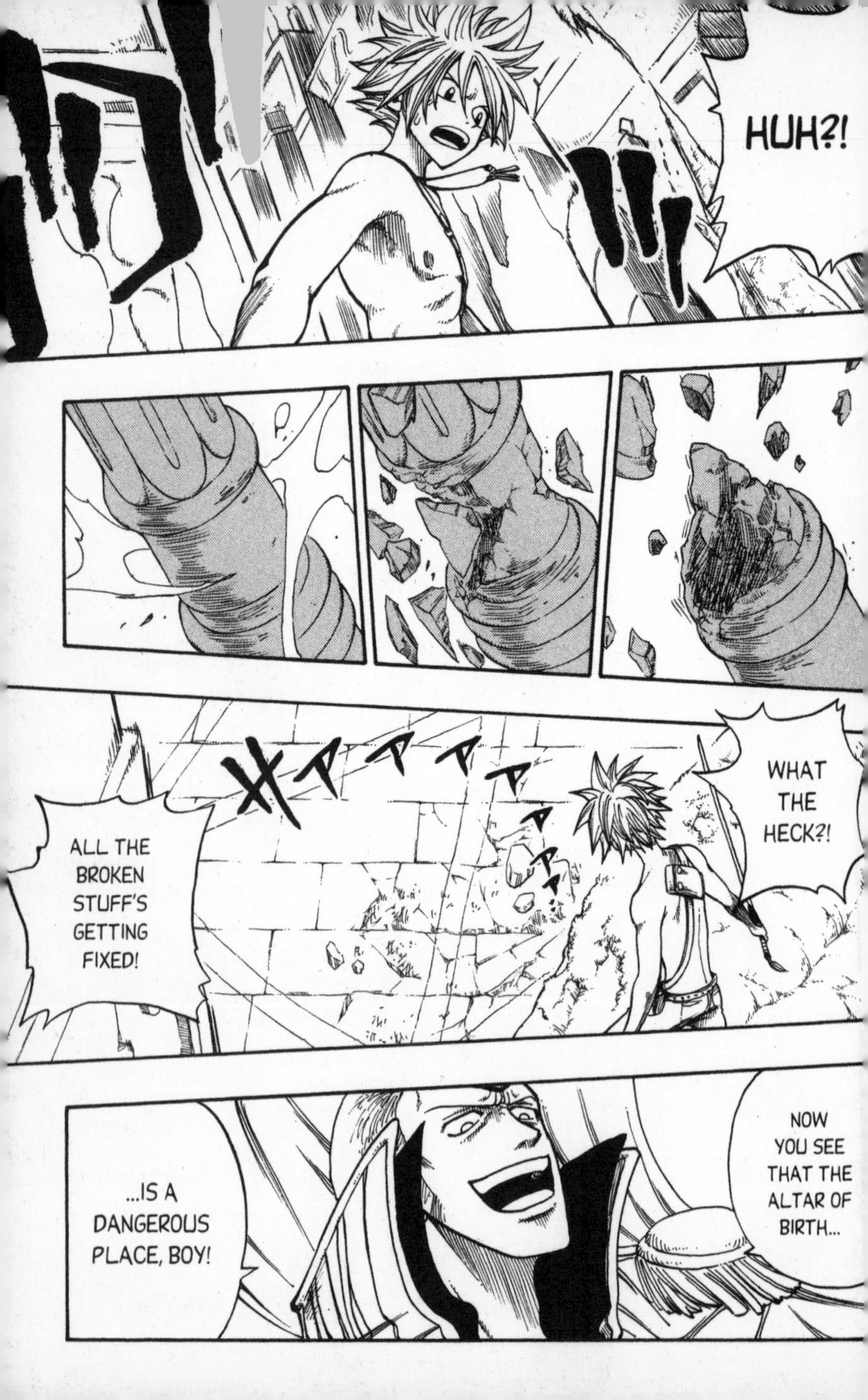
HUH?!
WHAT THE HECK?!
ALL THE BROKEN STUFF'S GETTING FIXED!
NOW YOU SEE THAT THE ALTAR OF BIRTH...
...IS A DANGEROUS PLACE, BOY!

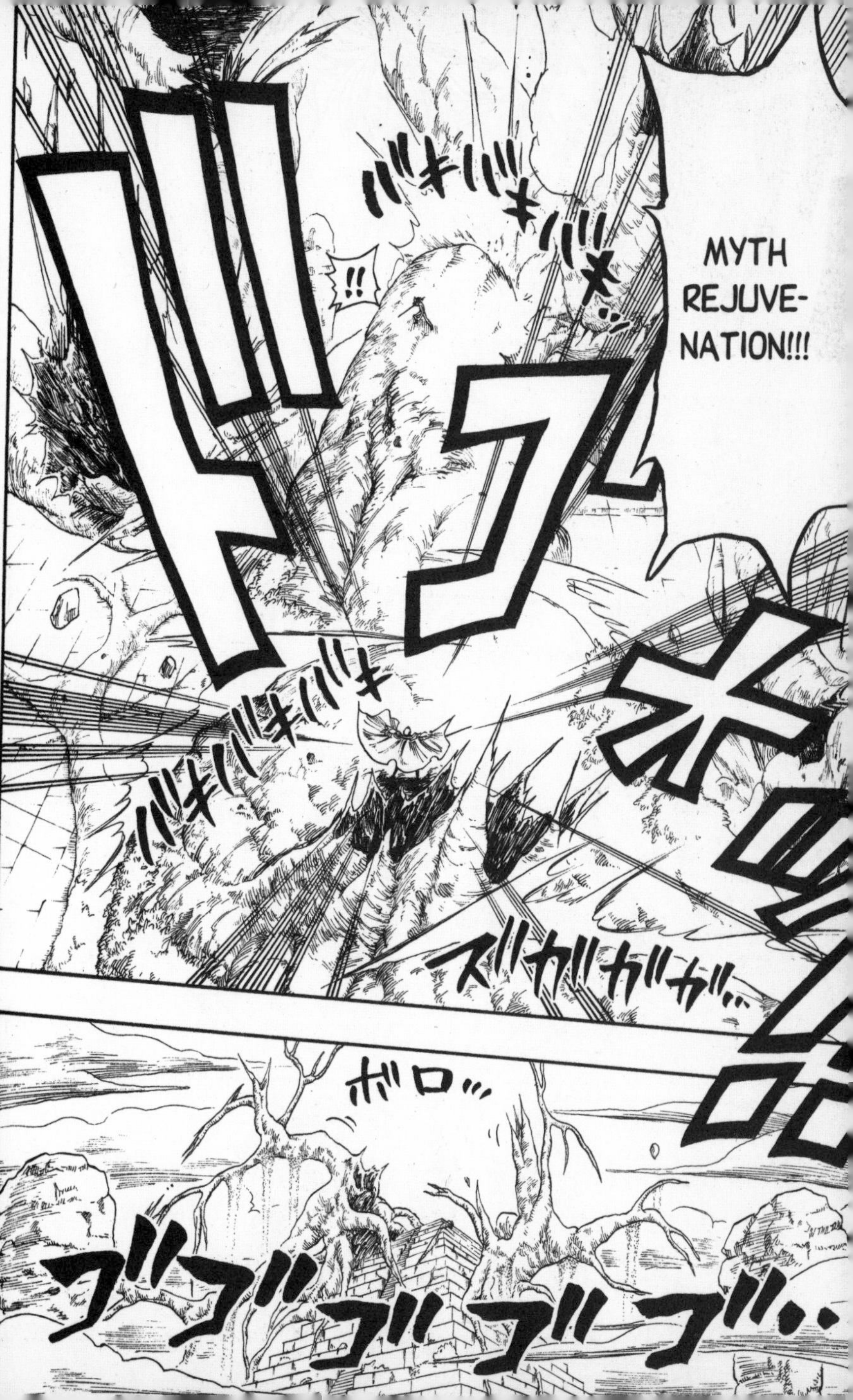
MYTH
REJUVE-
NATION!!!
バキバキ…
!!
ドン
バキバキバキ
ズガガガ…
ボロッ
ゴゴゴゴ…

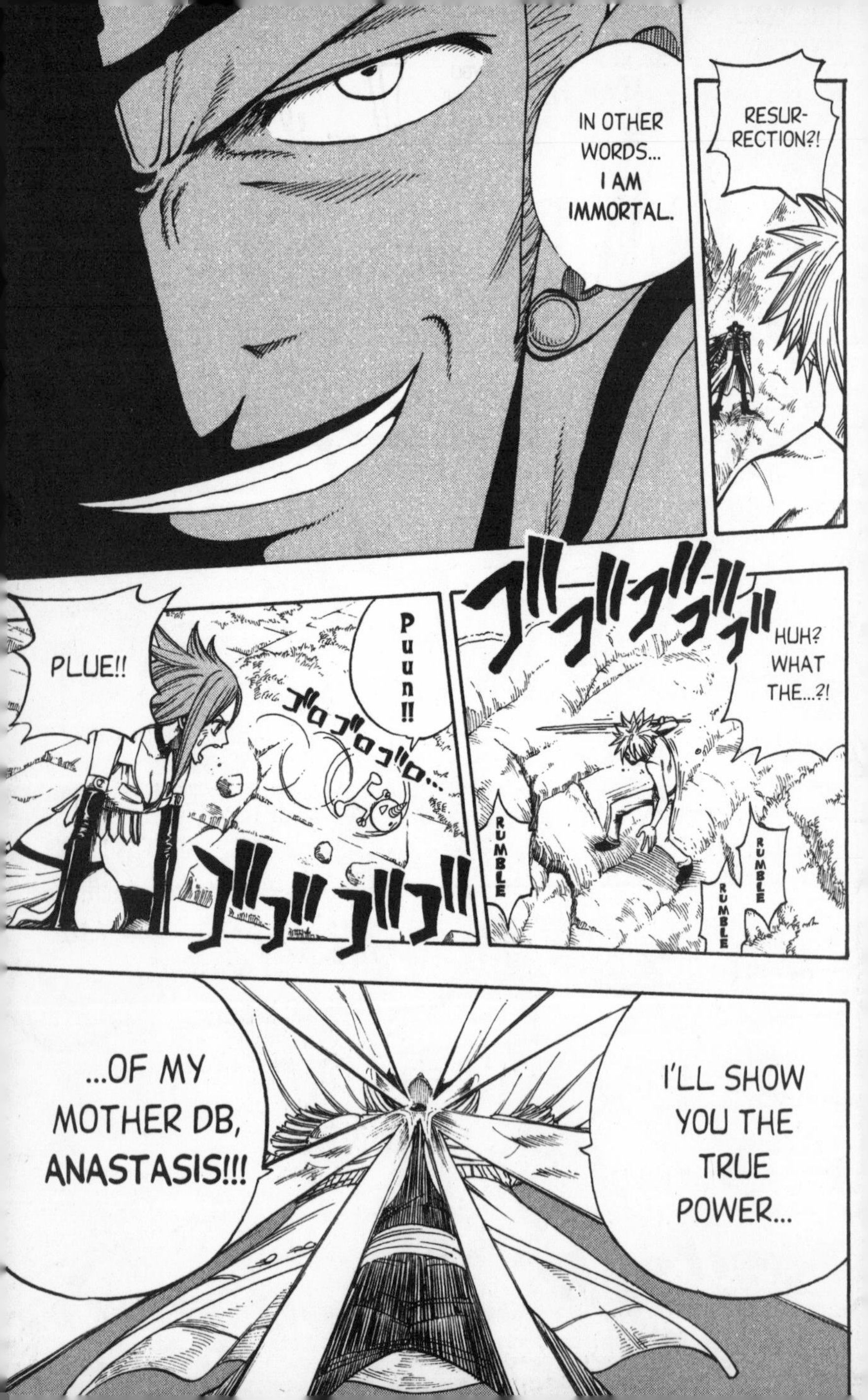
RESUR-
RECTION?!
IN OTHER WORDS... I AM IMMORTAL.
HUH? WHAT THE...?!
RUMBLE
RUMBLE
RUMBLE
Puun!!
ゴロゴロゴロ...
PLUE!!
I'LL SHOW YOU THE TRUE POWER...
...OF MY MOTHER DB, ANASTASIS!!!

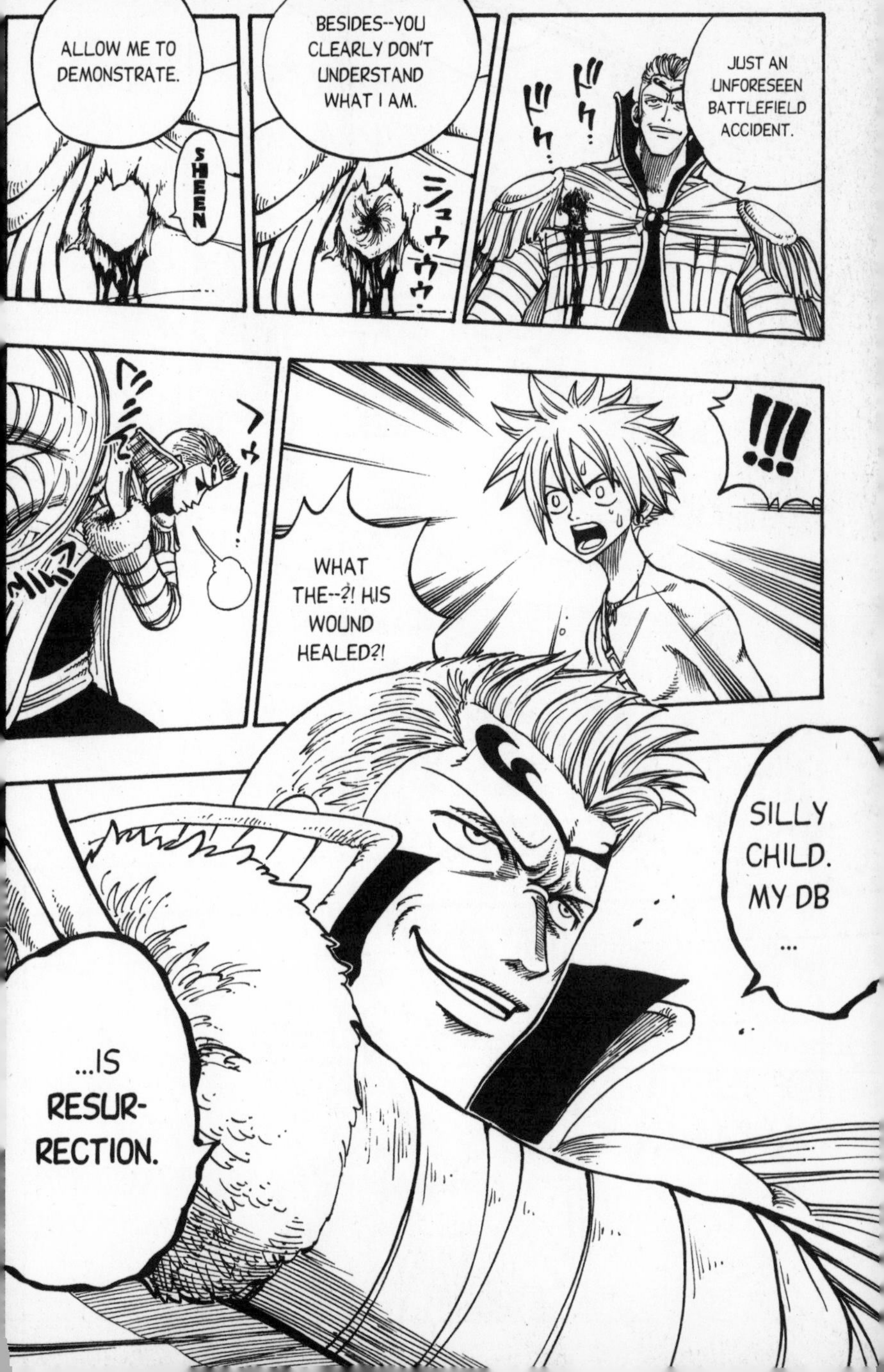
JUST AN UNFORESEEN BATTLEFIELD ACCIDENT.
BESIDES--YOU CLEARLY DON'T UNDERSTAND WHAT I AM.
ALLOW ME TO DEMONSTRATE.
SHEEN
!!!
WHAT THE--?! HIS WOUND HEALED?!
SILLY CHILD. MY DB ...
...IS RESURRECTION.

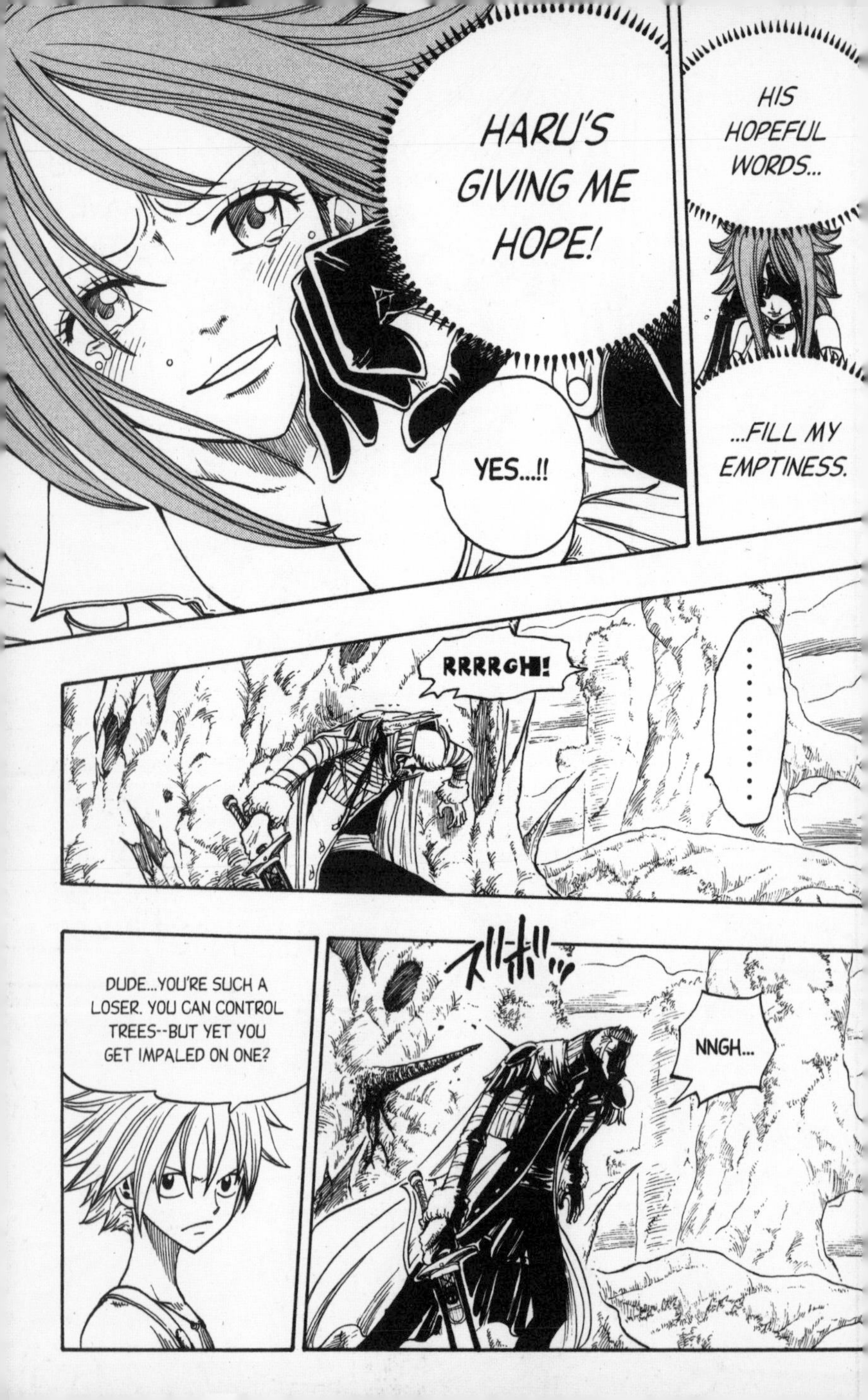
HIS HOPEFUL WORDS...
...FILL MY EMPTINESS.
HARU'S GIVING ME HOPE!
YES...!!
......
RRRRGH!
NNGH...
DUDE...YOU'RE SUCH A LOSER. YOU CAN CONTROL TREES--BUT YET YOU GET IMPALED ON ONE?

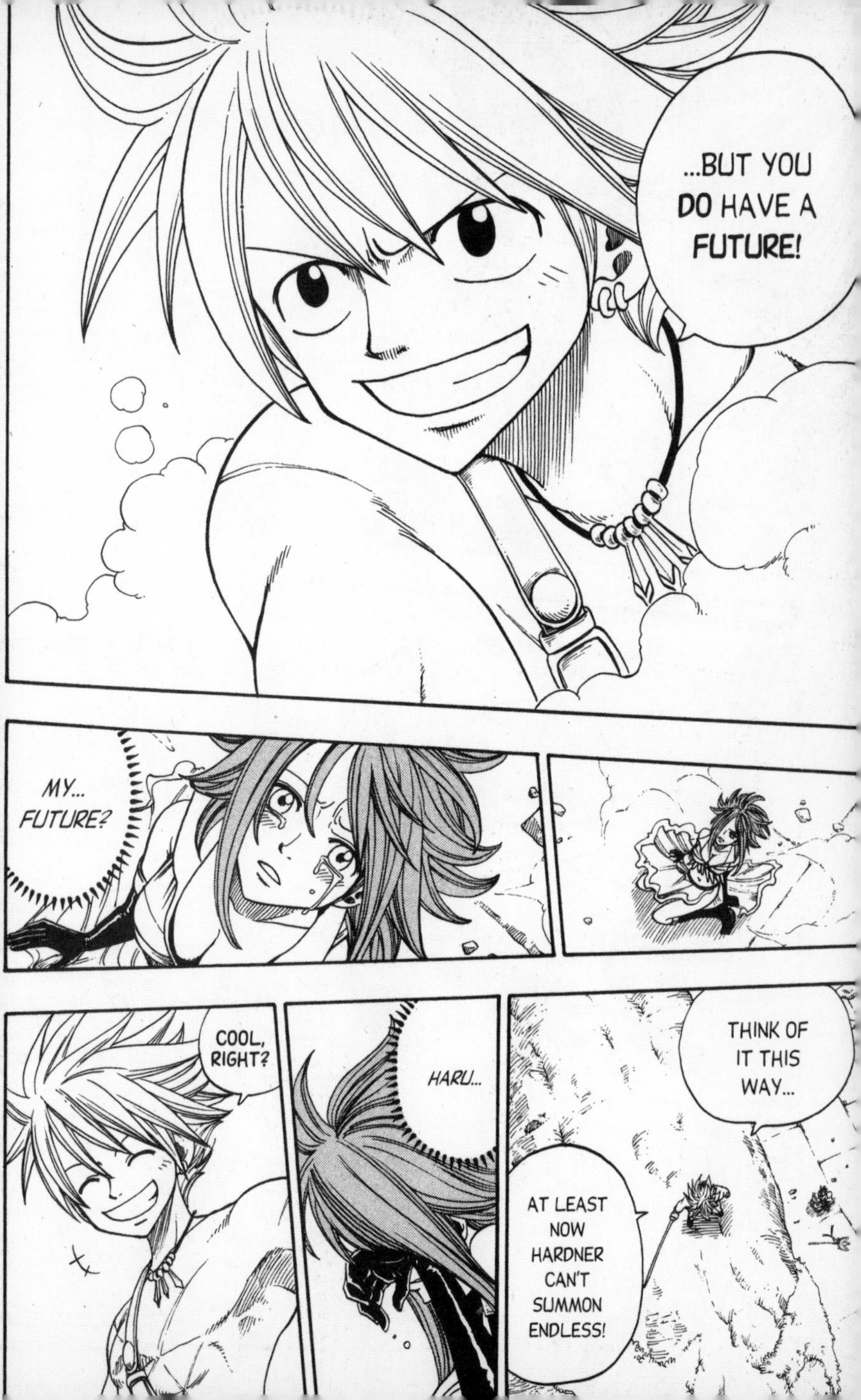
...BUT YOU DO HAVE A FUTURE!
MY... FUTURE?
THINK OF IT THIS WAY...
AT LEAST NOW HARDNER CAN'T SUMMON ENDLESS!
HARU...
COOL, RIGHT?

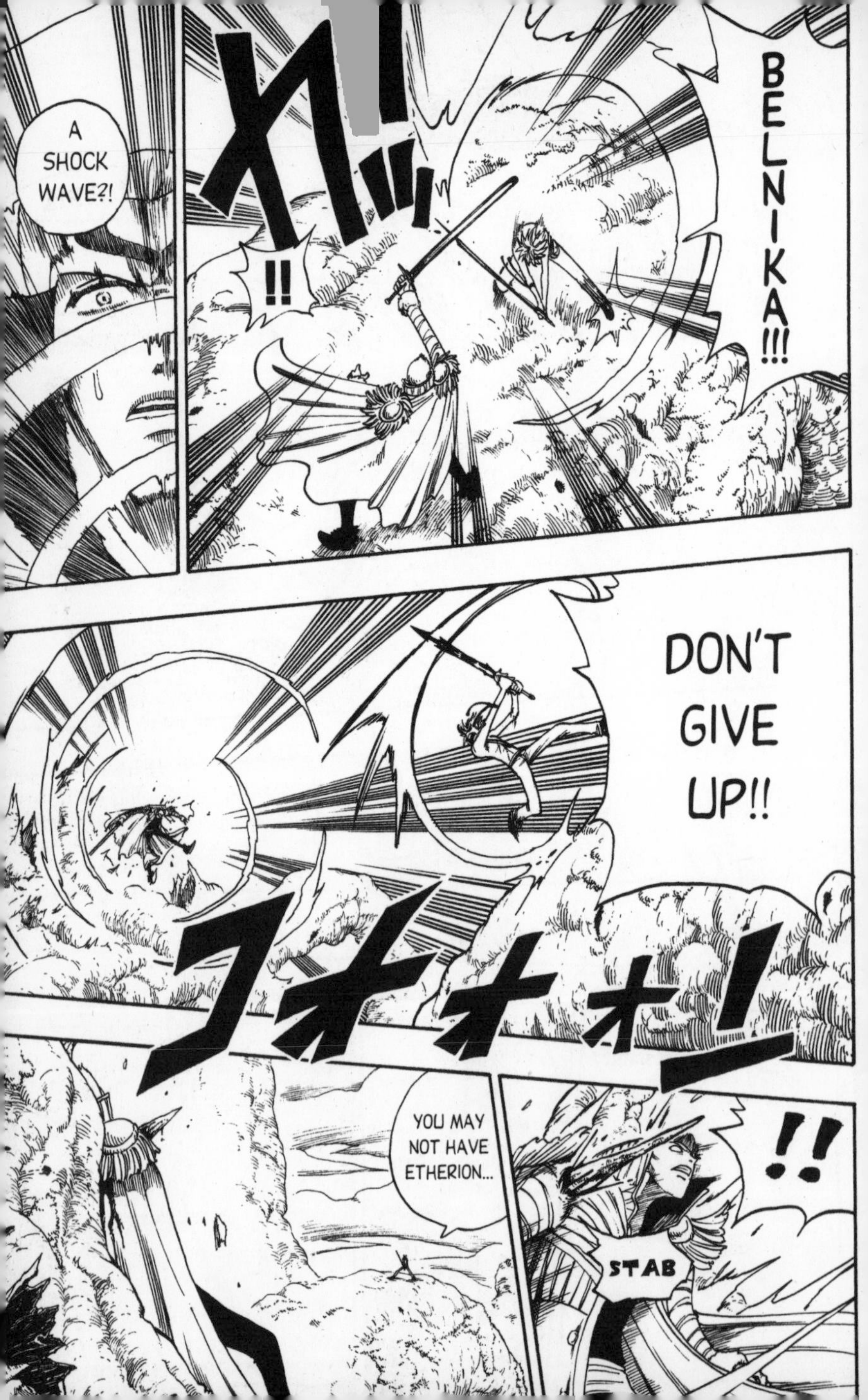
BELNIKA!!!
!!
A SHOCK WAVE?!
DON'T GIVE UP!!
!!
STAB
YOU MAY NOT HAVE ETHERION...

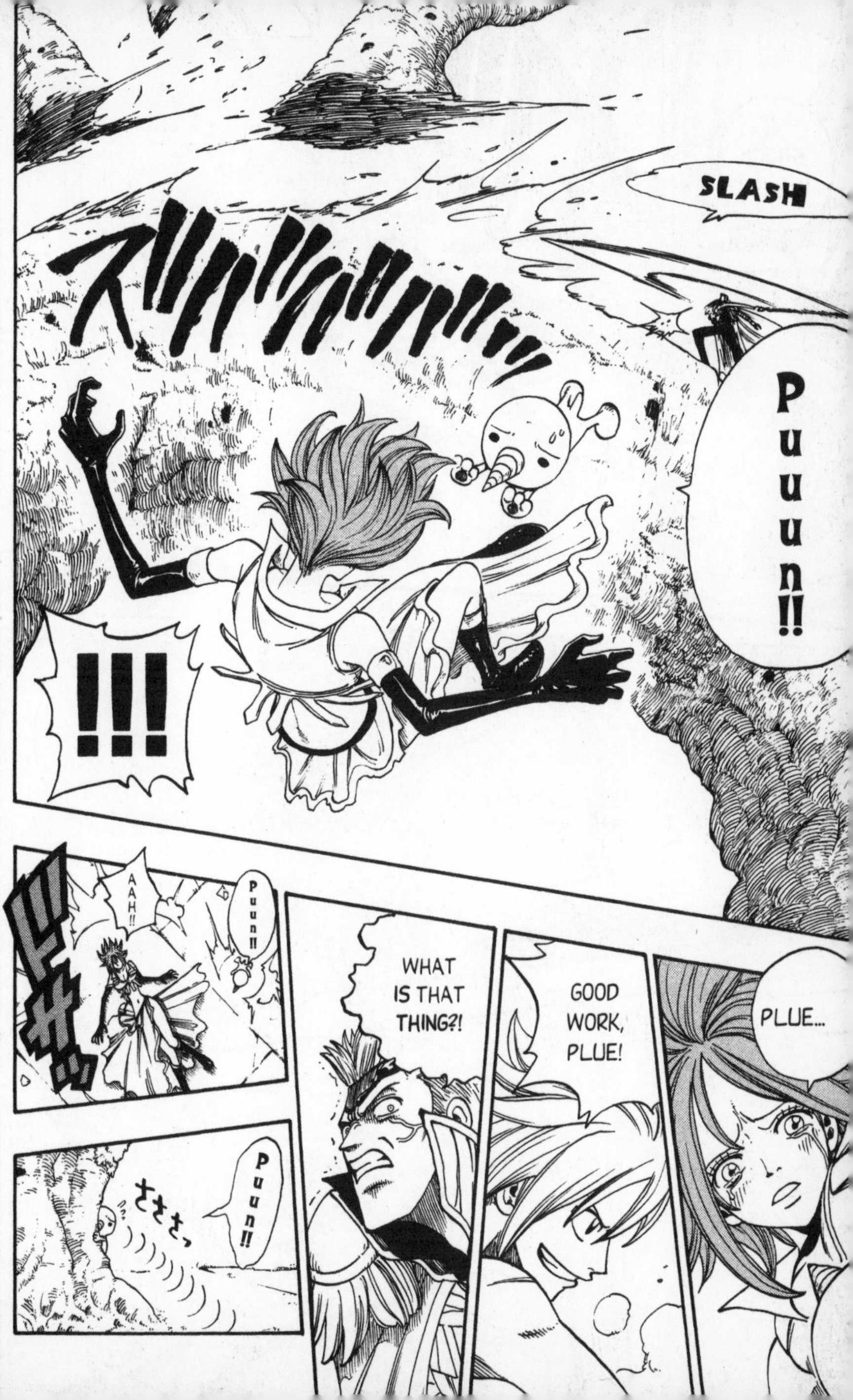

SLASH
Puuun!!
!!!
PLUE...
GOOD WORK, PLUE!
WHAT IS THAT THING?!
AAH!!
Puun!!
Puuun!!
さささっ

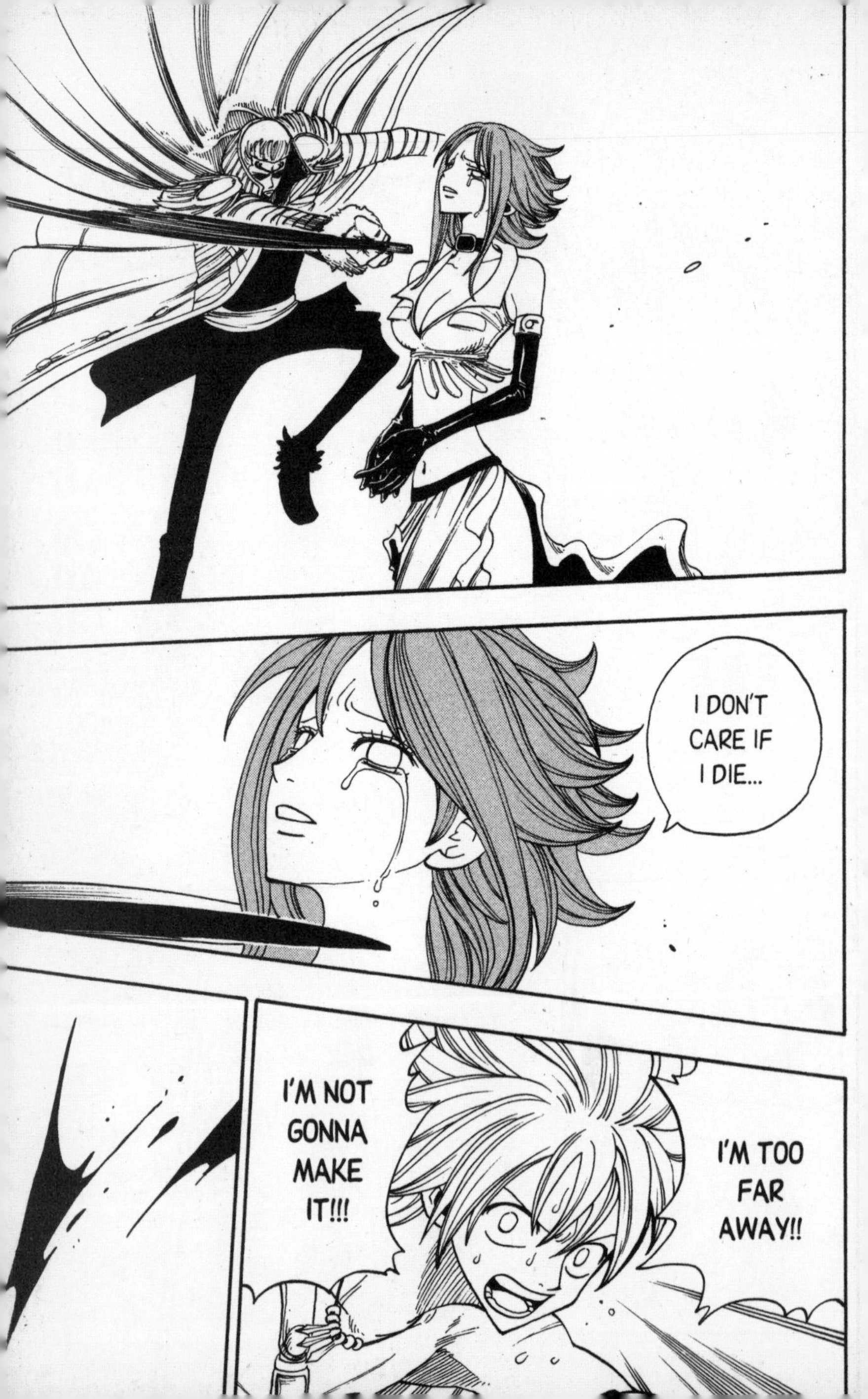
I DON'T CARE IF I DIE...
I'M TOO FAR AWAY!!
I'M NOT GONNA MAKE IT!!!

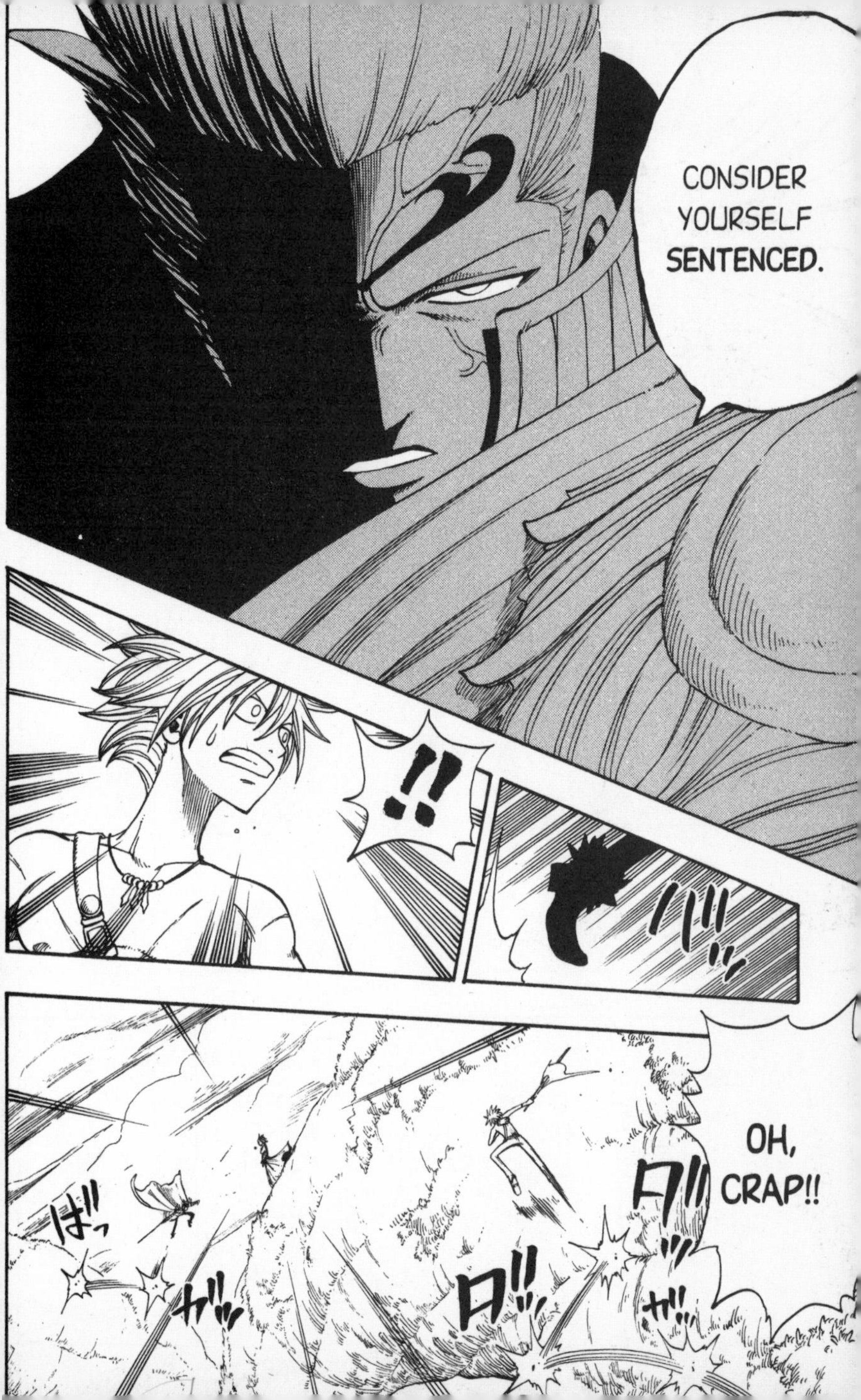
CONSIDER YOURSELF SENTENCED.
!!
OH, CRAP!!

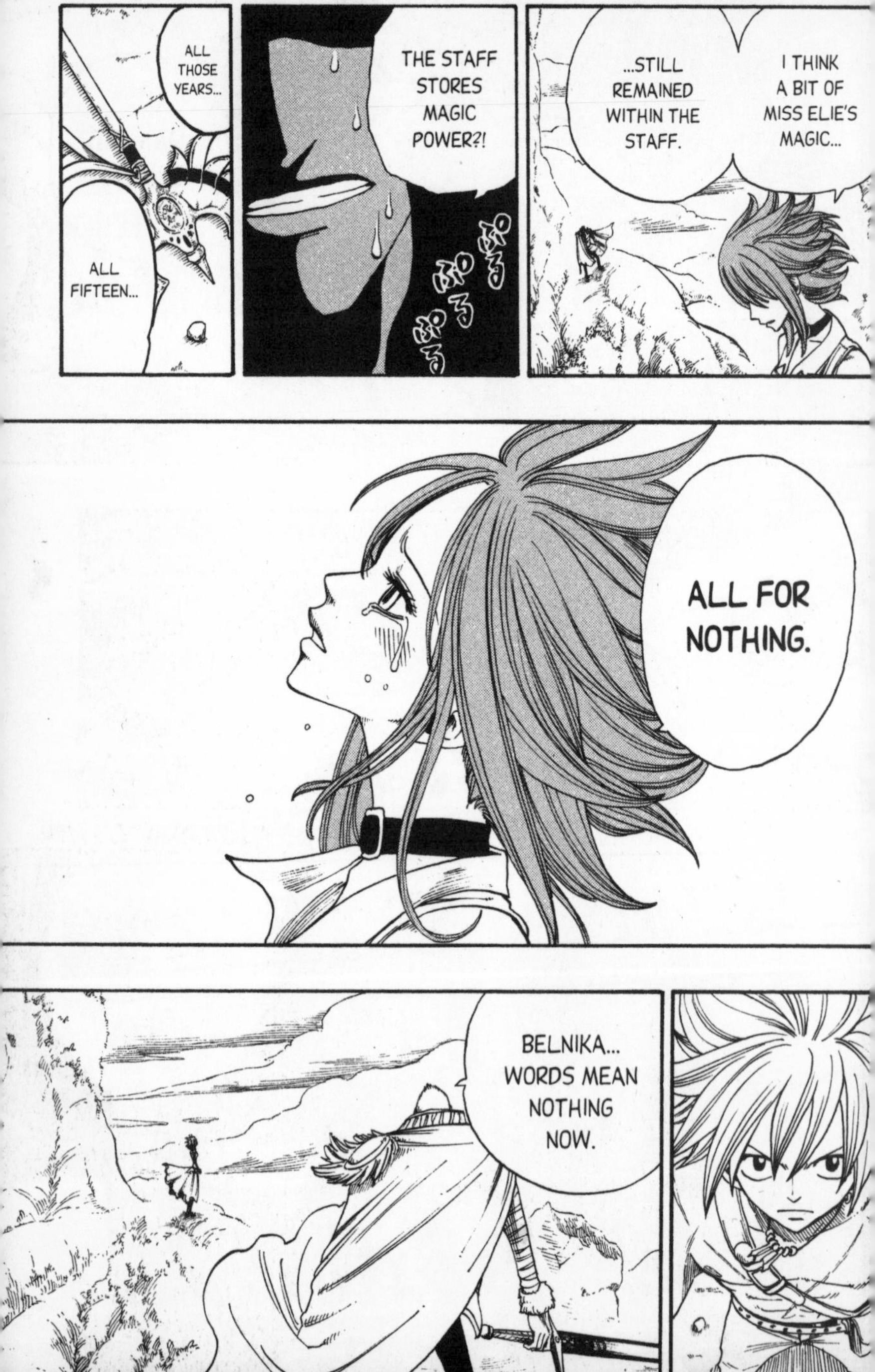
I THINK A BIT OF MISS ELIE'S MAGIC...
...STILL REMAINED WITHIN THE STAFF.
THE STAFF STORES MAGIC POWER?!
ぷる ぷる ぷる
ALL THOSE YEARS...
ALL FIFTEEN...
ALL FOR NOTHING.
BELNIKA... WORDS MEAN NOTHING NOW.

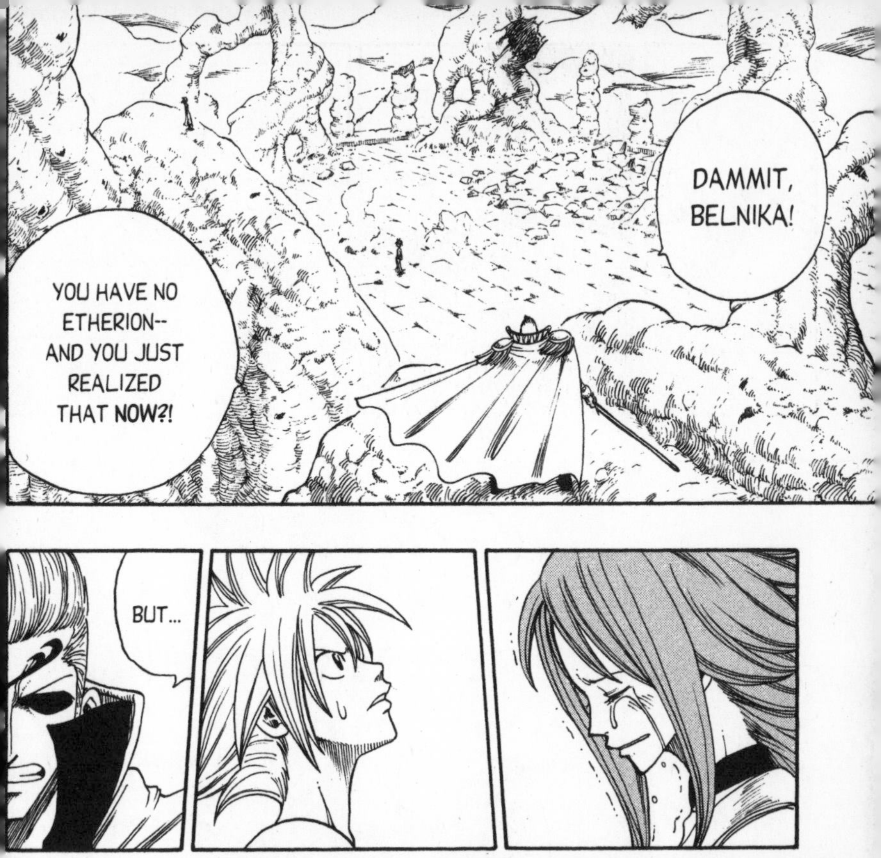
DAMMIT, BELNIKA!
YOU HAVE NO ETHERION-- AND YOU JUST REALIZED THAT NOW?!
BUT...

RAVE:217 ✚ "AMBITION" RESURRECTED!

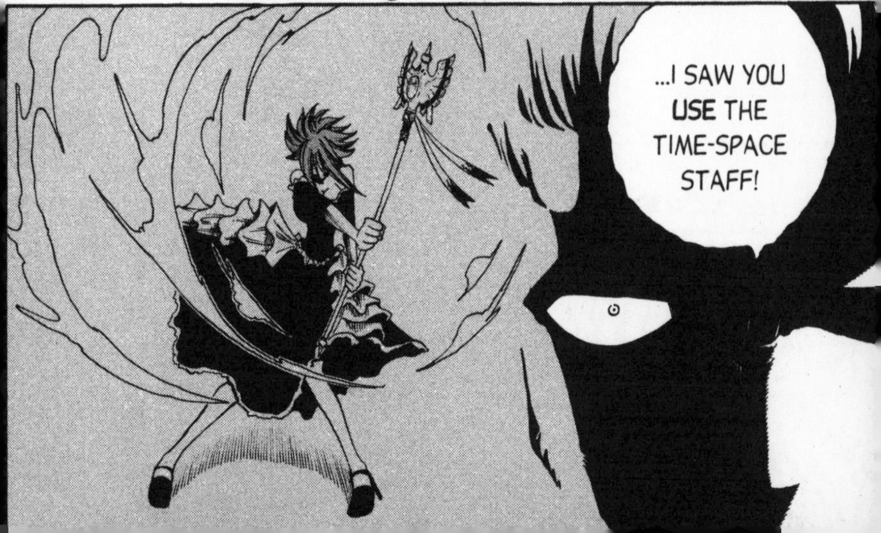
...I SAW YOU USE THE TIME-SPACE STAFF!

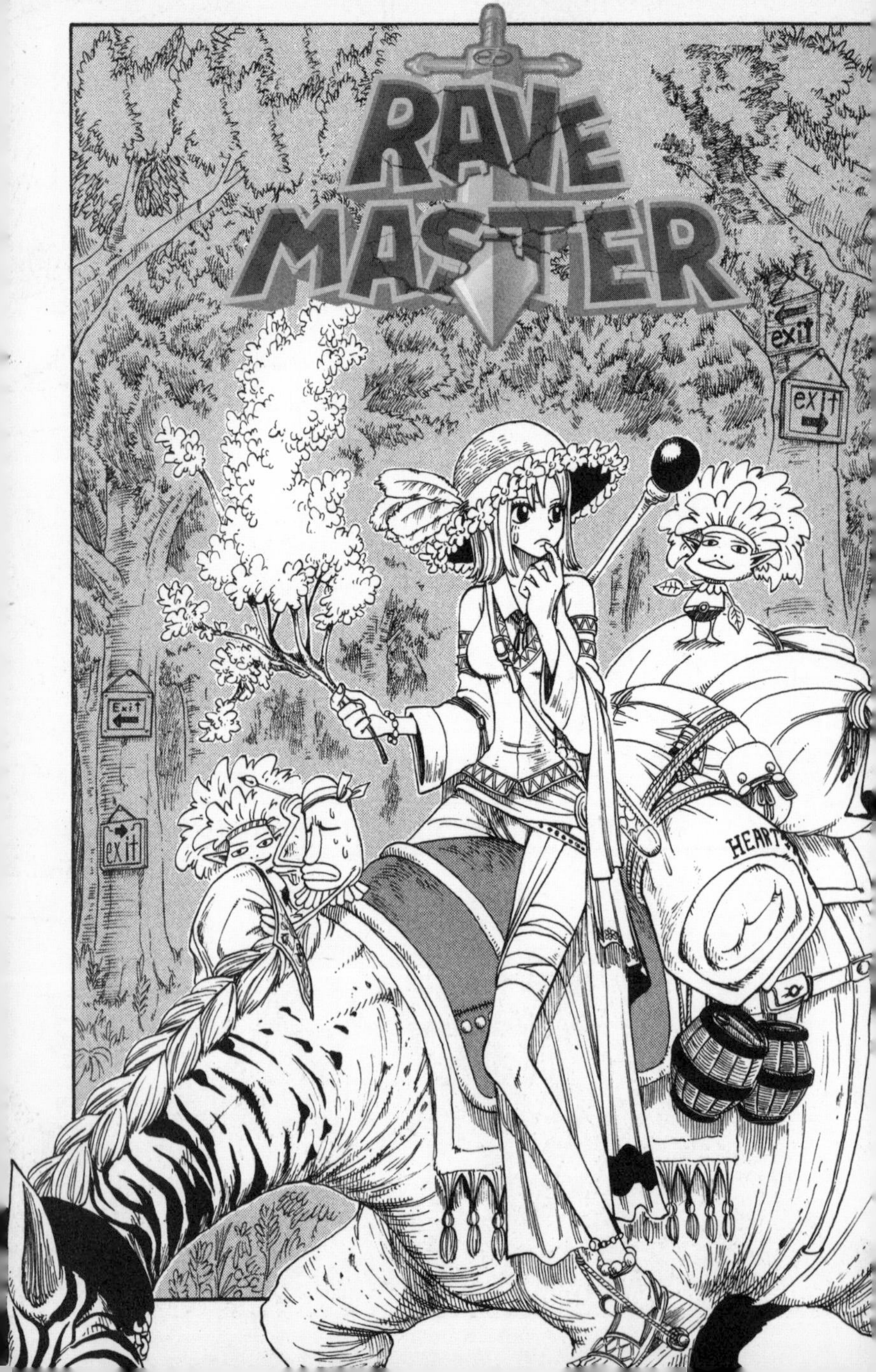
RAVE MASTER
exit
exit
Exit
exit
HEART

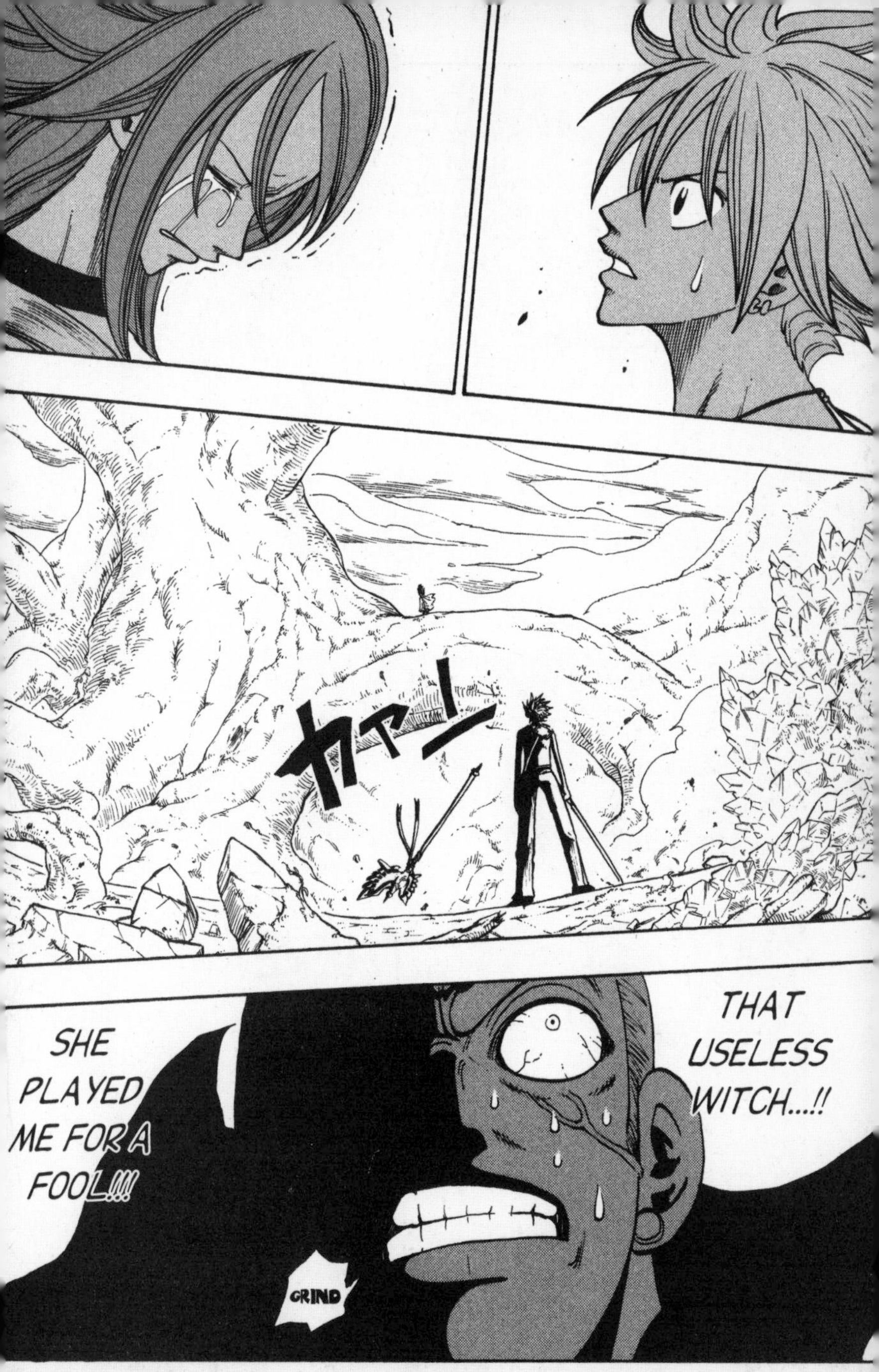
カァーン
THAT USELESS WITCH...!!
SHE PLAYED ME FOR A FOOL!!!
GRIND

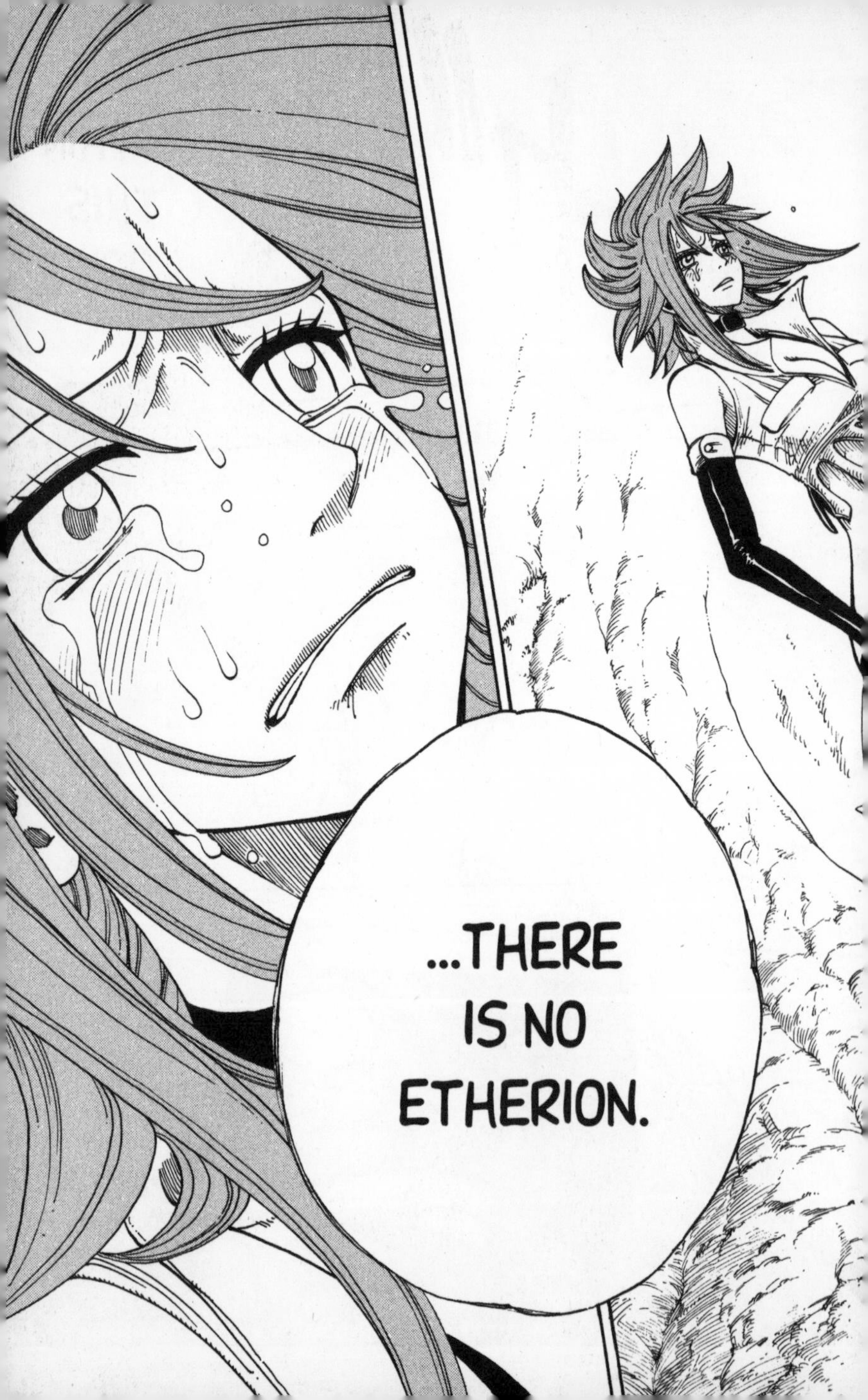
...THERE IS NO ETHERION.

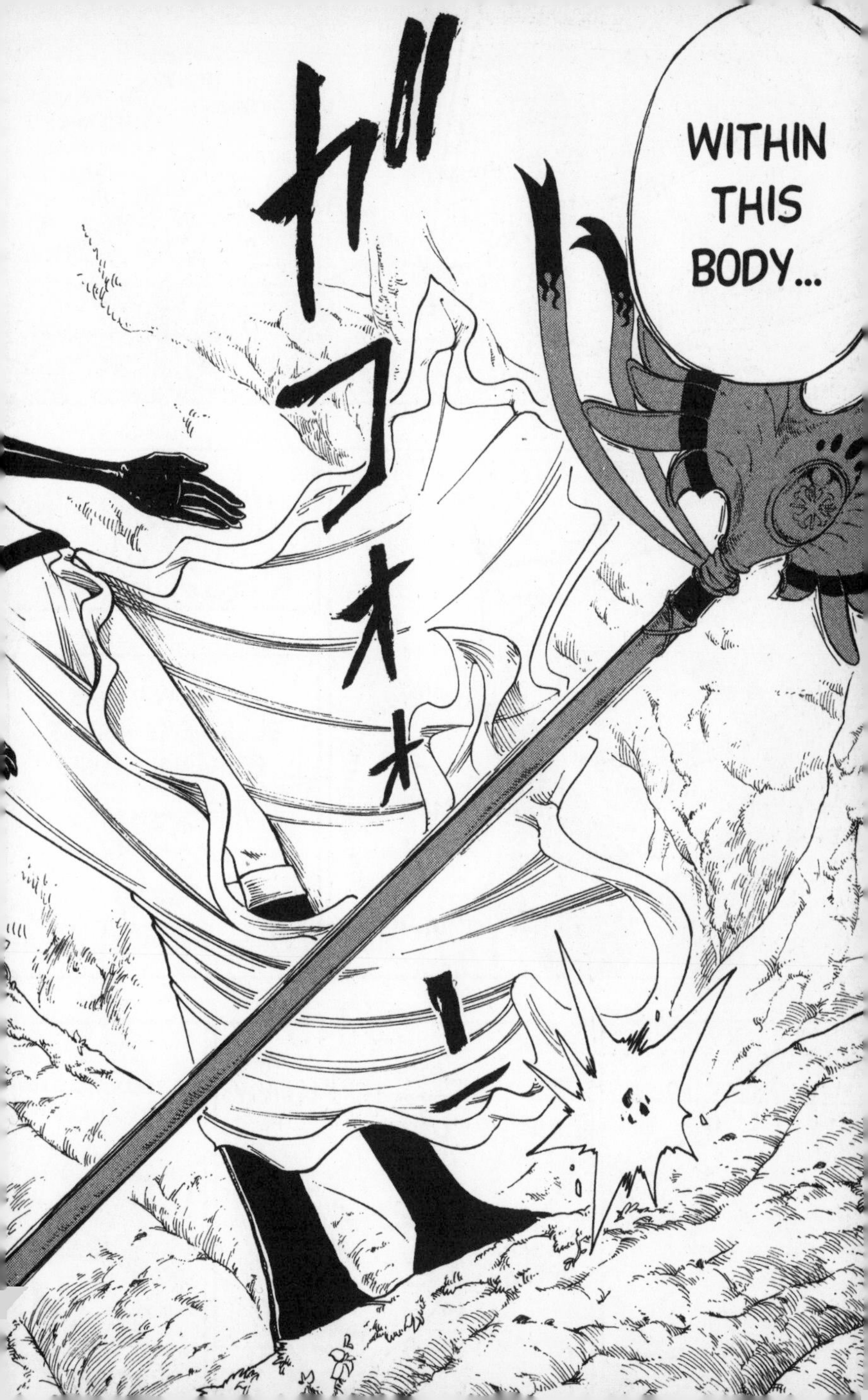
WITHIN THIS BODY...

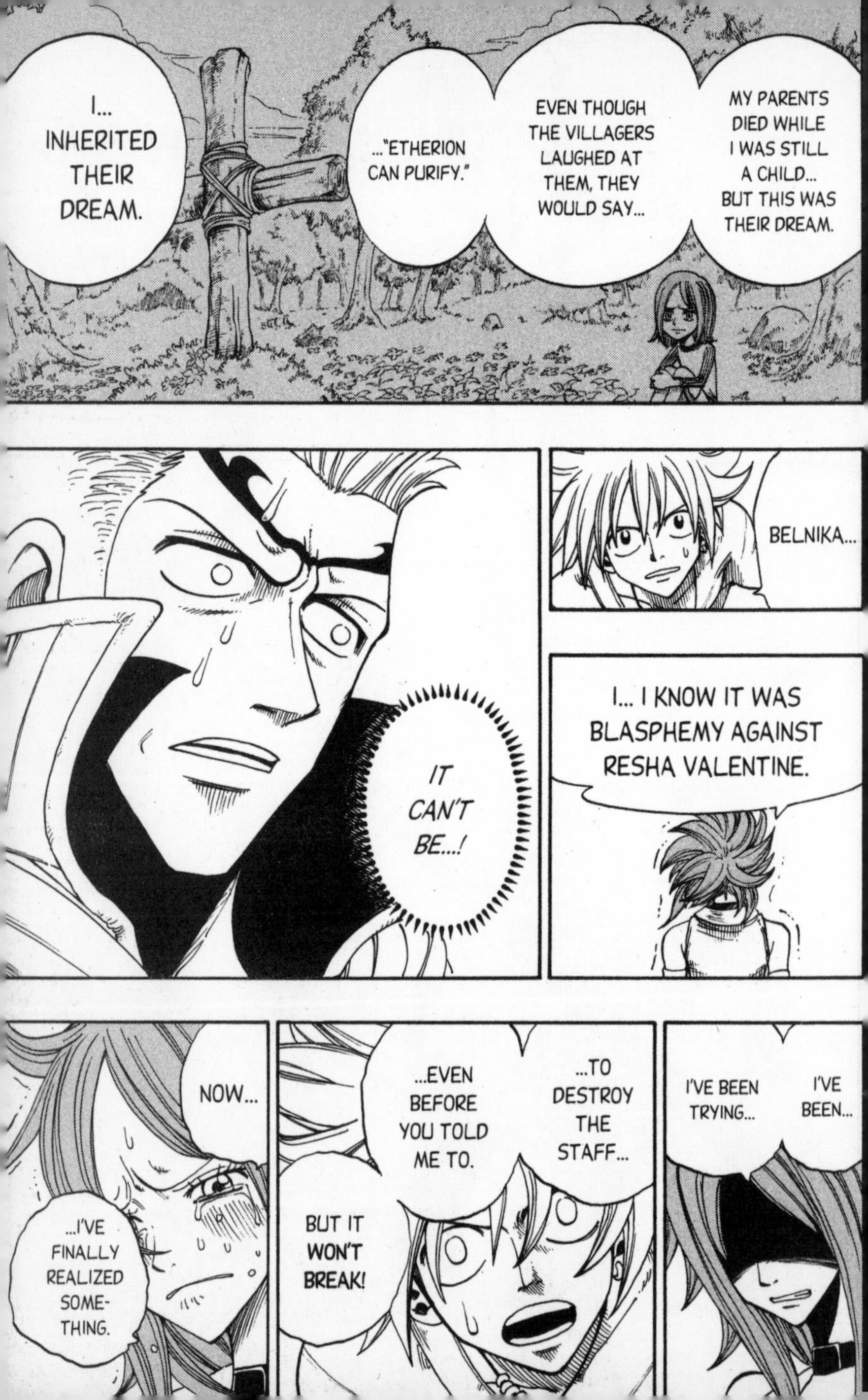
MY PARENTS DIED WHILE I WAS STILL A CHILD... BUT THIS WAS THEIR DREAM.
EVEN THOUGH THE VILLAGERS LAUGHED AT THEM, THEY WOULD SAY...
..."ETHERION CAN PURIFY."
I... INHERITED THEIR DREAM.
BELNIKA...
I... I KNOW IT WAS BLASPHEMY AGAINST RESHA VALENTINE.
IT CAN'T BE...!
I'VE BEEN...
I'VE BEEN TRYING...
...TO DESTROY THE STAFF...
...EVEN BEFORE YOU TOLD ME TO.
BUT IT WON'T BREAK!
NOW...
...I'VE FINALLY REALIZED SOME-THING.

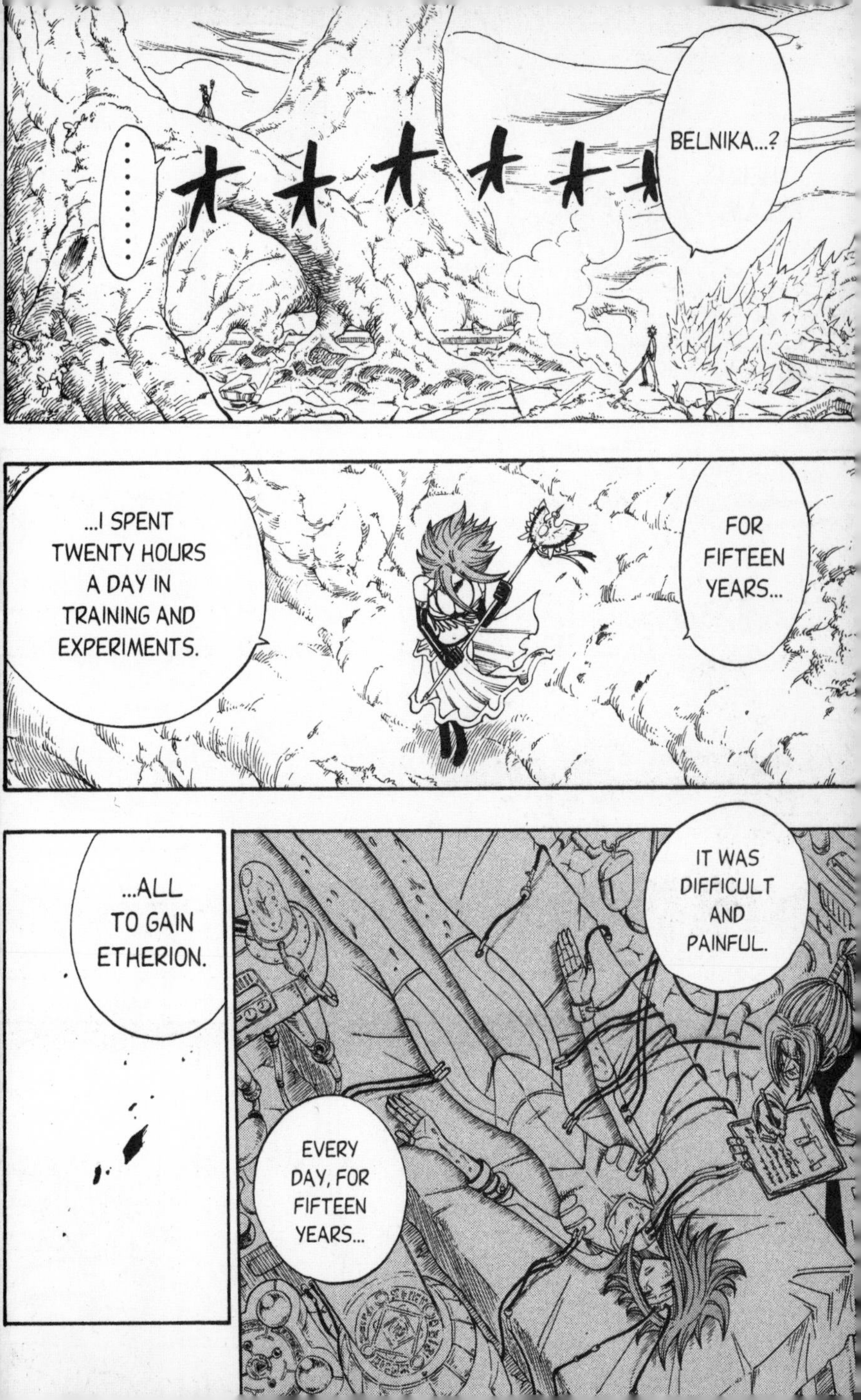
BELNIKA...?
......
FOR FIFTEEN YEARS...
...I SPENT TWENTY HOURS A DAY IN TRAINING AND EXPERIMENTS.
IT WAS DIFFICULT AND PAINFUL.
EVERY DAY, FOR FIFTEEN YEARS...
...ALL TO GAIN ETHERION.

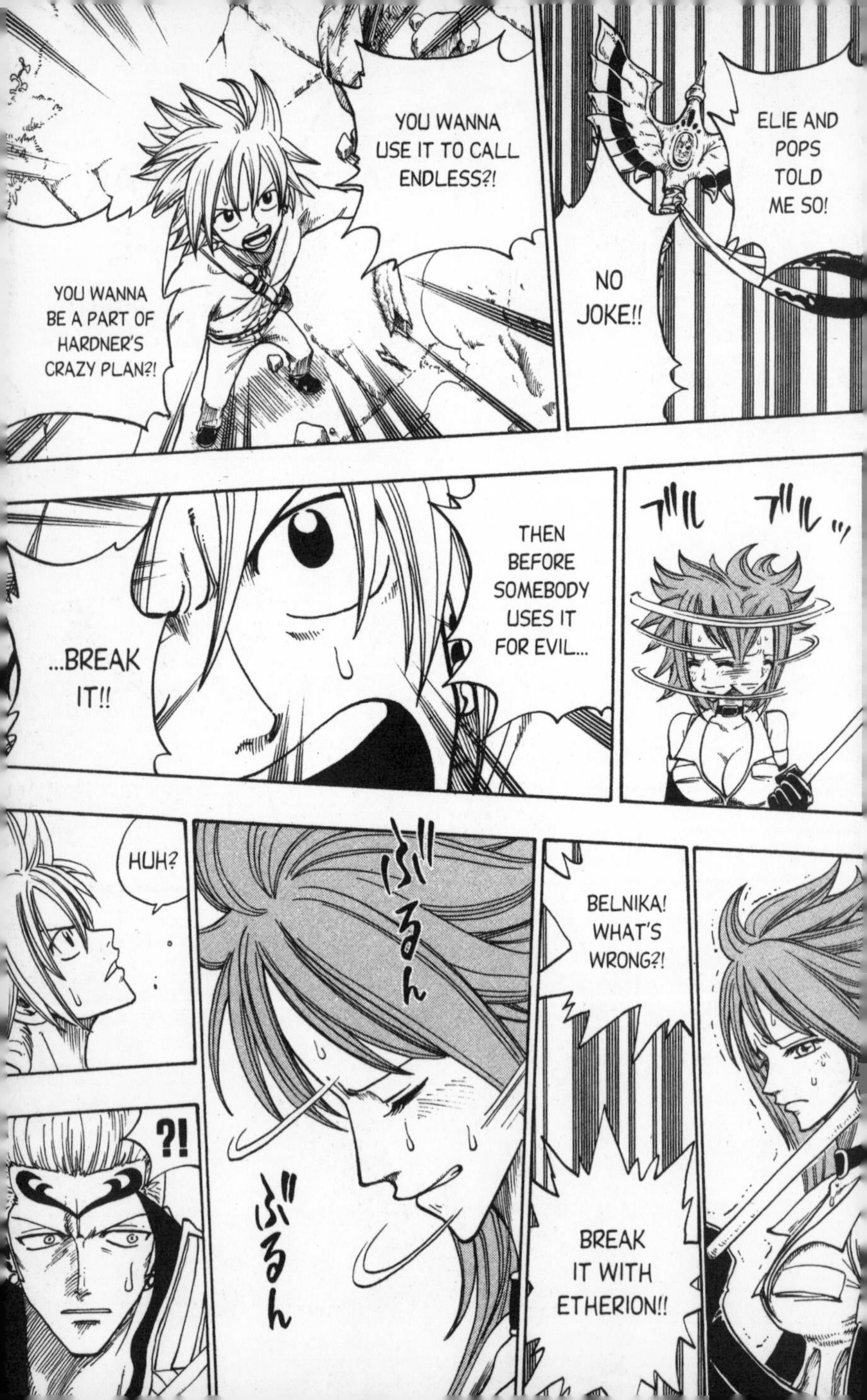
ELIE AND POPS TOLD ME SO!
NO JOKE!!
YOU WANNA USE IT TO CALL ENDLESS?!
YOU WANNA BE A PART OF HARDNER'S CRAZY PLAN?!
ブル ブルッ
THEN BEFORE SOMEBODY USES IT FOR EVIL...
...BREAK IT!!
BELNIKA! WHAT'S WRONG?!
BREAK IT WITH ETHERION!!
ぷるん
ぷるん
HUH?
?!

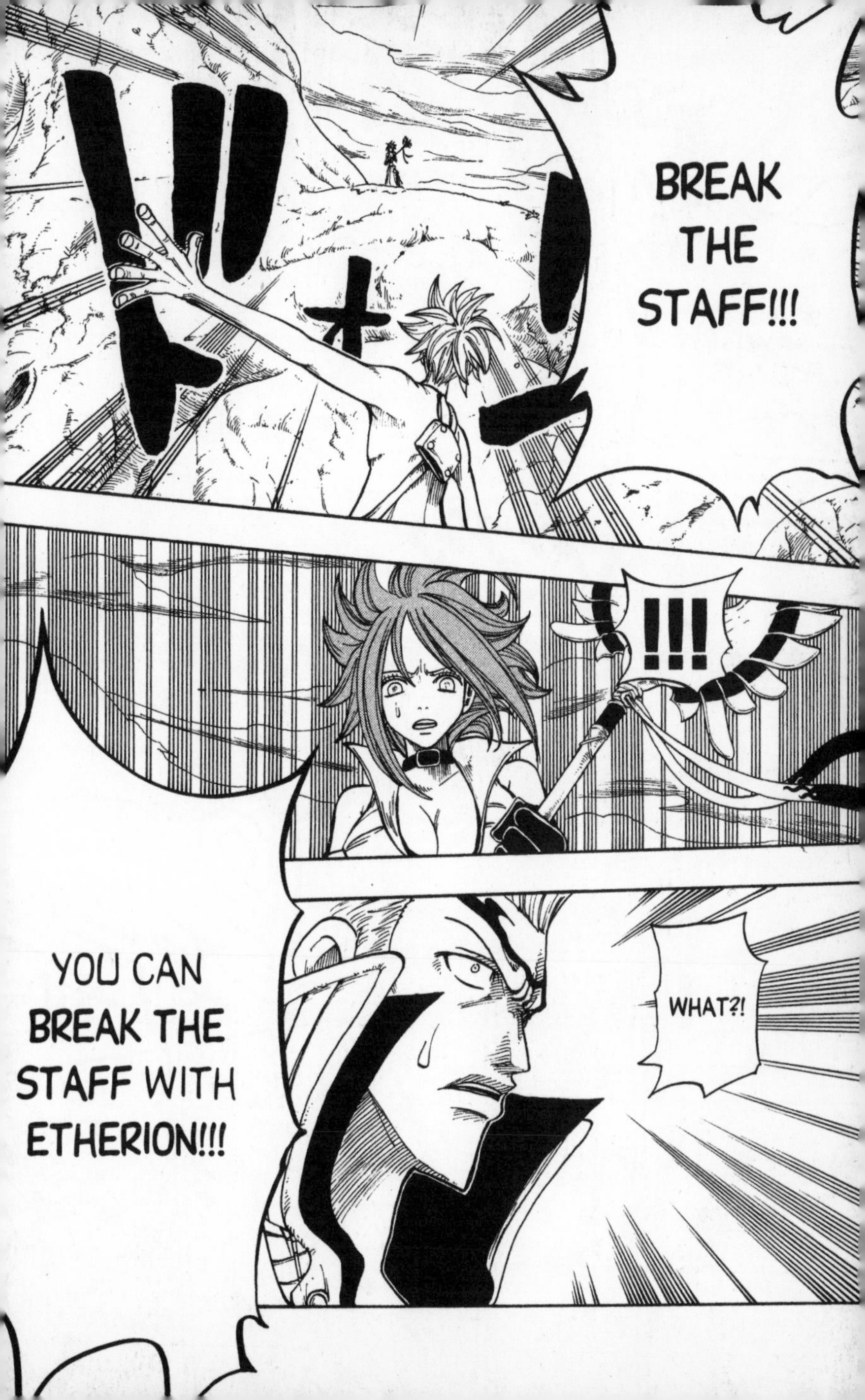
BREAK THE STAFF!!!
!!!
YOU CAN BREAK THE STAFF WITH ETHERION!!!
WHAT?!

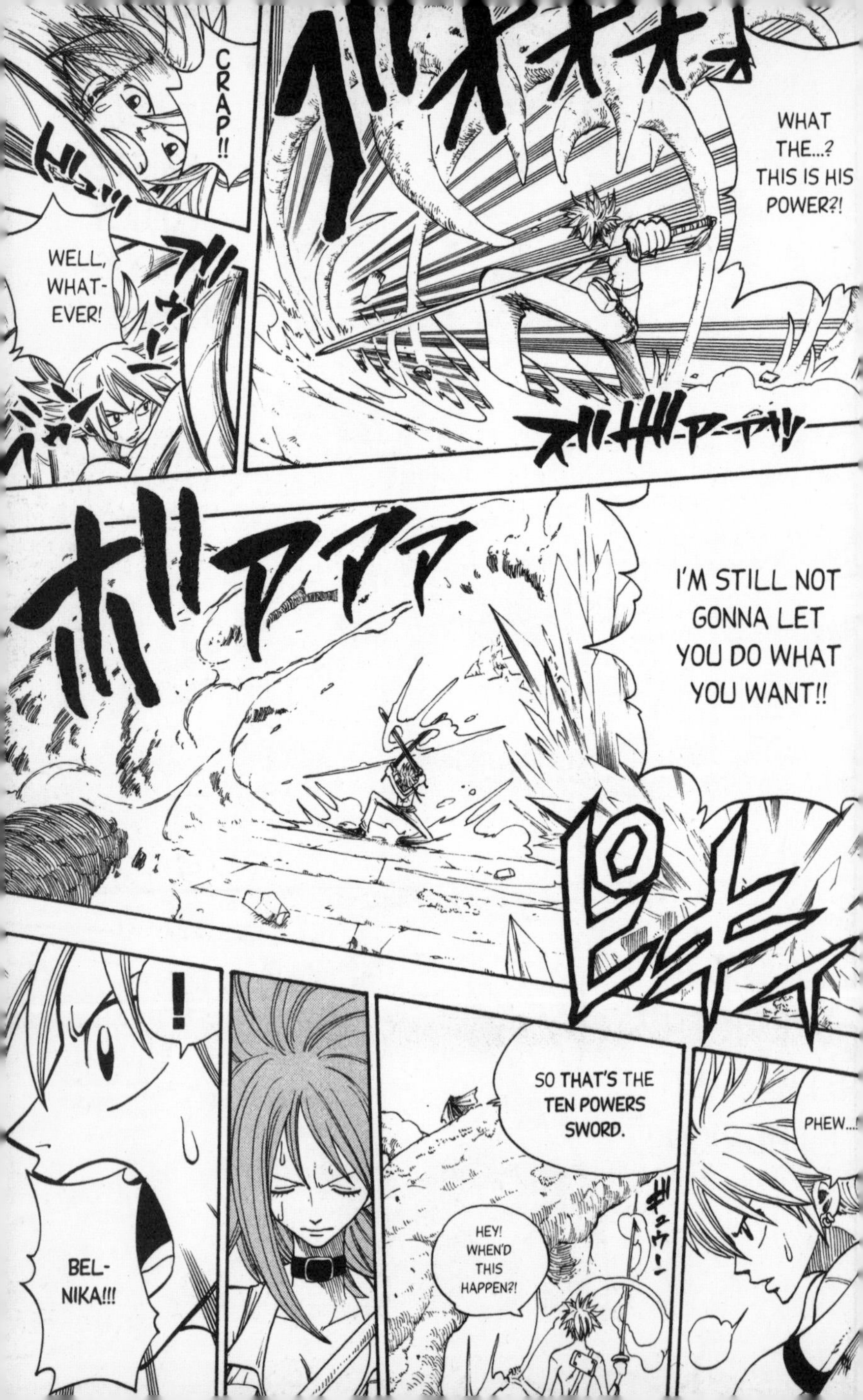

WHAT THE...? THIS IS HIS POWER?!
CRAP!!
WELL, WHAT-EVER!
I'M STILL NOT GONNA LET YOU DO WHAT YOU WANT!!
PHEW...!
SO THAT'S THE TEN POWERS SWORD.
HEY! WHEN'D THIS HAPPEN?!
!
BEL-NIKA!!!

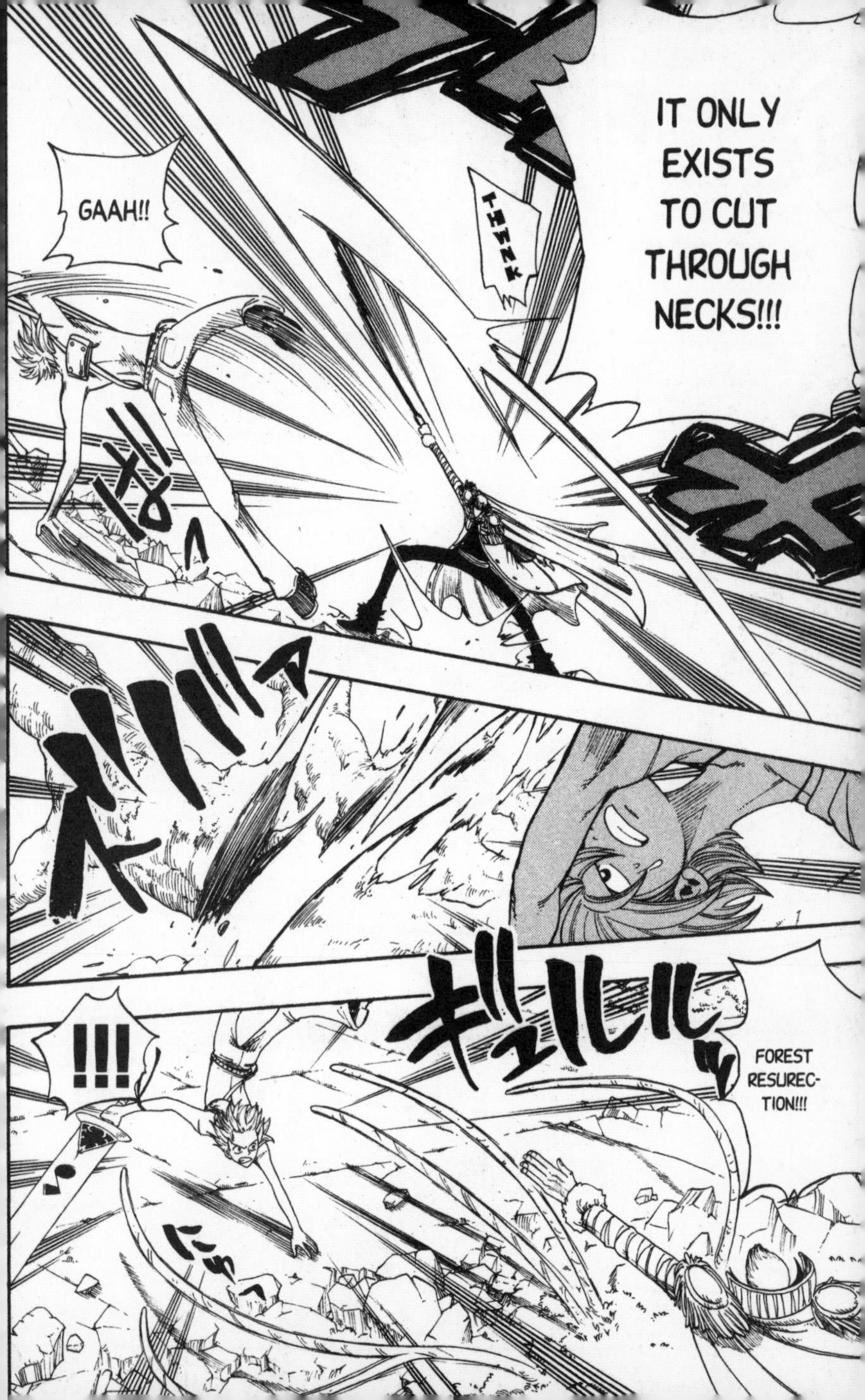
IT ONLY EXISTS TO CUT THROUGH NECKS!!!
THWNK
GAAH!!
FOREST RESURECTION!!!
!!!

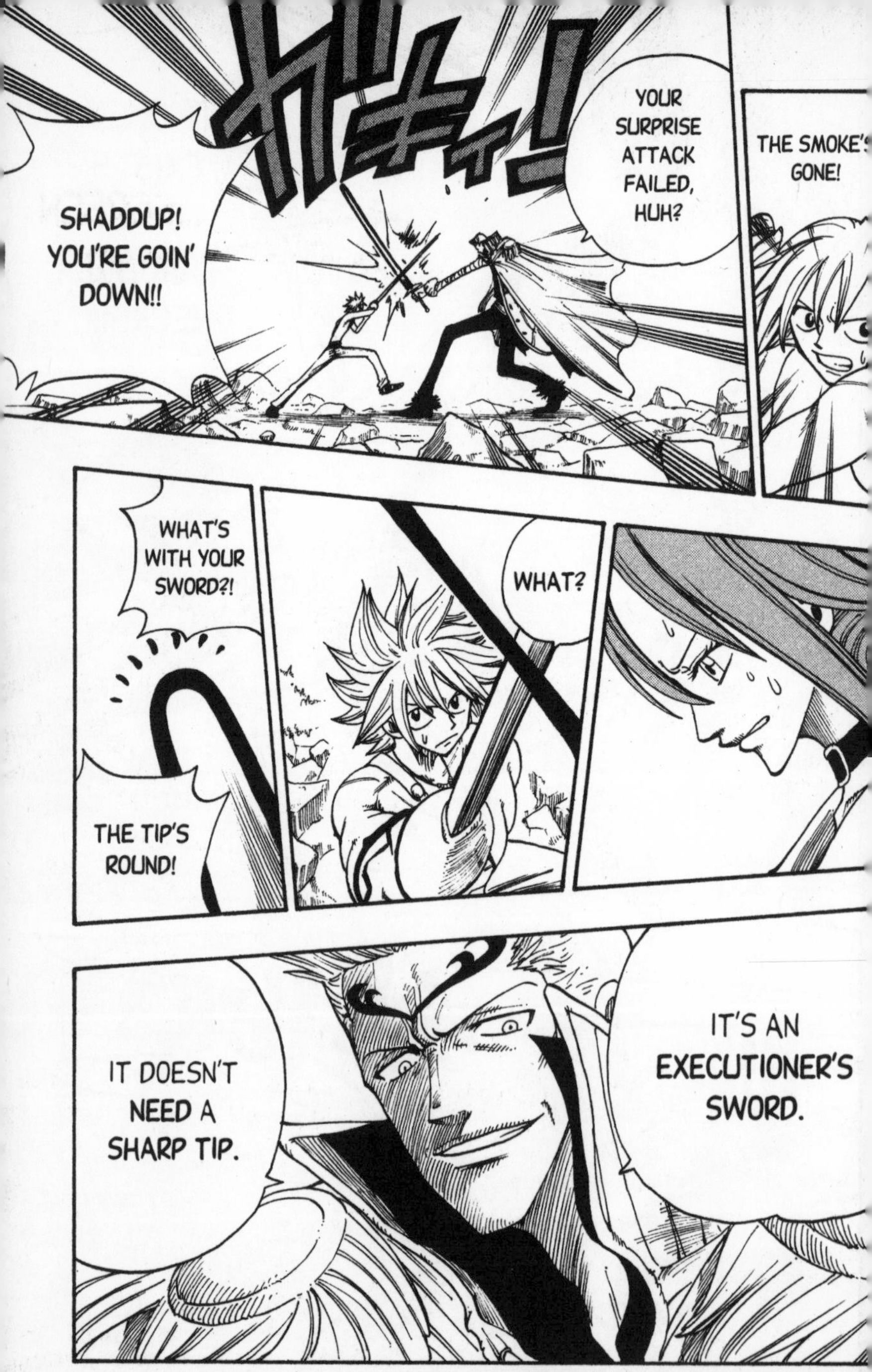

THE SMOKE'S GONE!
ガキィ!
YOUR SURPRISE ATTACK FAILED, HUH?
SHADDUP! YOU'RE GOIN' DOWN!!
WHAT?
WHAT'S WITH YOUR SWORD?!
THE TIP'S ROUND!
IT'S AN EXECUTIONER'S SWORD.
IT DOESN'T NEED A SHARP TIP.

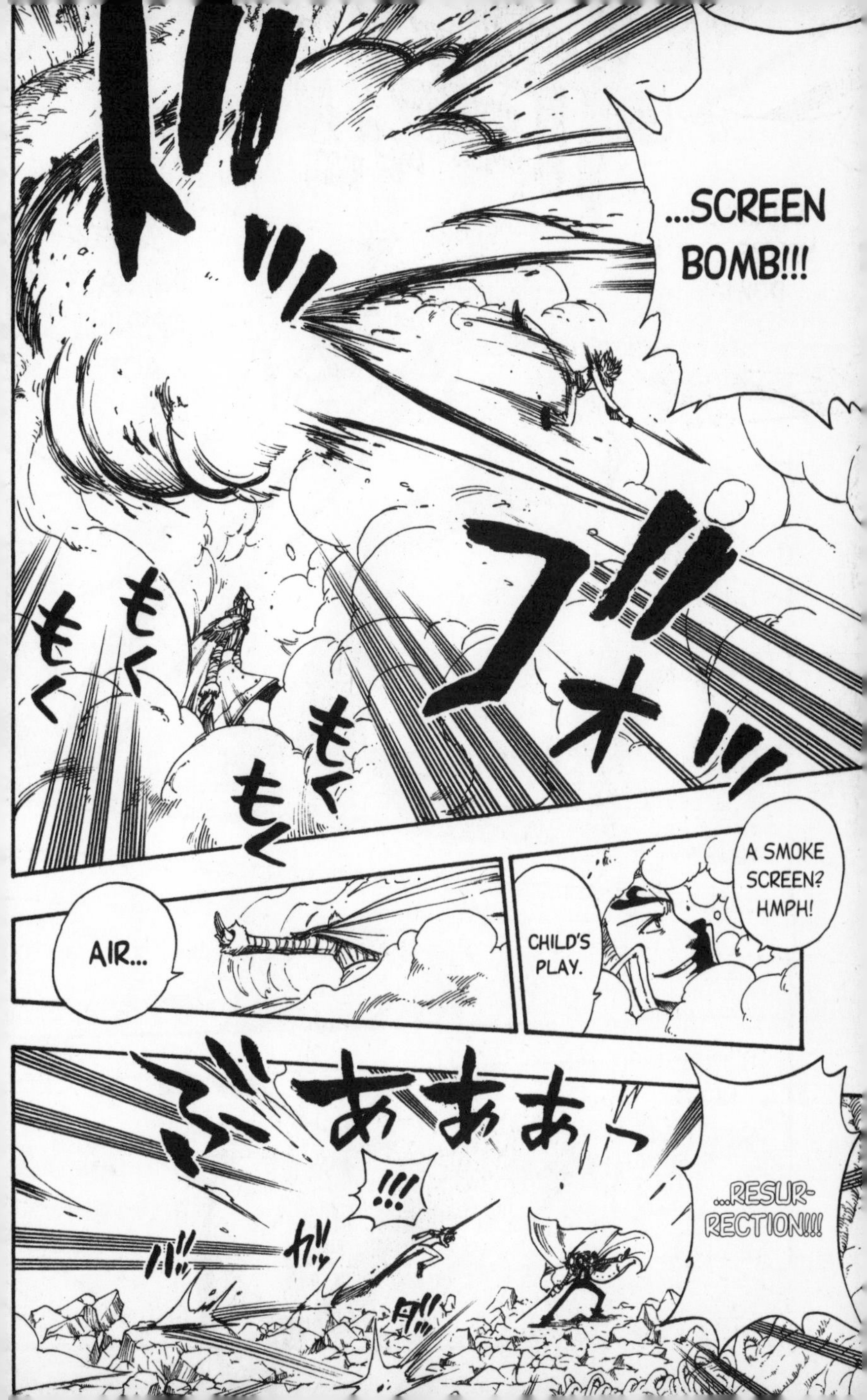
...SCREEN BOMB!!!
もくもく
もくもく
A SMOKE SCREEN? HMPH!
CHILD'S PLAY.
AIR...
...RESUR-RECTION!!!
!!!
ぶあああ〜

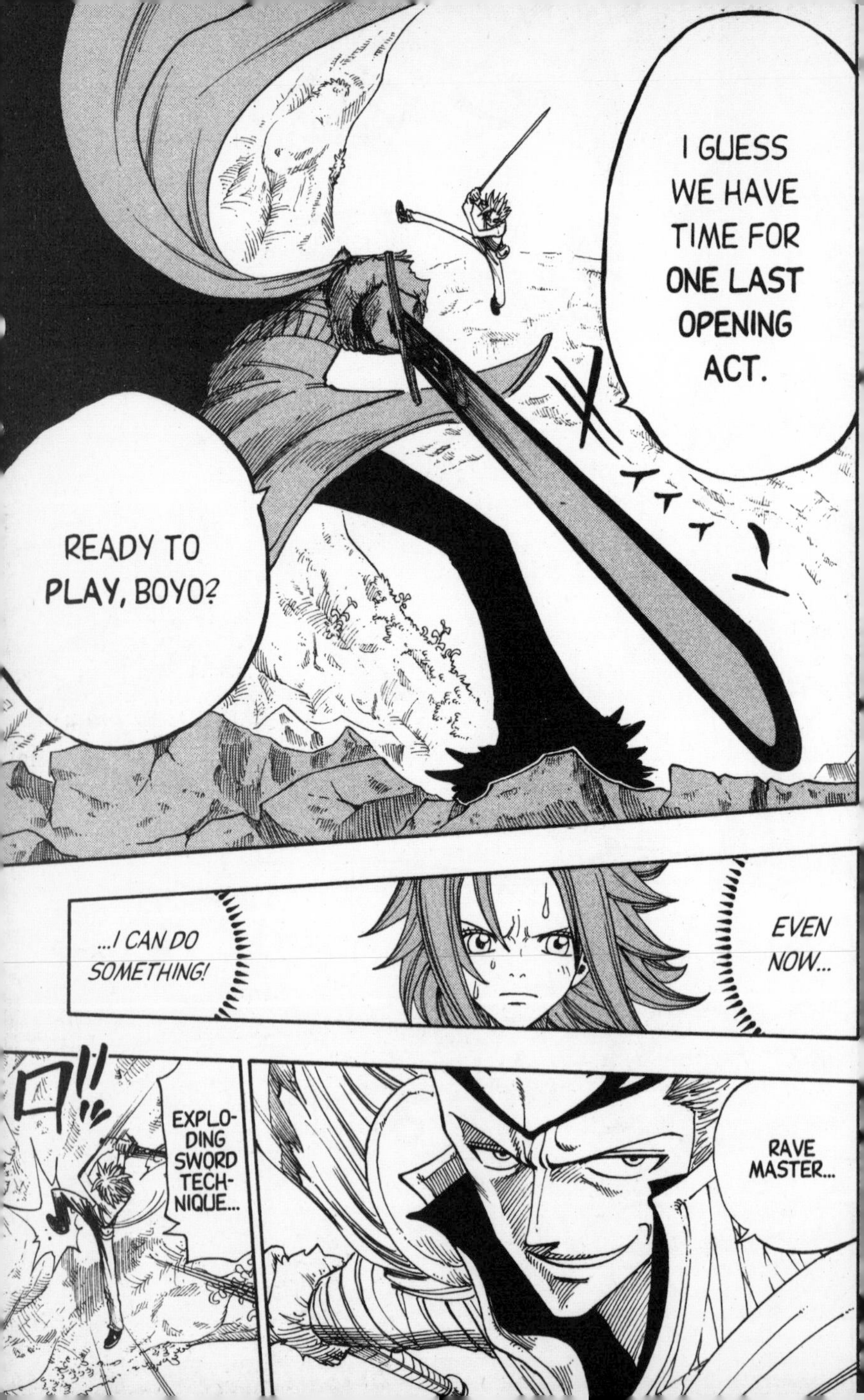
I GUESS WE HAVE TIME FOR ONE LAST OPENING ACT.
READY TO PLAY, BOYO?
EVEN NOW...
...I CAN DO SOMETHING!
RAVE MASTER...
EXPLODING SWORD TECHNIQUE...

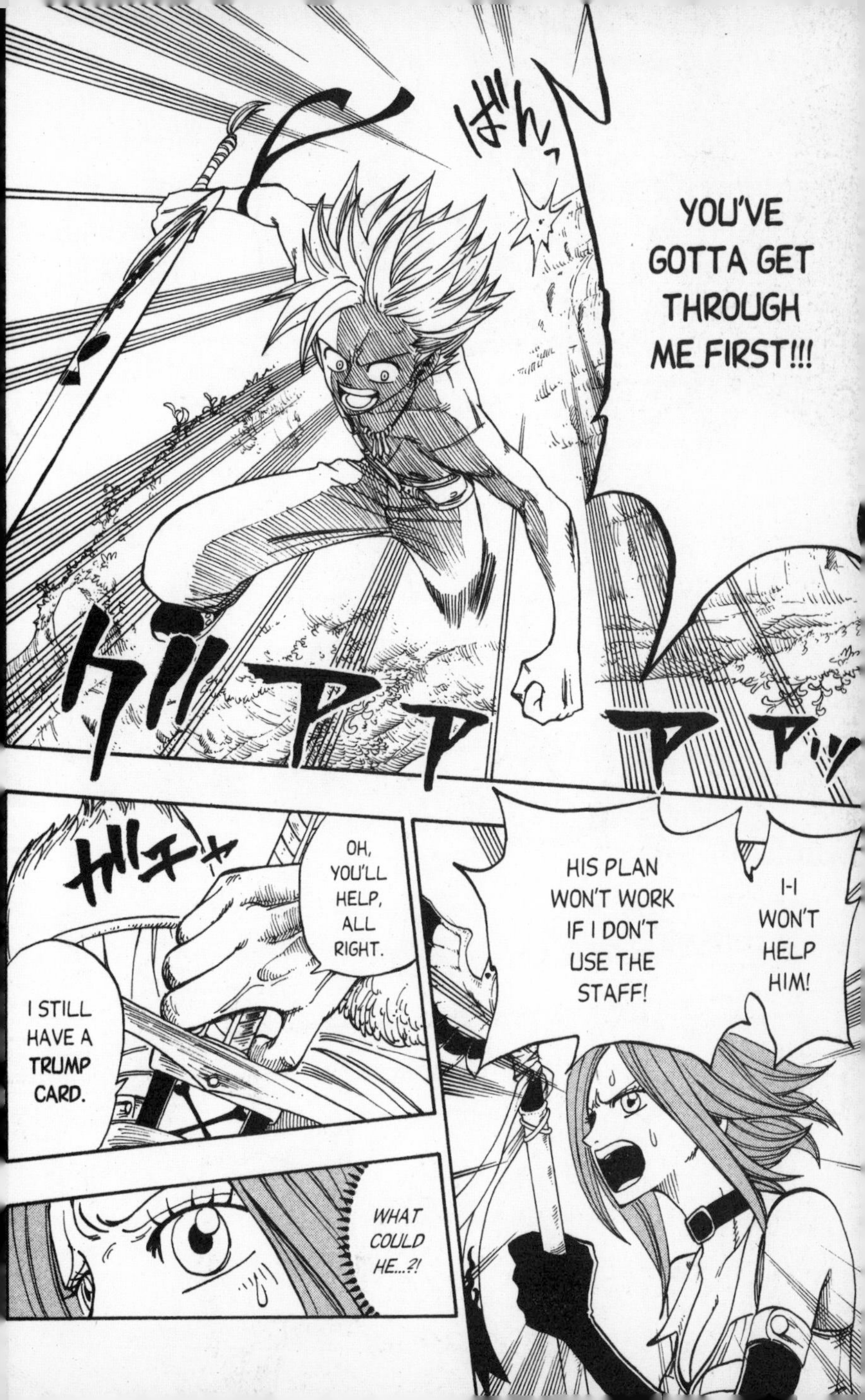
ばんっ
YOU'VE GOTTA GET THROUGH ME FIRST!!!
I-I WON'T HELP HIM!
HIS PLAN WON'T WORK IF I DON'T USE THE STAFF!
ガチャ
OH, YOU'LL HELP, ALL RIGHT.
I STILL HAVE A TRUMP CARD.
WHAT COULD HE...?!

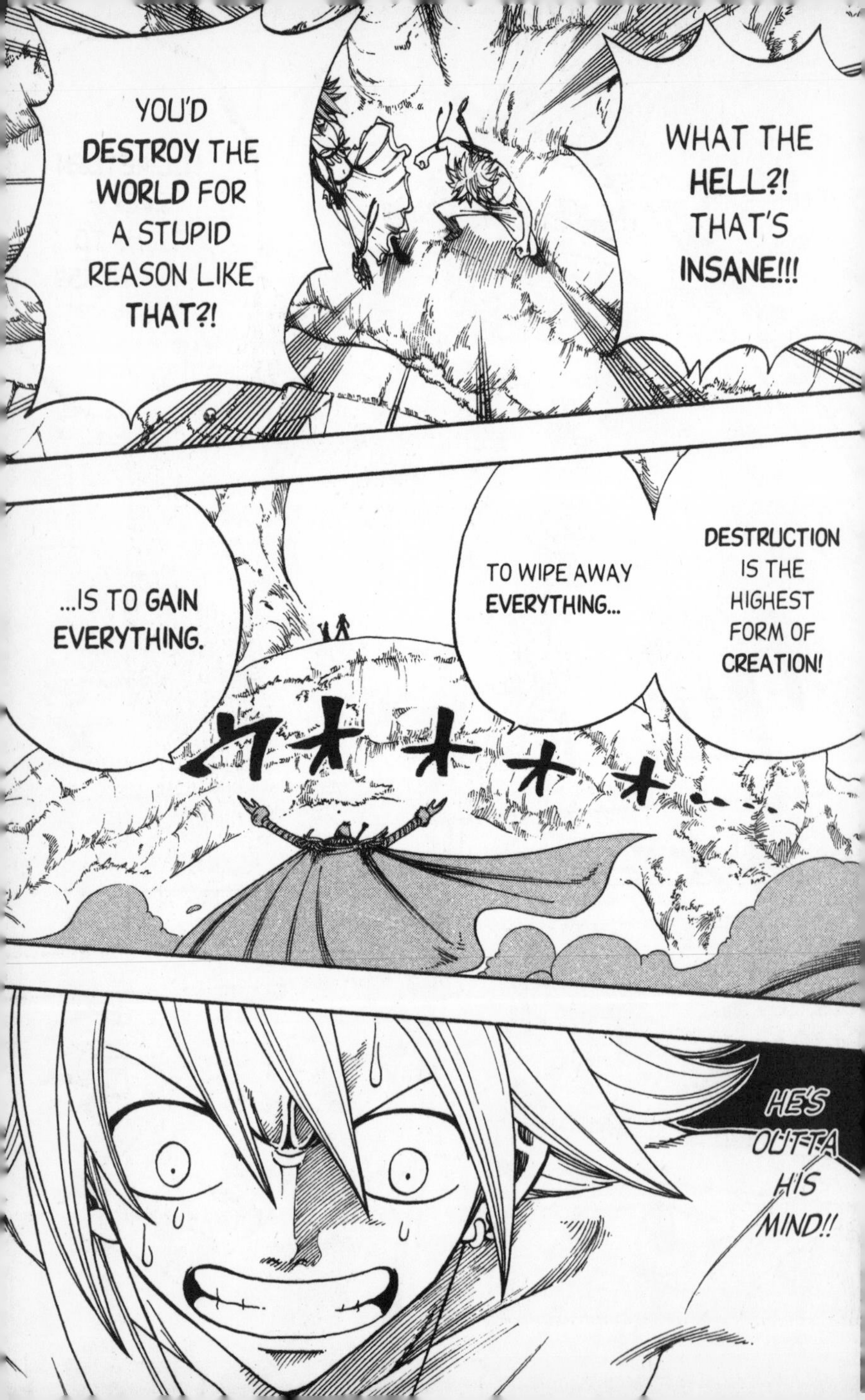
WHAT THE HELL?! THAT'S INSANE!!!
YOU'D DESTROY THE WORLD FOR A STUPID REASON LIKE THAT?!
DESTRUCTION IS THE HIGHEST FORM OF CREATION!
TO WIPE AWAY EVERYTHING...
...IS TO GAIN EVERYTHING.
ウオオオオ…
HE'S OUTTA HIS MIND!!

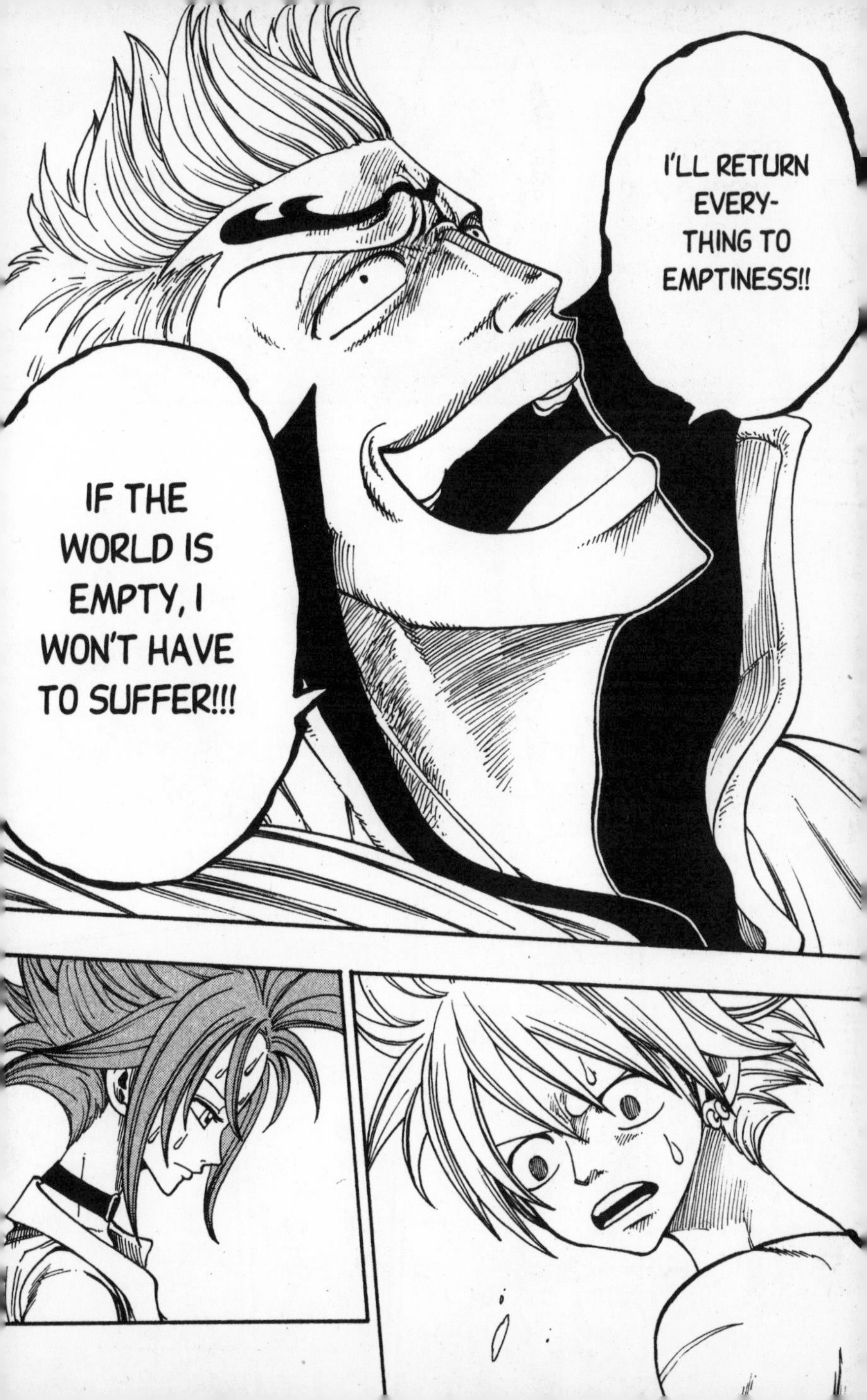
I'LL RETURN EVERY-THING TO EMPTINESS!!
IF THE WORLD IS EMPTY, I WON'T HAVE TO SUFFER!!!

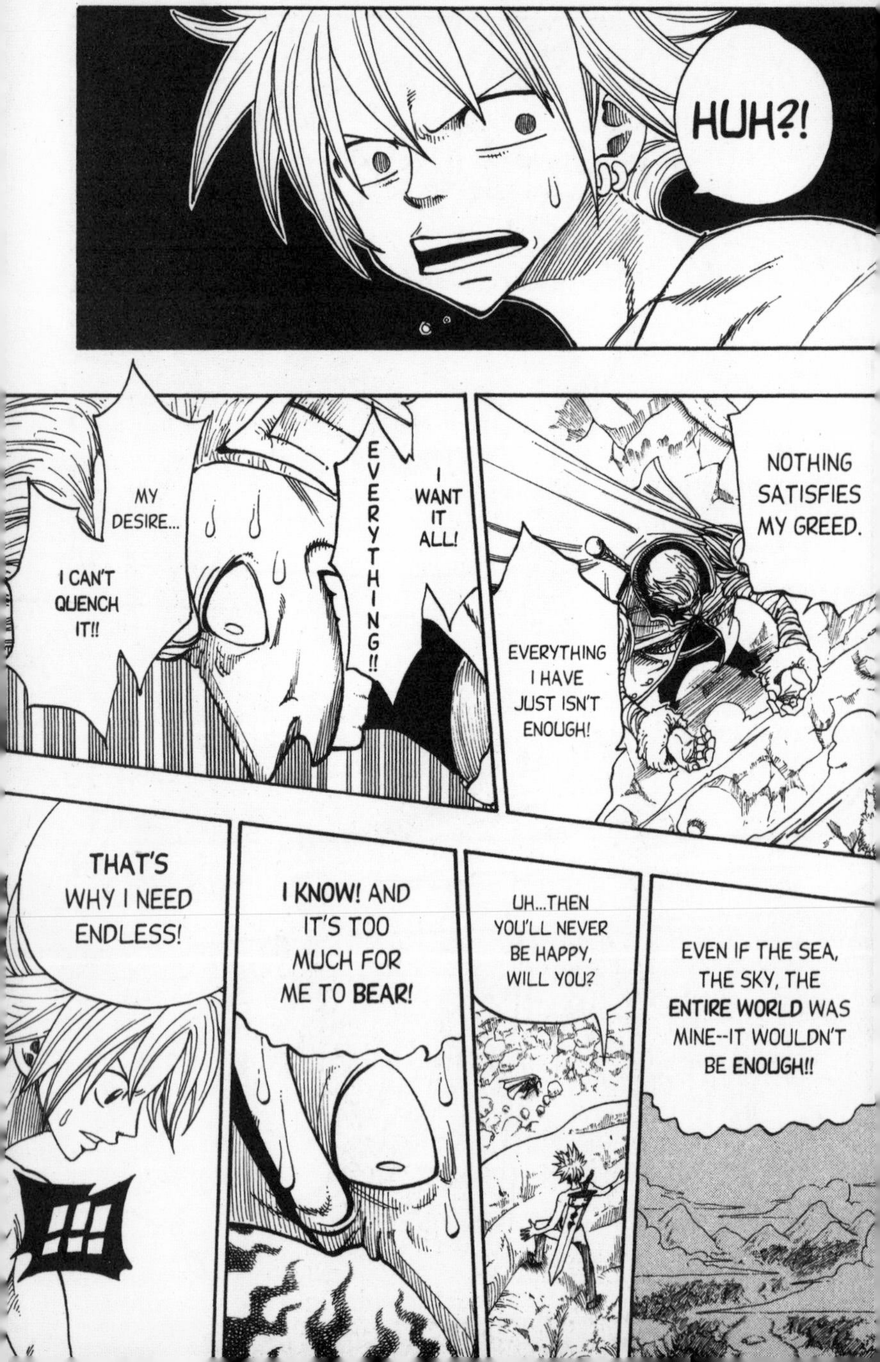
HUH?!
NOTHING SATISFIES MY GREED.
EVERYTHING I HAVE JUST ISN'T ENOUGH!
I WANT IT ALL!
EVERYTHING!!
MY DESIRE...
I CAN'T QUENCH IT!!
EVEN IF THE SEA, THE SKY, THE ENTIRE WORLD WAS MINE--IT WOULDN'T BE ENOUGH!!
UH...THEN YOU'LL NEVER BE HAPPY, WILL YOU?
I KNOW! AND IT'S TOO MUCH FOR ME TO BEAR!
THAT'S WHY I NEED ENDLESS!

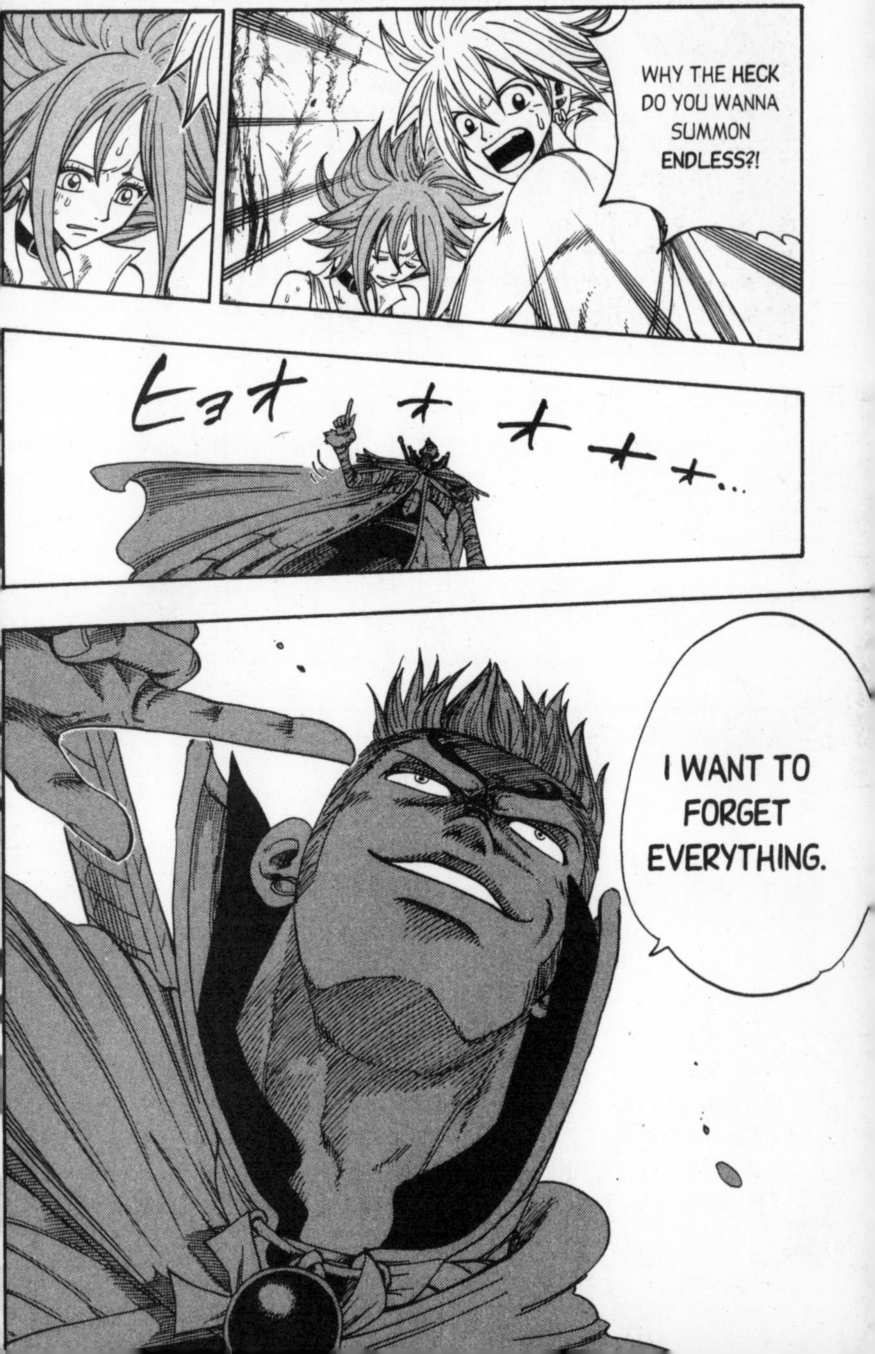
WHY THE HECK DO YOU WANNA SUMMON ENDLESS?!
ヒョオオオオオ...
I WANT TO FORGET EVERYTHING.

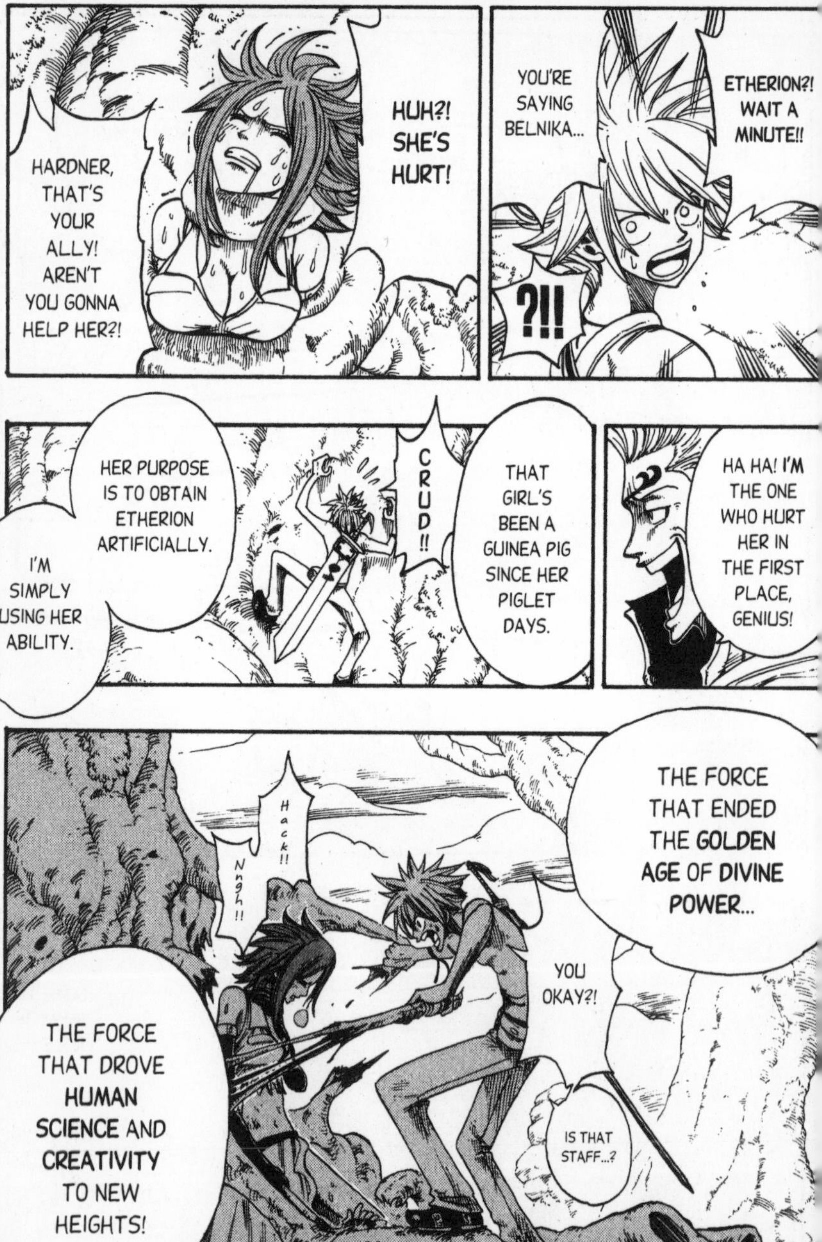
ETHERION?! WAIT A MINUTE!!
YOU'RE SAYING BELNIKA...
?!!
HUH?! SHE'S HURT!
HARDNER, THAT'S YOUR ALLY! AREN'T YOU GONNA HELP HER?!
HA HA! I'M THE ONE WHO HURT HER IN THE FIRST PLACE, GENIUS!
THAT GIRL'S BEEN A GUINEA PIG SINCE HER PIGLET DAYS.
CRUD!!
HER PURPOSE IS TO OBTAIN ETHERION ARTIFICIALLY.
I'M SIMPLY USING HER ABILITY.
THE FORCE THAT ENDED THE GOLDEN AGE OF DIVINE POWER...
Hack!!
Nngh!!
YOU OKAY?!
IS THAT STAFF...?
THE FORCE THAT DROVE HUMAN SCIENCE AND CREATIVITY TO NEW HEIGHTS!

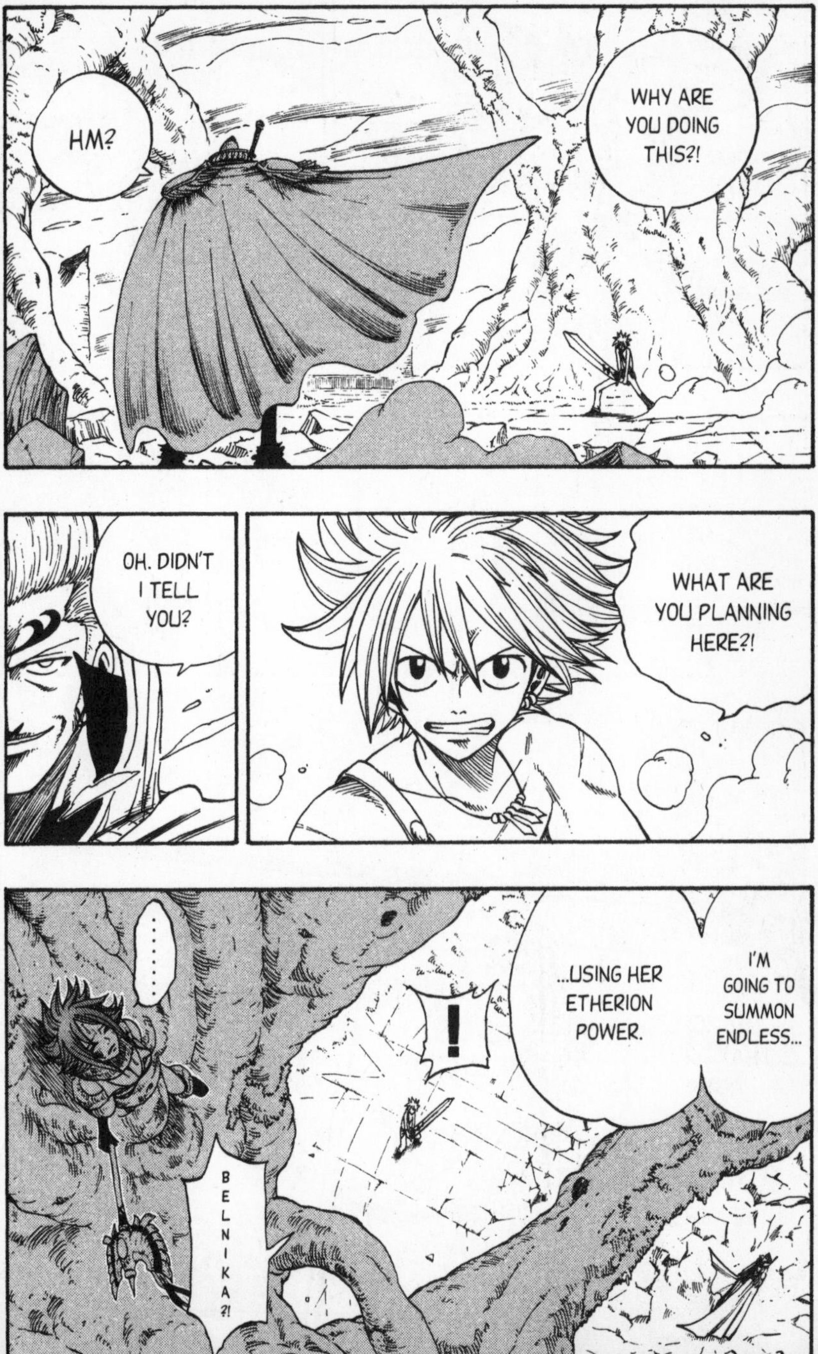
WHY ARE YOU DOING THIS?!
HM?
WHAT ARE YOU PLANNING HERE?!
OH. DIDN'T I TELL YOU?
I'M GOING TO SUMMON ENDLESS...
...USING HER ETHERION POWER.
!
......
BELNIKA?!

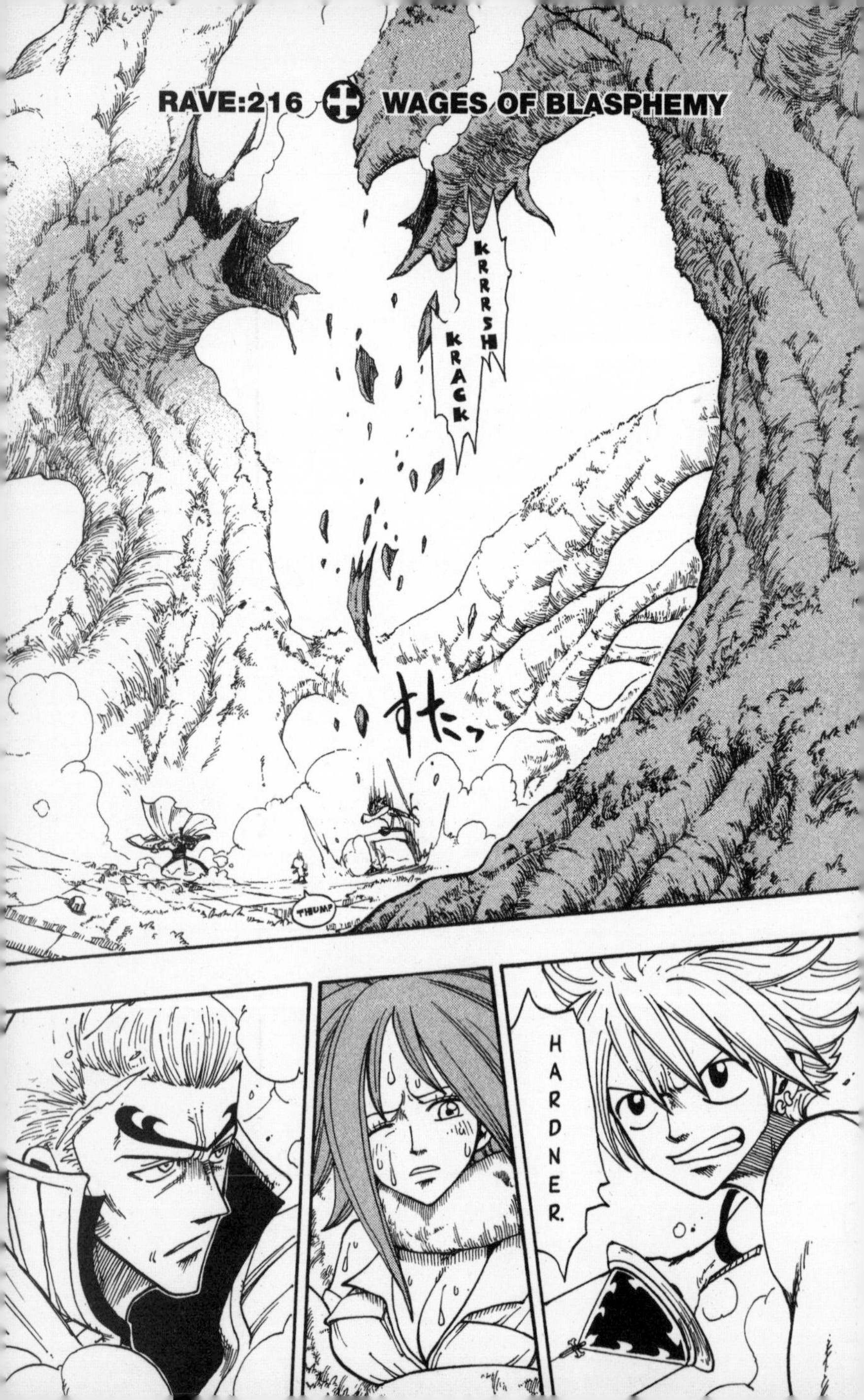
RAVE:216 WAGES OF BLASPHEMY
KRRRSH
KRACK
すたっ
THUMP
HARDNER.

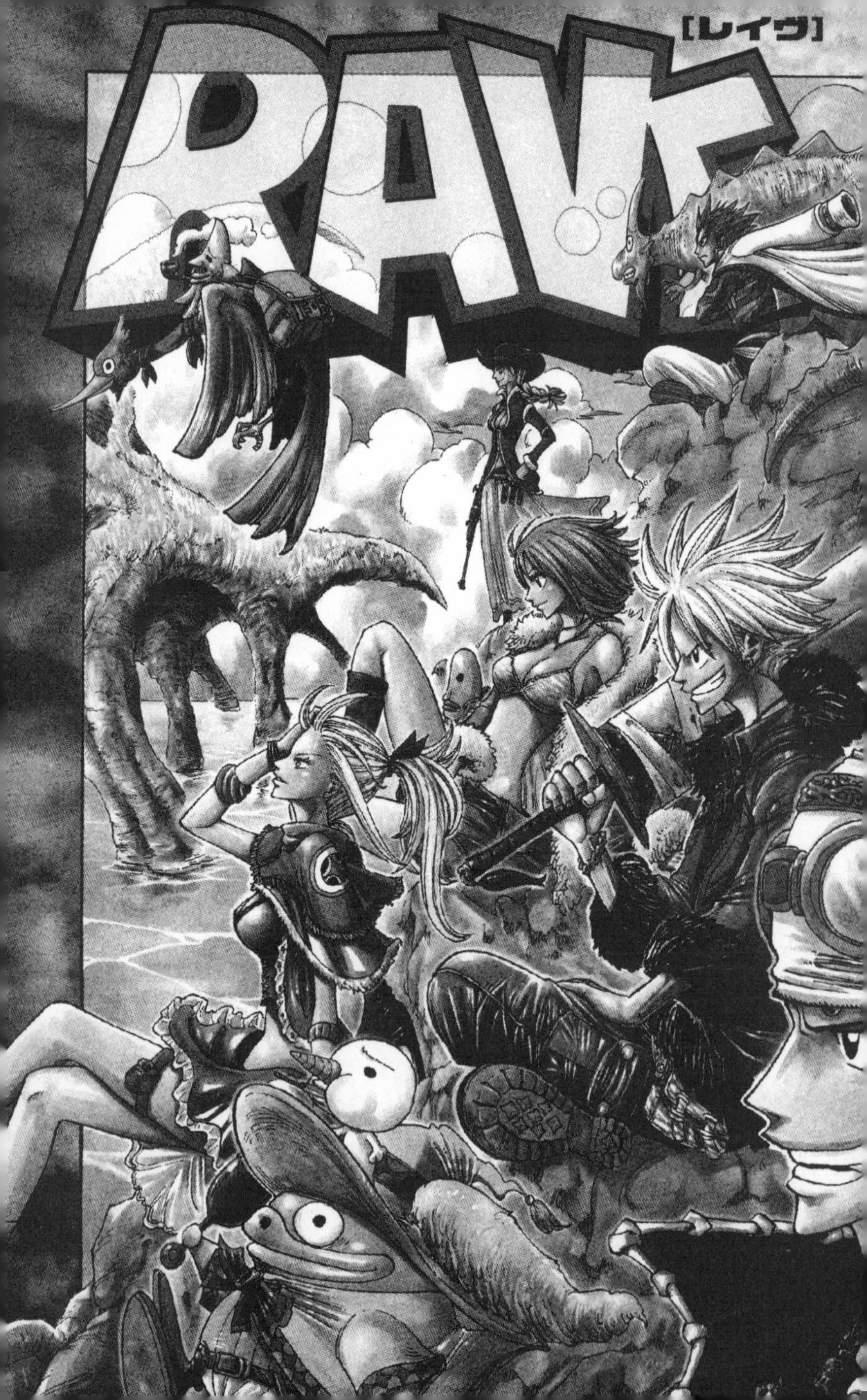
RAVE
[レイヴ]

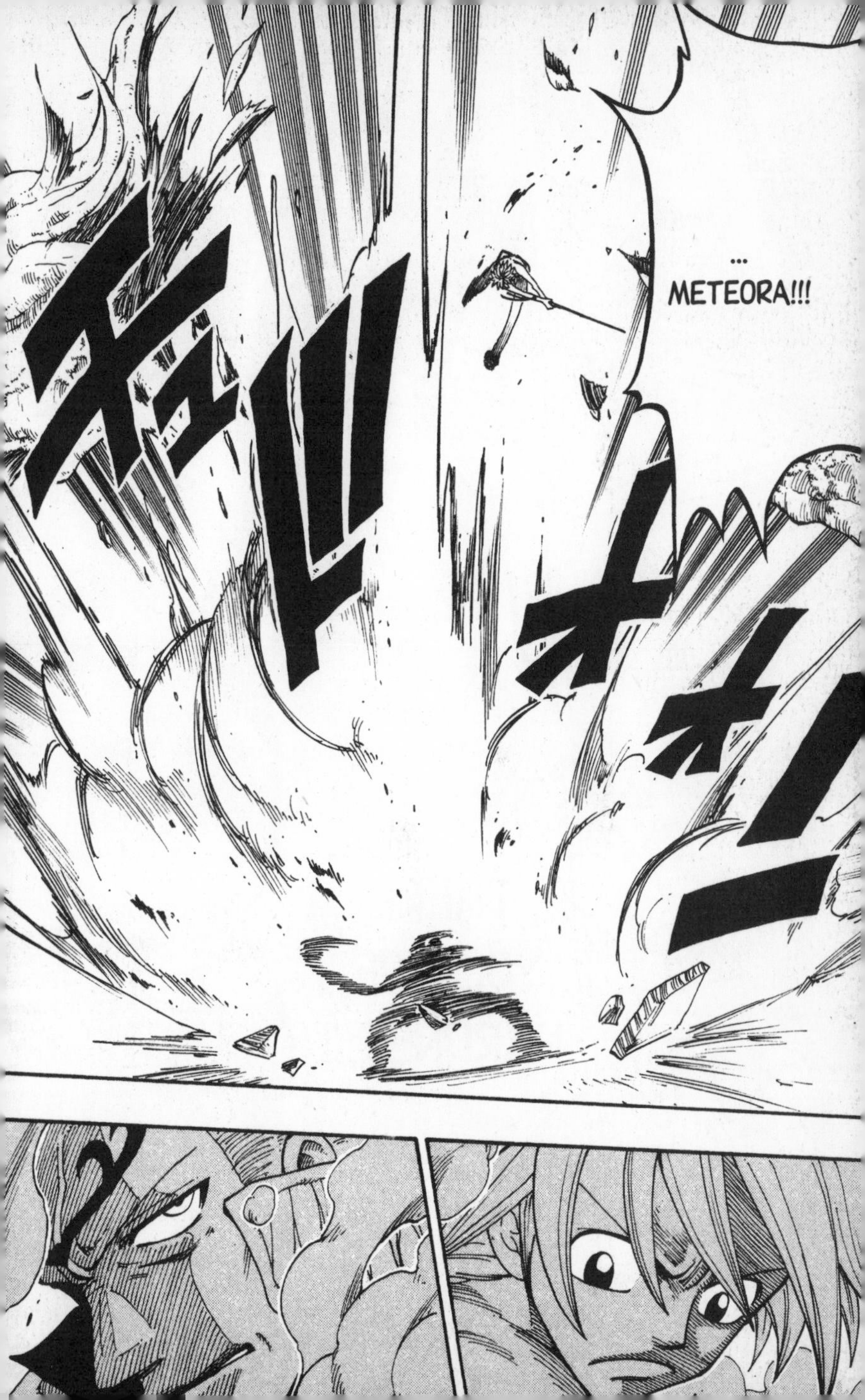
... METEORA!!!

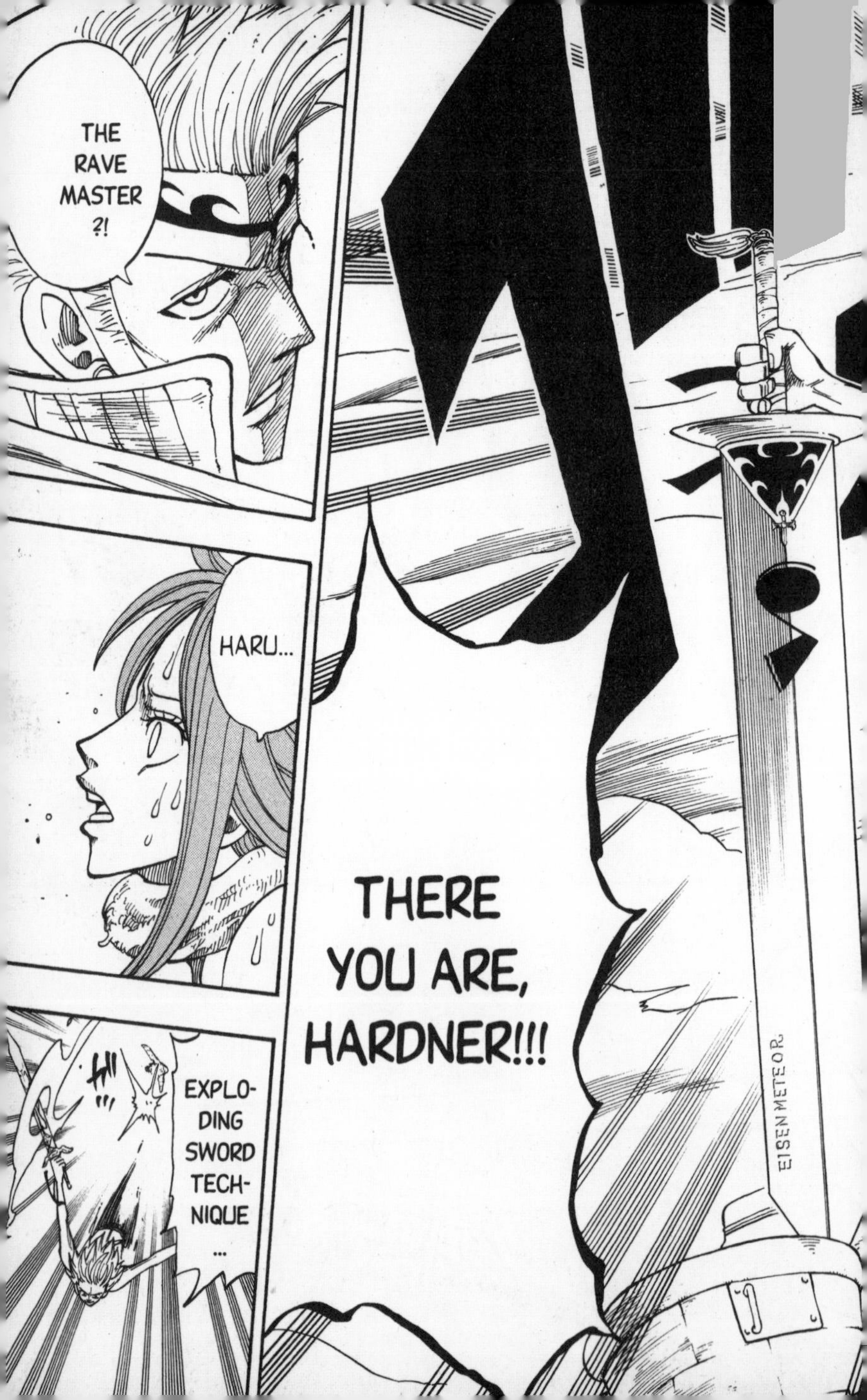
THERE YOU ARE, HARDNER!!!
EISENMETEOR
THE RAVE MASTER ?!
HARU...
EXPLO- DING SWORD TECH- NIQUE ...

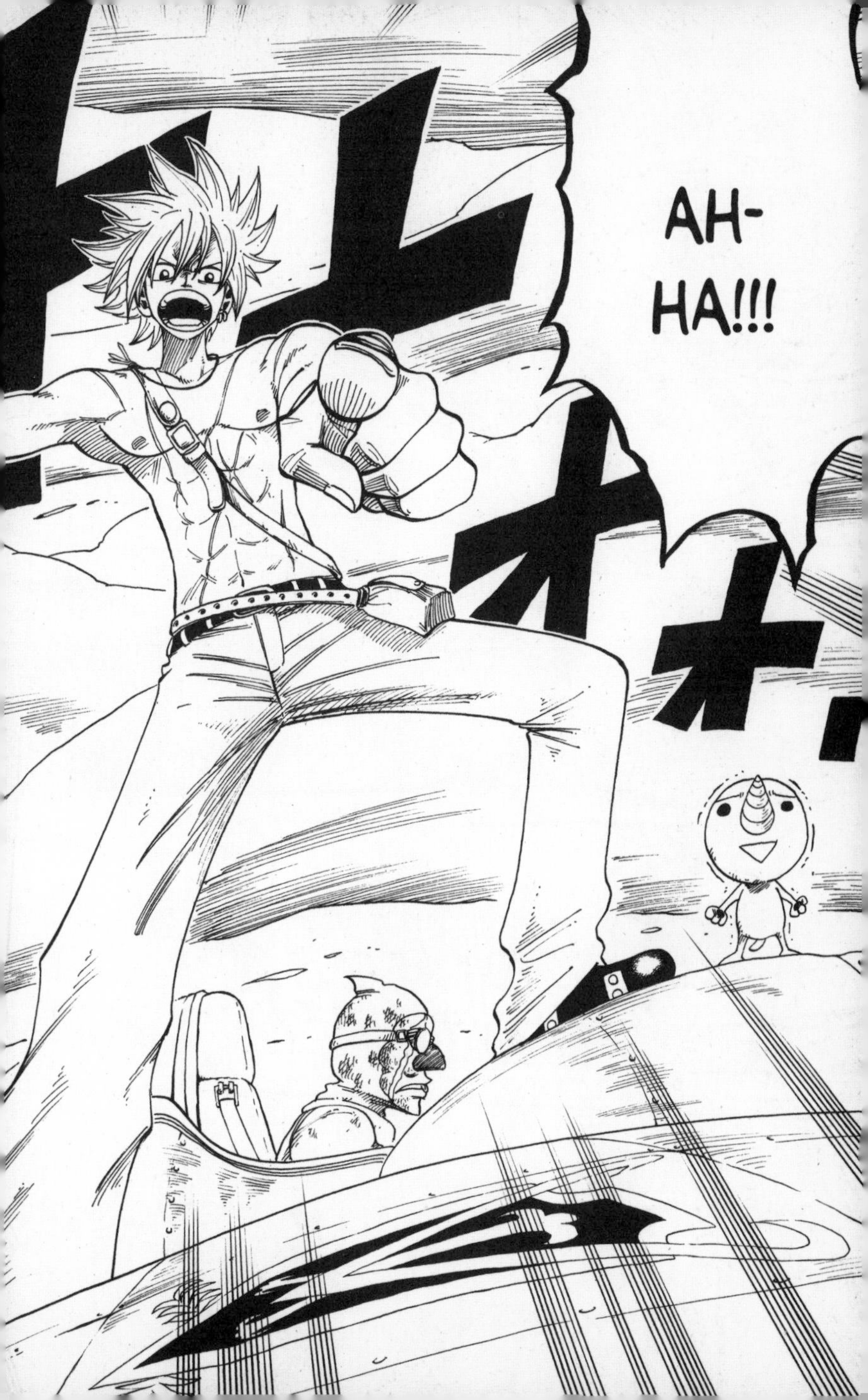
AH-
HA!!!

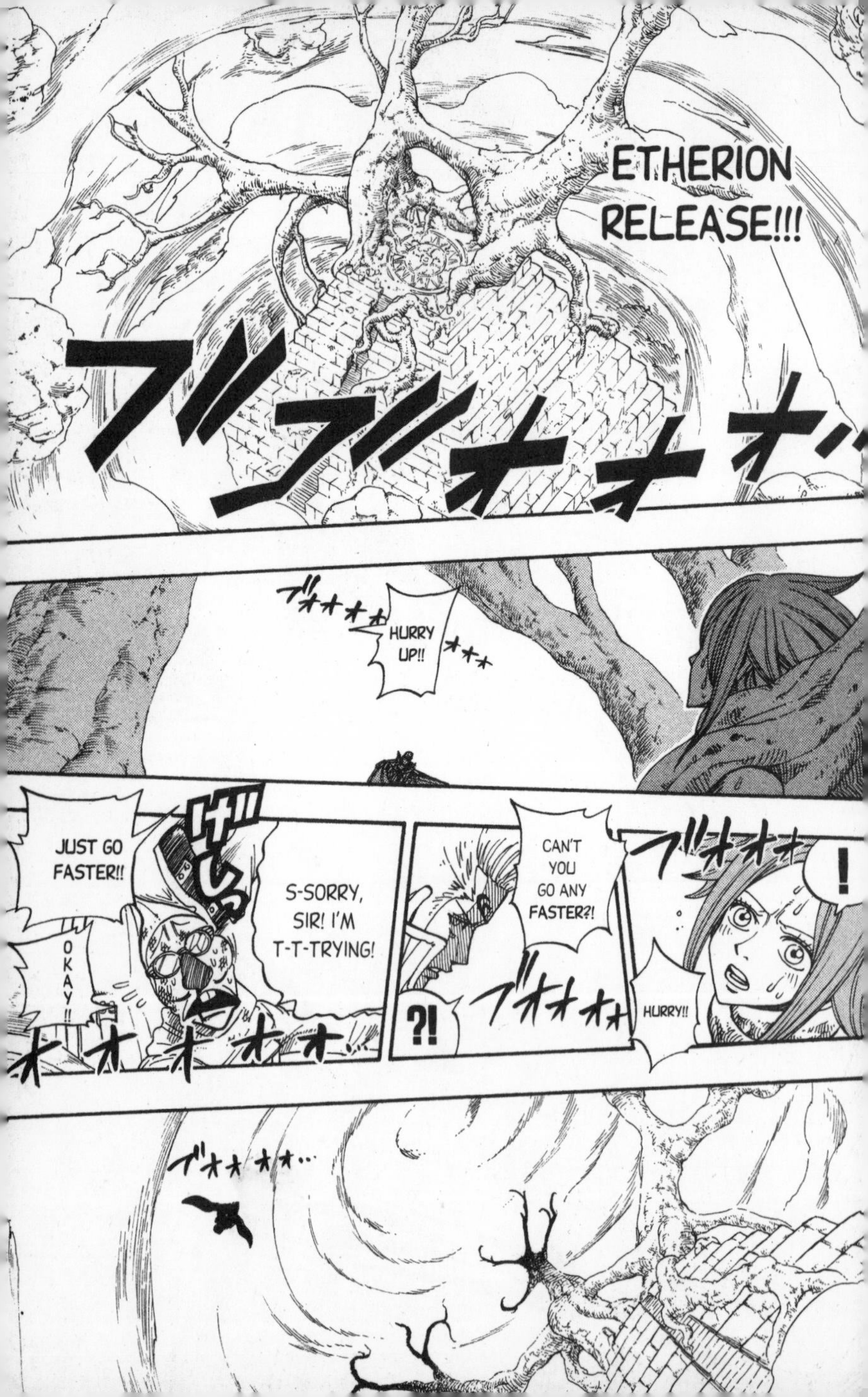
ETHERION RELEASE!!!
HURRY UP!!
!
HURRY!!
CAN'T YOU GO ANY FASTER?!
?!
S-SORRY, SIR! I'M T-T-TRYING!
JUST GO FASTER!!
OKAY!!

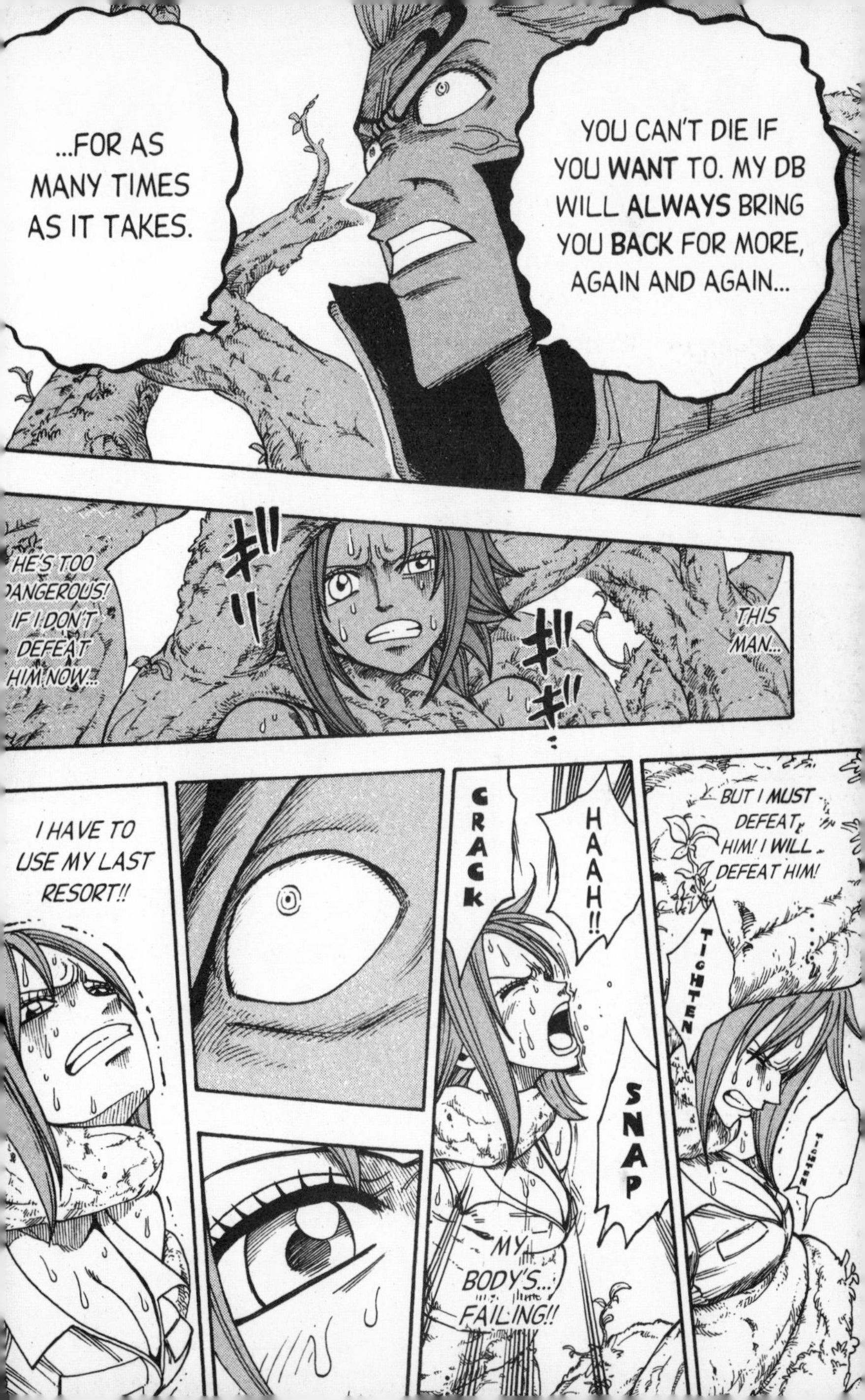
YOU CAN'T DIE IF YOU WANT TO. MY DB WILL ALWAYS BRING YOU BACK FOR MORE, AGAIN AND AGAIN...
...FOR AS MANY TIMES AS IT TAKES.
THIS MAN...
ギリギリ
ギリ
HE'S TOO DANGEROUS! IF I DON'T DEFEAT HIM NOW...
BUT I MUST DEFEAT HIM! I WILL DEFEAT HIM!
TIGHTEN
TIGHTEN
HAAAH!!
CRACK
SNAP
MY BODY'S... FAILING!!
I HAVE TO USE MY LAST RESORT!!

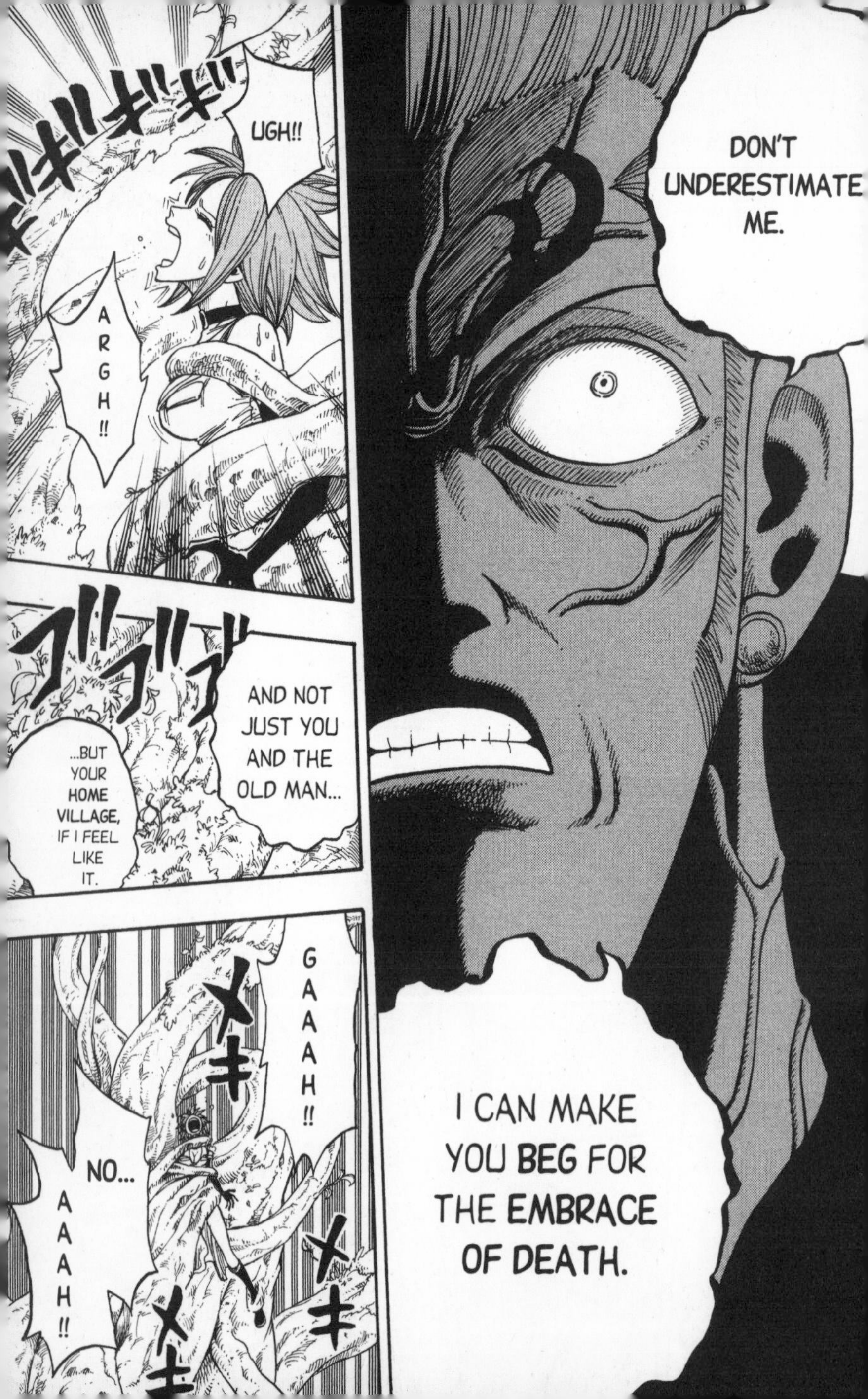
DON'T UNDERESTIMATE ME.
I CAN MAKE YOU BEG FOR THE EMBRACE OF DEATH.
UGH!!
ARGH!!
AND NOT JUST YOU AND THE OLD MAN...
...BUT YOUR HOME VILLAGE, IF I FEEL LIKE IT.
GAAAAH!!
NO...
AAAAH!!

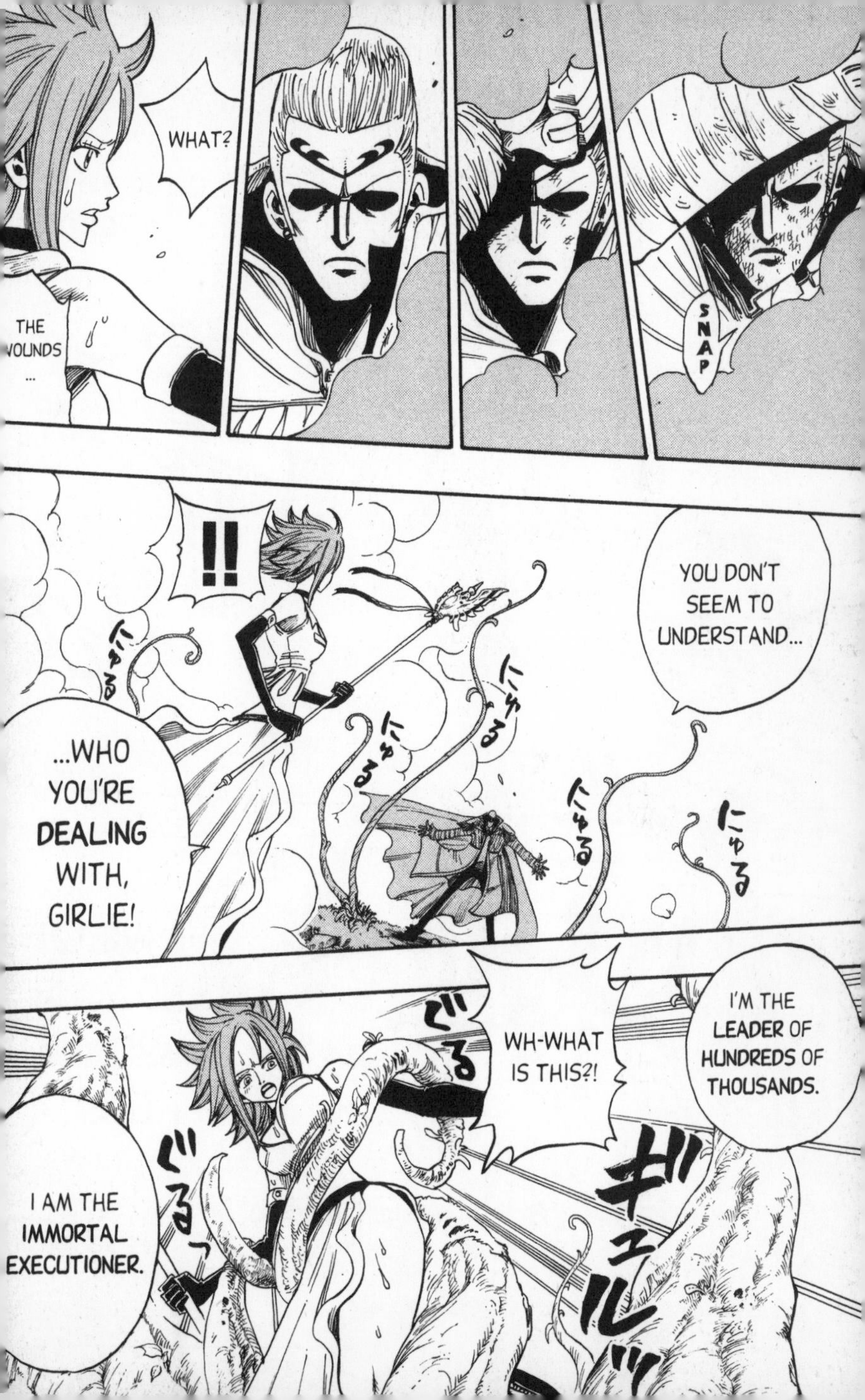
SNAP
WHAT?
THE WOUNDS ...
YOU DON'T SEEM TO UNDERSTAND...
にゅる
にゅる
にゅる
にゅる
!!
にゅる
...WHO YOU'RE DEALING WITH, GIRLIE!
I'M THE LEADER OF HUNDREDS OF THOUSANDS.
ギュルッ
WH-WHAT IS THIS?!
ぐる
ぐるっ
I AM THE IMMORTAL EXECUTIONER.

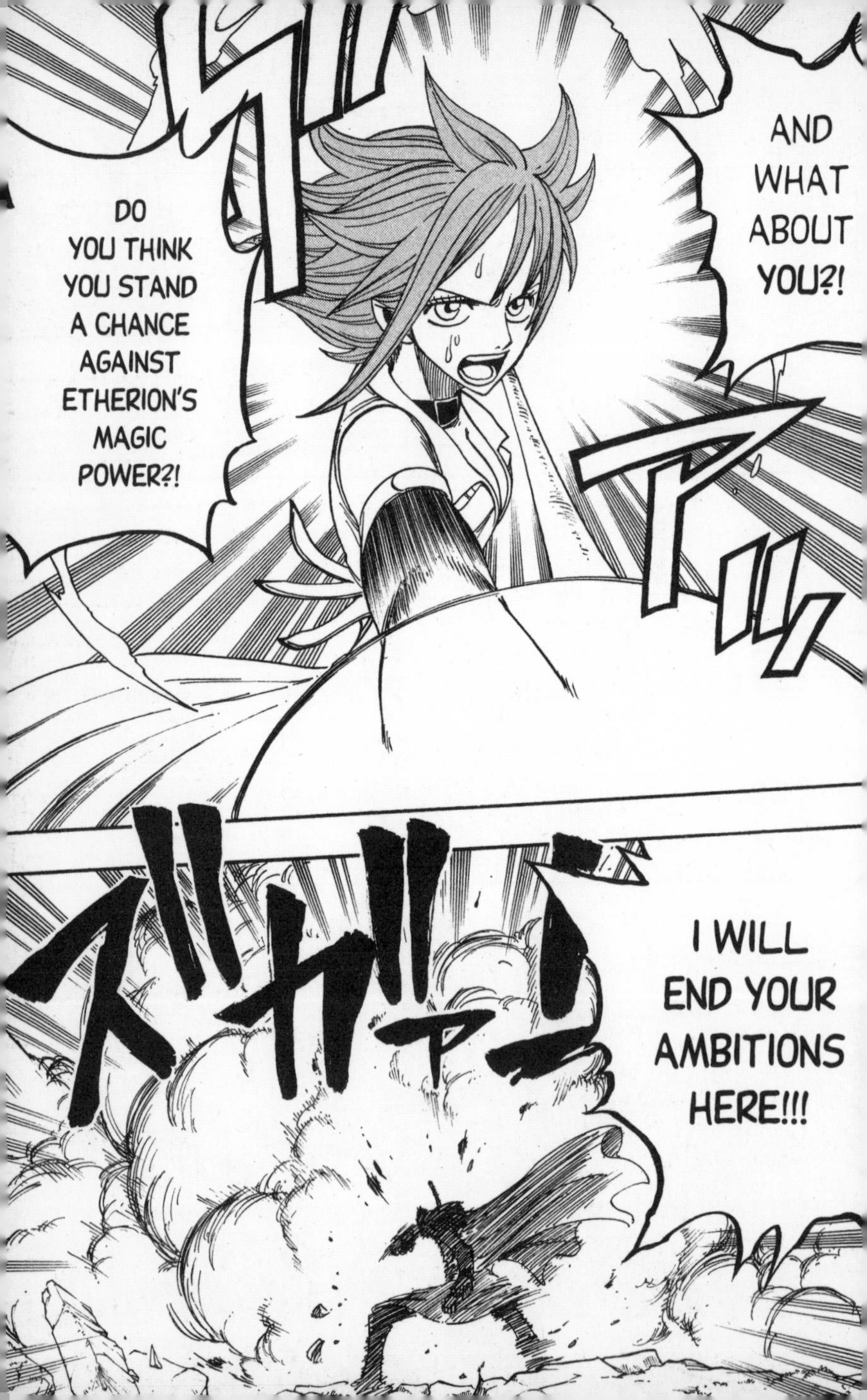
AND WHAT ABOUT YOU?!
DO YOU THINK YOU STAND A CHANCE AGAINST ETHERION'S MAGIC POWER?!
I WILL END YOUR AMBITIONS HERE!!!

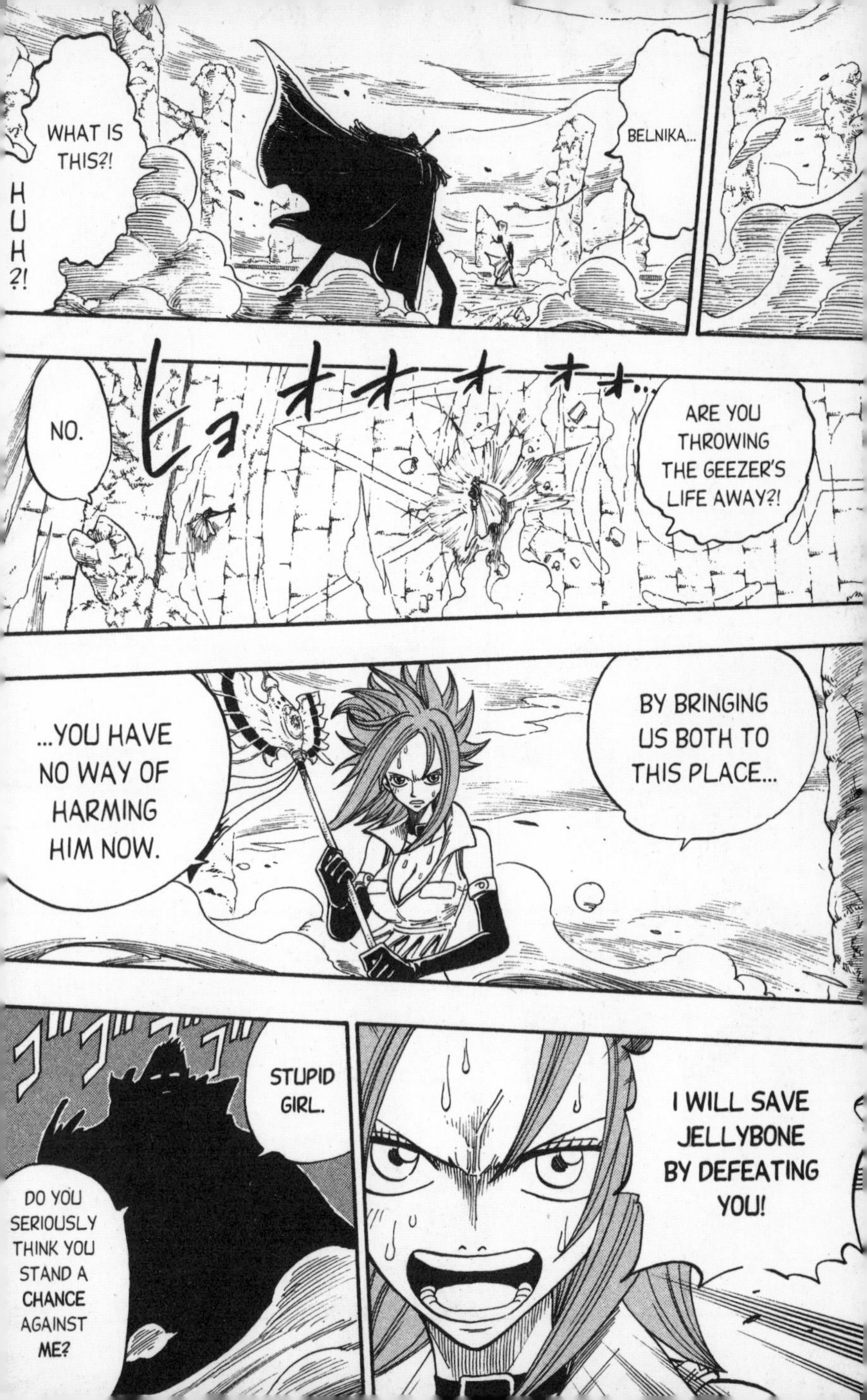
BELNIKA...
WHAT IS THIS?!
HUH?!
ARE YOU THROWING THE GEEZER'S LIFE AWAY?!
ヒョオオオオオ…
NO.
BY BRINGING US BOTH TO THIS PLACE...
...YOU HAVE NO WAY OF HARMING HIM NOW.
I WILL SAVE JELLYBONE BY DEFEATING YOU!
STUPID GIRL.
ゴゴゴゴ
DO YOU SERIOUSLY THINK YOU STAND A CHANCE AGAINST ME?

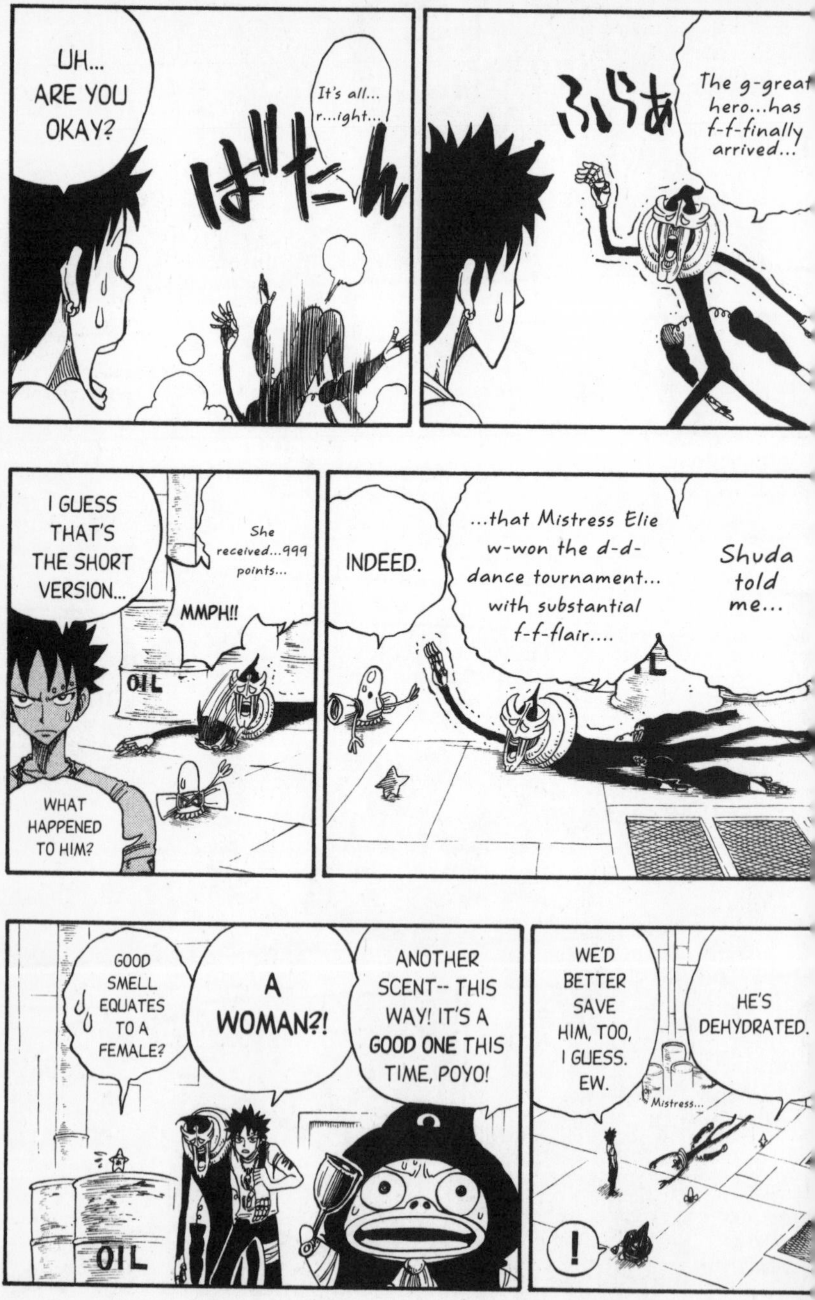
ふらあ
The g-great hero...has f-f-finally arrived...
It's all... r...ight...
ばたーん
UH... ARE YOU OKAY?
Shuda told me...
...that Mistress Elie w-won the d-d-dance tournament... with substantial f-f-flair....
INDEED.
She received...999 points...
I GUESS THAT'S THE SHORT VERSION...
MMPH!!
WHAT HAPPENED TO HIM?
OIL
HE'S DEHYDRATED.
WE'D BETTER SAVE HIM, TOO, I GUESS. EW.
Mistress...
!
ANOTHER SCENT-- THIS WAY! IT'S A GOOD ONE THIS TIME, POYO!
A WOMAN?!
GOOD SMELL EQUATES TO A FEMALE?
OIL

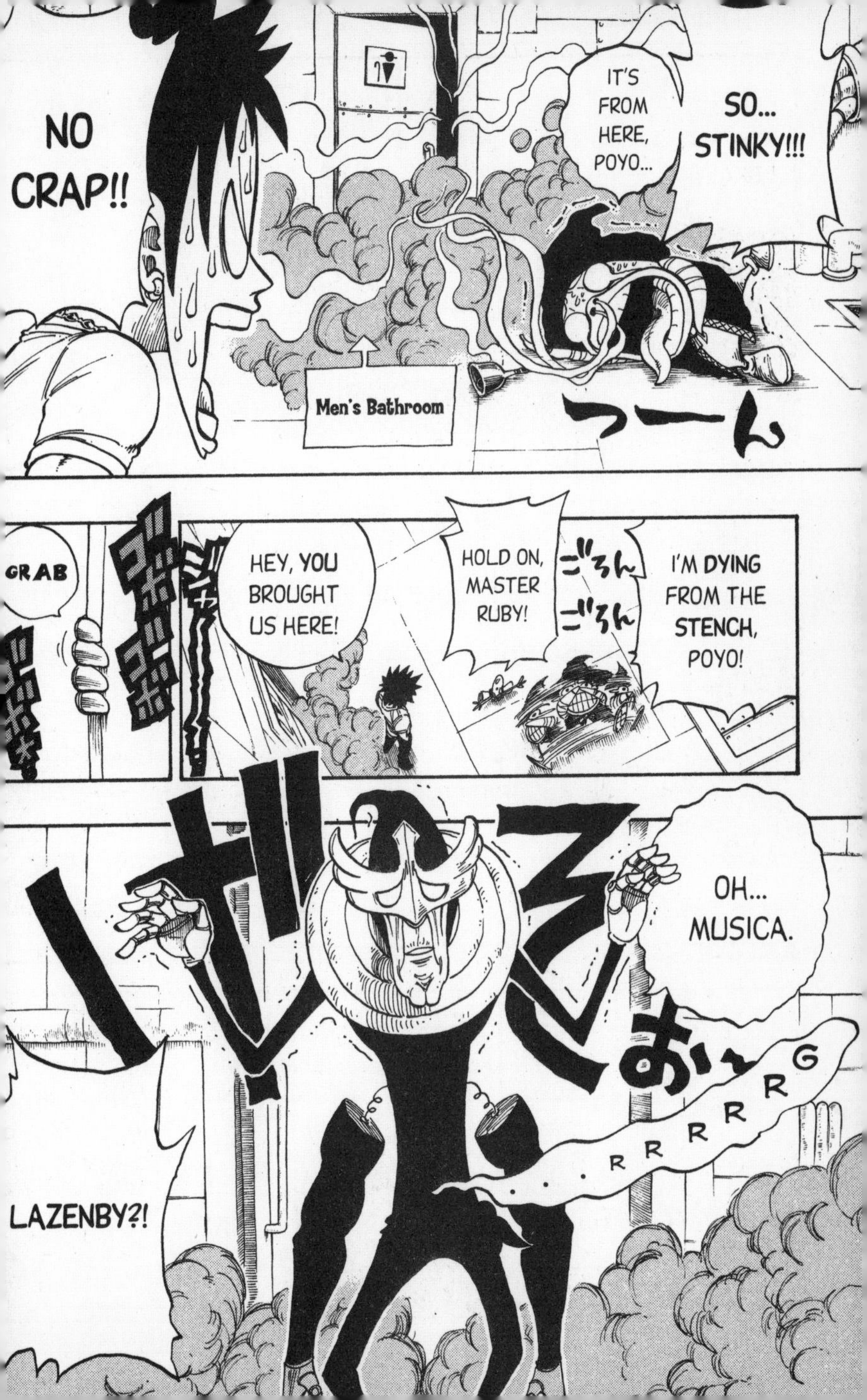
SO... STINKY!!!
IT'S FROM HERE, POYO...
NO CRAP!!
Men's Bathroom
つーん
I'M DYING FROM THE STENCH, POYO!
ごろん
ごろん
HOLD ON, MASTER RUBY!
HEY, YOU BROUGHT US HERE!
GRAB
OH... MUSICA.
お
...RRRRRRG
LAZENBY?!

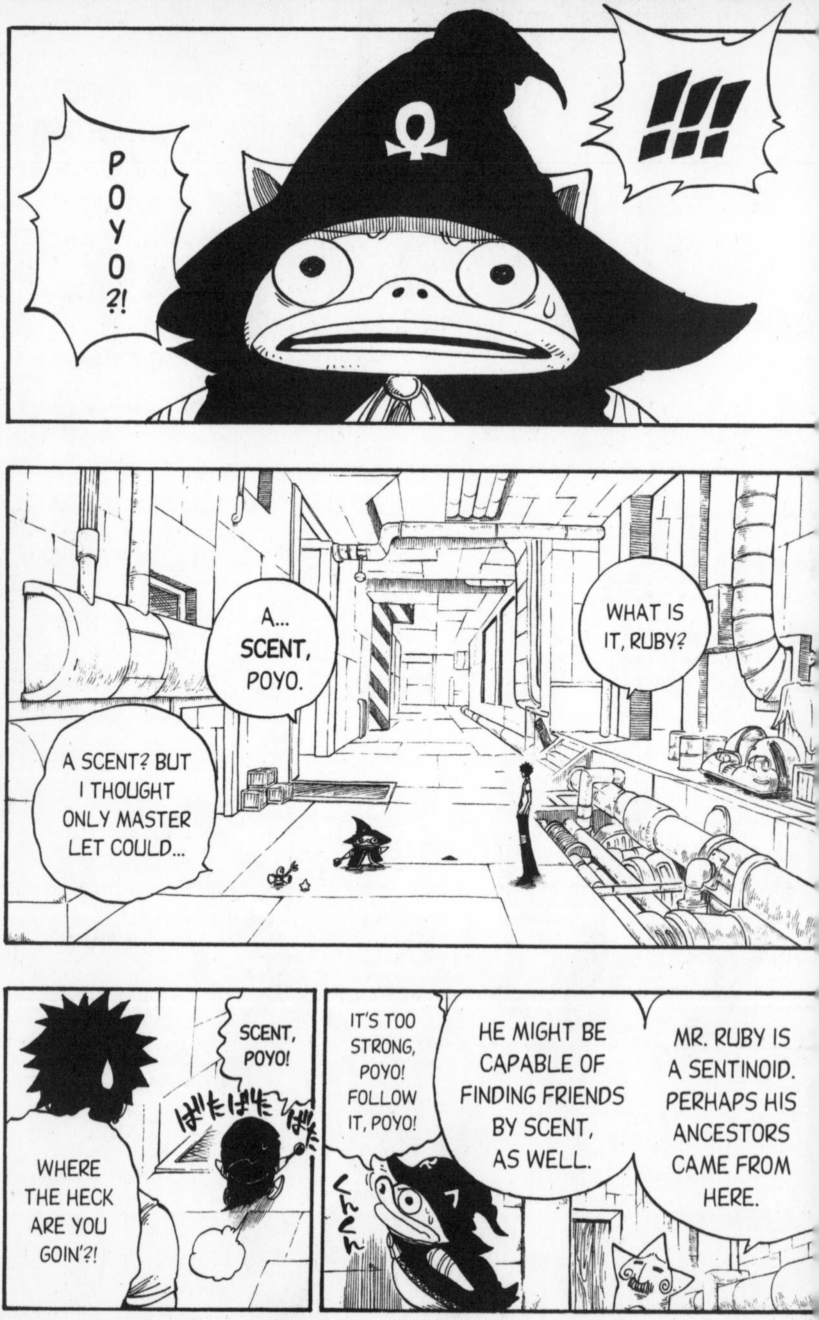
!!!
POYO?!
WHAT IS IT, RUBY?
A... SCENT, POYO.
A SCENT? BUT I THOUGHT ONLY MASTER LET COULD...
MR. RUBY IS A SENTINOID. PERHAPS HIS ANCESTORS CAME FROM HERE.
HE MIGHT BE CAPABLE OF FINDING FRIENDS BY SCENT, AS WELL.
IT'S TOO STRONG, POYO! FOLLOW IT, POYO!
くんくん
SCENT, POYO!
ぱたぱた
ぱた
WHERE THE HECK ARE YOU GOIN'?!

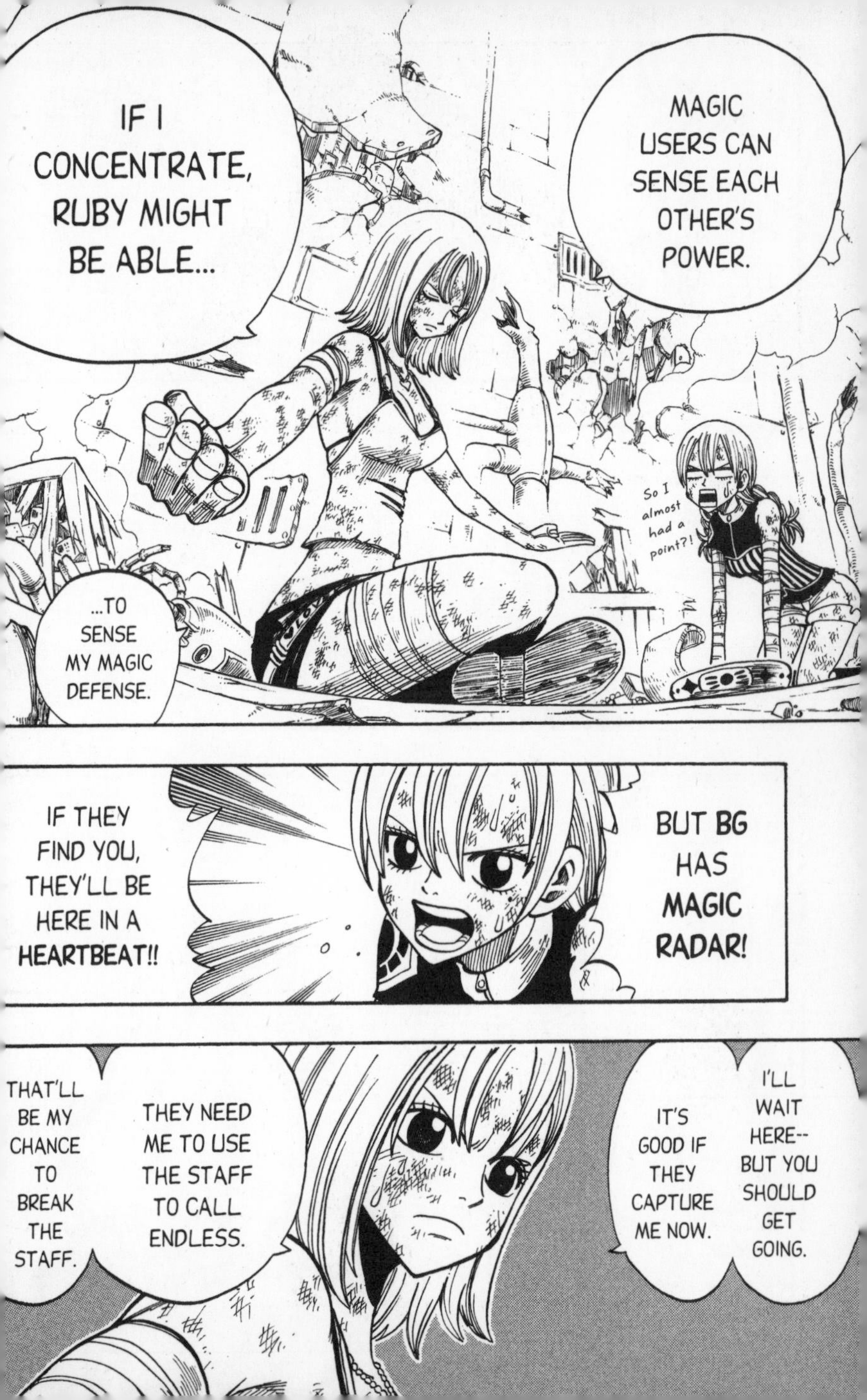
MAGIC USERS CAN SENSE EACH OTHER'S POWER.
IF I CONCENTRATE, RUBY MIGHT BE ABLE...
So I almost had a point?!
...TO SENSE MY MAGIC DEFENSE.
BUT BG HAS MAGIC RADAR!
IF THEY FIND YOU, THEY'LL BE HERE IN A HEARTBEAT!!
I'LL WAIT HERE-- BUT YOU SHOULD GET GOING.
IT'S GOOD IF THEY CAPTURE ME NOW.
THEY NEED ME TO USE THE STAFF TO CALL ENDLESS.
THAT'LL BE MY CHANCE TO BREAK THE STAFF.

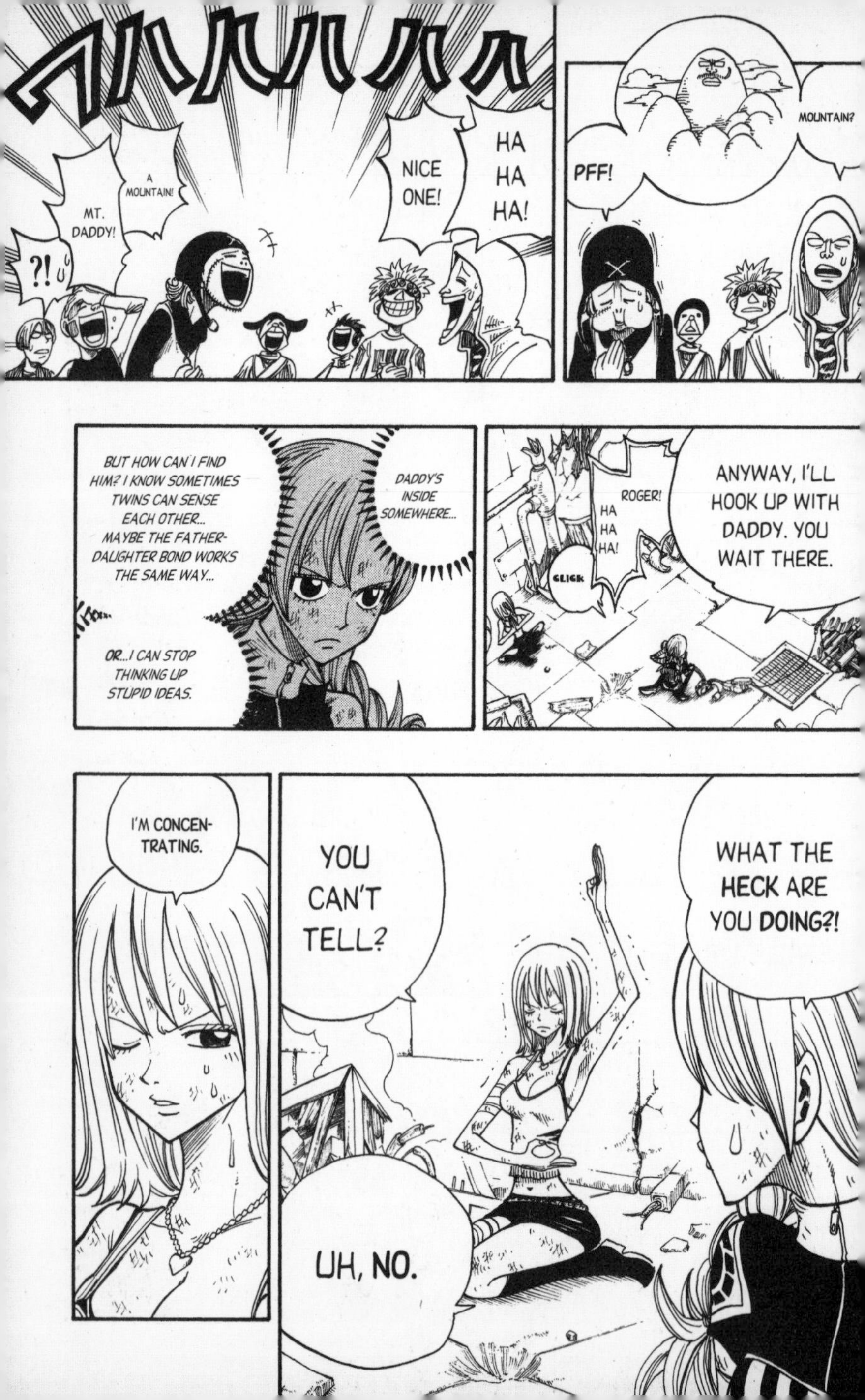
MOUNTAIN?
PFF!
HA HA HA!
NICE ONE!
A MOUNTAIN!
MT. DADDY!
?!
ANYWAY, I'LL HOOK UP WITH DADDY. YOU WAIT THERE.
ROGER!
HA HA HA!
CLICK
DADDY'S INSIDE SOMEWHERE...
BUT HOW CAN I FIND HIM? I KNOW SOMETIMES TWINS CAN SENSE EACH OTHER... MAYBE THE FATHER-DAUGHTER BOND WORKS THE SAME WAY...
OR...I CAN STOP THINKING UP STUPID IDEAS.
WHAT THE HECK ARE YOU DOING?!
YOU CAN'T TELL?
UH, NO.
I'M CONCEN-TRATING.

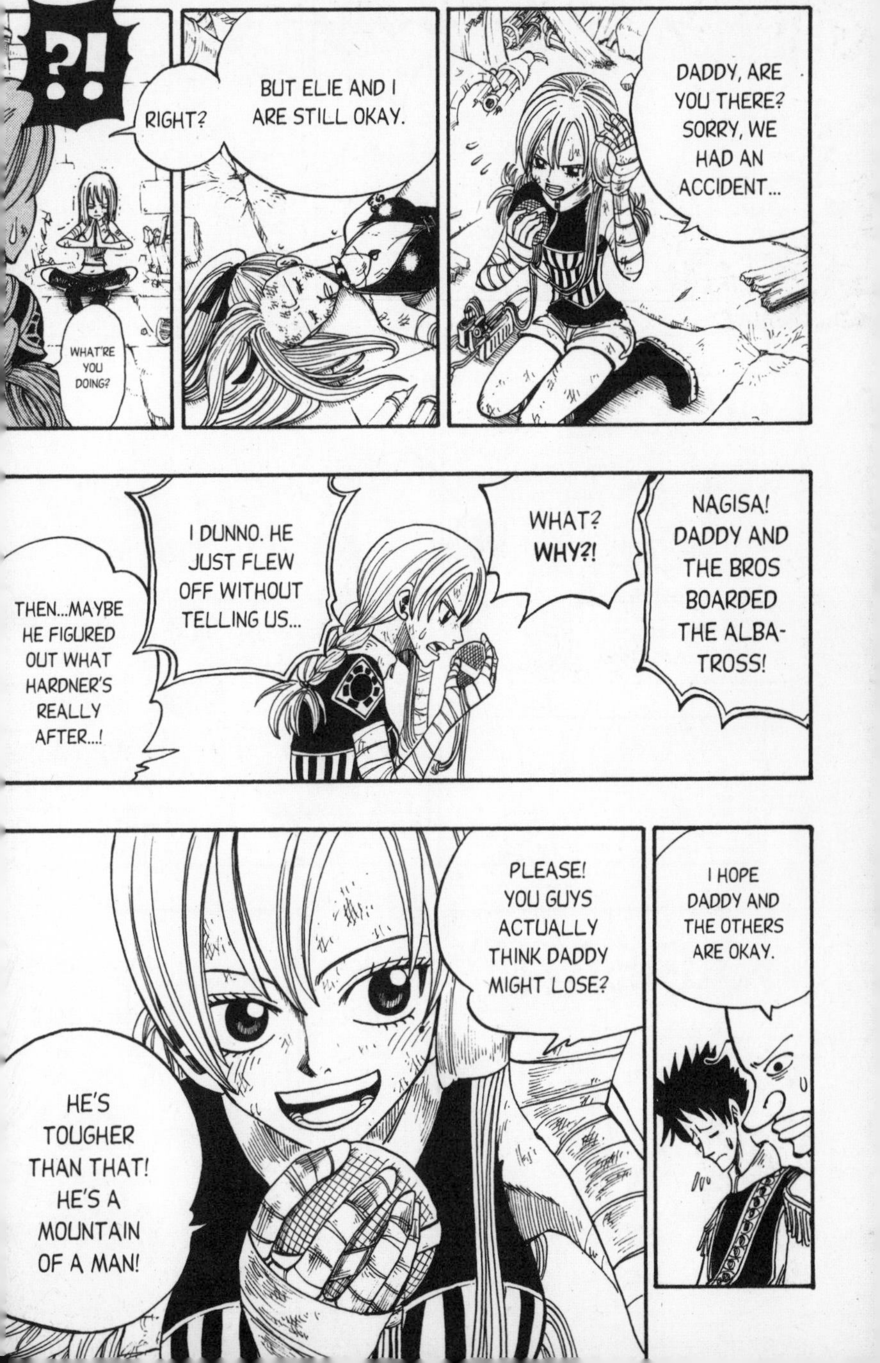
DADDY, ARE YOU THERE? SORRY, WE HAD AN ACCIDENT...
BUT ELIE AND I ARE STILL OKAY.
RIGHT?
?!
WHAT'RE YOU DOING?
NAGISA! DADDY AND THE BROS BOARDED THE ALBA-TROSS!
WHAT? WHY?!
I DUNNO. HE JUST FLEW OFF WITHOUT TELLING US...
THEN...MAYBE HE FIGURED OUT WHAT HARDNER'S REALLY AFTER...!
I HOPE DADDY AND THE OTHERS ARE OKAY.
PLEASE! YOU GUYS ACTUALLY THINK DADDY MIGHT LOSE?
HE'S TOUGHER THAN THAT! HE'S A MOUNTAIN OF A MAN!

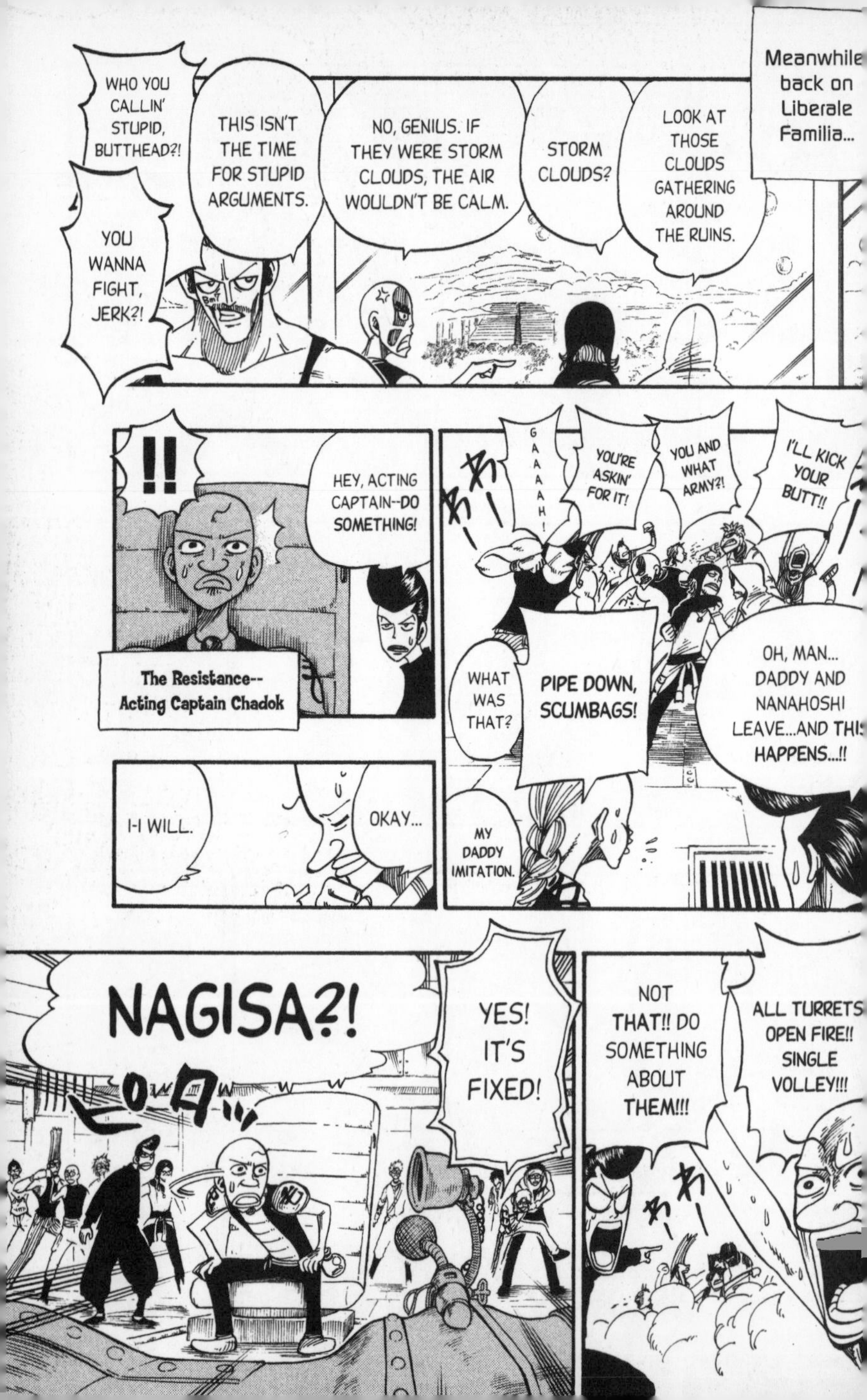
Meanwhile back on Liberale Familia...
LOOK AT THOSE CLOUDS GATHERING AROUND THE RUINS.
STORM CLOUDS?
NO, GENIUS. IF THEY WERE STORM CLOUDS, THE AIR WOULDN'T BE CALM.
THIS ISN'T THE TIME FOR STUPID ARGUMENTS.
WHO YOU CALLIN' STUPID, BUTTHEAD?!
YOU WANNA FIGHT, JERK?!
I'LL KICK YOUR BUTT!!
YOU AND WHAT ARMY?!
YOU'RE ASKIN' FOR IT!
GAAAAH!
OH, MAN... DADDY AND NANAHOSHI LEAVE...AND THI HAPPENS...!!
PIPE DOWN, SCUMBAGS!
WHAT WAS THAT?
MY DADDY IMITATION.
!!
HEY, ACTING CAPTAIN--DO SOMETHING!
The Resistance-- Acting Captain Chadok
OKAY...
I-I WILL.
ALL TURRETS OPEN FIRE!! SINGLE VOLLEY!!!
NOT THAT!! DO SOMETHING ABOUT THEM!!!
YES! IT'S FIXED!
NAGISA?!

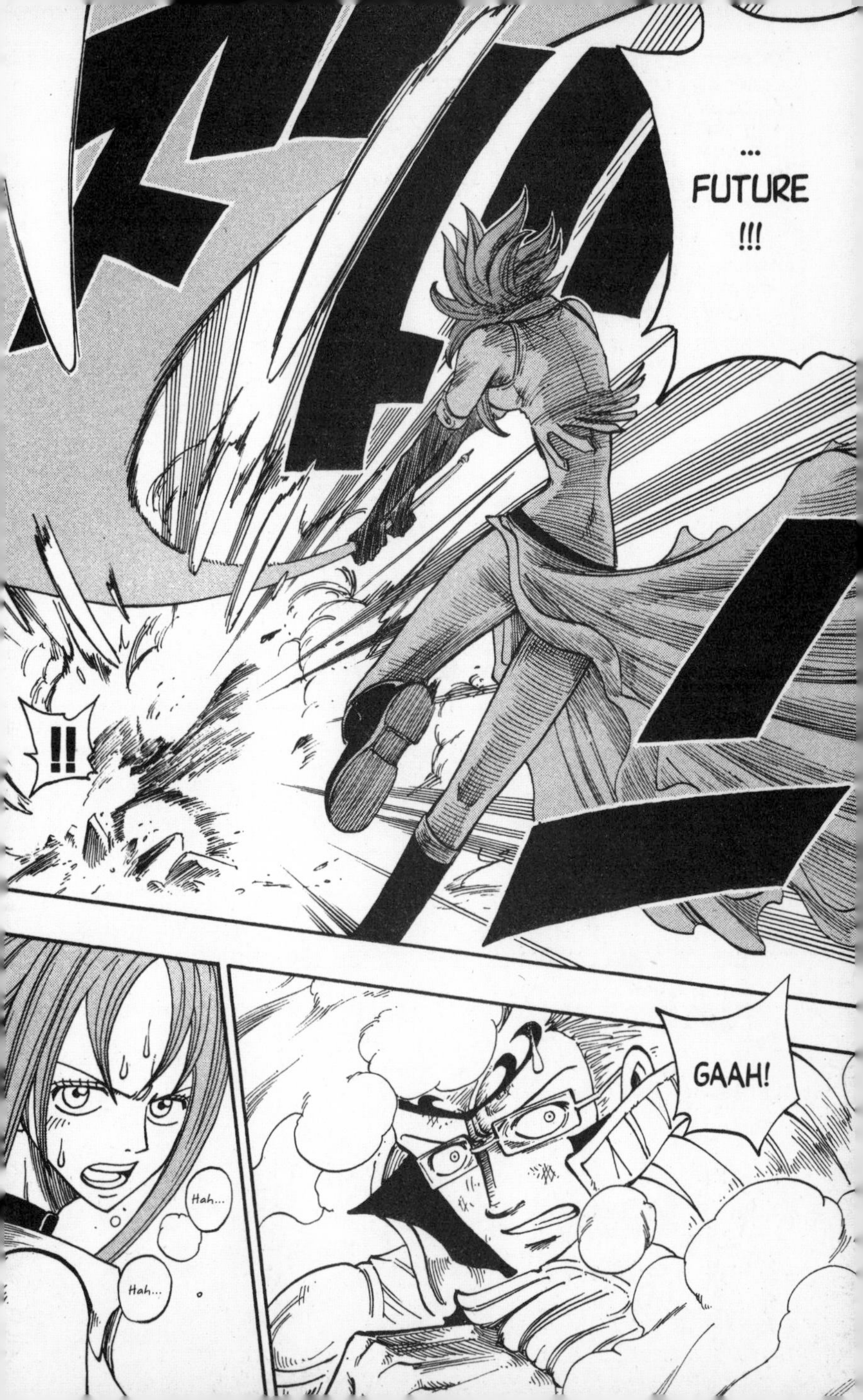
... FUTURE !!!
!!
GAAH!
Hah...
Hah...

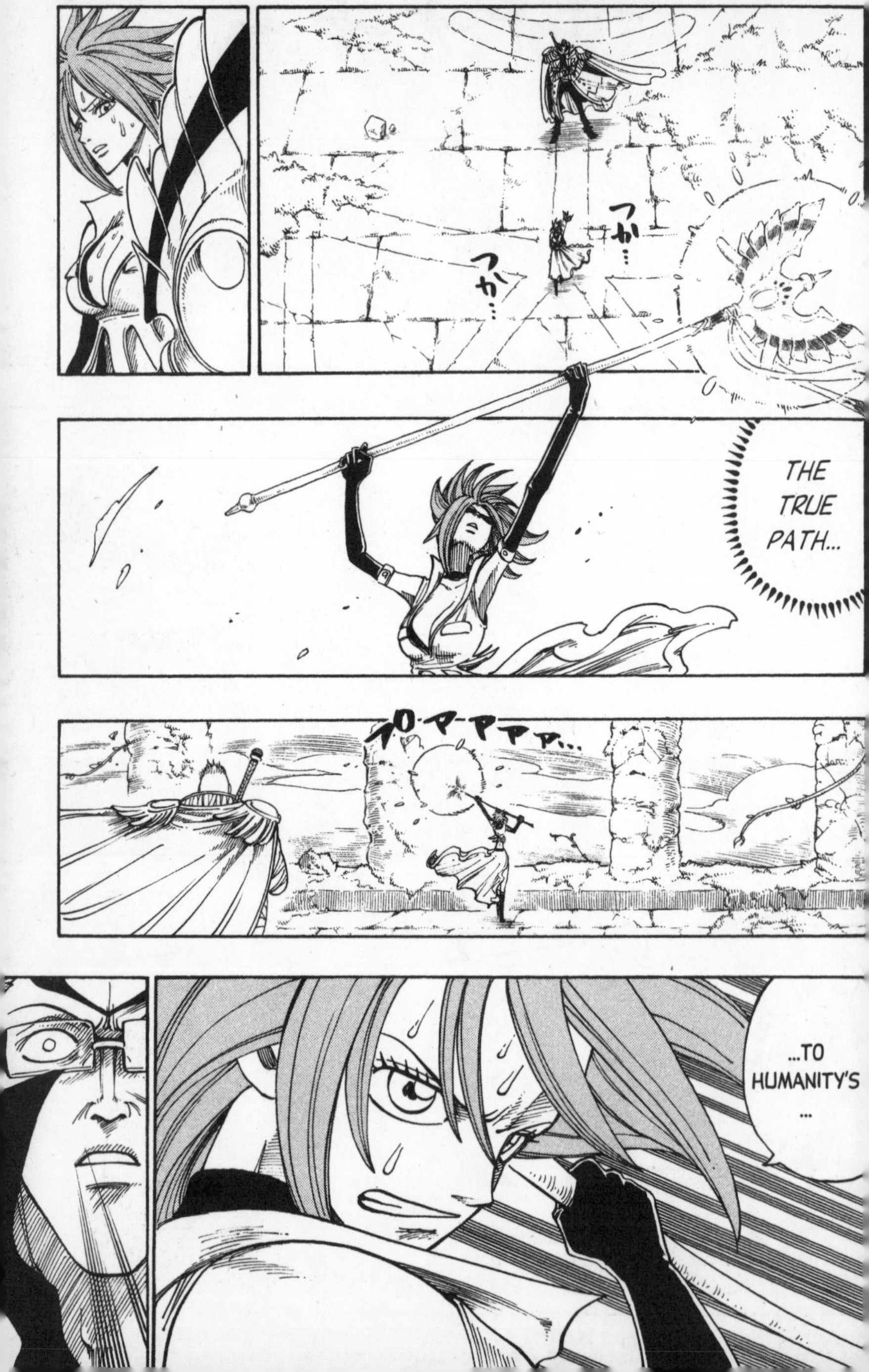
つか…
つか…
THE TRUE PATH...
フワアアアア...
...TO HUMANITY'S ...

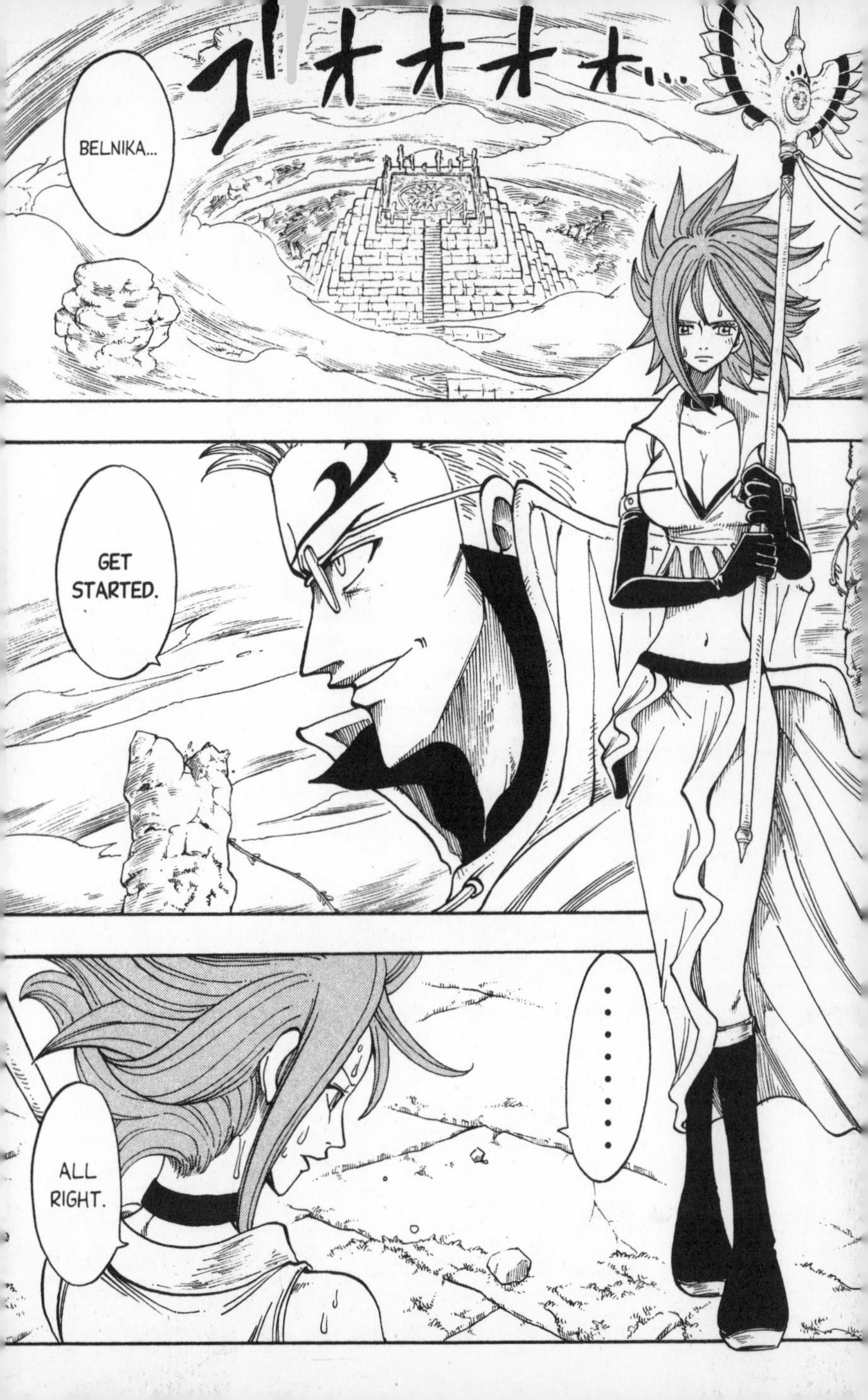

ゴオオオオ…
BELNIKA...
GET STARTED.
....
ALL RIGHT.

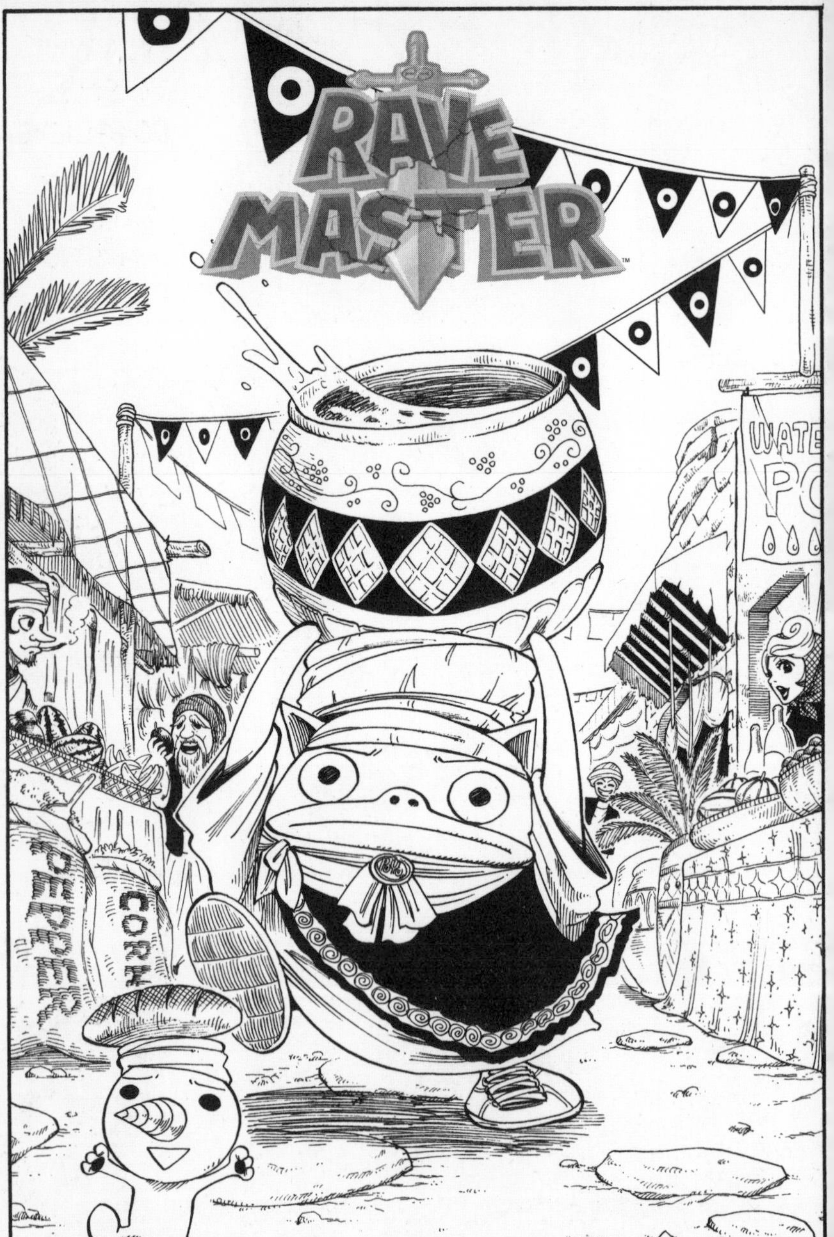
RAVE MASTER
PEPPER
CORN

RAVE:215 IN PURSUIT OF JUSTICE

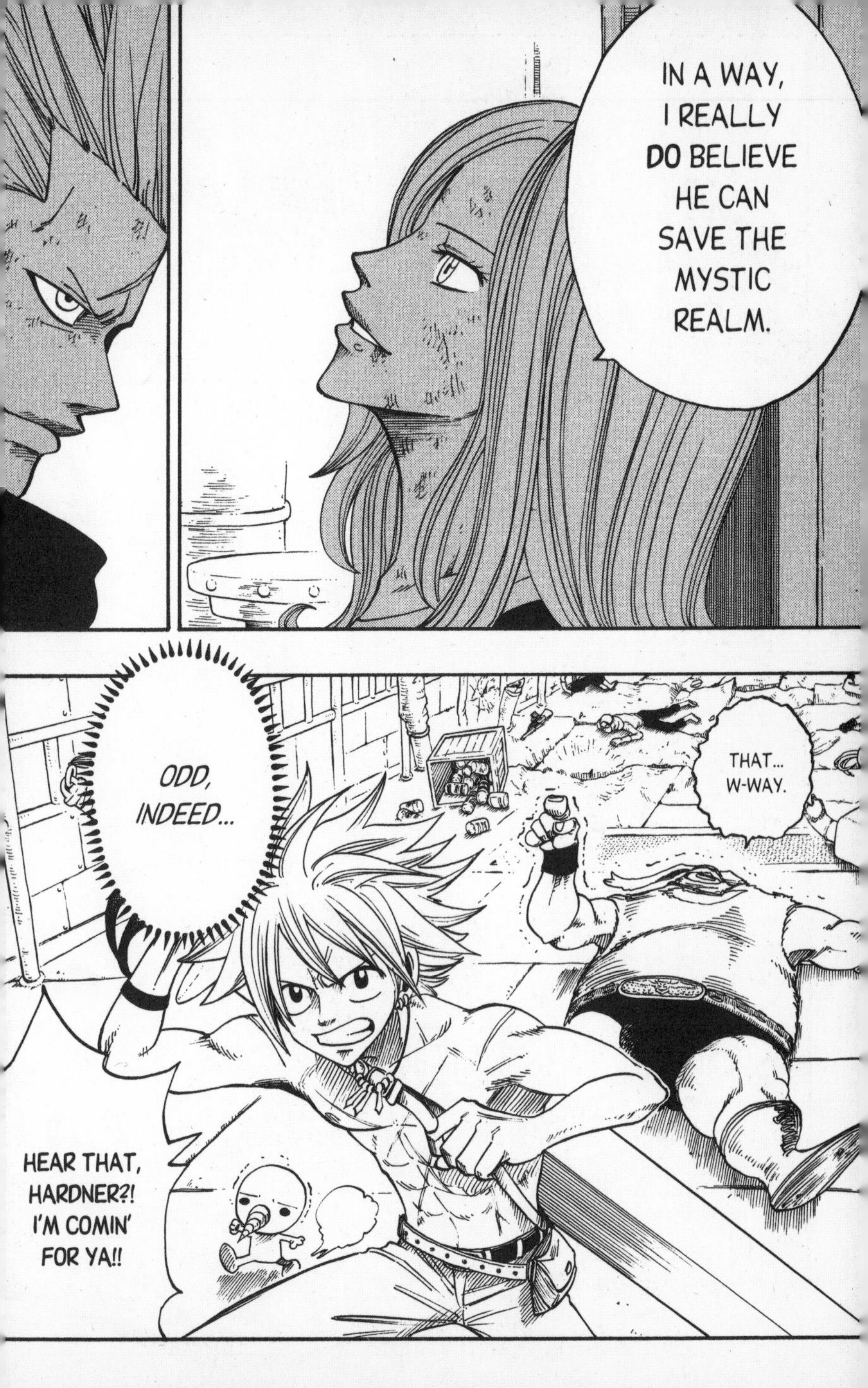
IN A WAY, I REALLY DO BELIEVE HE CAN SAVE THE MYSTIC REALM.
THAT... W-WAY.
ODD, INDEED...
HEAR THAT, HARDNER?! I'M COMIN' FOR YA!!

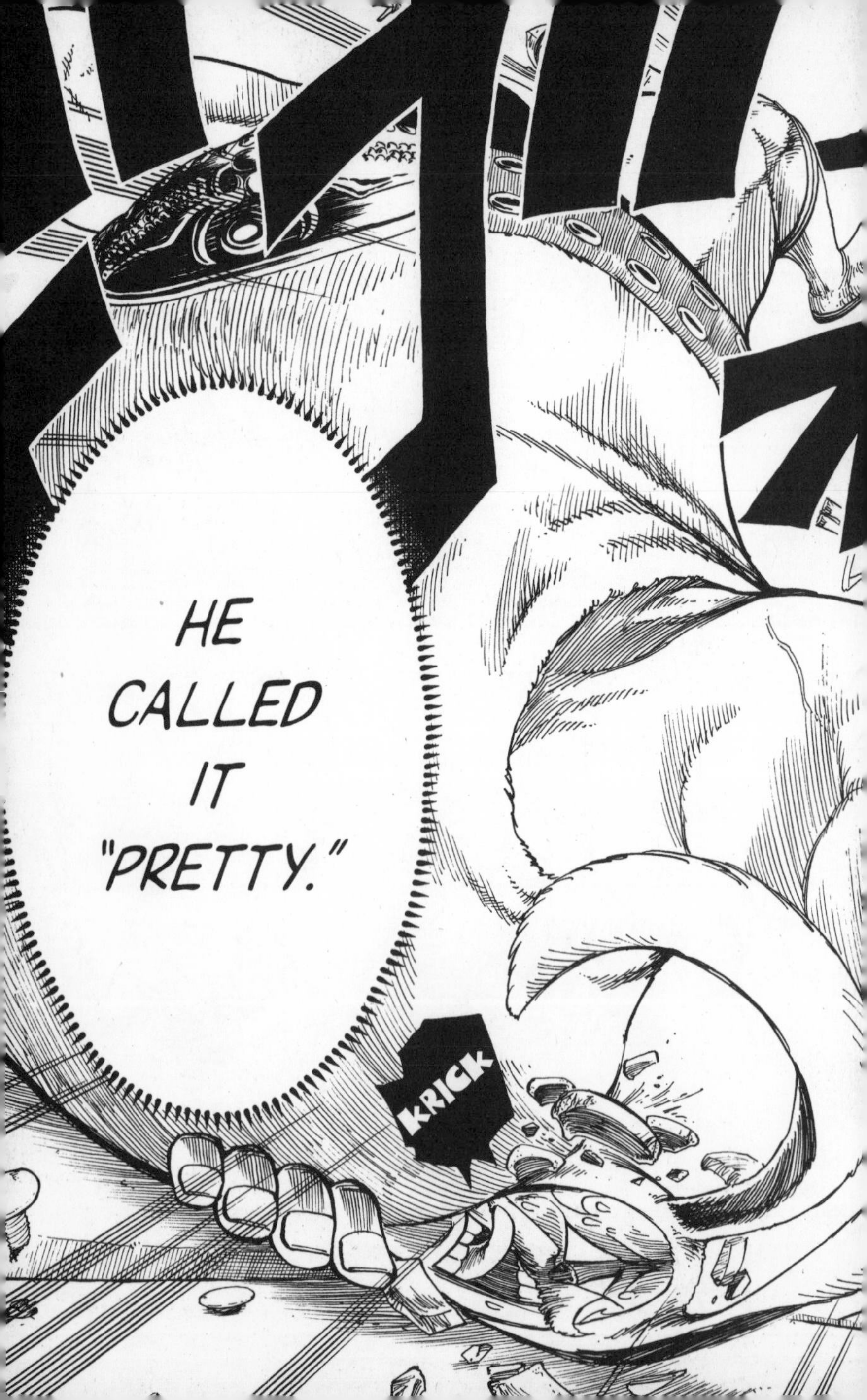
HE CALLED IT "PRETTY."
KRICK

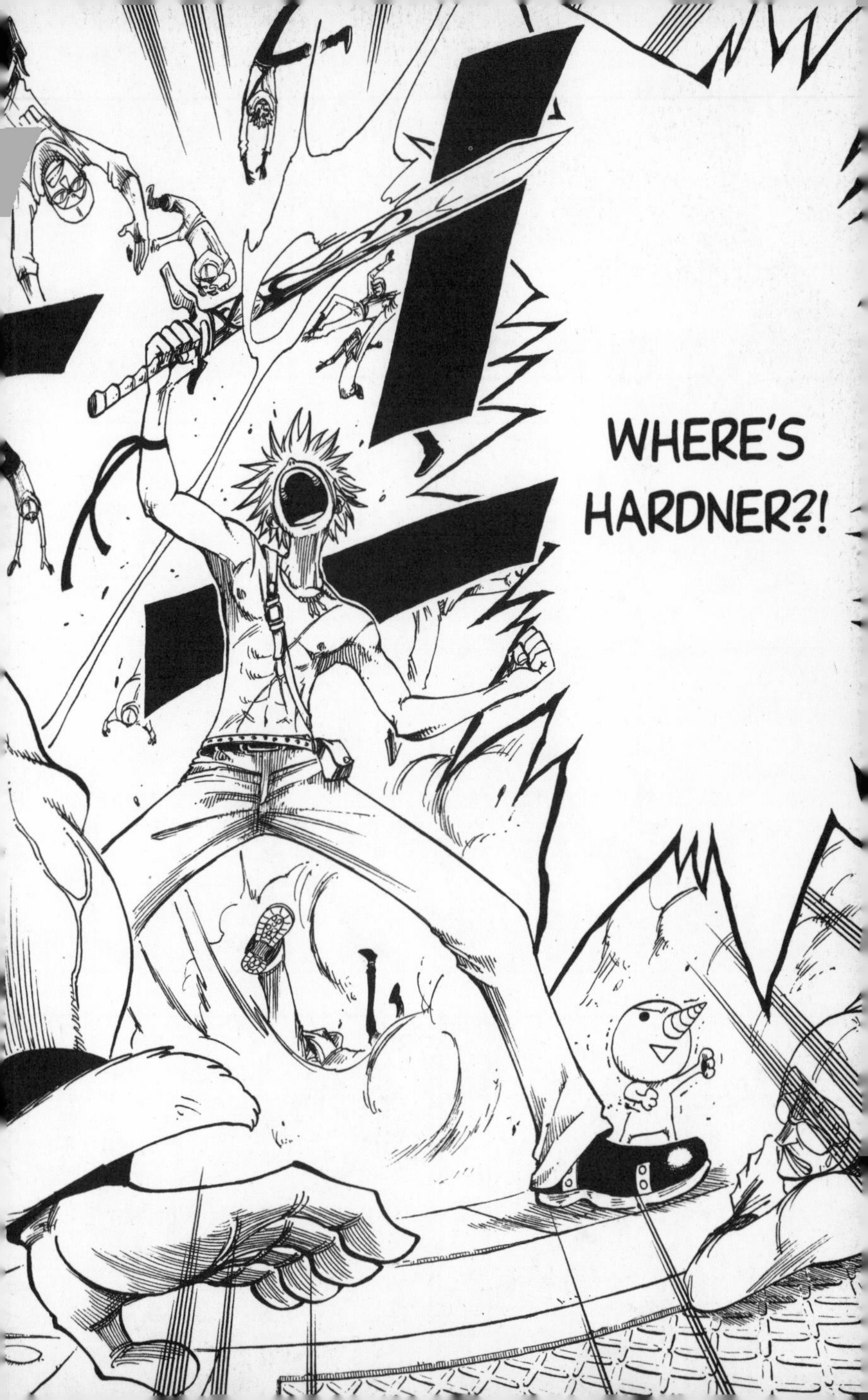
WHERE'S HARDNER?!

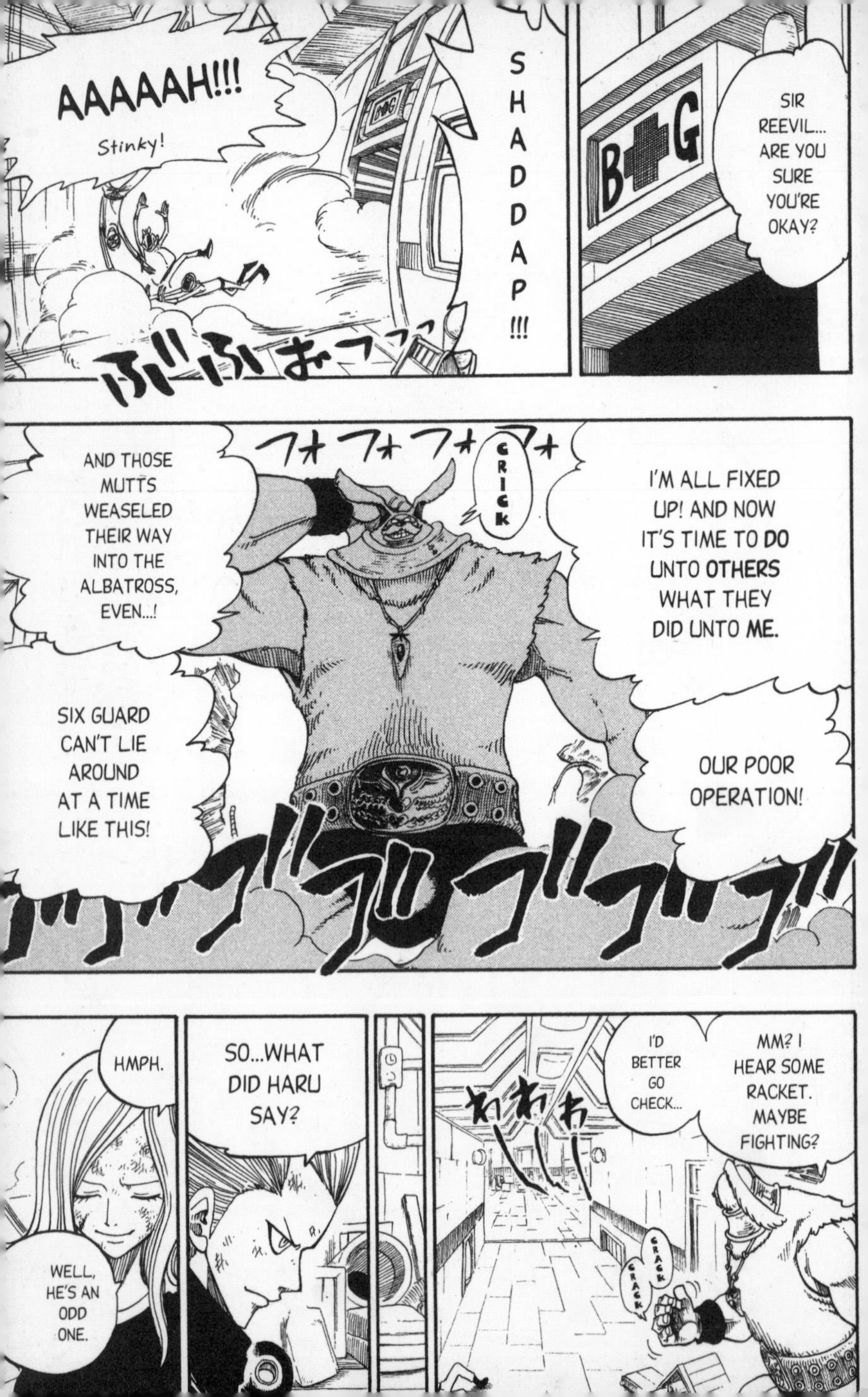
SIR REEVIL... ARE YOU SURE YOU'RE OKAY?
SHADDAP!!!
AAAAAH!!!
Stinky!
I'M ALL FIXED UP! AND NOW IT'S TIME TO DO UNTO OTHERS WHAT THEY DID UNTO ME.
CRICK
フォフォフォフォ
OUR POOR OPERATION!
AND THOSE MUTTS WEASELED THEIR WAY INTO THE ALBATROSS, EVEN...!
SIX GUARD CAN'T LIE AROUND AT A TIME LIKE THIS!
MM? I HEAR SOME RACKET. MAYBE FIGHTING?
I'D BETTER GO CHECK...
CRACK
CRACK
CRACK
SO...WHAT DID HARU SAY?
HMPH.
WELL, HE'S AN ODD ONE.

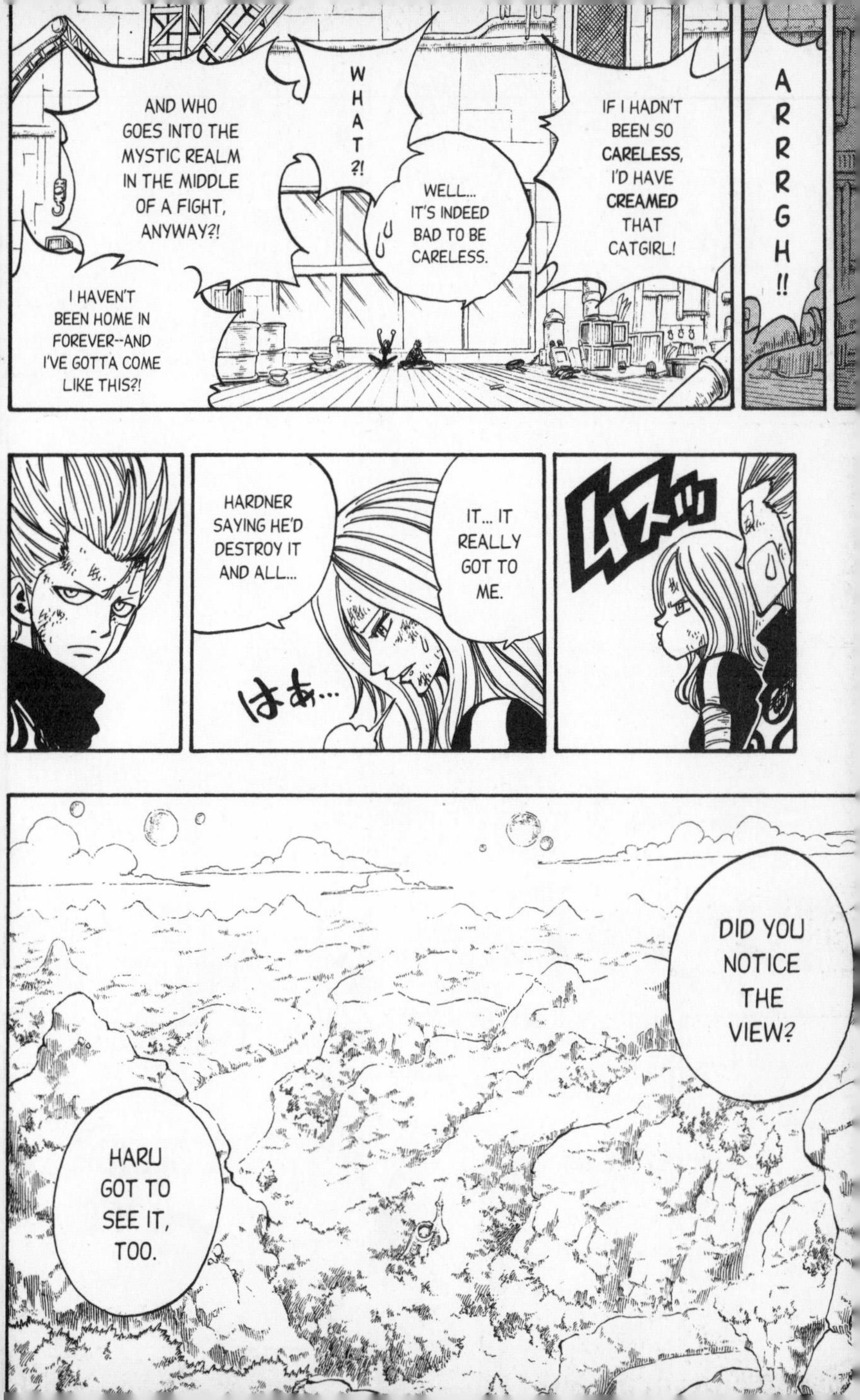
ARRRGH!!
IF I HADN'T BEEN SO CARELESS, I'D HAVE CREAMED THAT CATGIRL!
WELL... IT'S INDEED BAD TO BE CARELESS.
WHAT?!
AND WHO GOES INTO THE MYSTIC REALM IN THE MIDDLE OF A FIGHT, ANYWAY?!
I HAVEN'T BEEN HOME IN FOREVER--AND I'VE GOTTA COME LIKE THIS?!
ムスッ
IT... IT REALLY GOT TO ME.
HARDNER SAYING HE'D DESTROY IT AND ALL...
はぁ…
DID YOU NOTICE THE VIEW?
HARU GOT TO SEE IT, TOO.

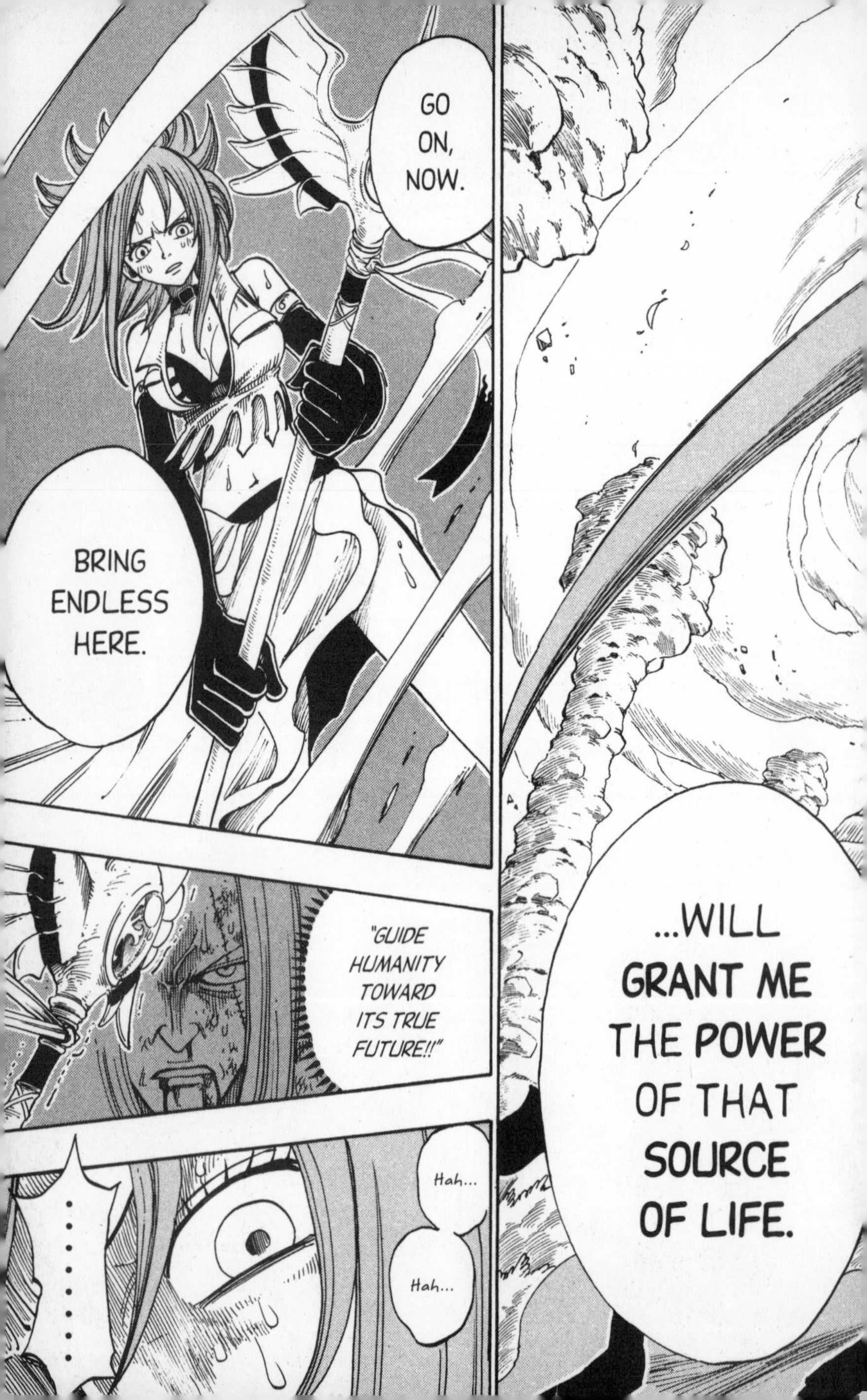
...WILL GRANT ME THE POWER OF THAT SOURCE OF LIFE.
GO ON, NOW.
BRING ENDLESS HERE.
"GUIDE HUMANITY TOWARD ITS TRUE FUTURE!!"
Hah...
Hah...
......

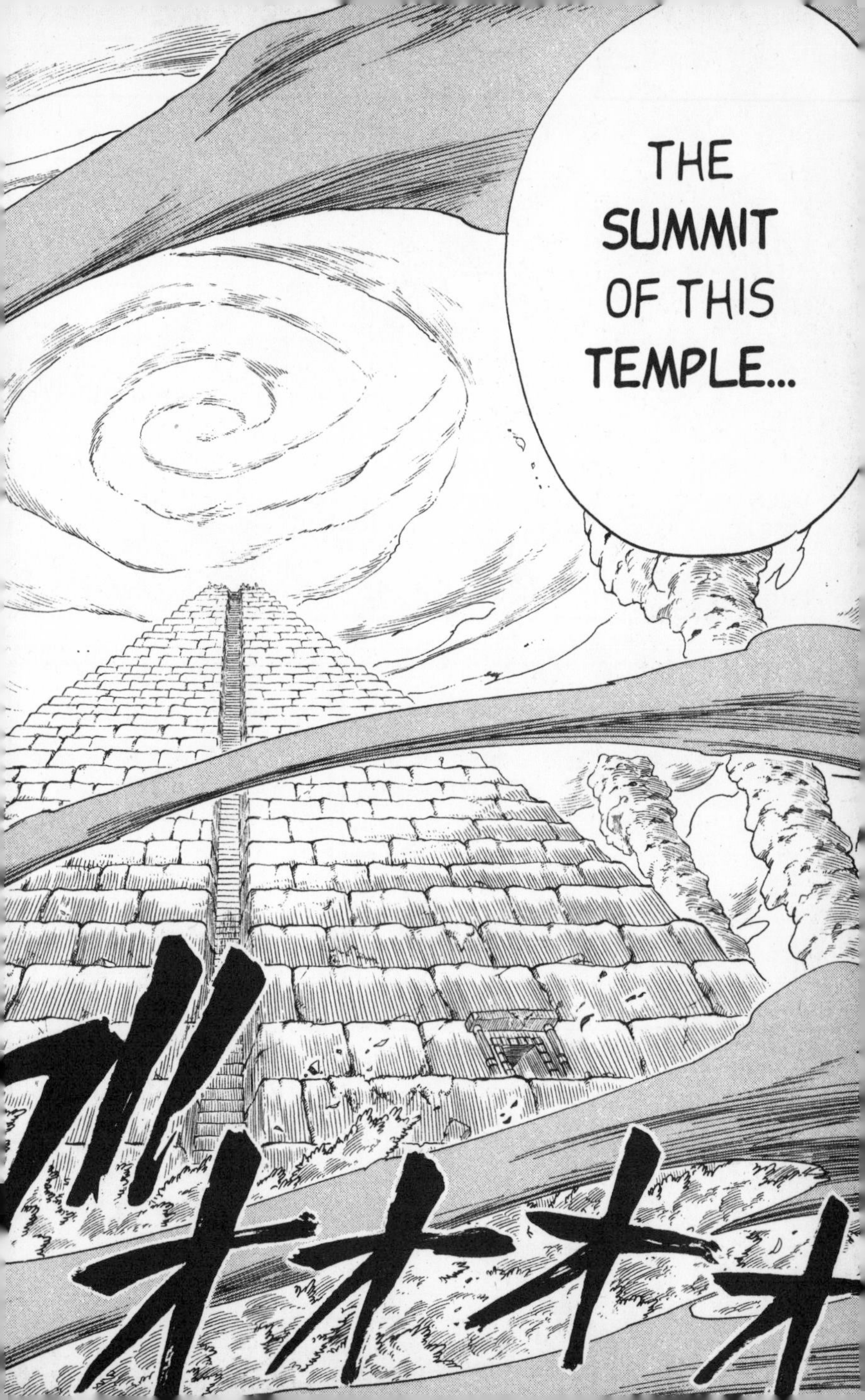
THE SUMMIT OF THIS TEMPLE...

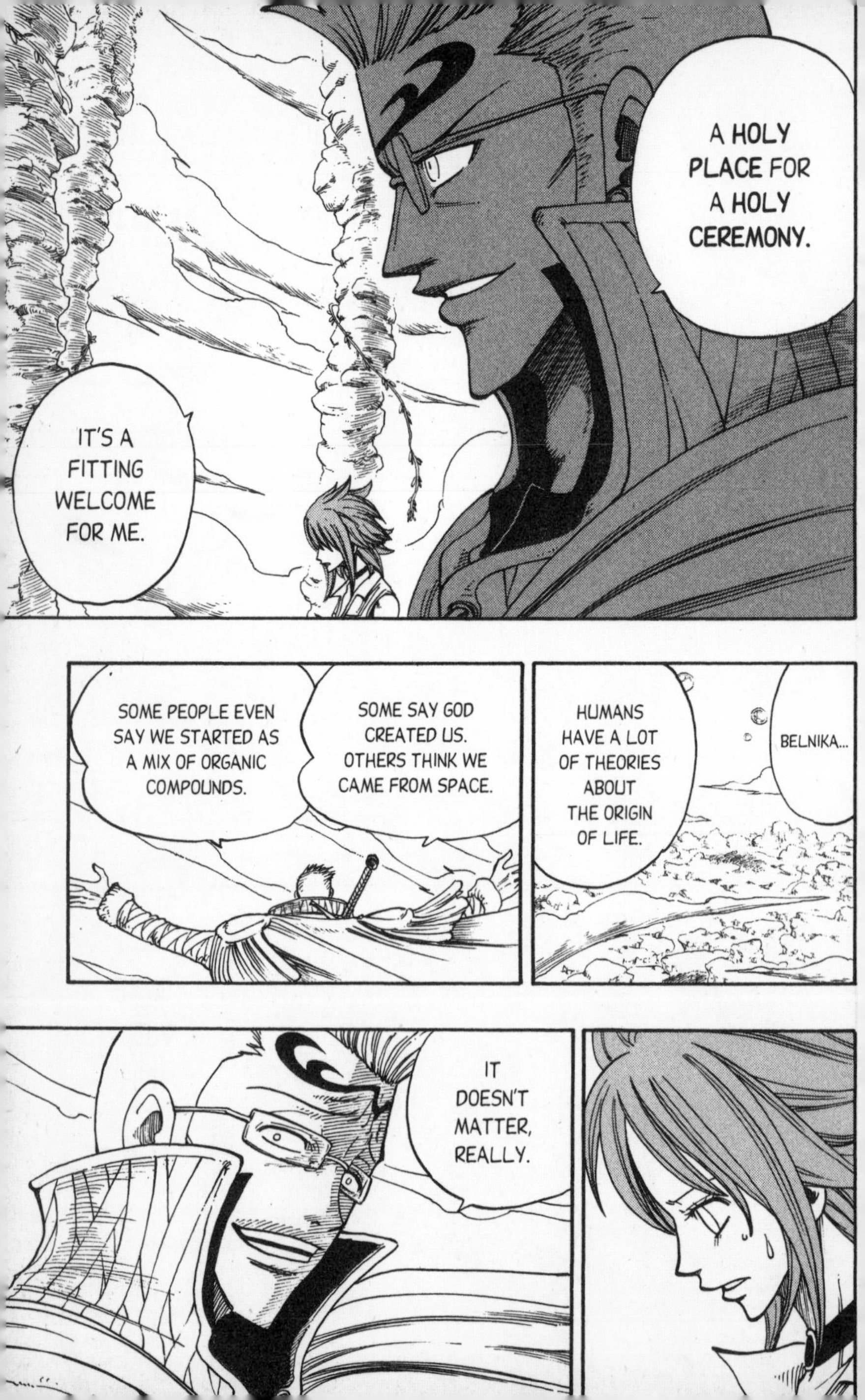
A HOLY PLACE FOR A HOLY CEREMONY.
IT'S A FITTING WELCOME FOR ME.
BELNIKA...
HUMANS HAVE A LOT OF THEORIES ABOUT THE ORIGIN OF LIFE.
SOME SAY GOD CREATED US. OTHERS THINK WE CAME FROM SPACE.
SOME PEOPLE EVEN SAY WE STARTED AS A MIX OF ORGANIC COMPOUNDS.
IT DOESN'T MATTER, REALLY.

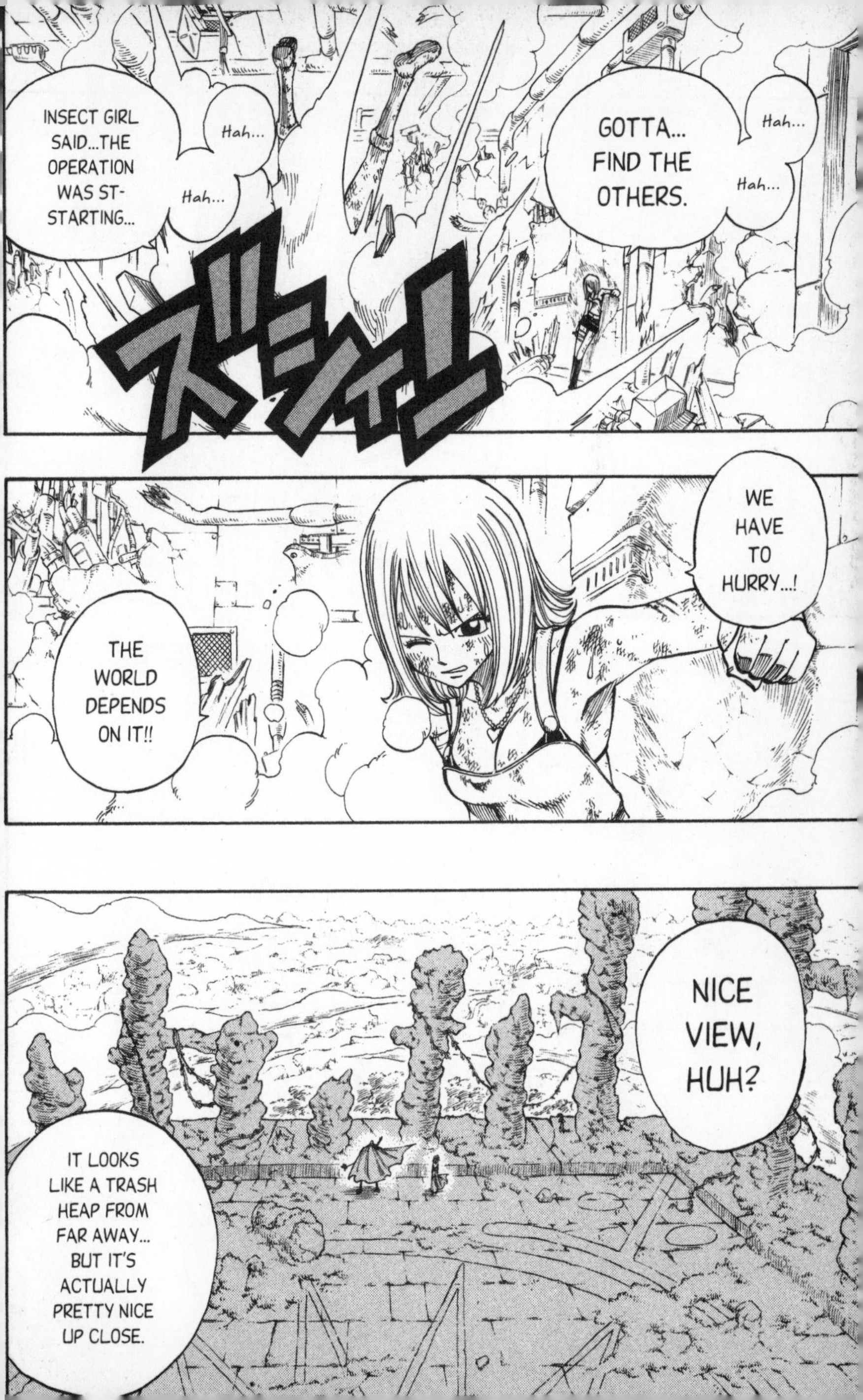
Hah...
Hah...
GOTTA... FIND THE OTHERS.
Hah...
Hah...
INSECT GIRL SAID...THE OPERATION WAS ST-STARTING...
WE HAVE TO HURRY...!
THE WORLD DEPENDS ON IT!!
NICE VIEW, HUH?
IT LOOKS LIKE A TRASH HEAP FROM FAR AWAY... BUT IT'S ACTUALLY PRETTY NICE UP CLOSE.

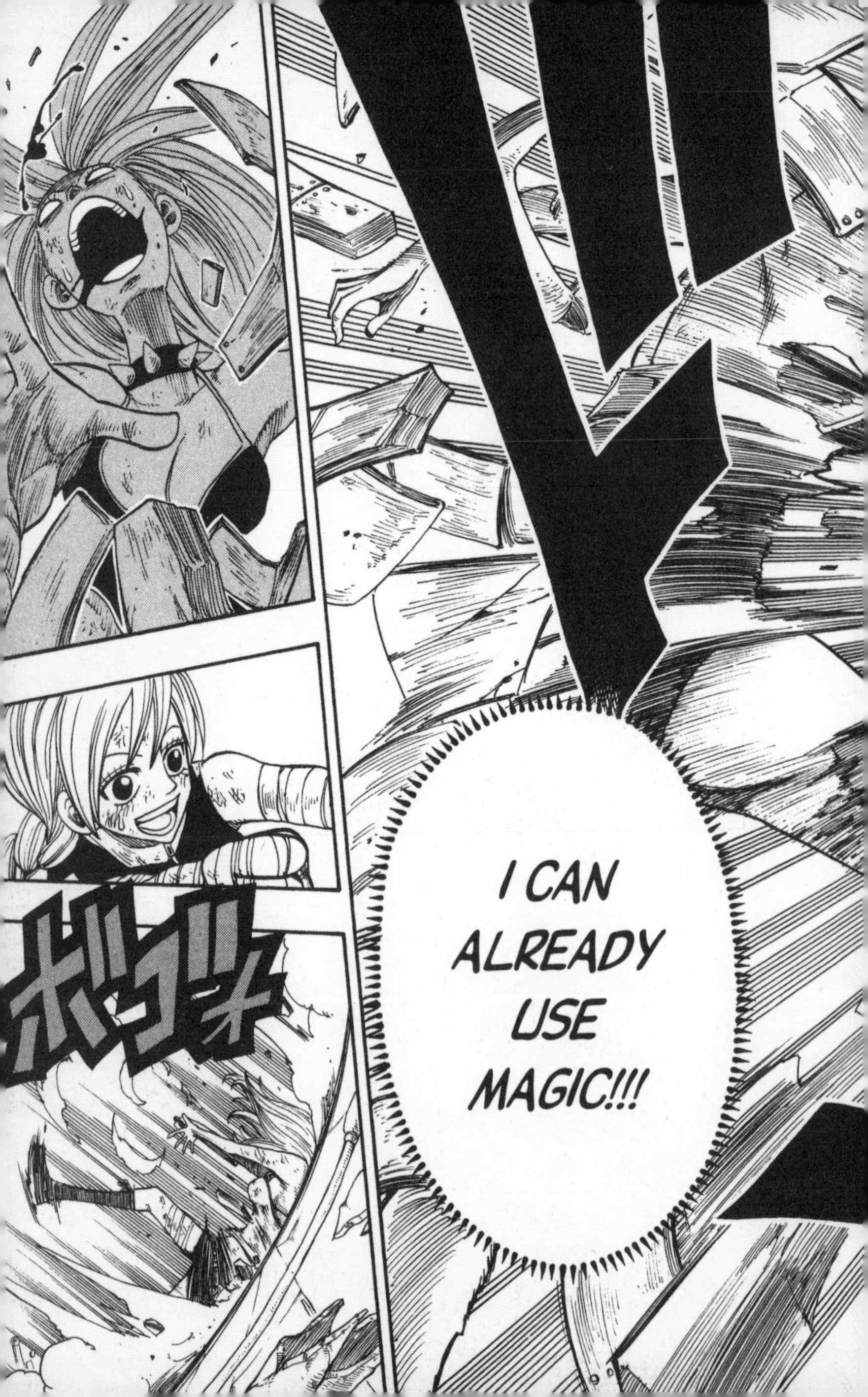
I CAN ALREADY USE MAGIC!!!

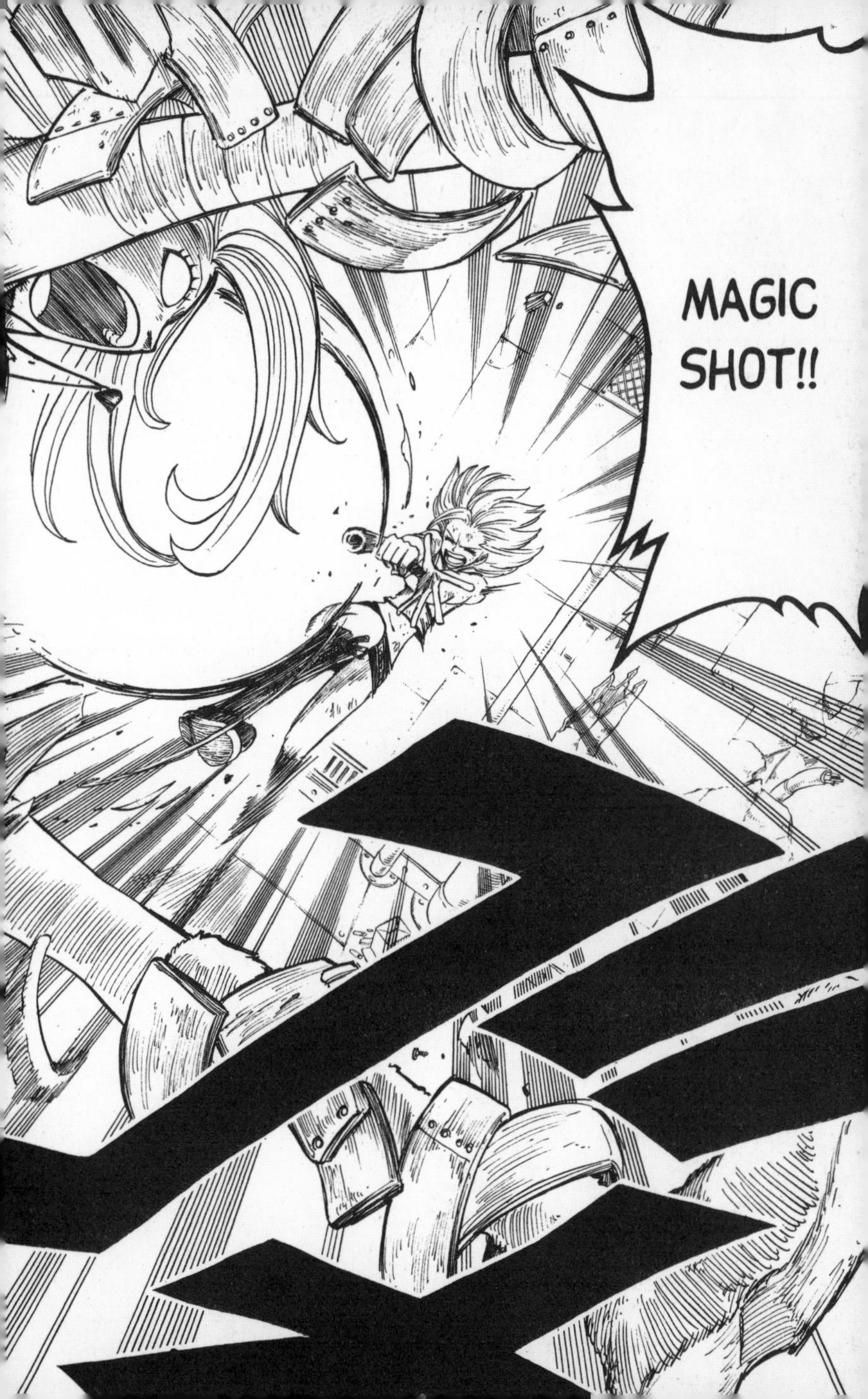
MAGIC SHOT!!

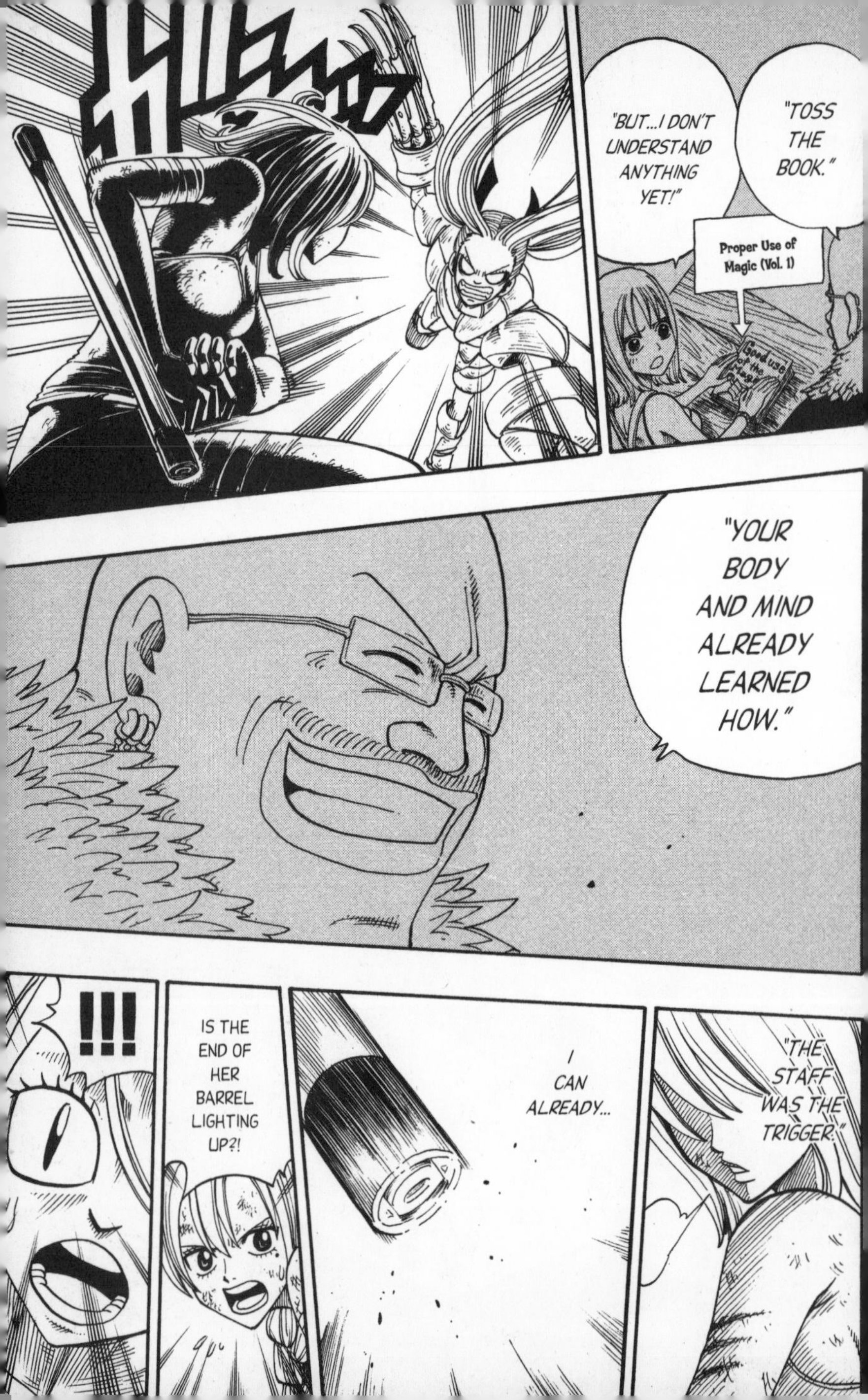
"TOSS THE BOOK."
"BUT...I DON'T UNDERSTAND ANYTHING YET!"
Proper Use of Magic (Vol. 1)
"YOUR BODY AND MIND ALREADY LEARNED HOW."
"THE STAFF WAS THE TRIGGER."
I CAN ALREADY...
IS THE END OF HER BARREL LIGHTING UP?!
!!!

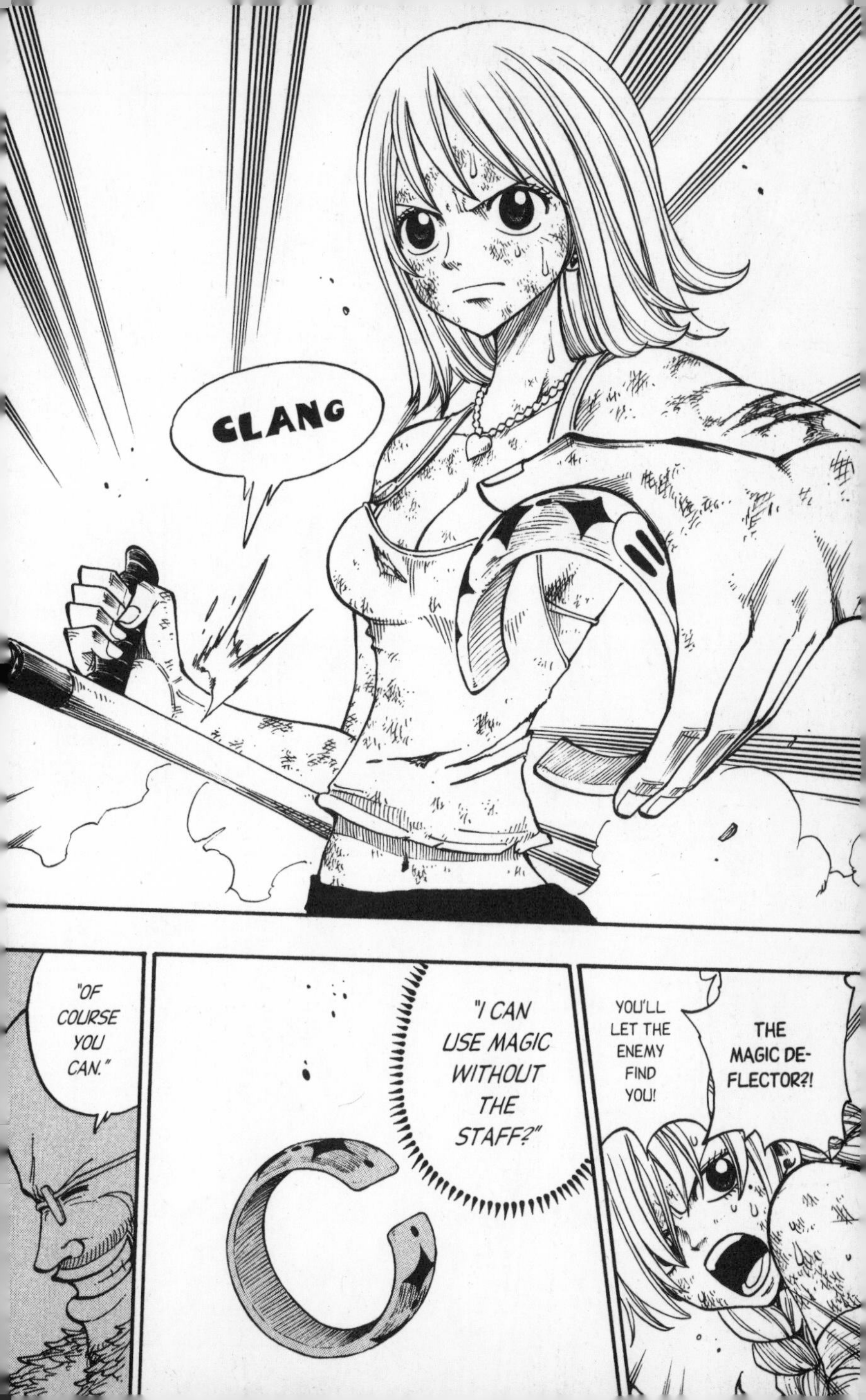
CLANG
THE MAGIC DE-FLECTOR?!
YOU'LL LET THE ENEMY FIND YOU!
"I CAN USE MAGIC WITHOUT THE STAFF?"
"OF COURSE YOU CAN."

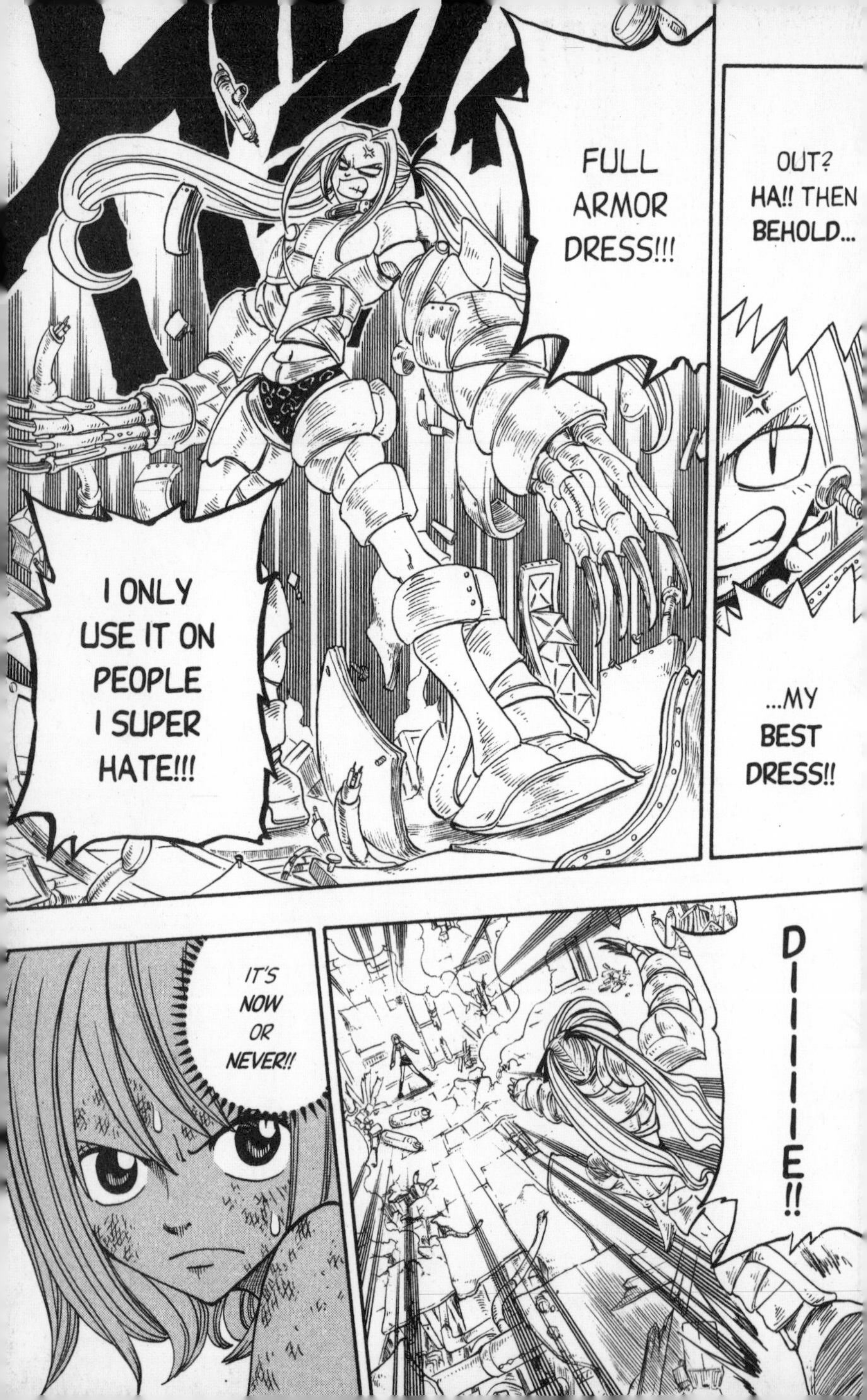
OUT? HA!! THEN BEHOLD...
...MY BEST DRESS!!
FULL ARMOR DRESS!!!
I ONLY USE IT ON PEOPLE I SUPER HATE!!!
DIIIIIE!!
IT'S NOW OR NEVER!!

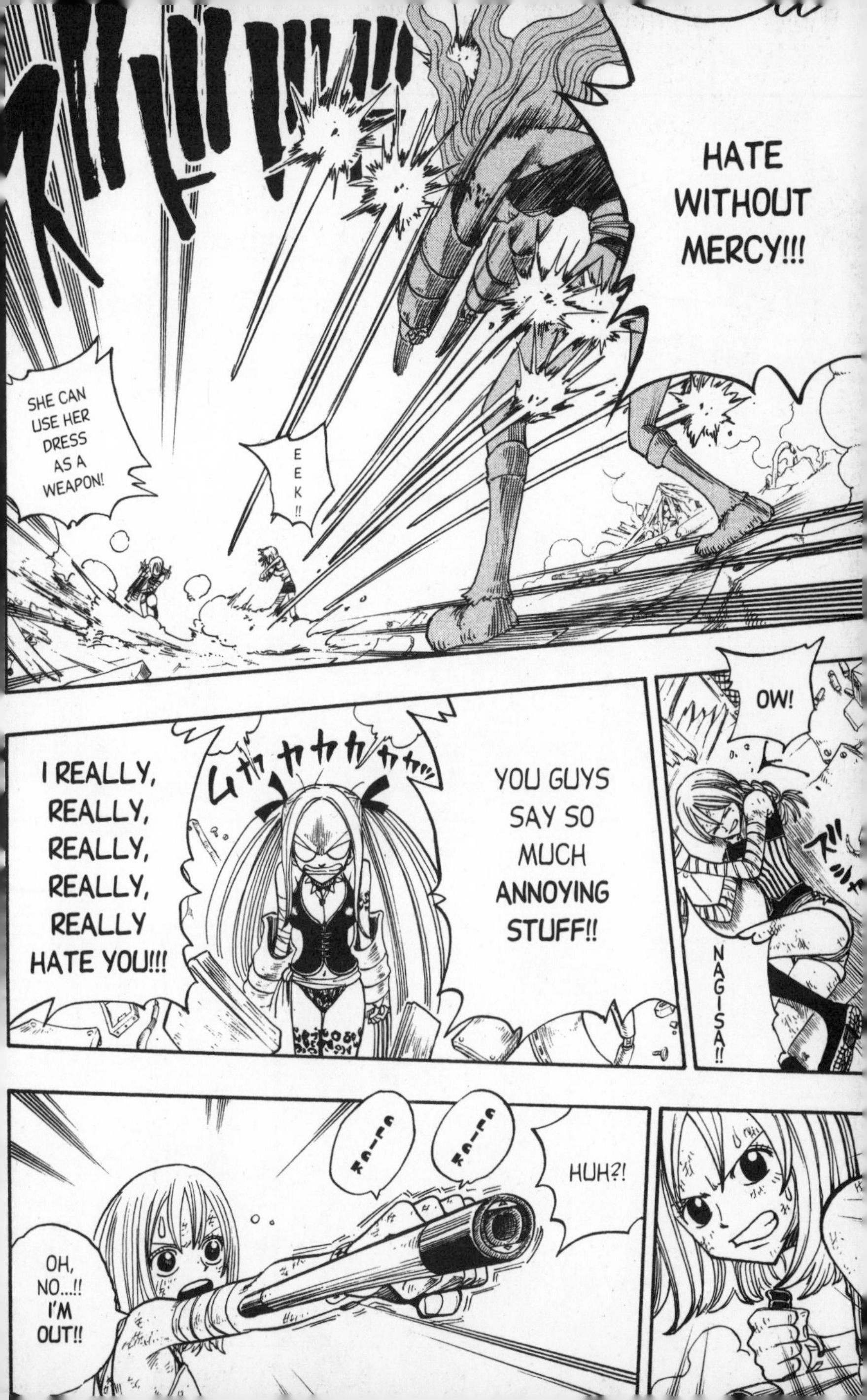
HATE WITHOUT MERCY!!!
EEK!!
SHE CAN USE HER DRESS AS A WEAPON!
OW!
NAGISA!!
YOU GUYS SAY SO MUCH ANNOYING STUFF!!
I REALLY, REALLY, REALLY, REALLY, REALLY HATE YOU!!!
HUH?!
OH, NO...!! I'M OUT!!

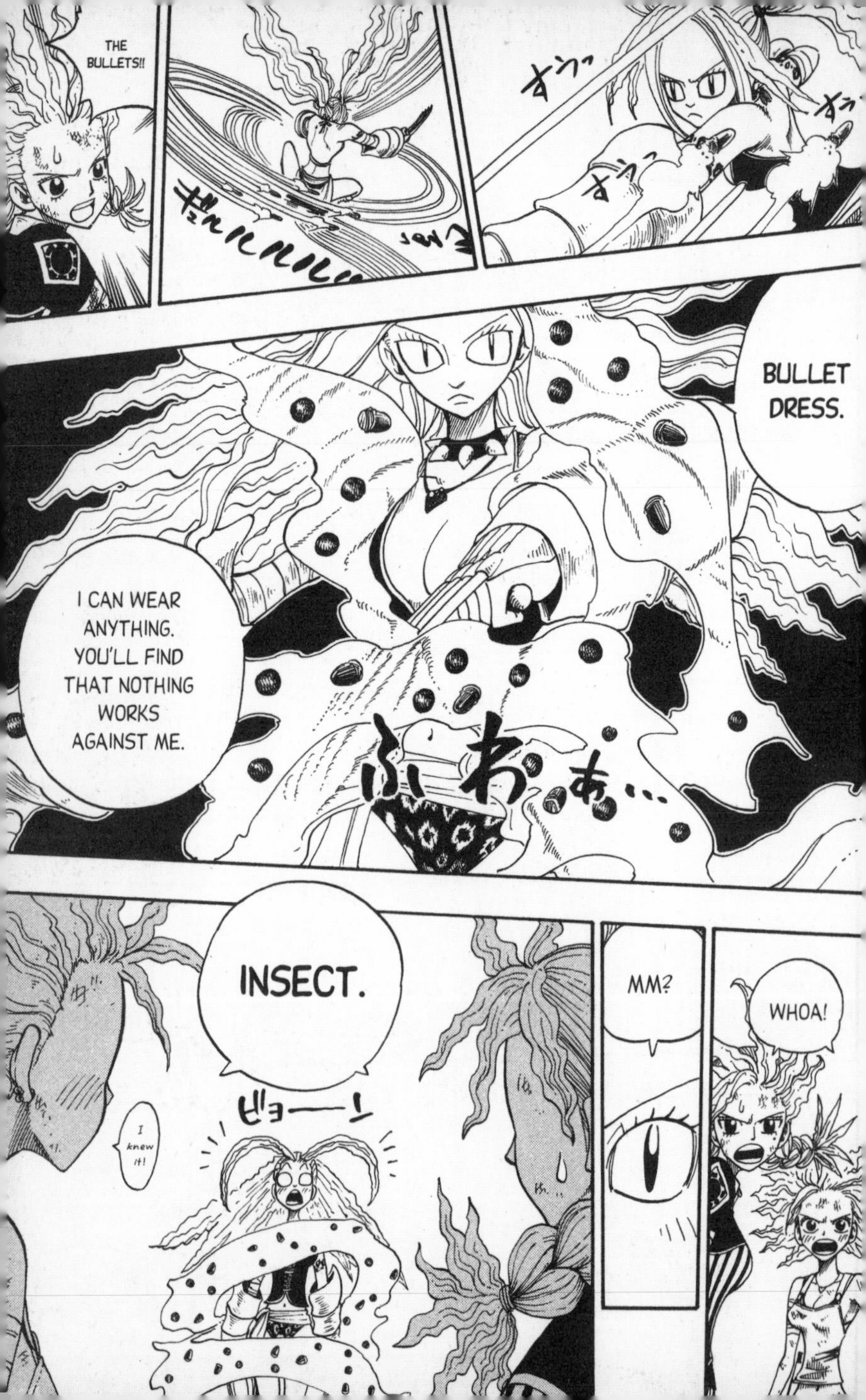
THE BULLETS!!
BULLET DRESS.
I CAN WEAR ANYTHING. YOU'LL FIND THAT NOTHING WORKS AGAINST ME.
ふわぁ…
WHOA!
MM?
INSECT.
ビョーー!
I knew it!

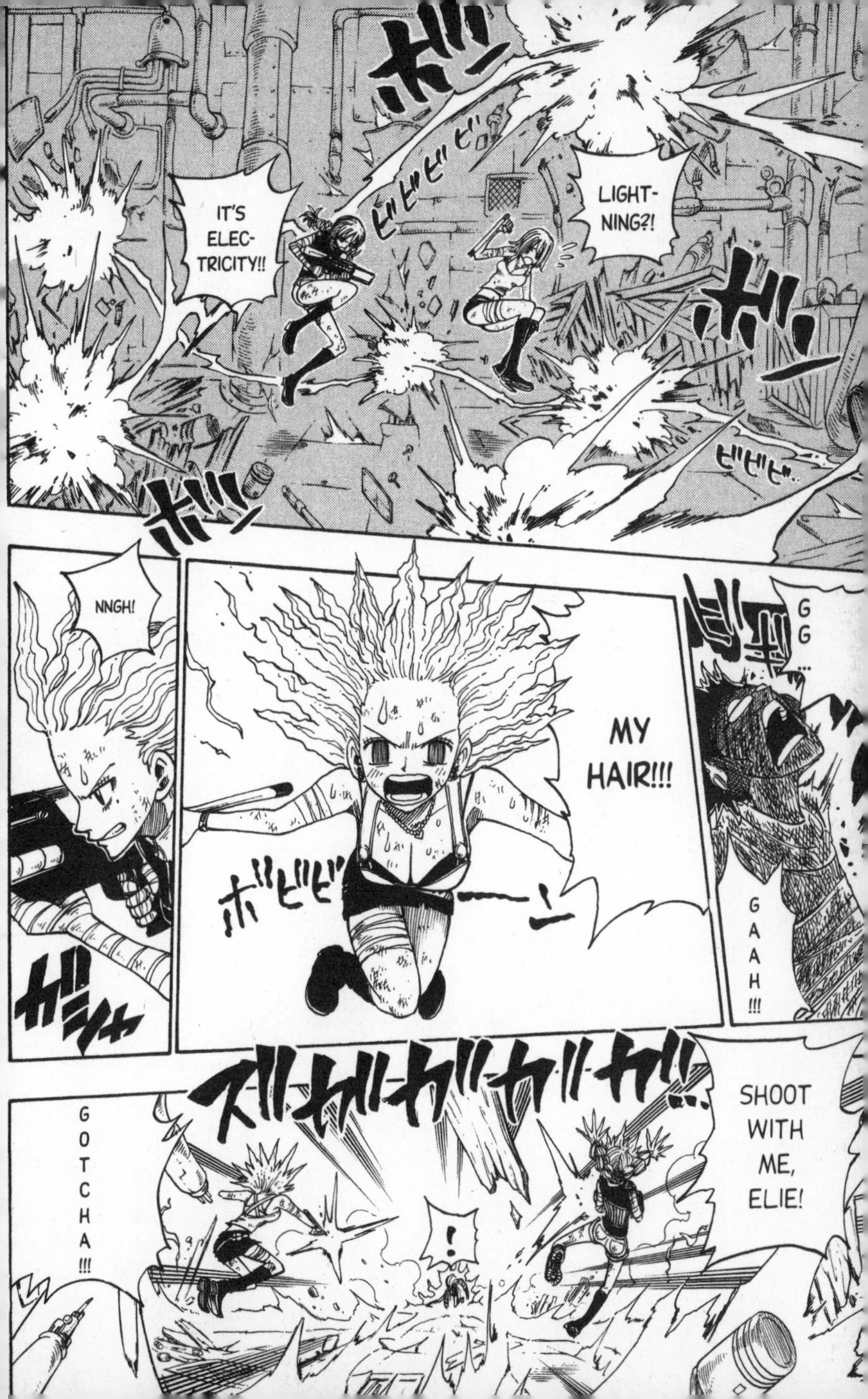
LIGHT-NING?!
IT'S ELEC-TRICITY!!
GG...
GAAH!!!
MY HAIR!!!
NNGH!
SHOOT WITH ME, ELIE!
!
GOTCHA!!!

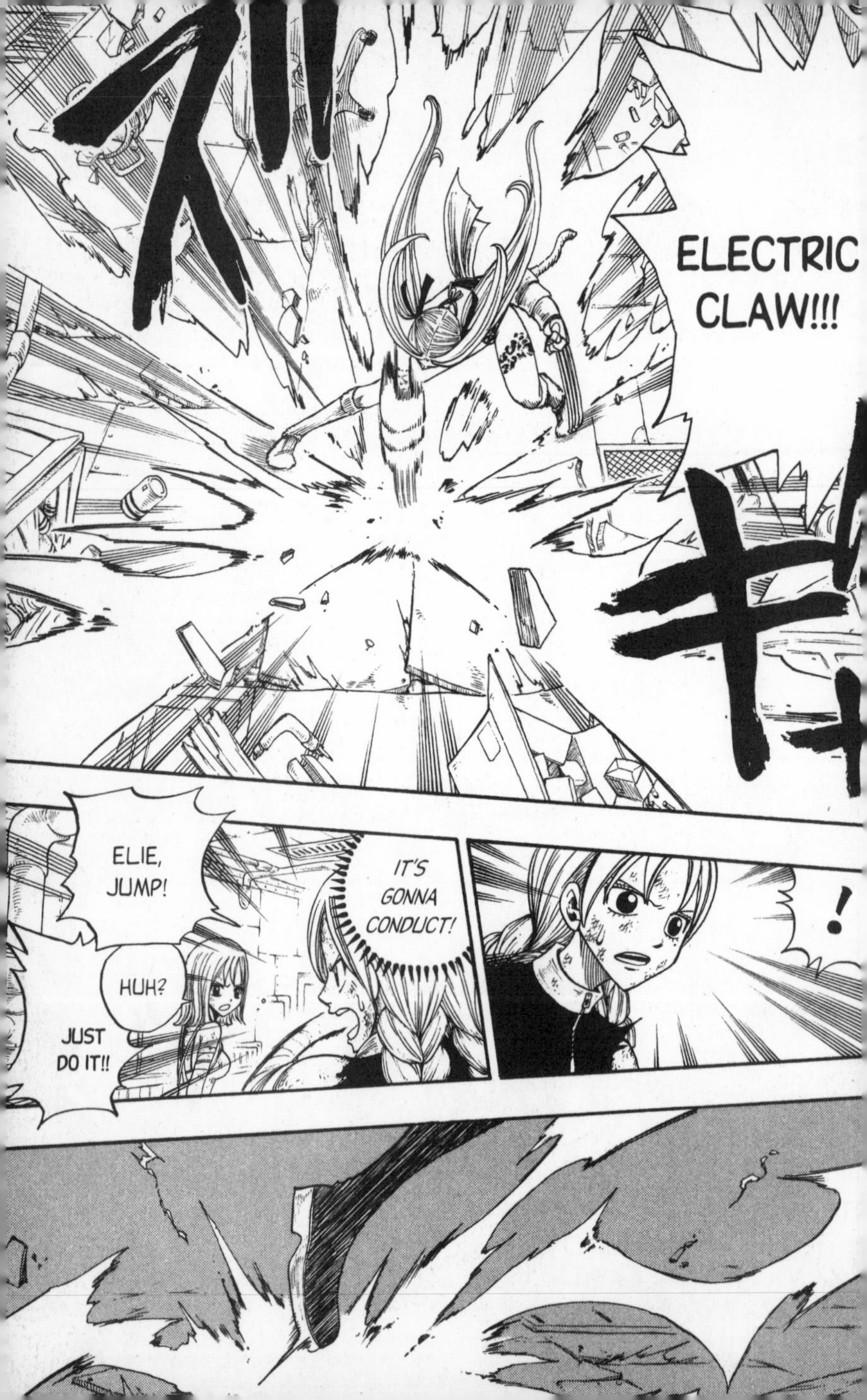
ELECTRIC CLAW!!!
!
IT'S GONNA CONDUCT!
ELIE, JUMP!
HUH?
JUST DO IT!!

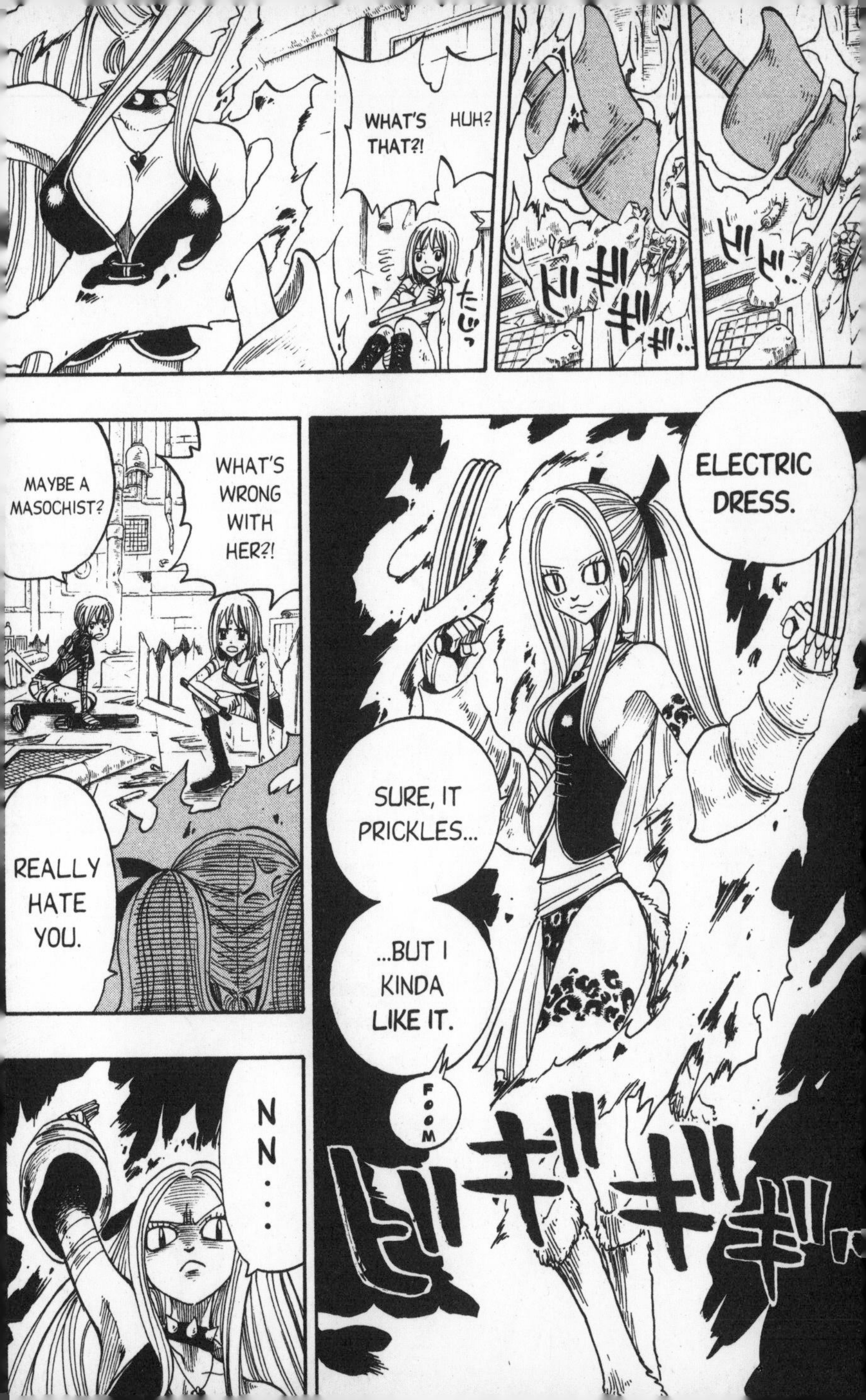
HUH?
WHAT'S THAT?!
WHAT'S WRONG WITH HER?!
MAYBE A MASOCHIST?
REALLY HATE YOU.
NN...
ELECTRIC DRESS.
SURE, IT PRICKLES...
...BUT I KINDA LIKE IT.
FOOM

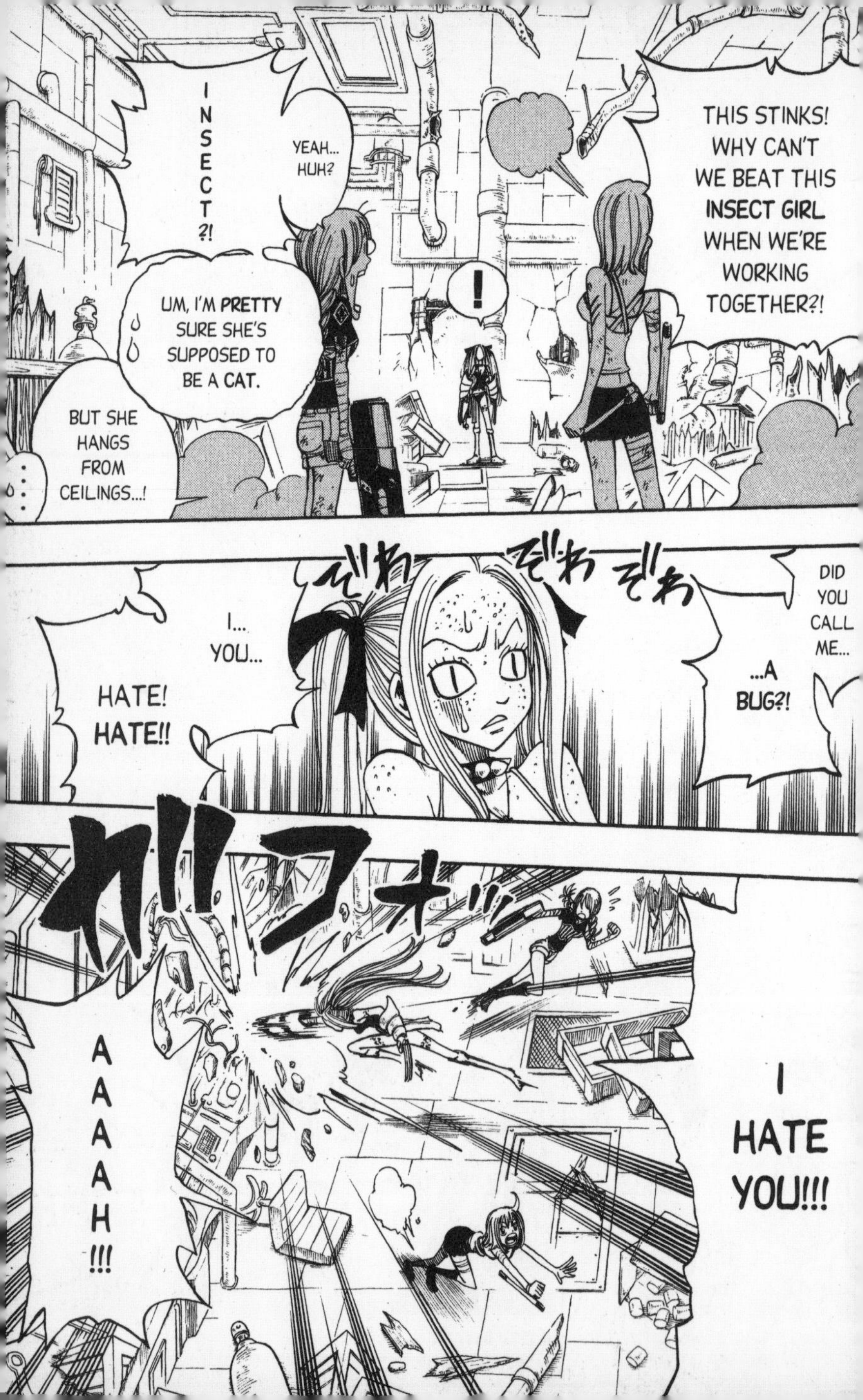
THIS STINKS! WHY CAN'T WE BEAT THIS INSECT GIRL WHEN WE'RE WORKING TOGETHER?!
!
YEAH... HUH?
INSECT?!
UM, I'M PRETTY SURE SHE'S SUPPOSED TO BE A CAT.
BUT SHE HANGS FROM CEILINGS...!
...
DID YOU CALL ME...
...A BUG?!
ざわざわざわ
I... YOU...
HATE! HATE!!
カ!!フォッ
I HATE YOU!!!
AAAAAH!!!

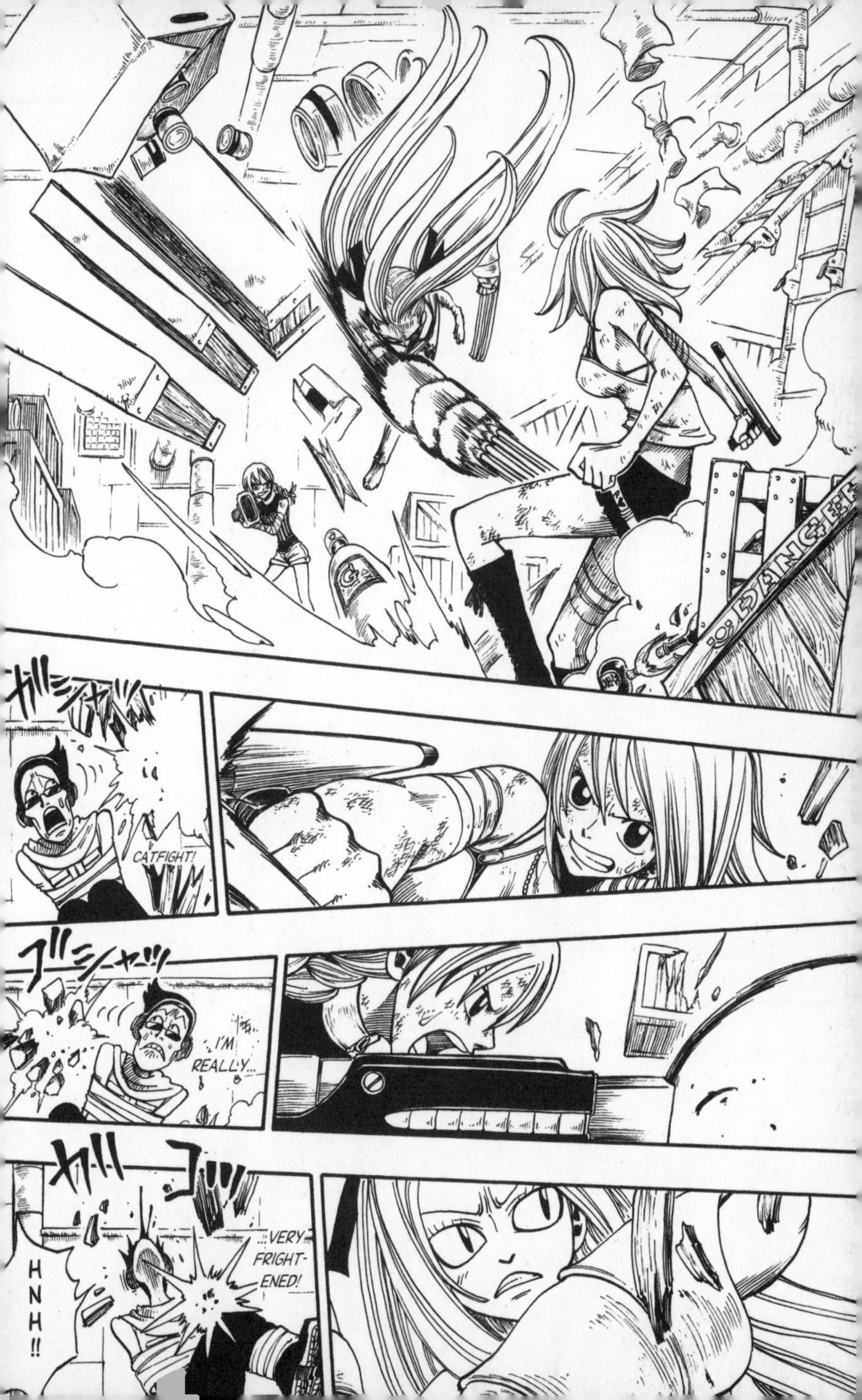
CATFIGHT!
I'M REALLY...
...VERY FRIGHT-ENED!
HNH!!

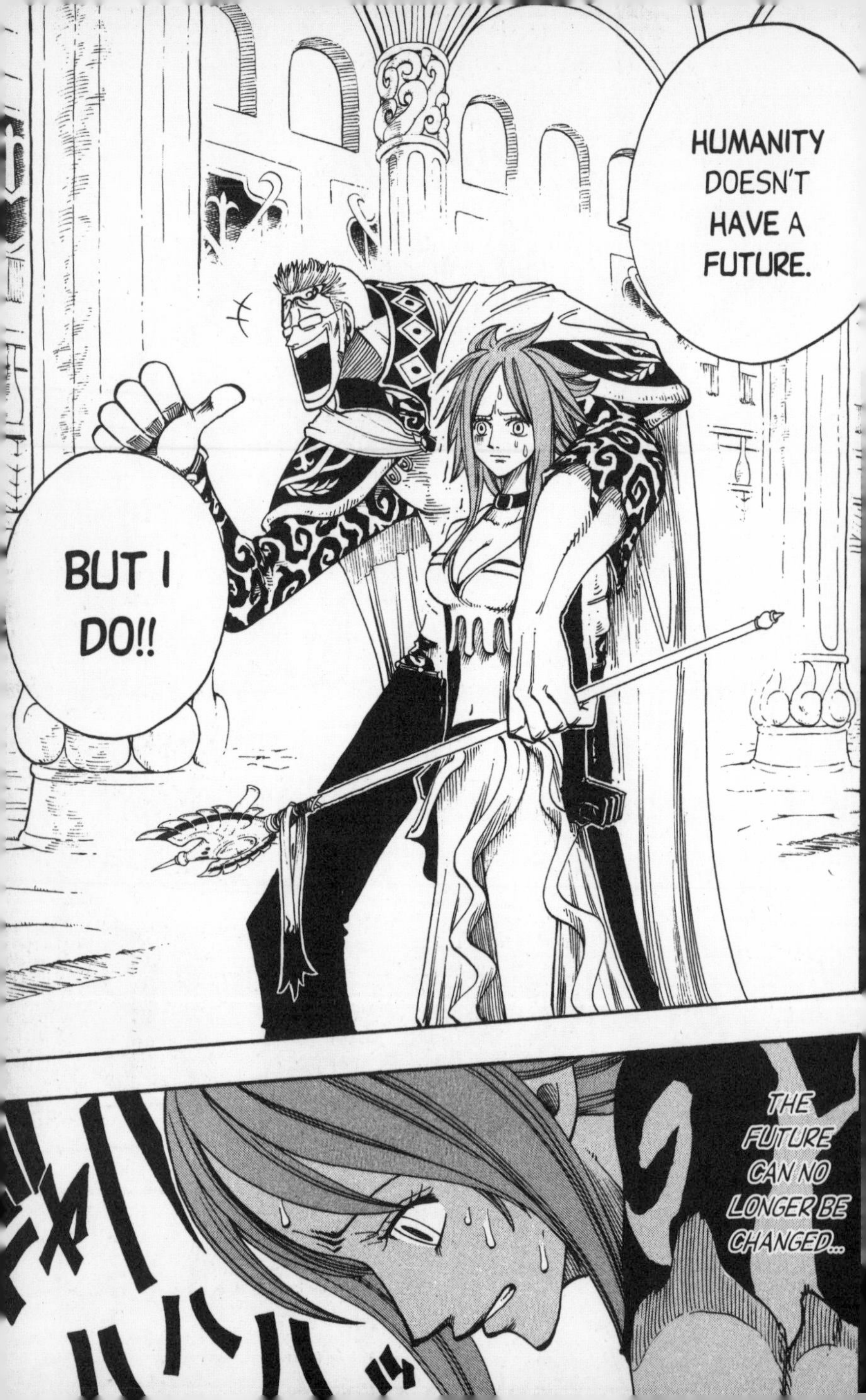
HUMANITY DOESN'T HAVE A FUTURE.
BUT I DO!!
THE FUTURE CAN NO LONGER BE CHANGED...

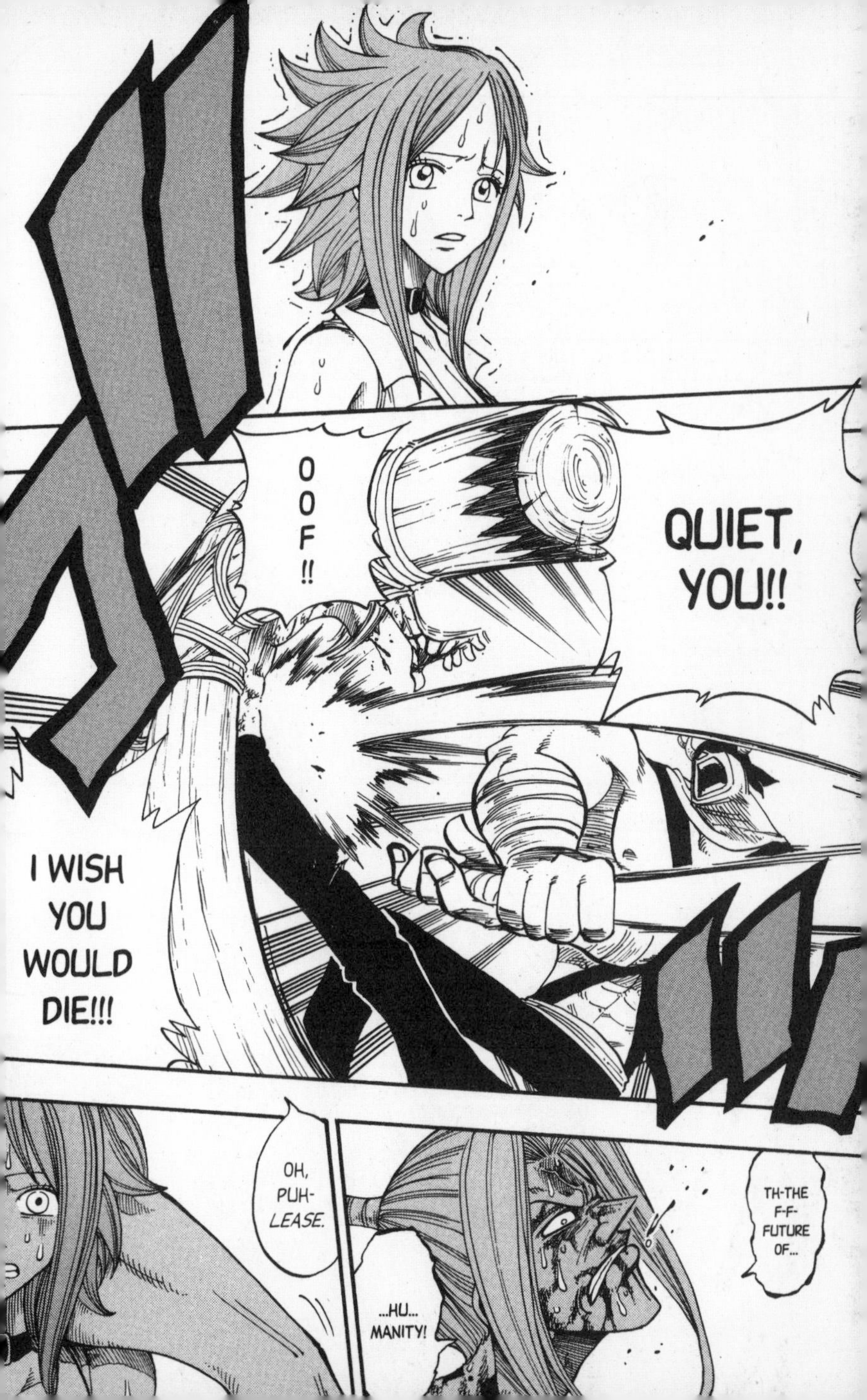
QUIET, YOU!!
OOF!!
I WISH YOU WOULD DIE!!!
TH-THE F-F-FUTURE OF...
...HU... MANITY!
OH, PUH-LEASE.

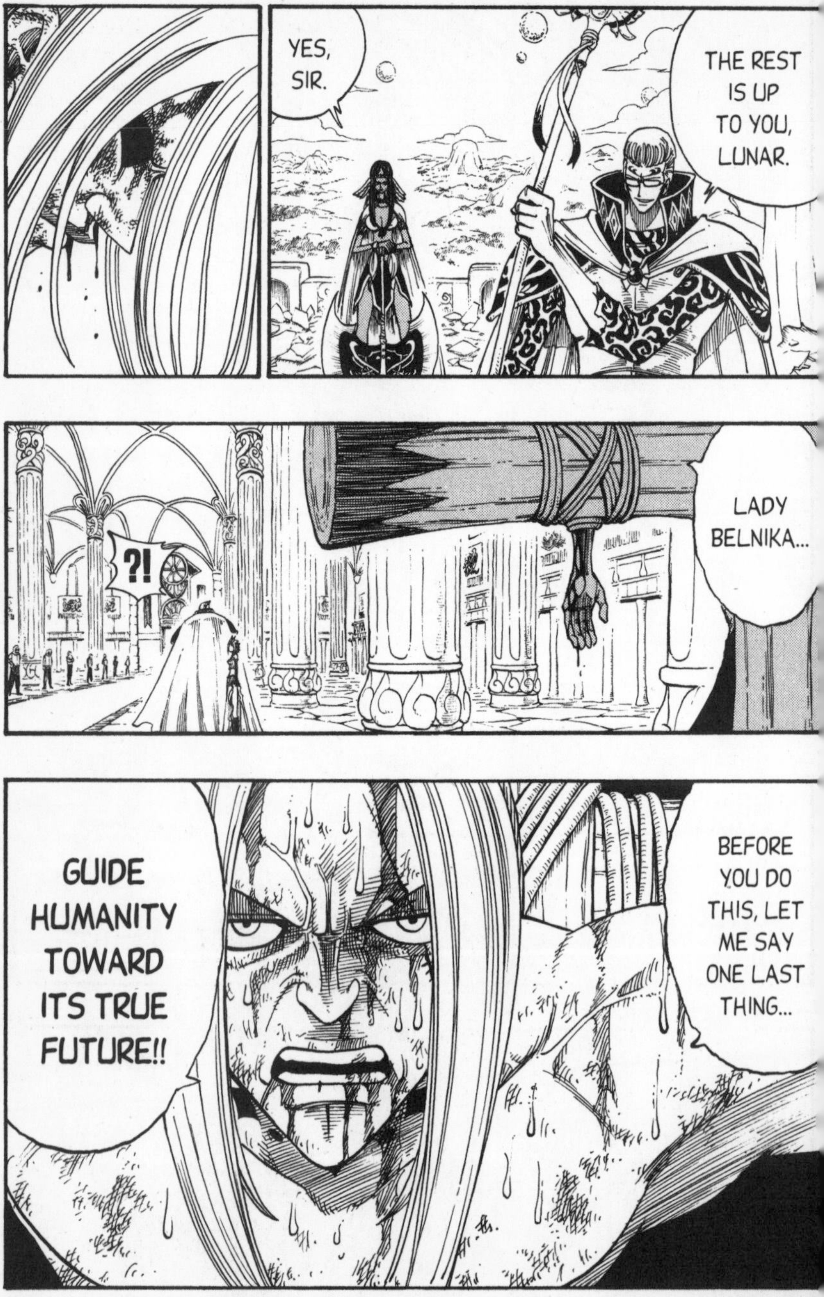
THE REST IS UP TO YOU, LUNAR.
YES, SIR.
LADY BELNIKA...
?!
BEFORE YOU DO THIS, LET ME SAY ONE LAST THING...
GUIDE HUMANITY TOWARD ITS TRUE FUTURE!!

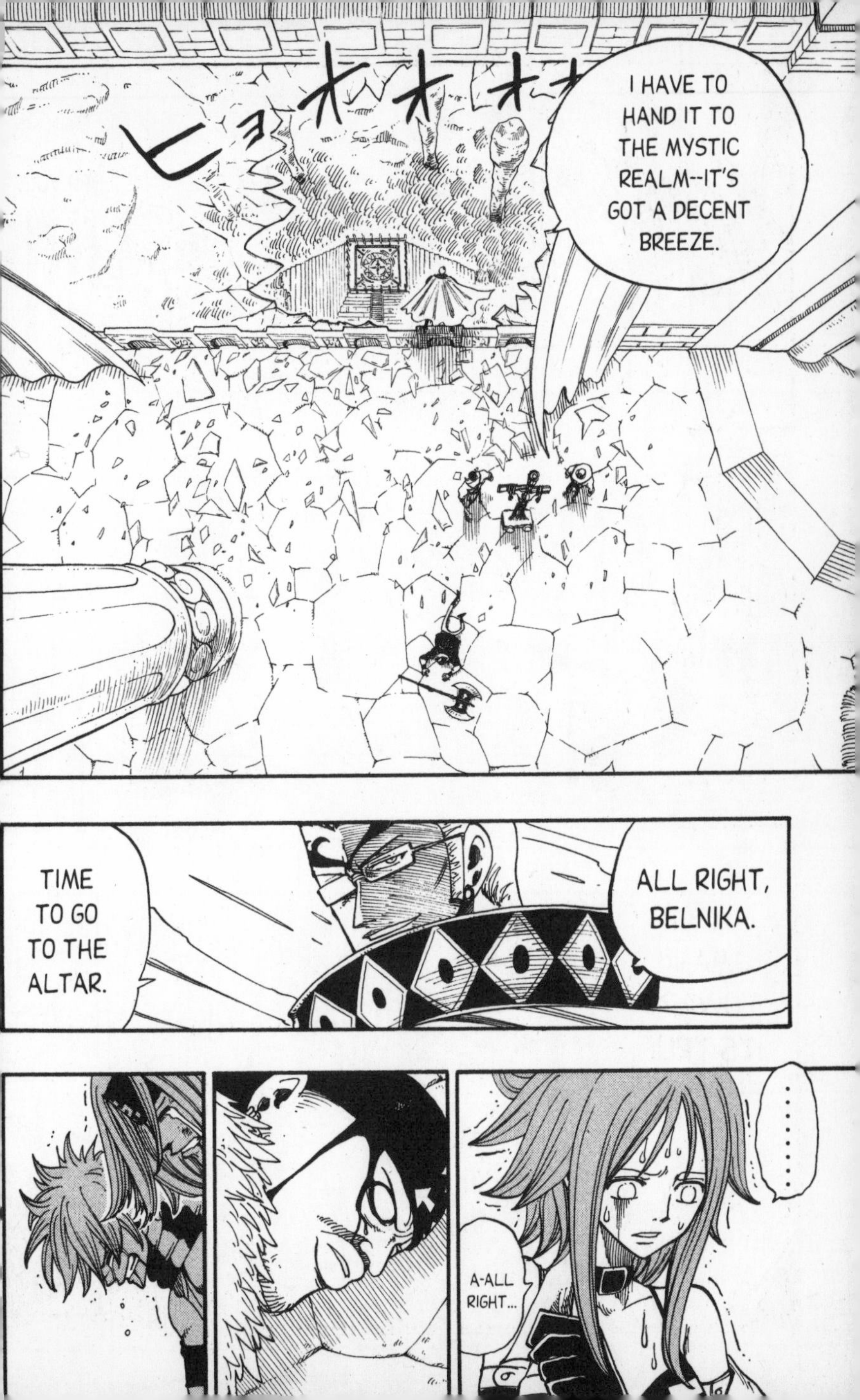
ヒョオオオ
I HAVE TO HAND IT TO THE MYSTIC REALM--IT'S GOT A DECENT BREEZE.
ALL RIGHT, BELNIKA.
TIME TO GO TO THE ALTAR.
......
A-ALL RIGHT...

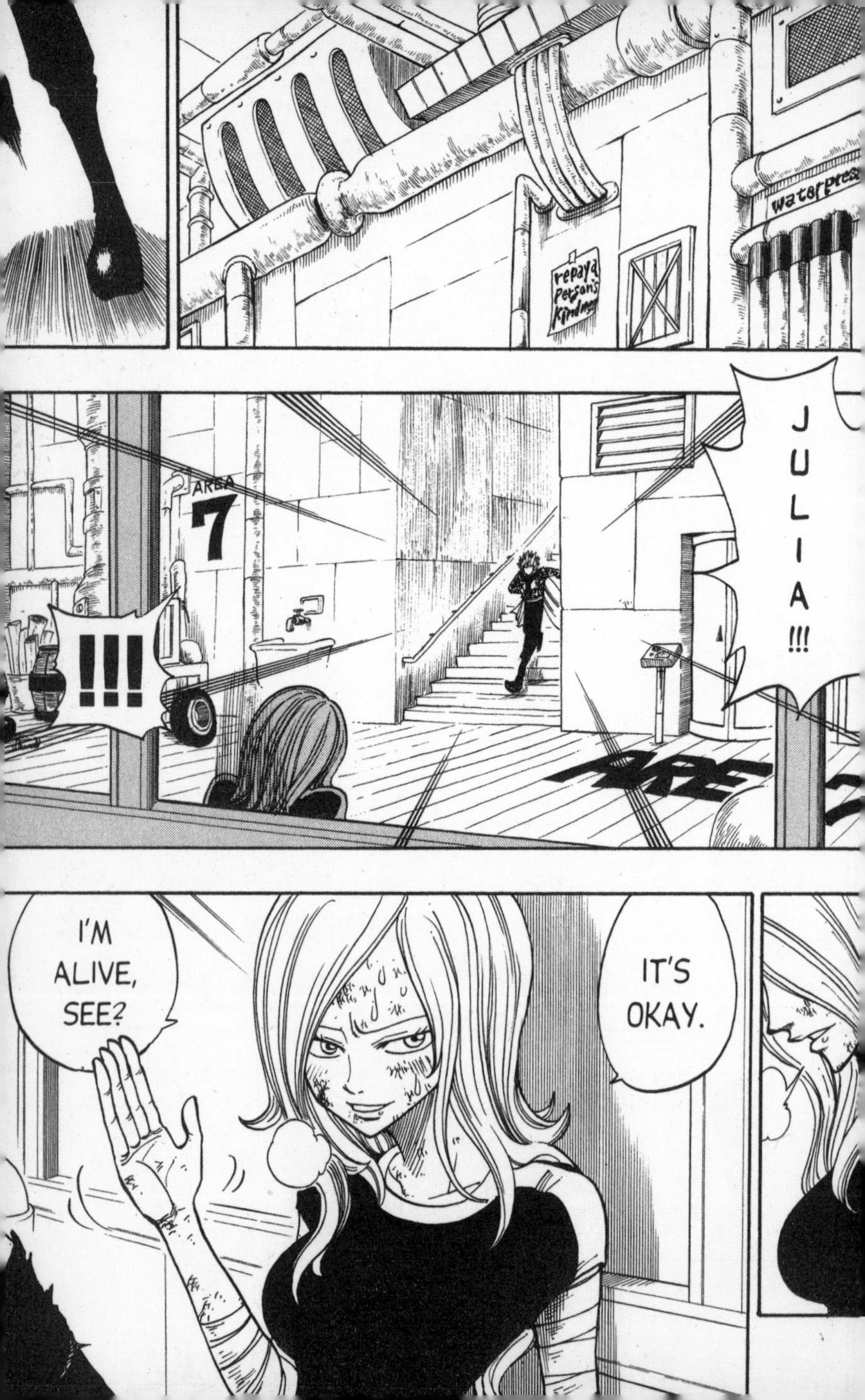
JULIA!!!
AREA 7
!!!
IT'S OKAY.
I'M ALIVE, SEE?

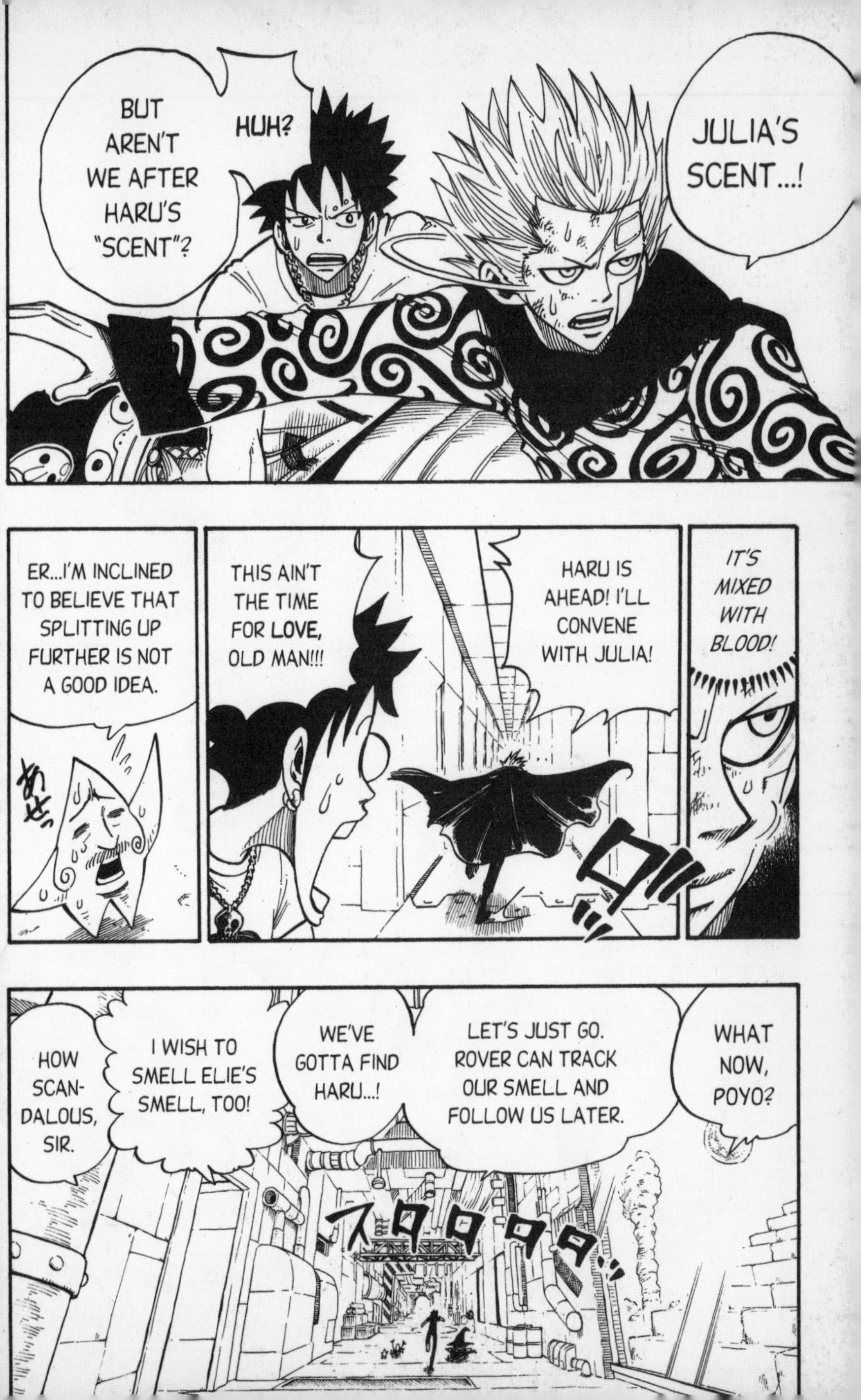
JULIA'S SCENT...!
HUH?
BUT AREN'T WE AFTER HARU'S "SCENT"?
IT'S MIXED WITH BLOOD!
HARU IS AHEAD! I'LL CONVENE WITH JULIA!
ダッ
THIS AIN'T THE TIME FOR LOVE, OLD MAN!!!
ER...I'M INCLINED TO BELIEVE THAT SPLITTING UP FURTHER IS NOT A GOOD IDEA.
WHAT NOW, POYO?
LET'S JUST GO. ROVER CAN TRACK OUR SMELL AND FOLLOW US LATER.
WE'VE GOTTA FIND HARU...!
I WISH TO SMELL ELIE'S SMELL, TOO!
HOW SCAN-DALOUS, SIR.

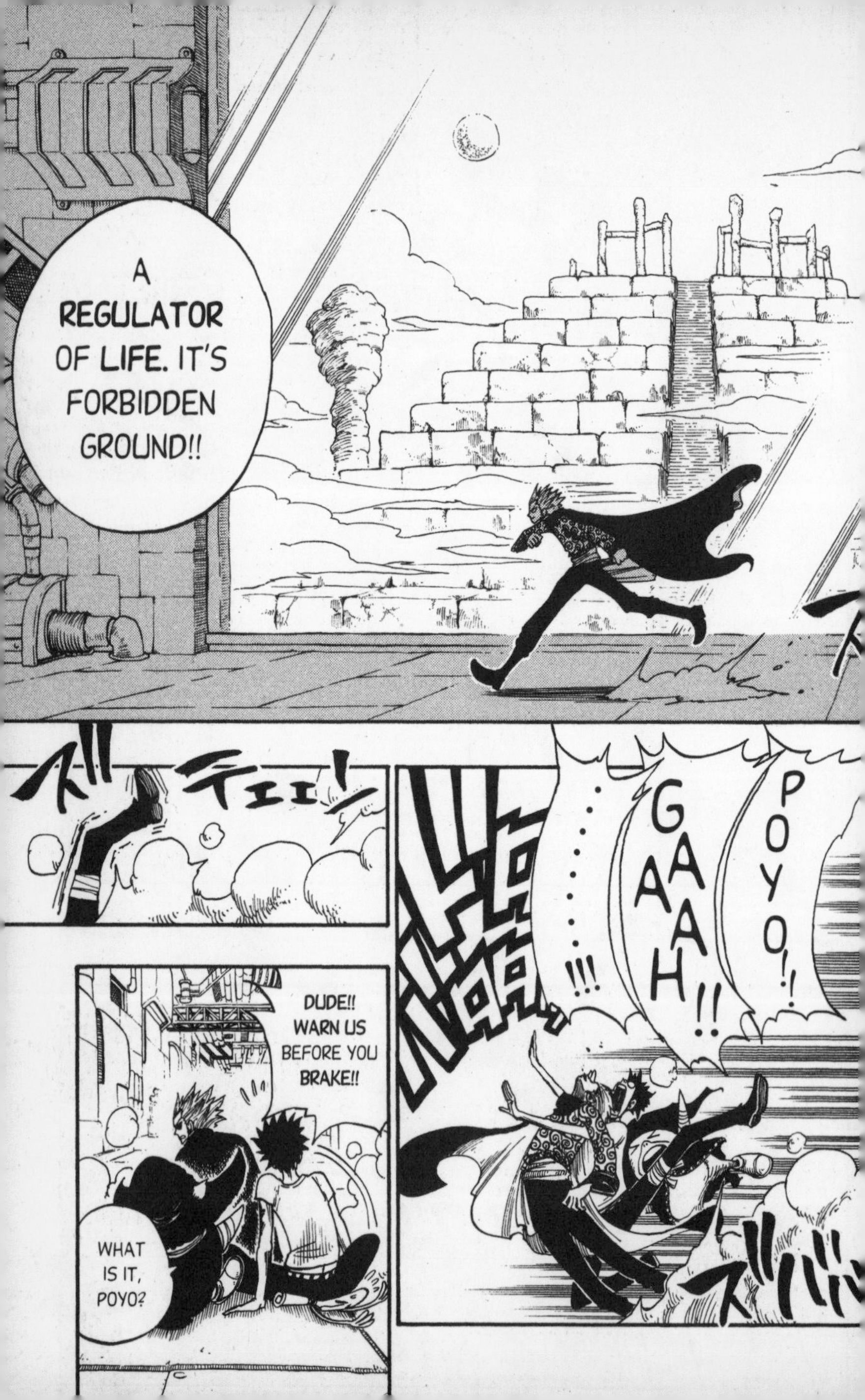
A REGULATOR OF LIFE. IT'S FORBIDDEN GROUND!!
POYO!!
GAAAH!!
...!!!
DUDE!! WARN US BEFORE YOU BRAKE!!
WHAT IS IT, POYO?

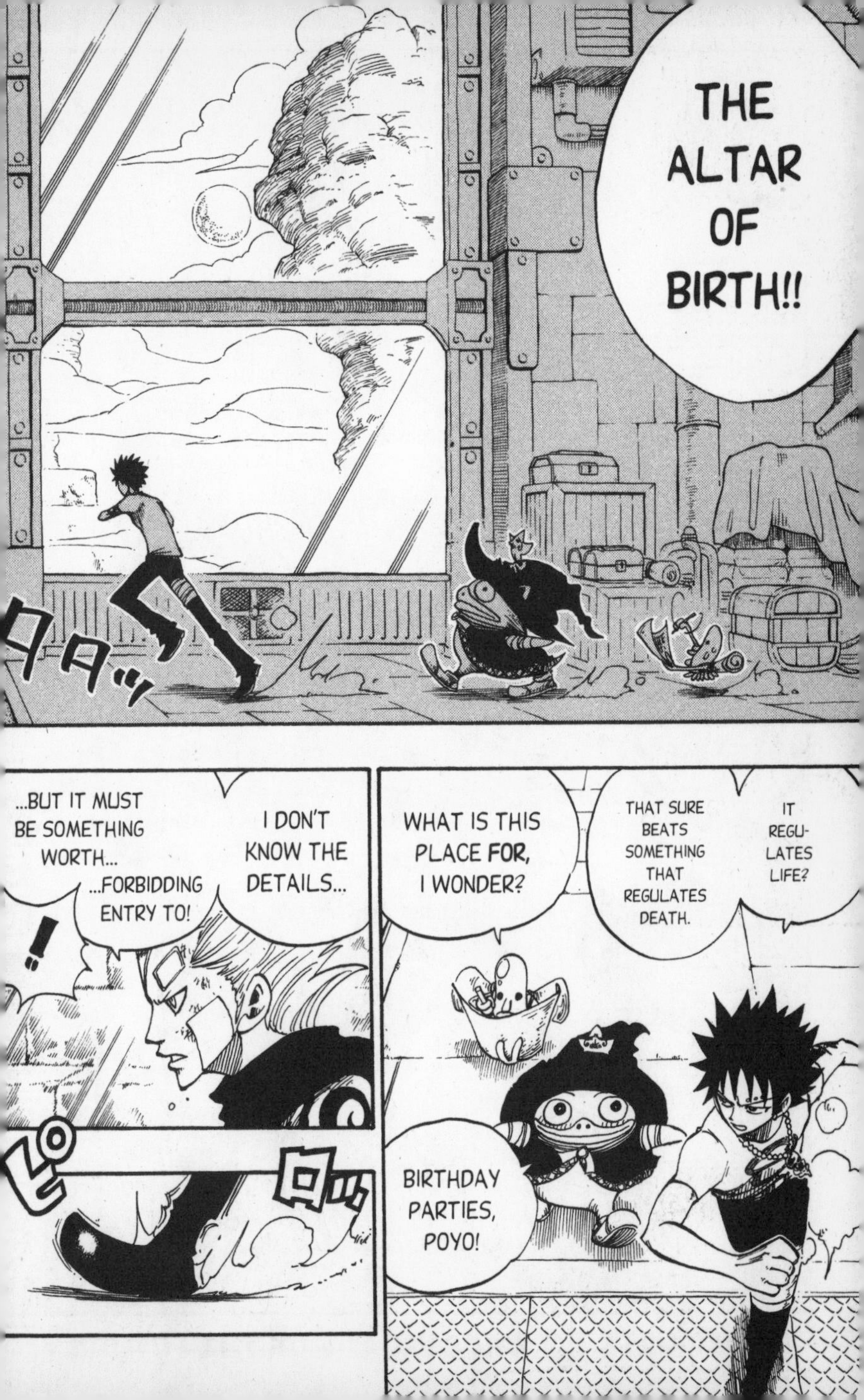
THE ALTAR OF BIRTH!!
タタッ
IT REGU-LATES LIFE?
THAT SURE BEATS SOMETHING THAT REGULATES DEATH.
WHAT IS THIS PLACE FOR, I WONDER?
BIRTHDAY PARTIES, POYO!
I DON'T KNOW THE DETAILS...
...BUT IT MUST BE SOMETHING WORTH... ...FORBIDDING ENTRY TO!
!
ピロッ

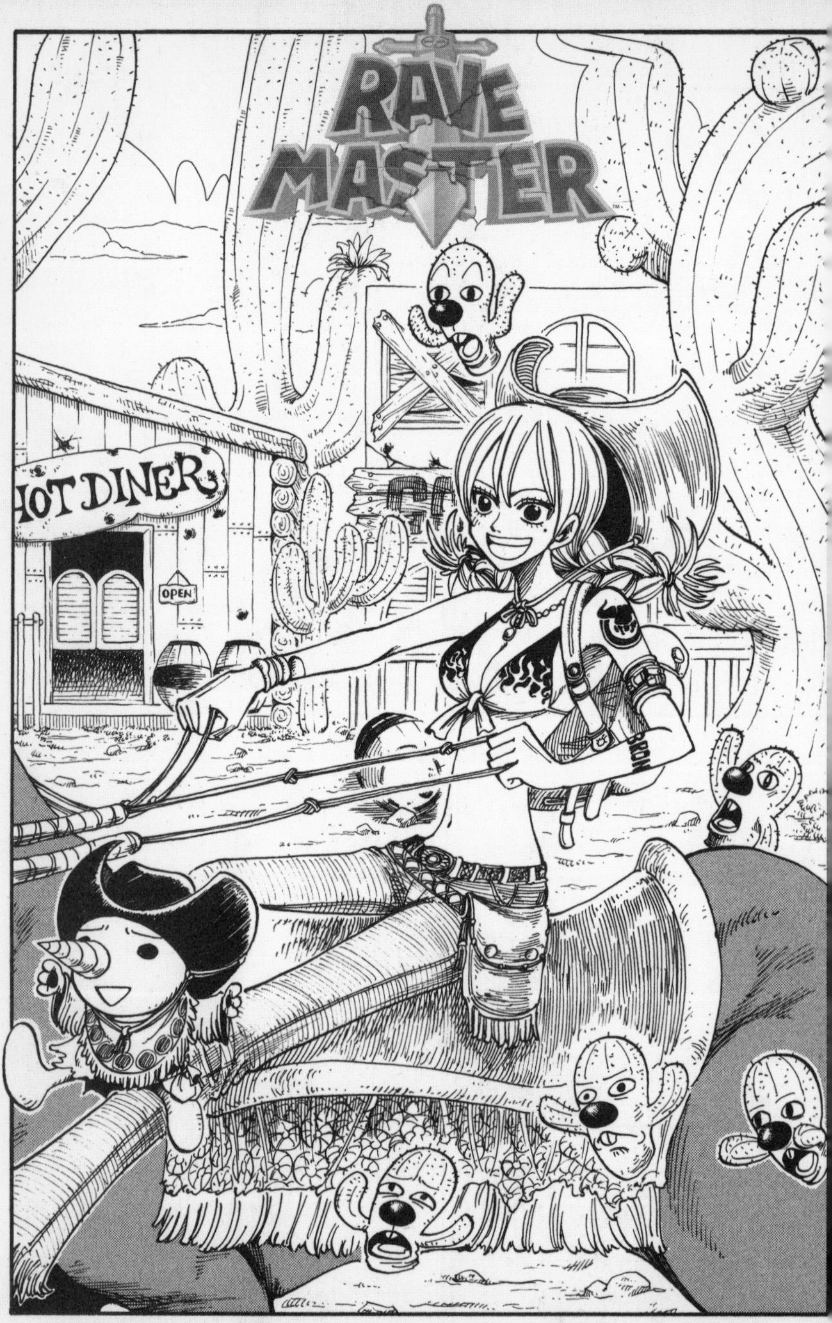
RAVE MASTER
HOT DINER
OPEN

RAVE:214 ✚ CROSSROADS OF THE FUTURE

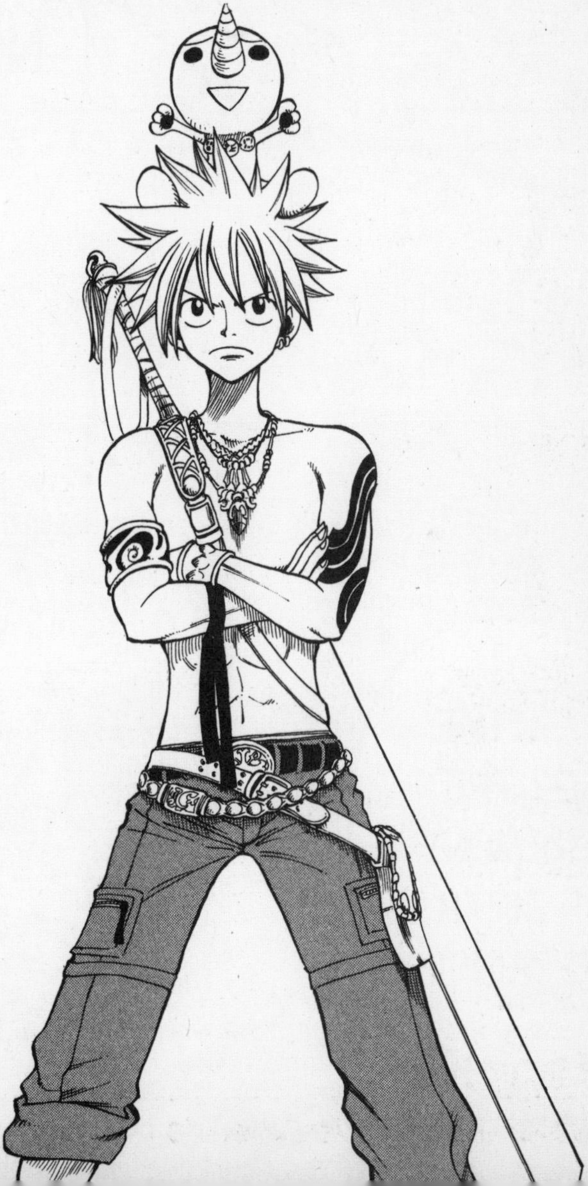

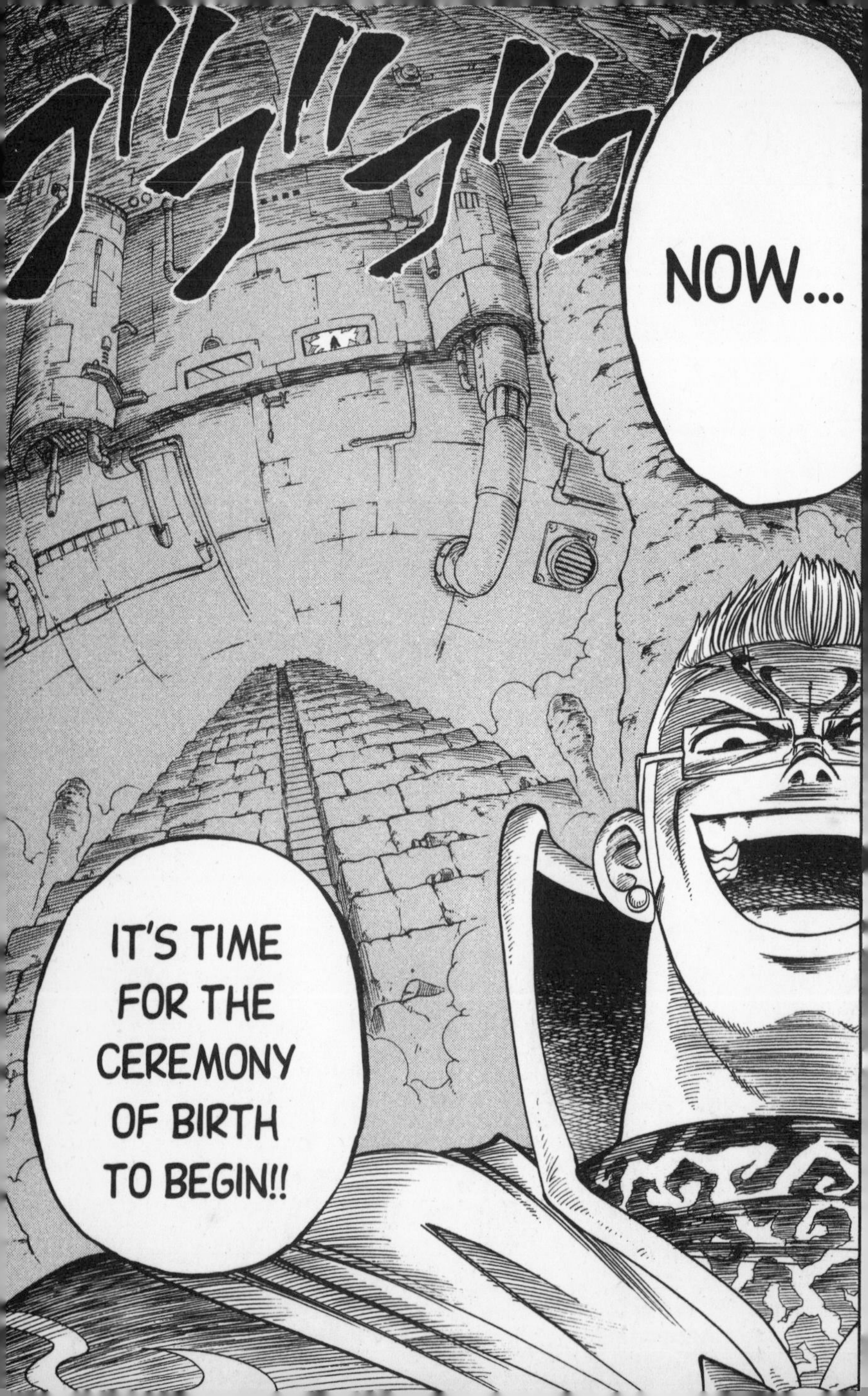
NOW...
IT'S TIME FOR THE CEREMONY OF BIRTH TO BEGIN!!

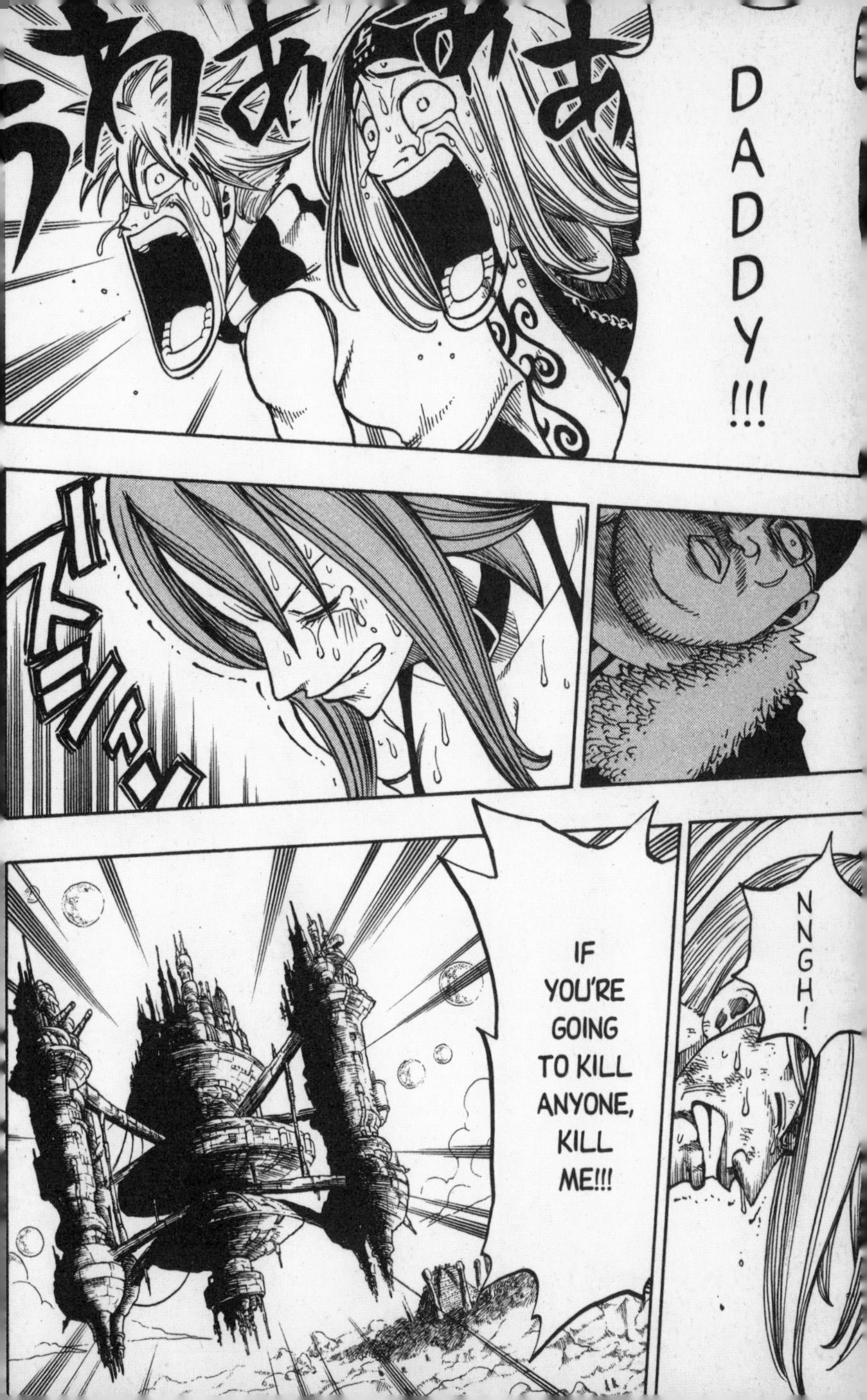
DADDY!!!
うわあああ
NNGH!
IF YOU'RE GOING TO KILL ANYONE, KILL ME!!!

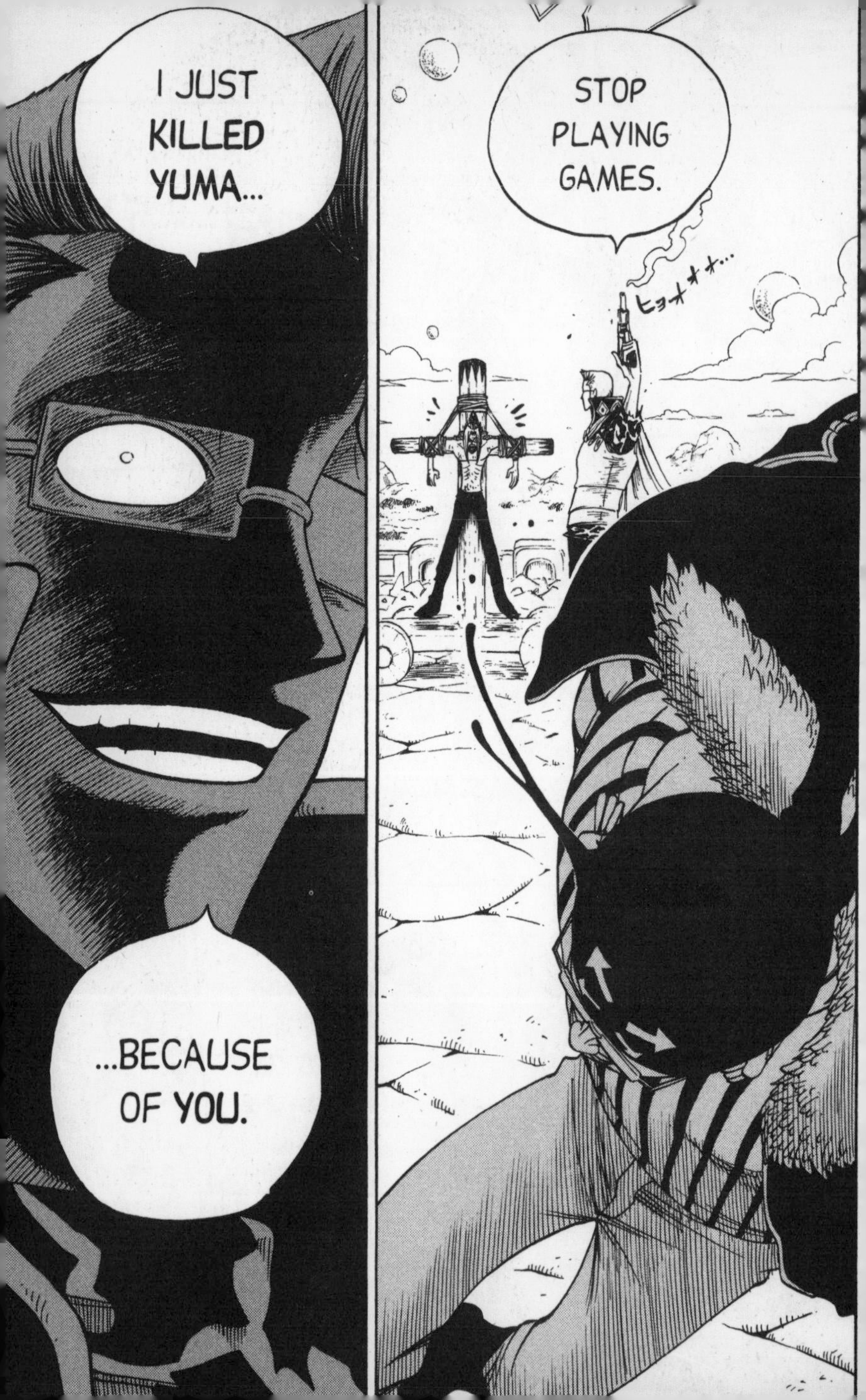
STOP PLAYING GAMES.
ヒョオオオ…
I JUST KILLED YUMA...
...BECAUSE OF YOU.

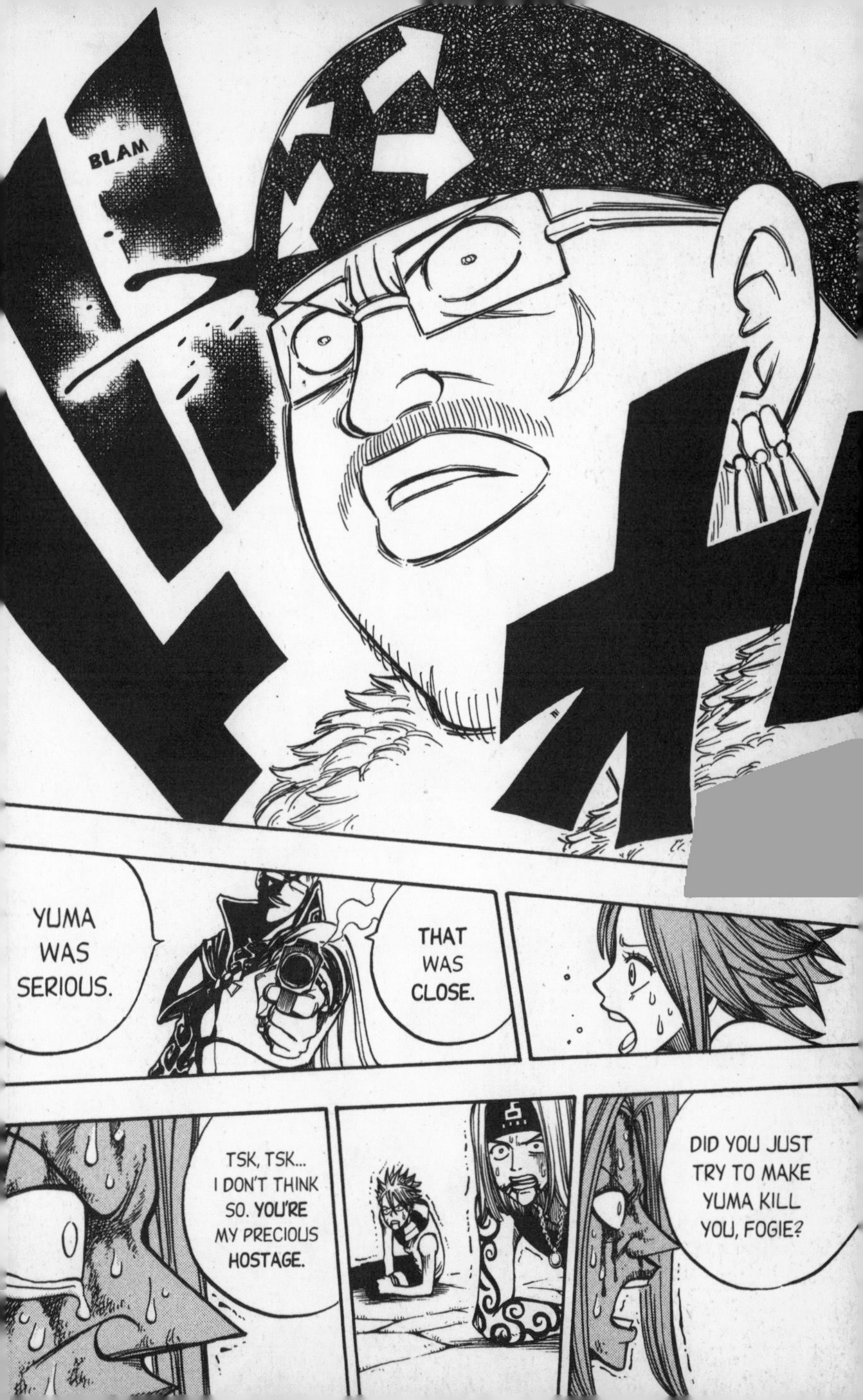
BLAM
THAT WAS CLOSE.
YUMA WAS SERIOUS.
DID YOU JUST TRY TO MAKE YUMA KILL YOU, FOGIE?
TSK, TSK... I DON'T THINK SO. YOU'RE MY PRECIOUS HOSTAGE.

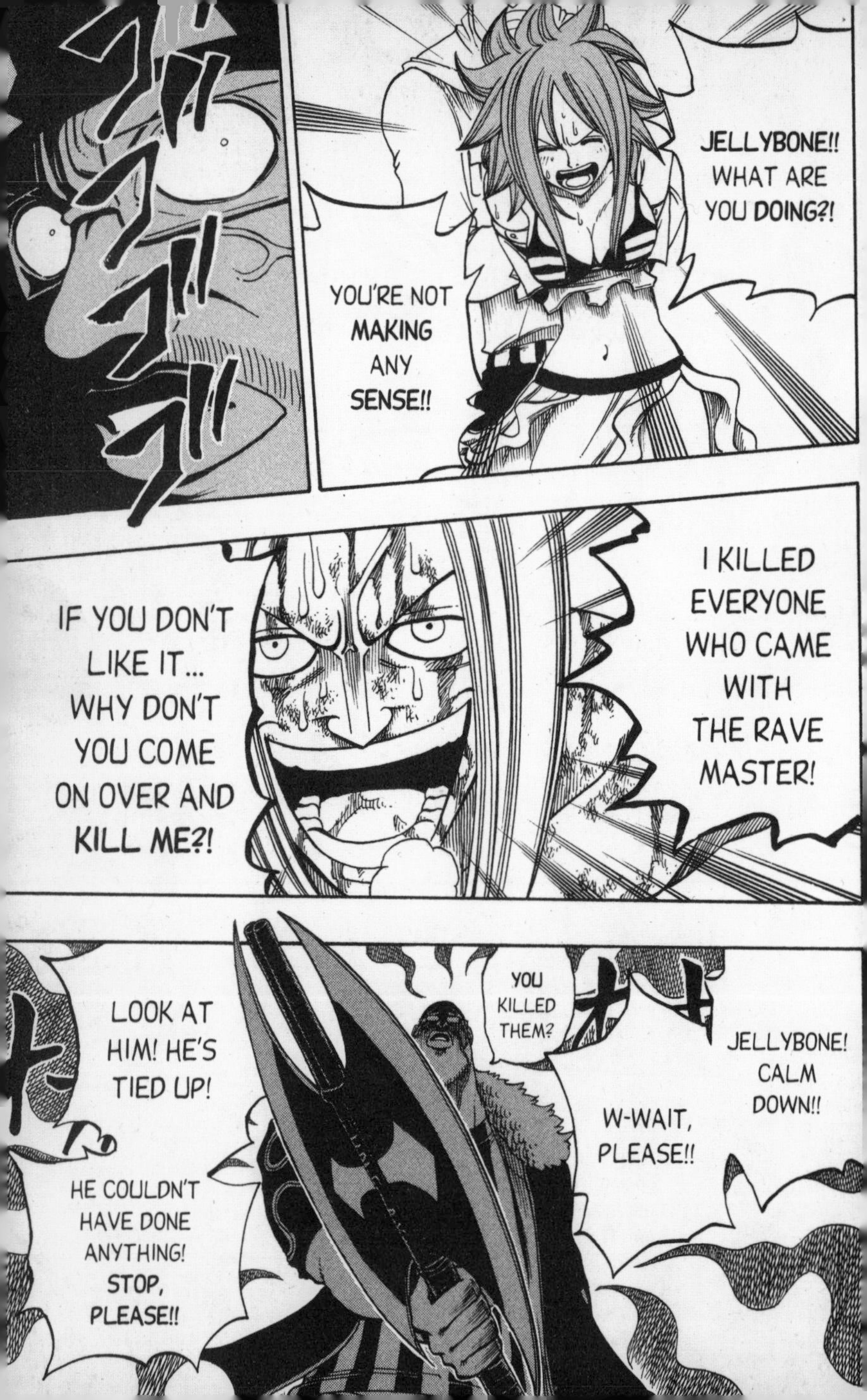
JELLYBONE!! WHAT ARE YOU DOING?!
YOU'RE NOT MAKING ANY SENSE!!
I KILLED EVERYONE WHO CAME WITH THE RAVE MASTER!
IF YOU DON'T LIKE IT... WHY DON'T YOU COME ON OVER AND KILL ME?!
JELLYBONE! CALM DOWN!!
YOU KILLED THEM?
W-WAIT, PLEASE!!
LOOK AT HIM! HE'S TIED UP!
HE COULDN'T HAVE DONE ANYTHING! STOP, PLEASE!!

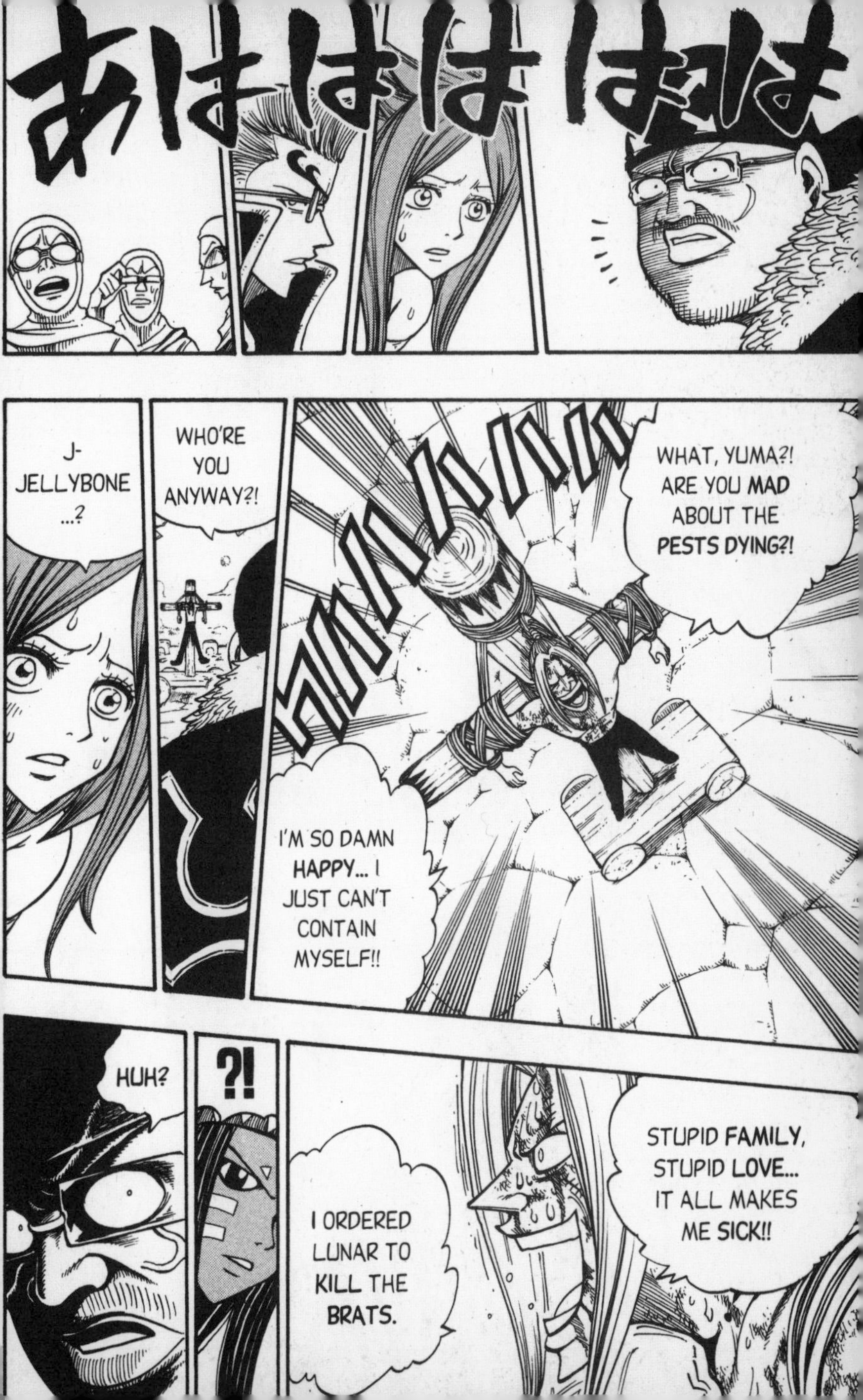
あははははは
WHAT, YUMA?! ARE YOU MAD ABOUT THE PESTS DYING?!
I'M SO DAMN HAPPY... I JUST CAN'T CONTAIN MYSELF!!
WHO'RE YOU ANYWAY?!
J-JELLYBONE ...?
STUPID FAMILY, STUPID LOVE... IT ALL MAKES ME SICK!!
I ORDERED LUNAR TO KILL THE BRATS.
?!
HUH?

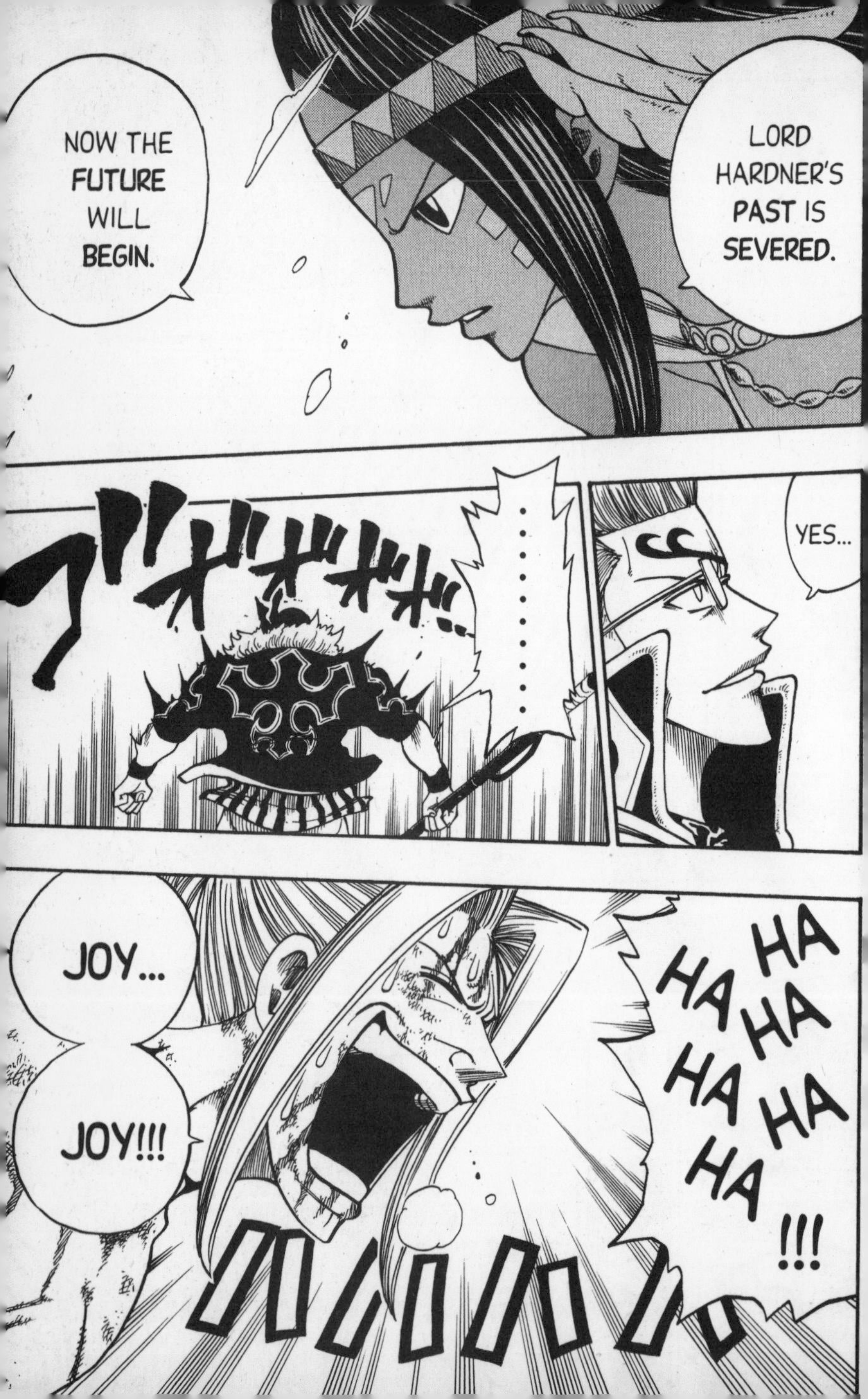
LORD HARDNER'S PAST IS SEVERED.
NOW THE FUTURE WILL BEGIN.
YES...
......
HA HA HA HA HA HA HA HA!!!
JOY...
JOY!!!

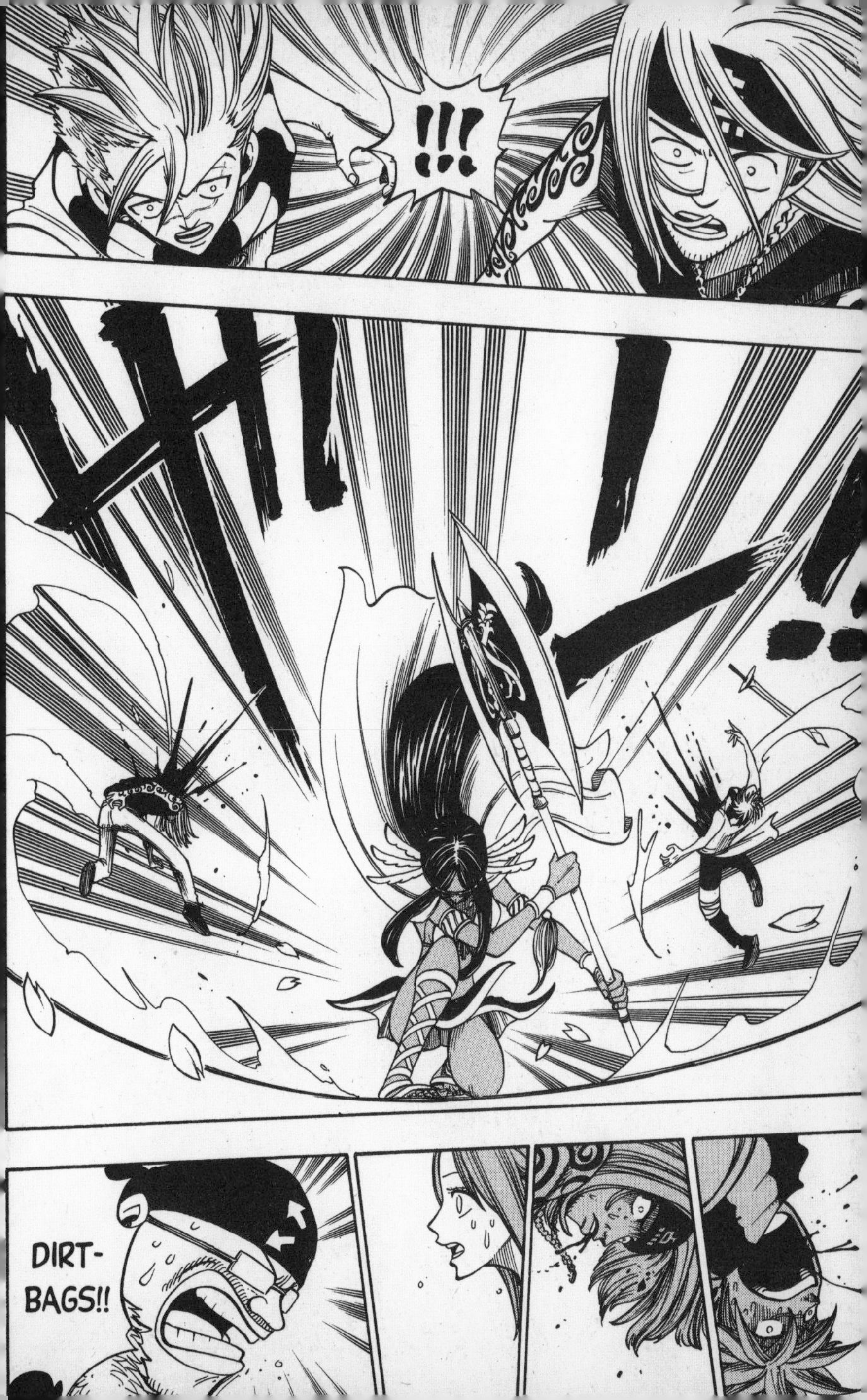
!!!
DIRT-
BAGS!!

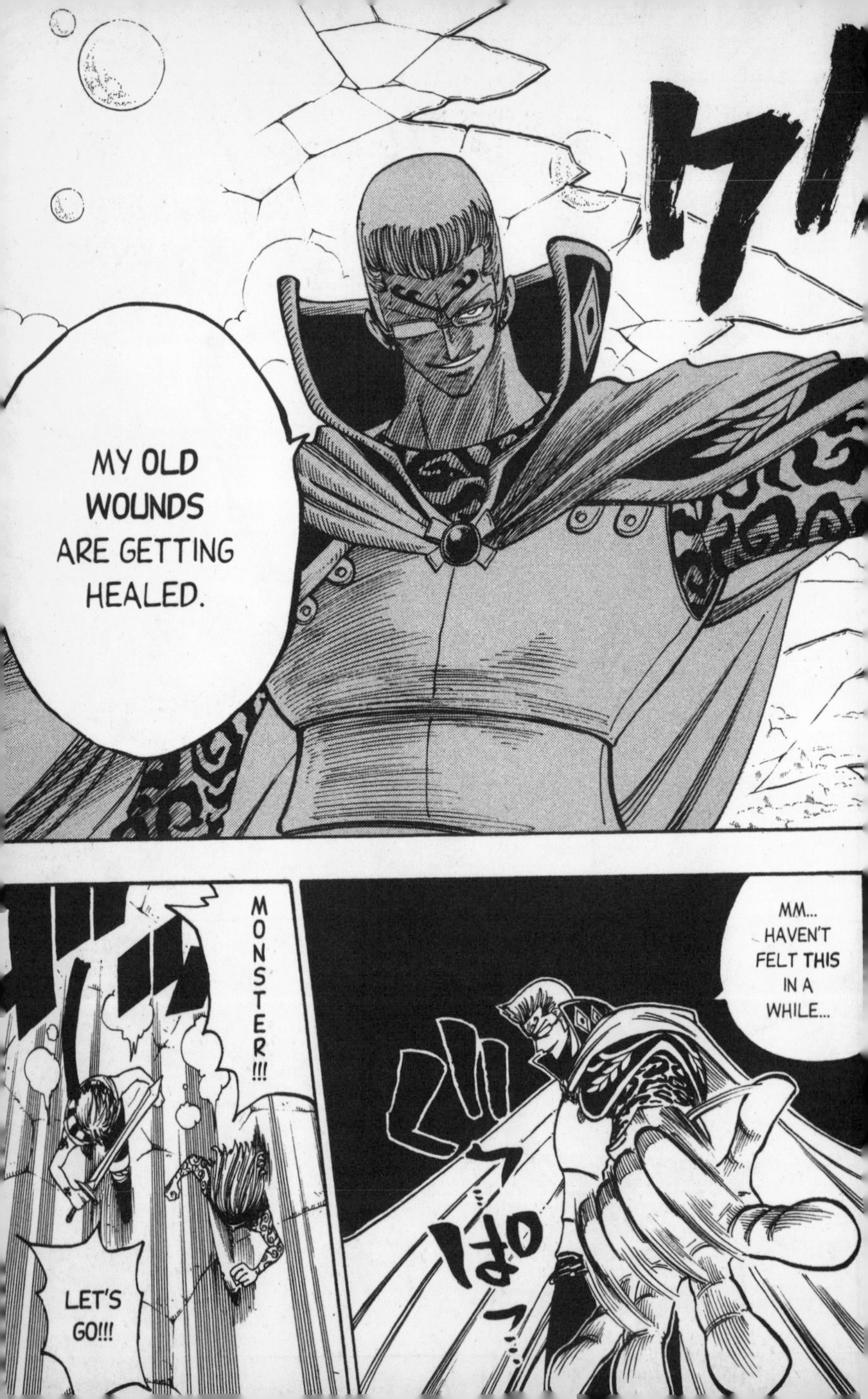
MY OLD WOUNDS ARE GETTING HEALED.
MM... HAVEN'T FELT THIS IN A WHILE...
MONSTER!!!
LET'S GO!!!

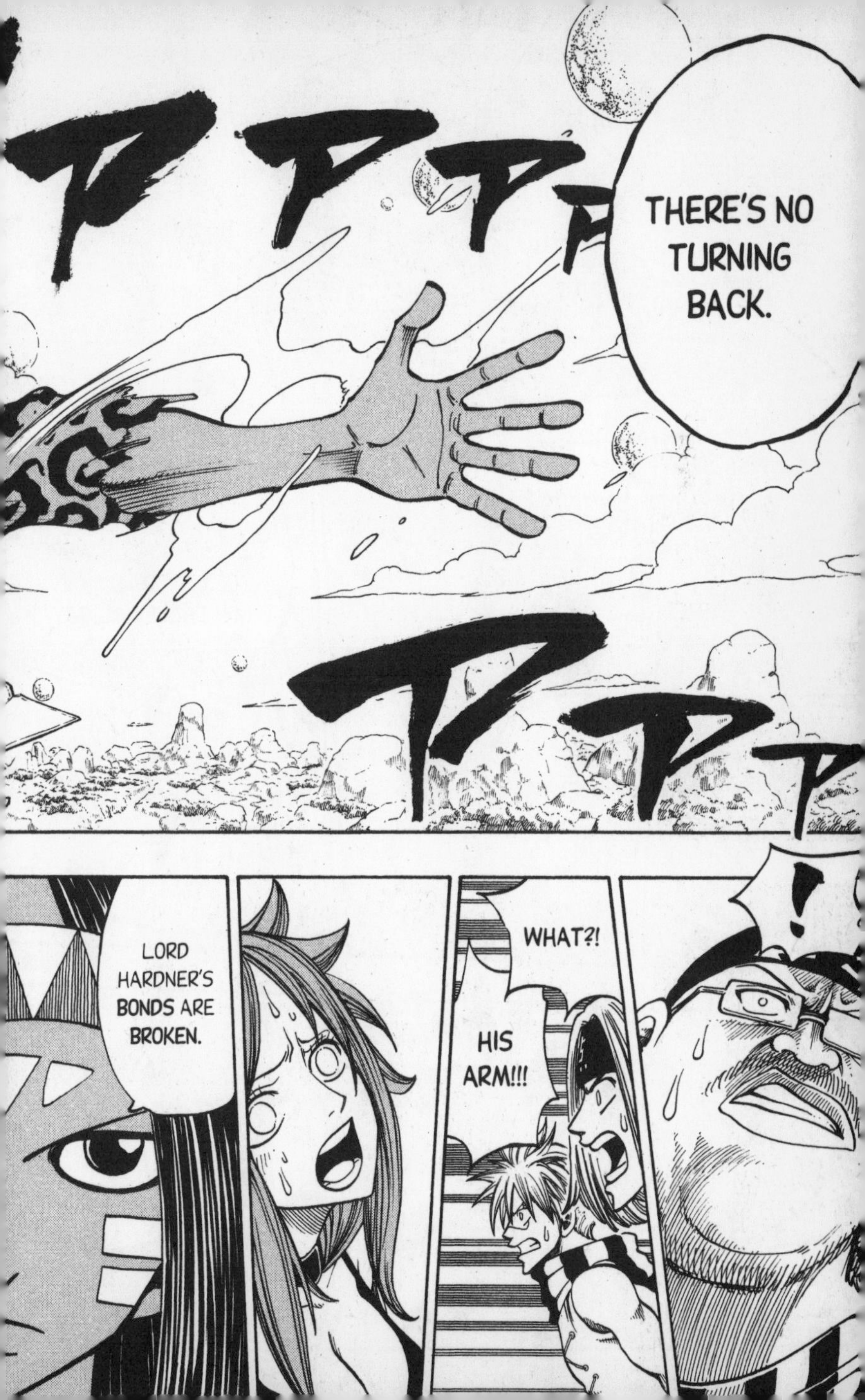
THERE'S NO TURNING BACK.
!
WHAT?!
HIS ARM!!!
LORD HARDNER'S BONDS ARE BROKEN.

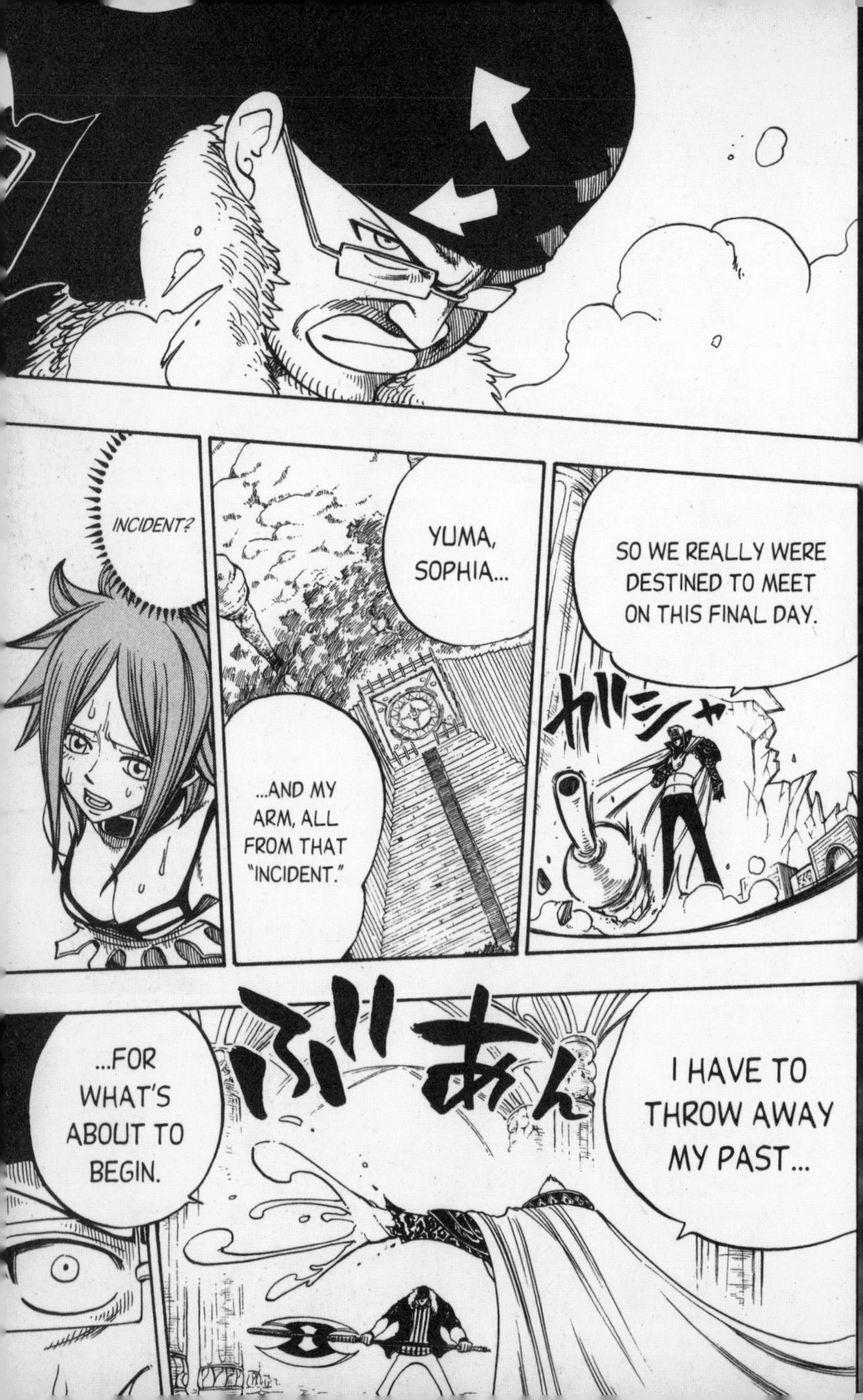
SO WE REALLY WERE DESTINED TO MEET ON THIS FINAL DAY.
ガシャ
YUMA, SOPHIA...
...AND MY ARM, ALL FROM THAT "INCIDENT."
INCIDENT?
I HAVE TO THROW AWAY MY PAST...
ぶあん
...FOR WHAT'S ABOUT TO BEGIN.

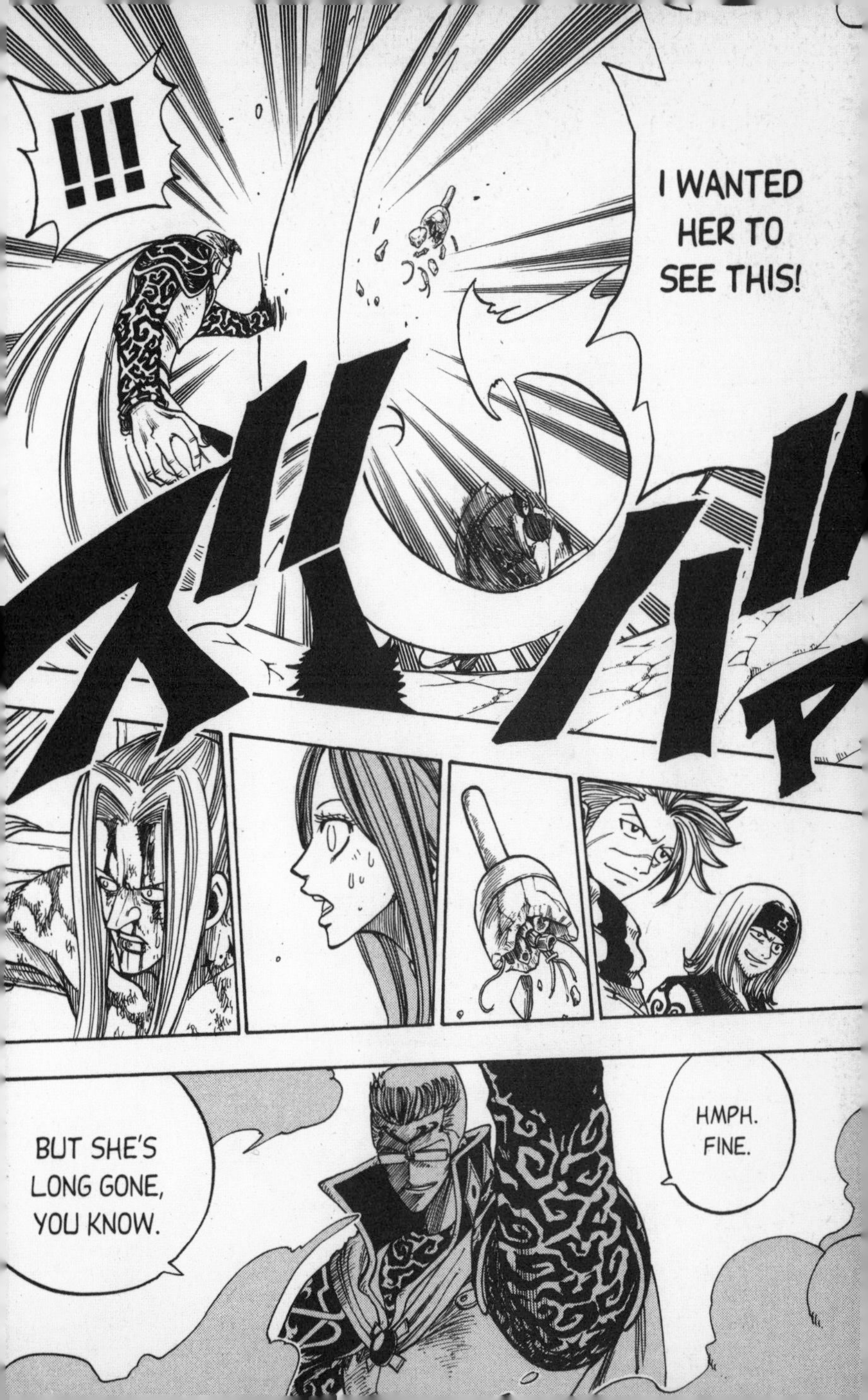
I WANTED HER TO SEE THIS!
!!!
HMPH. FINE.
BUT SHE'S LONG GONE, YOU KNOW.

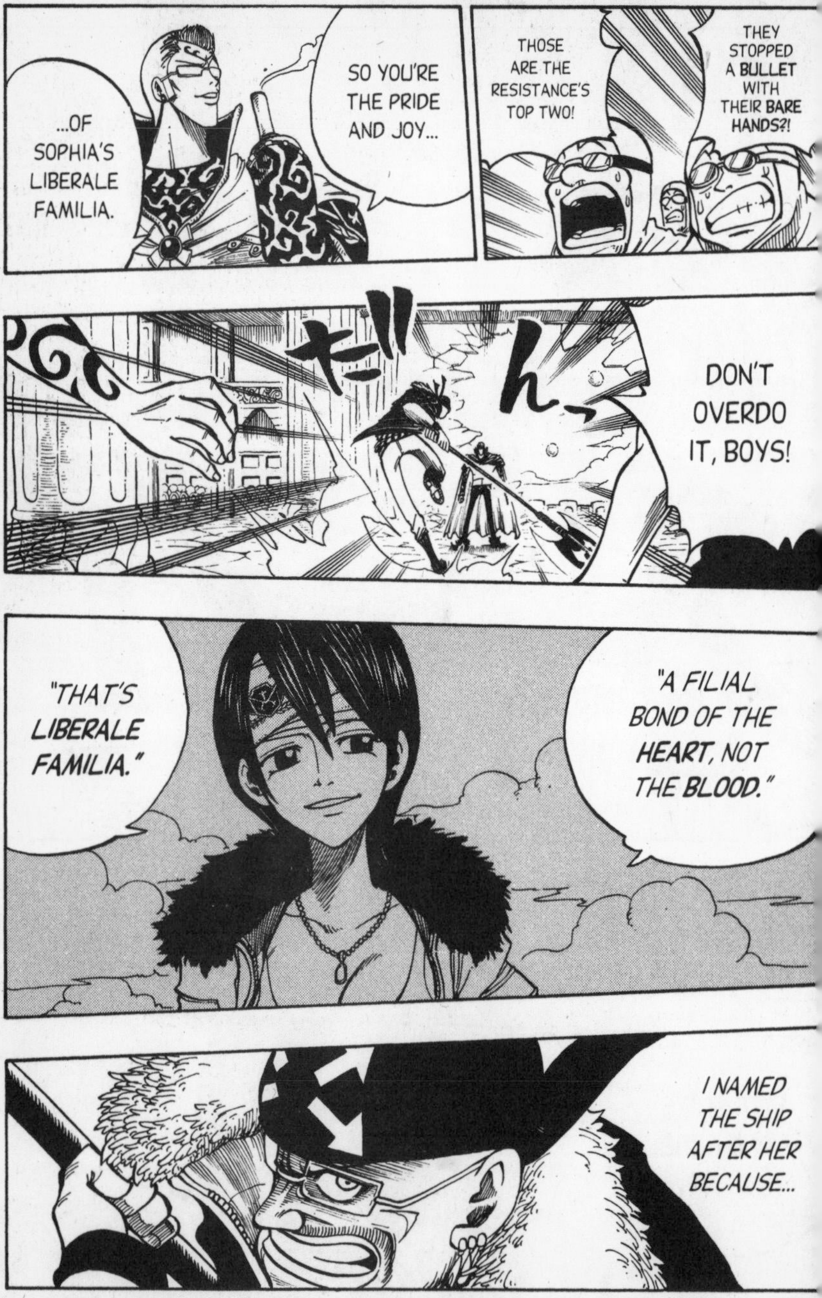
THEY STOPPED A BULLET WITH THEIR BARE HANDS?!
THOSE ARE THE RESISTANCE'S TOP TWO!
SO YOU'RE THE PRIDE AND JOY...
...OF SOPHIA'S LIBERALE FAMILIA.
DON'T OVERDO IT, BOYS!
"A FILIAL BOND OF THE HEART, NOT THE BLOOD."
"THAT'S LIBERALE FAMILIA."
I NAMED THE SHIP AFTER HER BECAUSE...

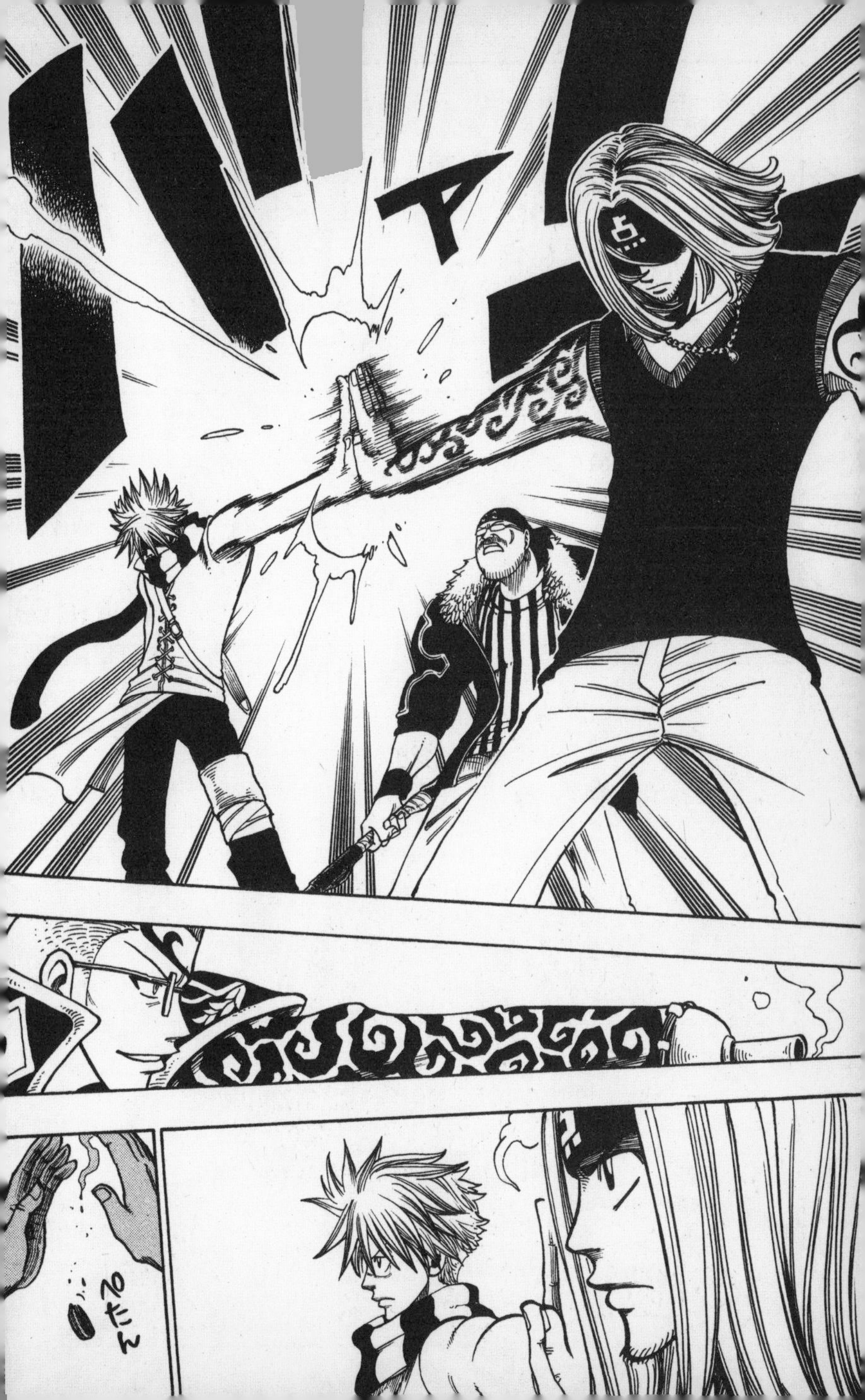
ぺたん

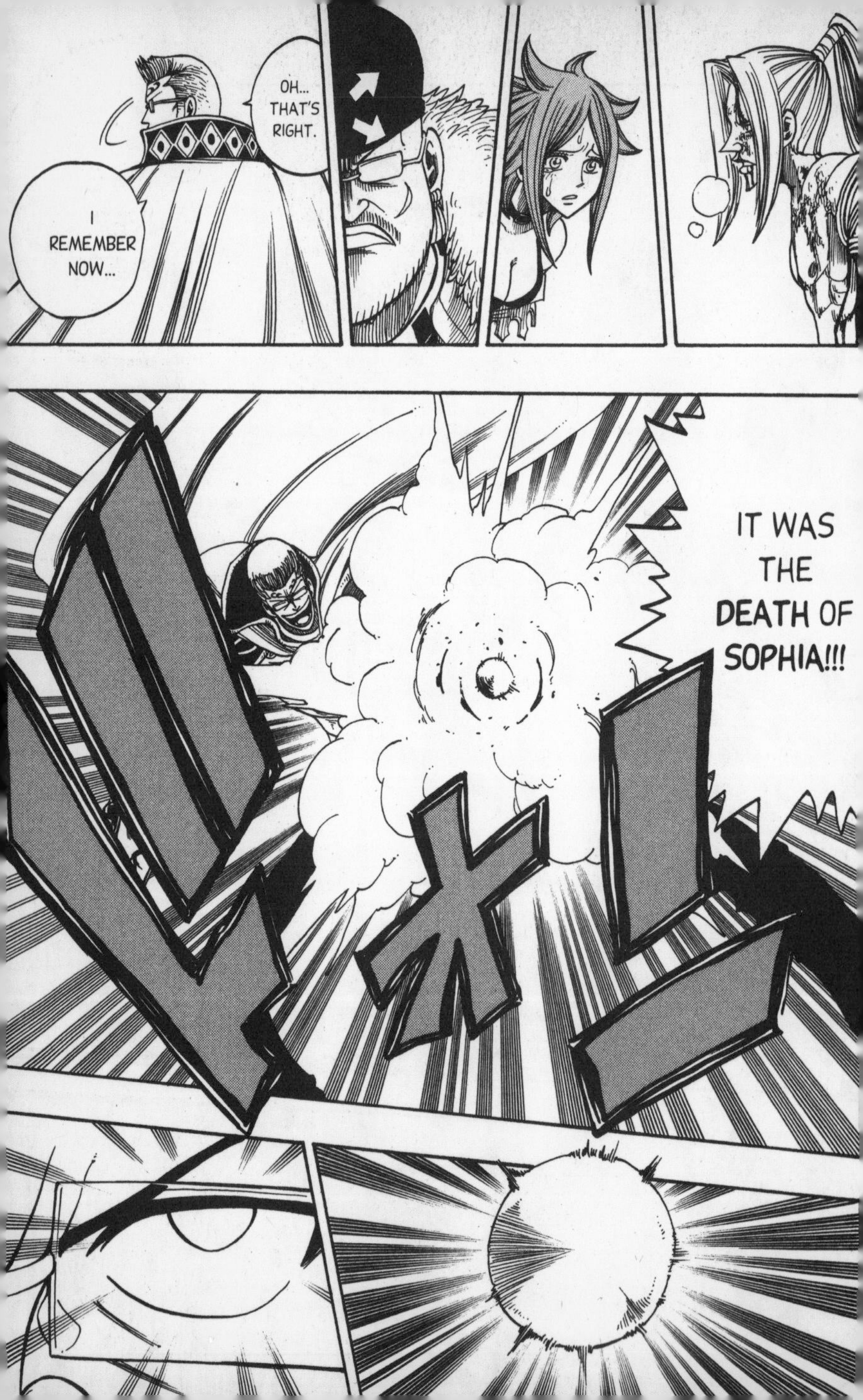
OH... THAT'S RIGHT.
I REMEMBER NOW...
IT WAS THE DEATH OF SOPHIA!!!

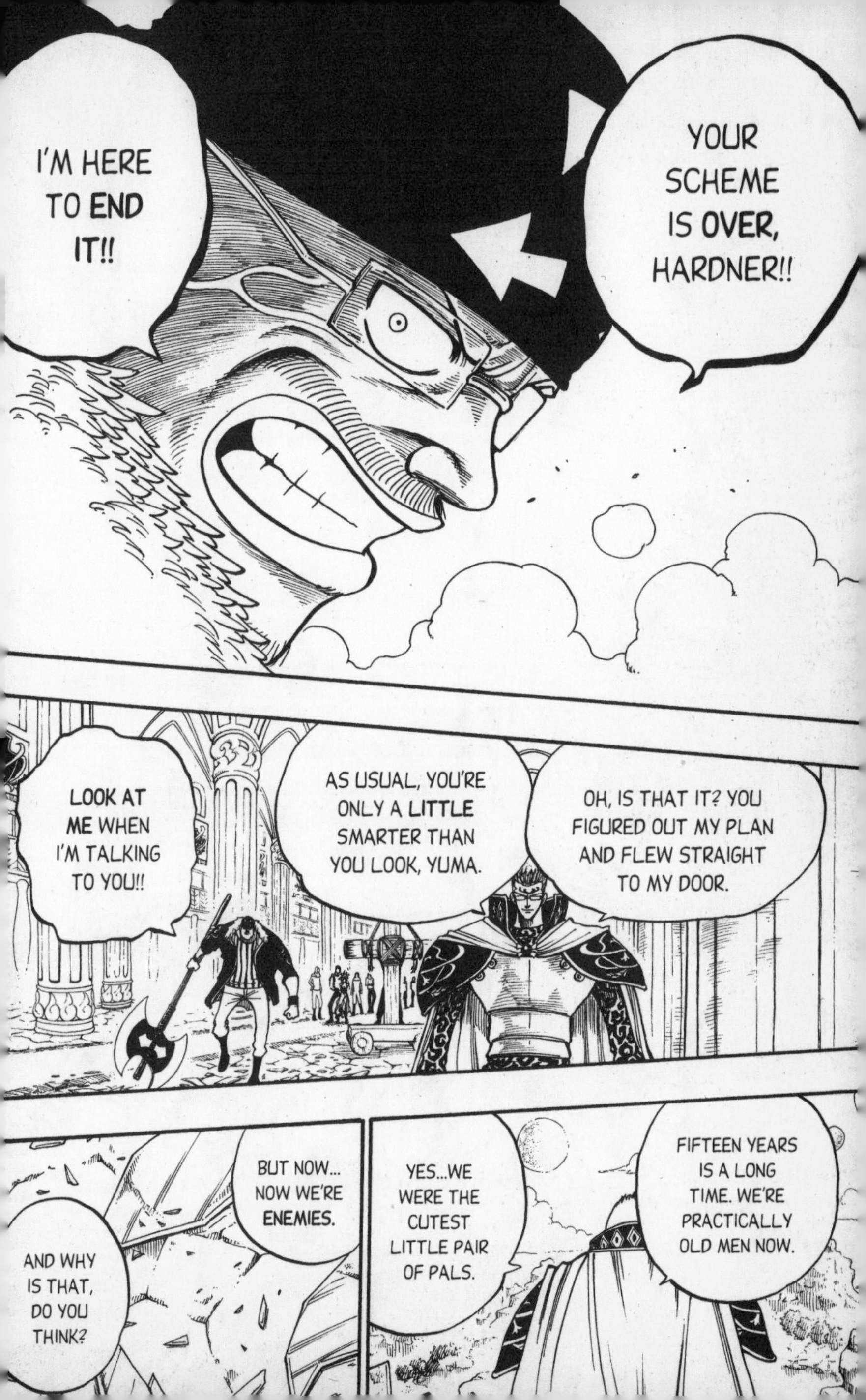
YOUR SCHEME IS OVER, HARDNER!!
I'M HERE TO END IT!!
OH, IS THAT IT? YOU FIGURED OUT MY PLAN AND FLEW STRAIGHT TO MY DOOR.
AS USUAL, YOU'RE ONLY A LITTLE SMARTER THAN YOU LOOK, YUMA.
LOOK AT ME WHEN I'M TALKING TO YOU!!
FIFTEEN YEARS IS A LONG TIME. WE'RE PRACTICALLY OLD MEN NOW.
YES...WE WERE THE CUTEST LITTLE PAIR OF PALS.
BUT NOW... NOW WE'RE ENEMIES.
AND WHY IS THAT, DO YOU THINK?

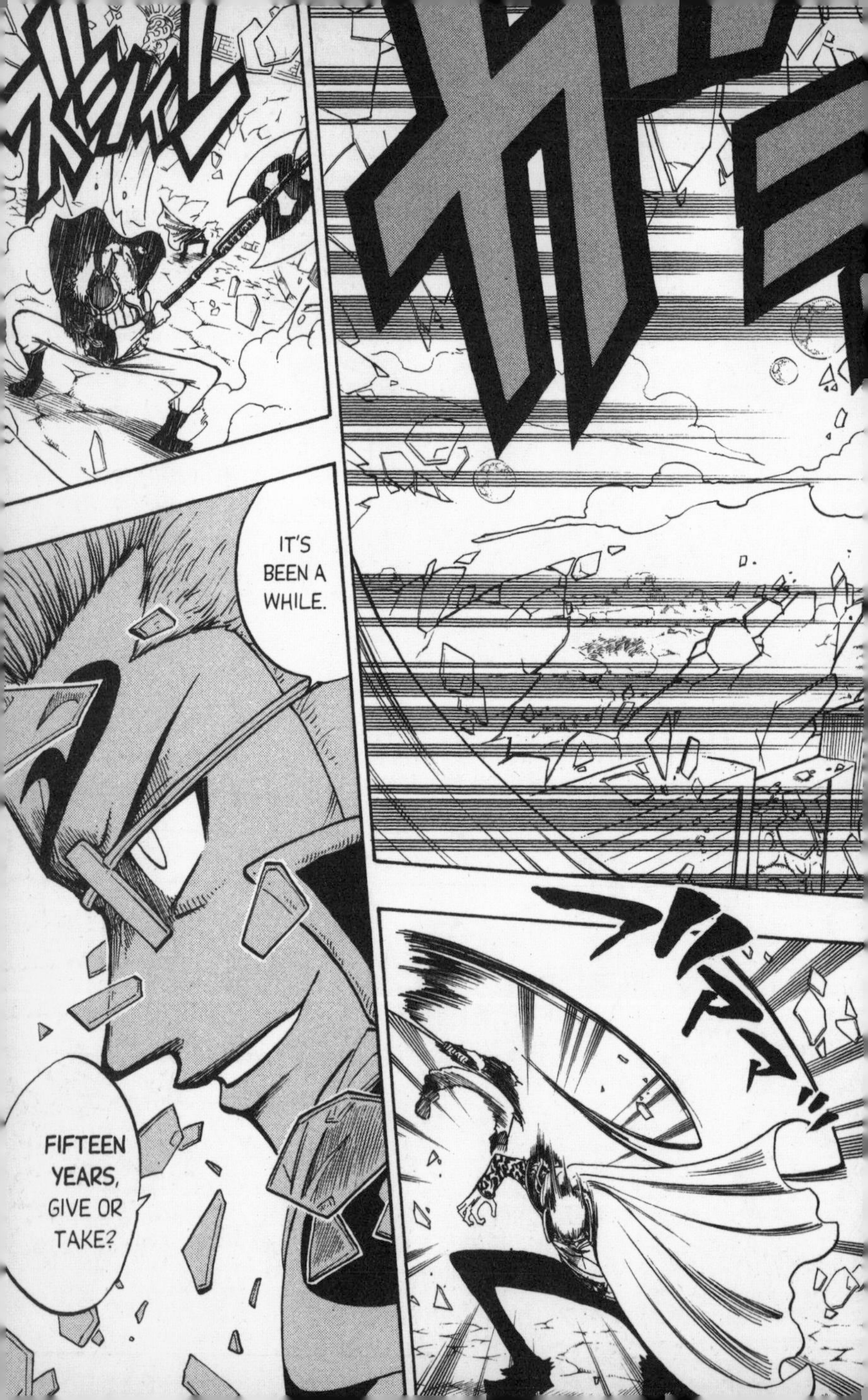
IT'S BEEN A WHILE.
FIFTEEN YEARS, GIVE OR TAKE?

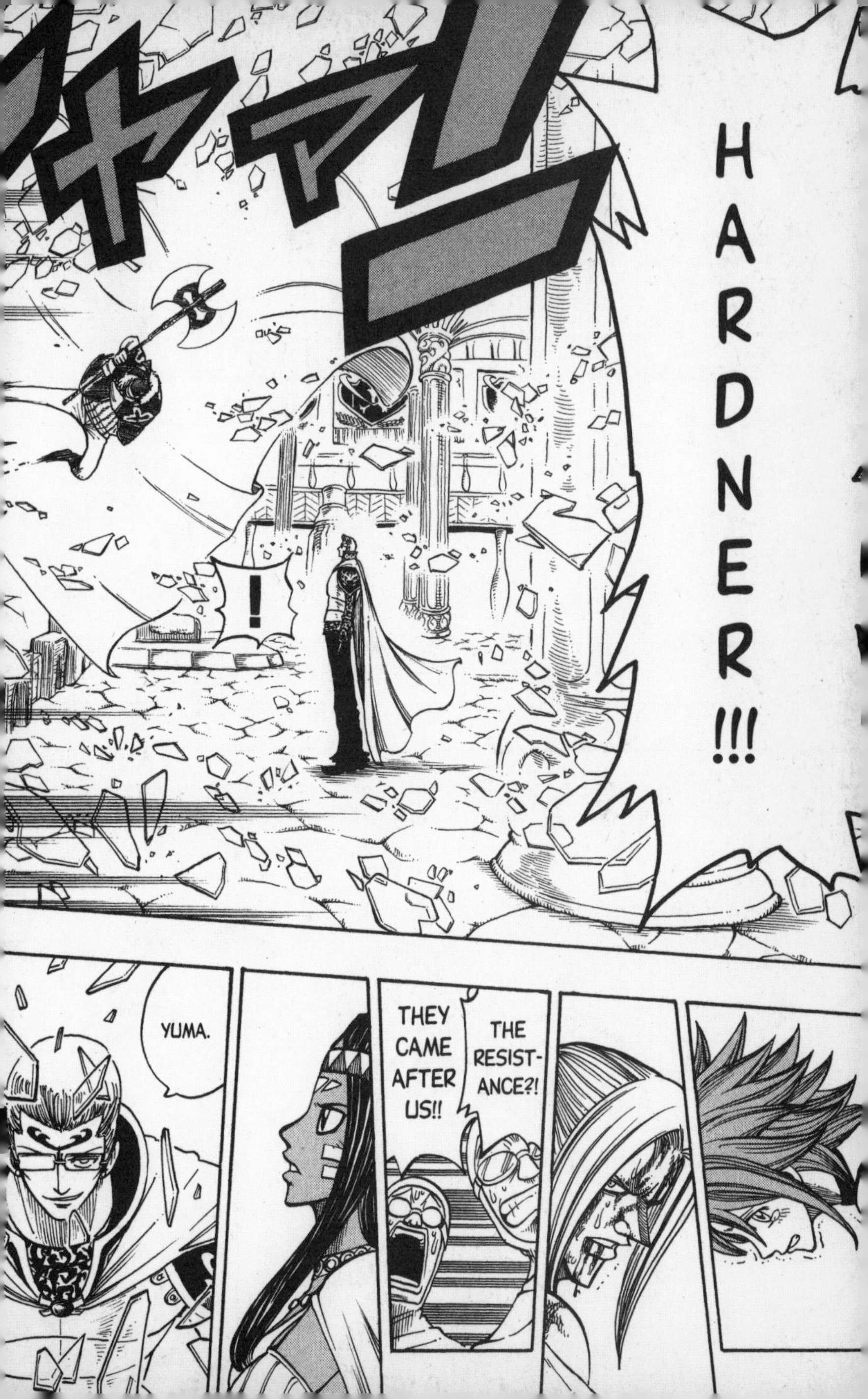
HARDNER!!!
!
THE RESIST-ANCE?!
THEY CAME AFTER US!!
YUMA.

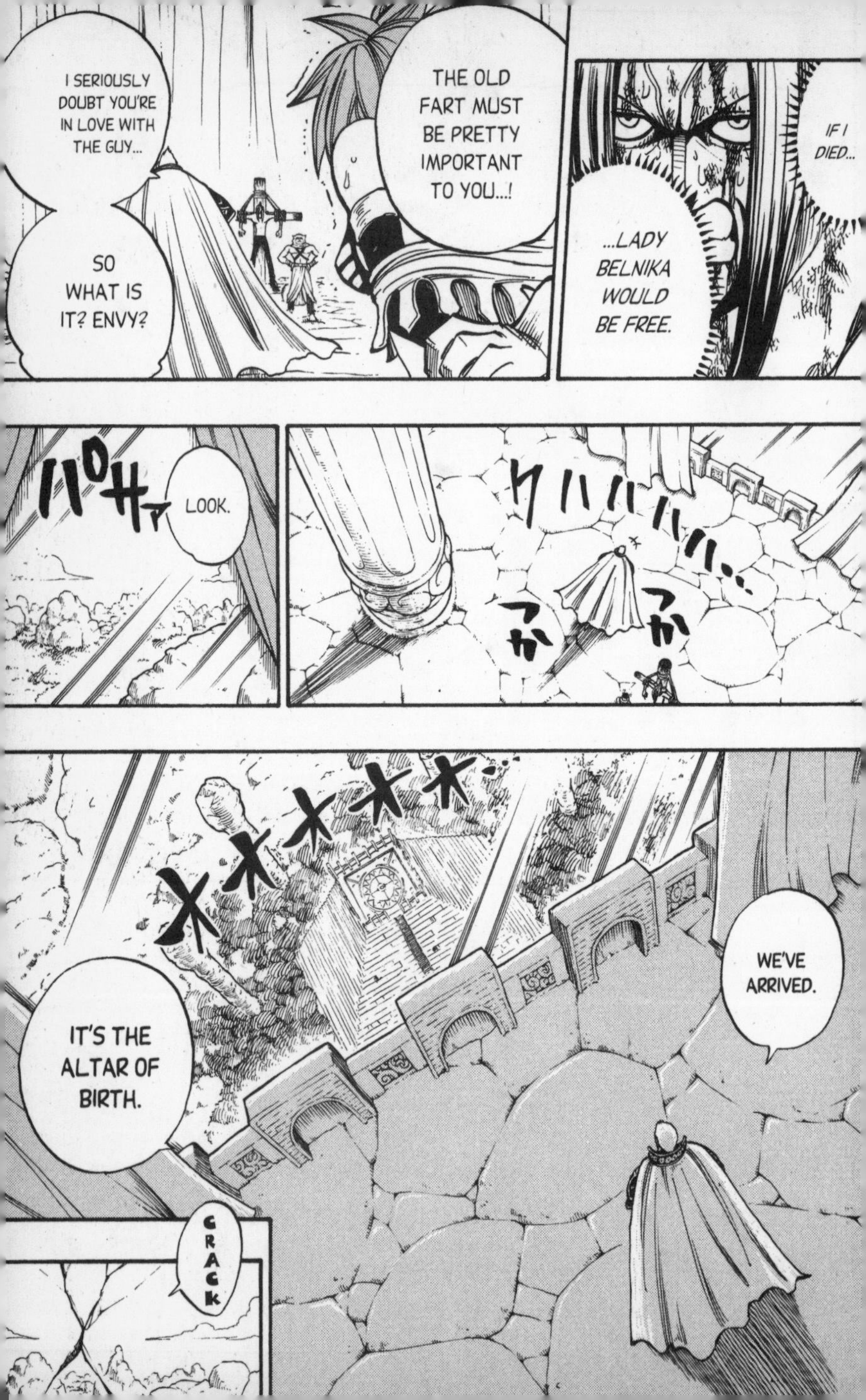
IF I DIED...
...LADY BELNIKA WOULD BE FREE.
THE OLD FART MUST BE PRETTY IMPORTANT TO YOU...!
I SERIOUSLY DOUBT YOU'RE IN LOVE WITH THE GUY...
SO WHAT IS IT? ENVY?
クハハハハ...
ふか
ふか
パサァ
LOOK.
WE'VE ARRIVED.
IT'S THE ALTAR OF BIRTH.
CRACK

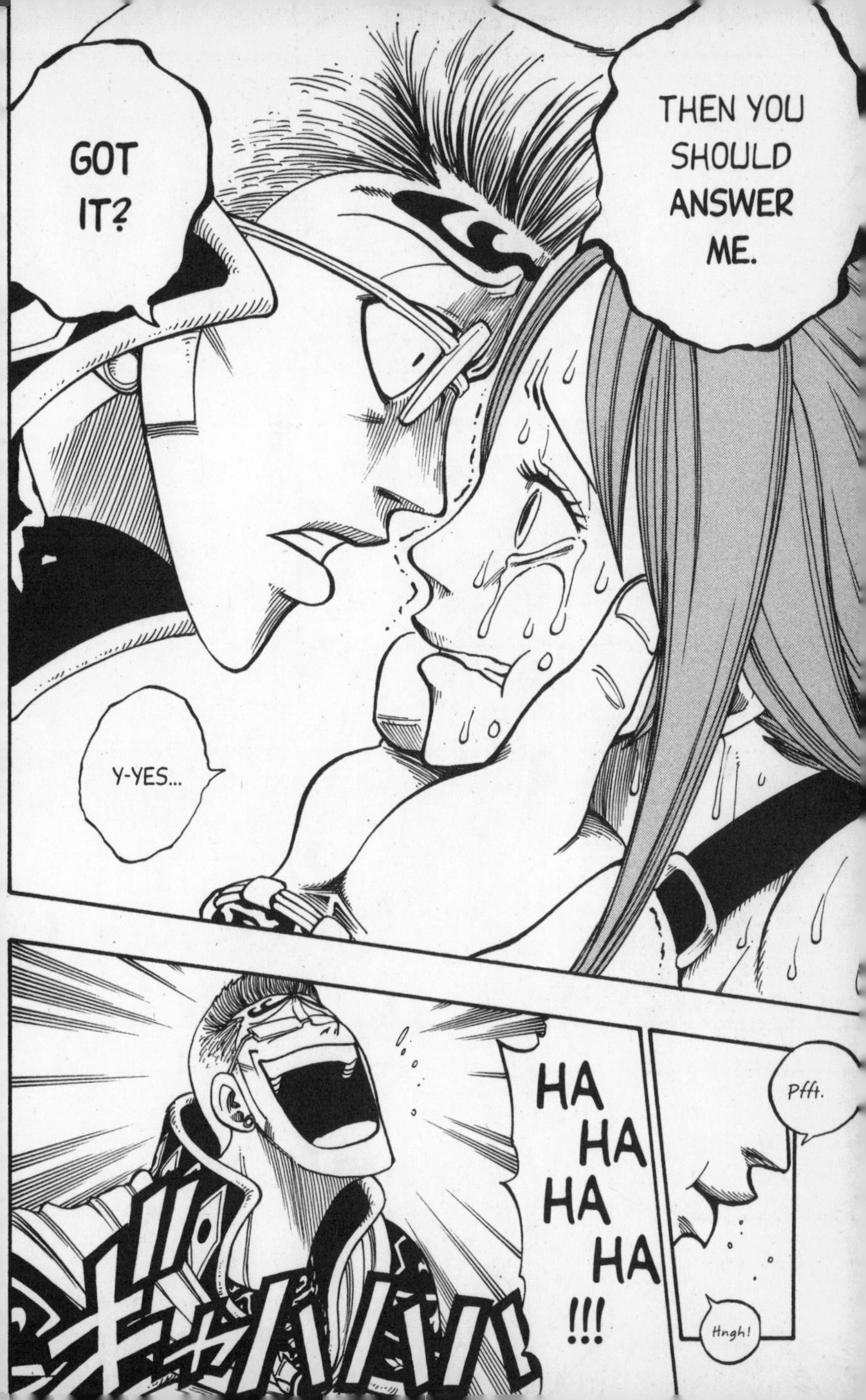
THEN YOU SHOULD ANSWER ME.
GOT IT?
Y-YES...
Pfft.
Hngh!
HA HA HA HA HA !!!

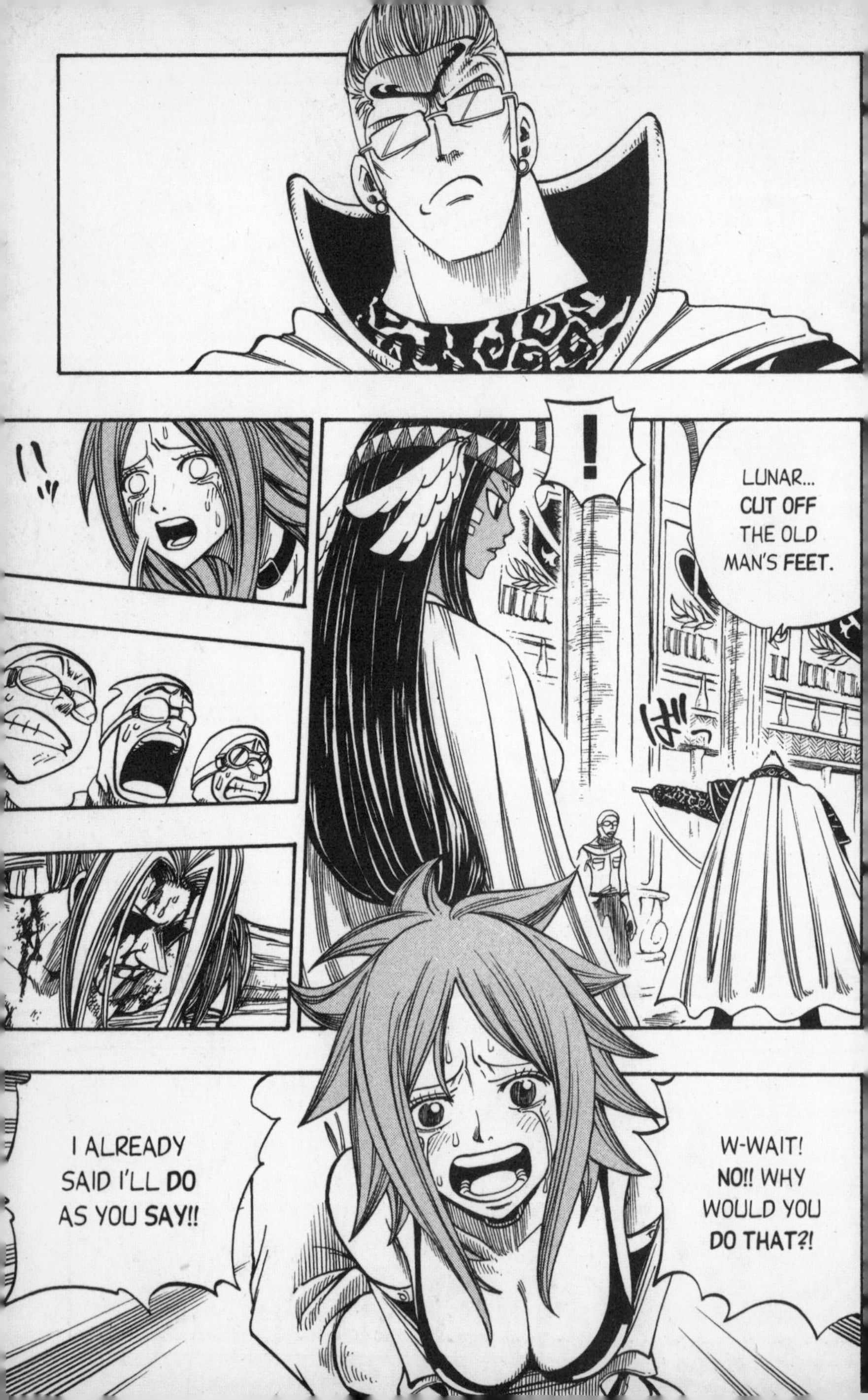
LUNAR... CUT OFF THE OLD MAN'S FEET.
!
ばっ
ハッ
W-WAIT! NO!! WHY WOULD YOU DO THAT?!
I ALREADY SAID I'LL DO AS YOU SAY!!

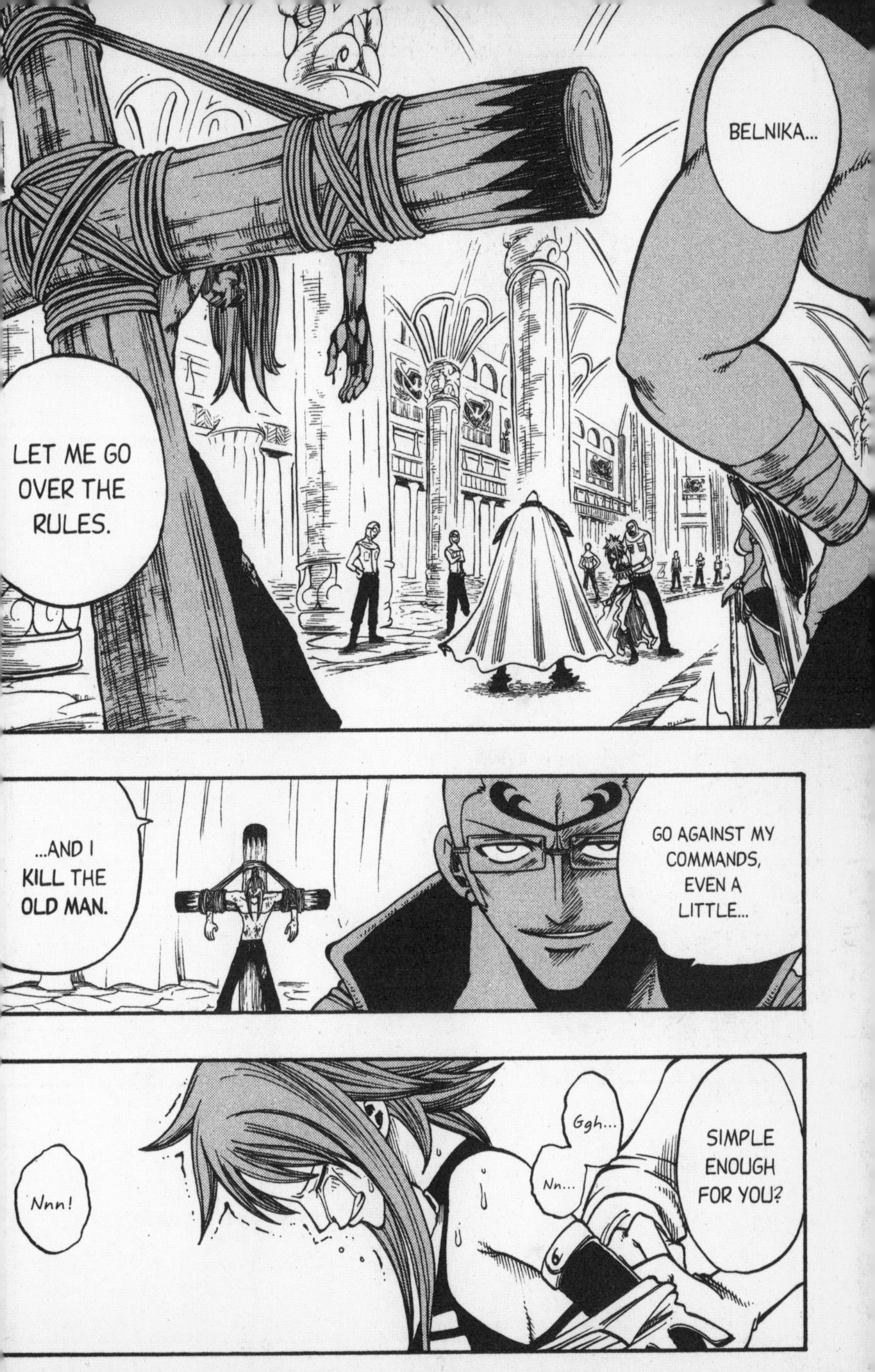
BELNIKA...
LET ME GO OVER THE RULES.
GO AGAINST MY COMMANDS, EVEN A LITTLE...
...AND I KILL THE OLD MAN.
SIMPLE ENOUGH FOR YOU?
Ggh...
Nn...
Nnn!

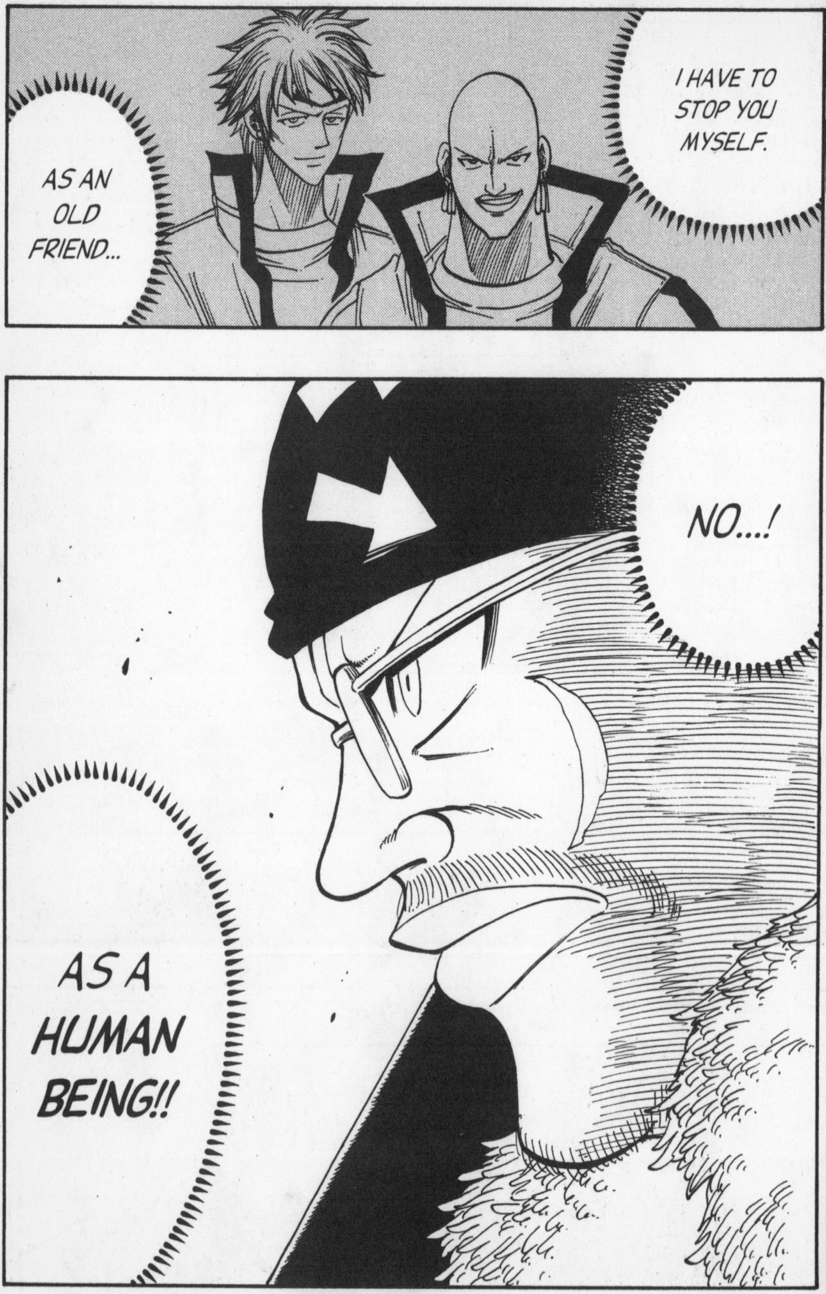
I HAVE TO STOP YOU MYSELF.
AS AN OLD FRIEND...
NO...!
AS A HUMAN BEING!!

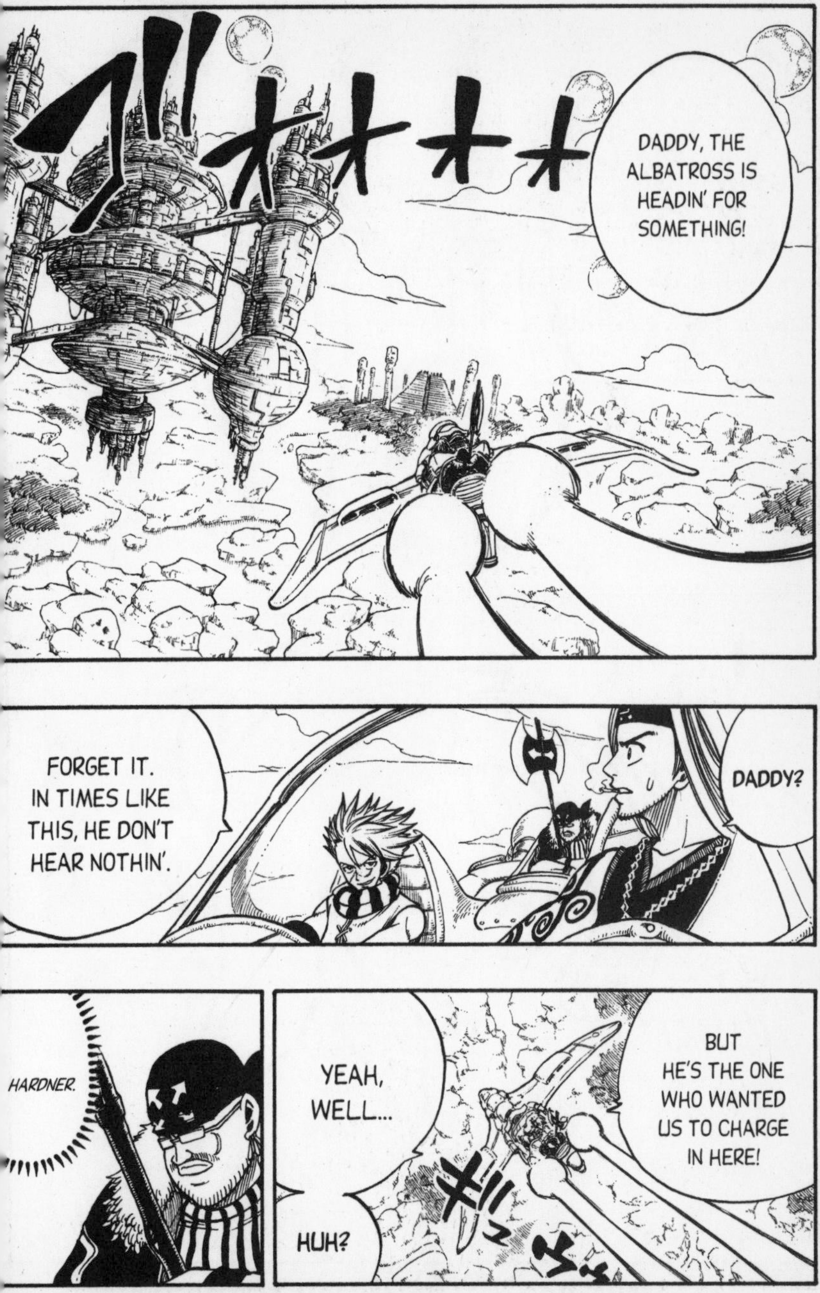
DADDY, THE ALBATROSS IS HEADIN' FOR SOMETHING!
DADDY?
FORGET IT. IN TIMES LIKE THIS, HE DON'T HEAR NOTHIN'.
BUT HE'S THE ONE WHO WANTED US TO CHARGE IN HERE!
YEAH, WELL...
HUH?
HARDNER.

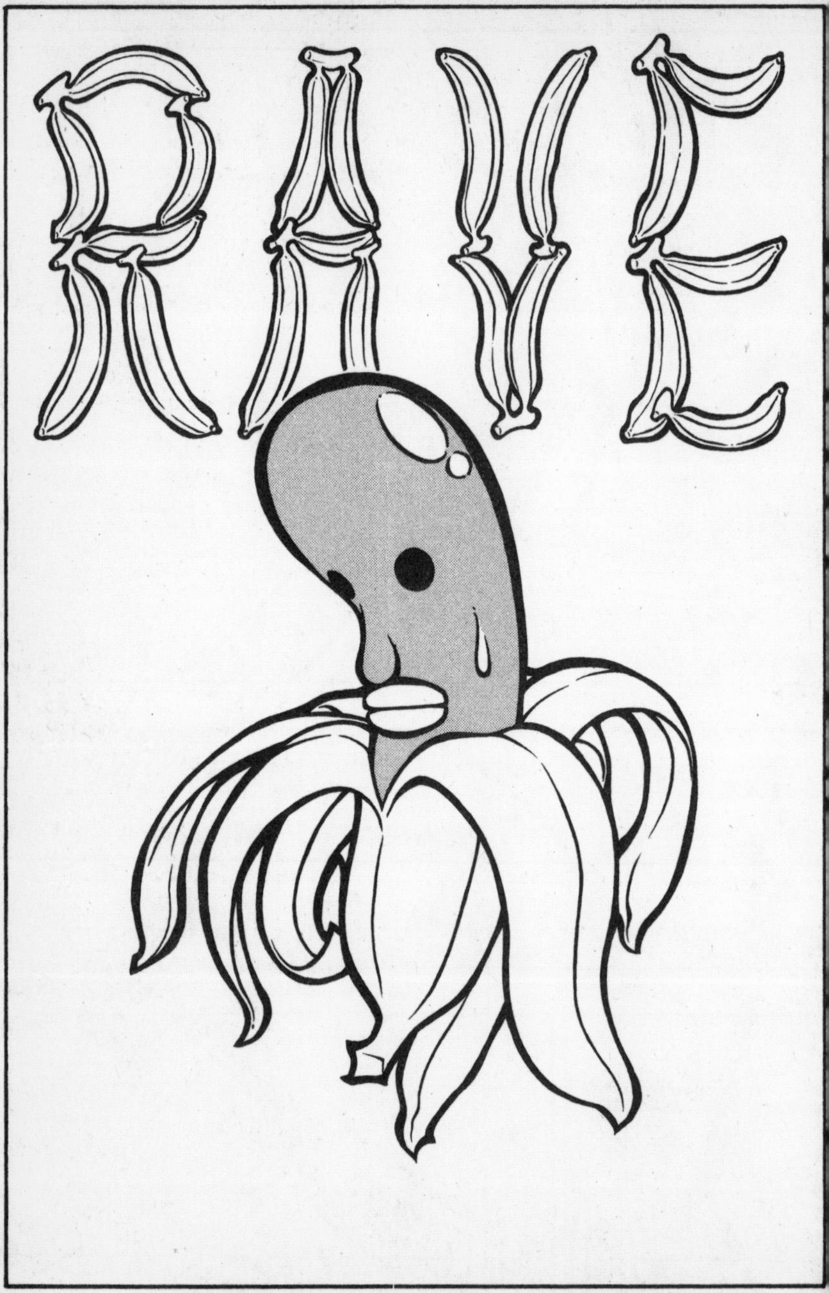
RAVE

RAVE:213 ✠ DEMONIC TRIGGER

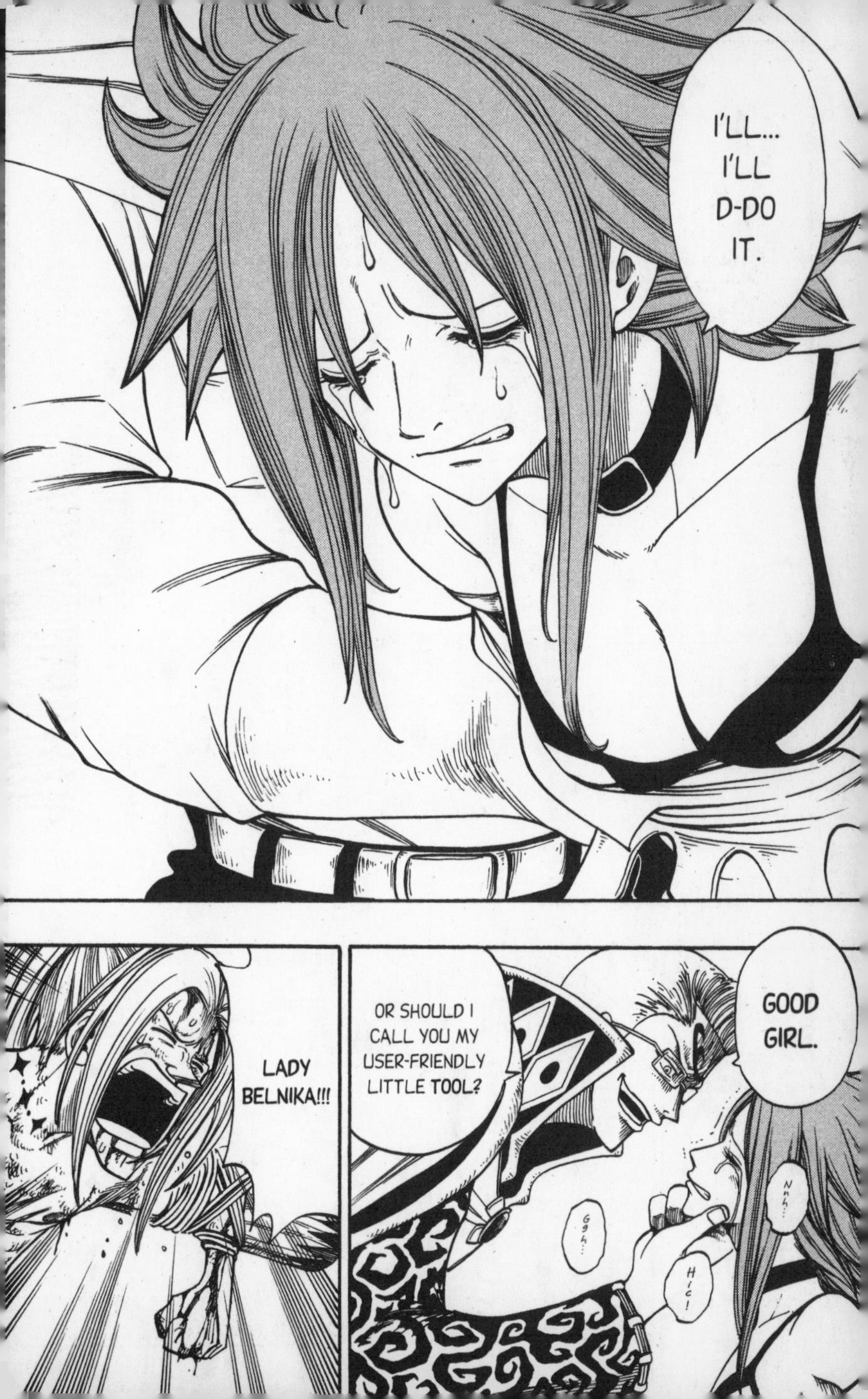
I'LL... I'LL D-DO IT.
GOOD GIRL.
OR SHOULD I CALL YOU MY USER-FRIENDLY LITTLE TOOL?
Nnh...
Ggh...
Hic!
LADY BELNIKA!!!

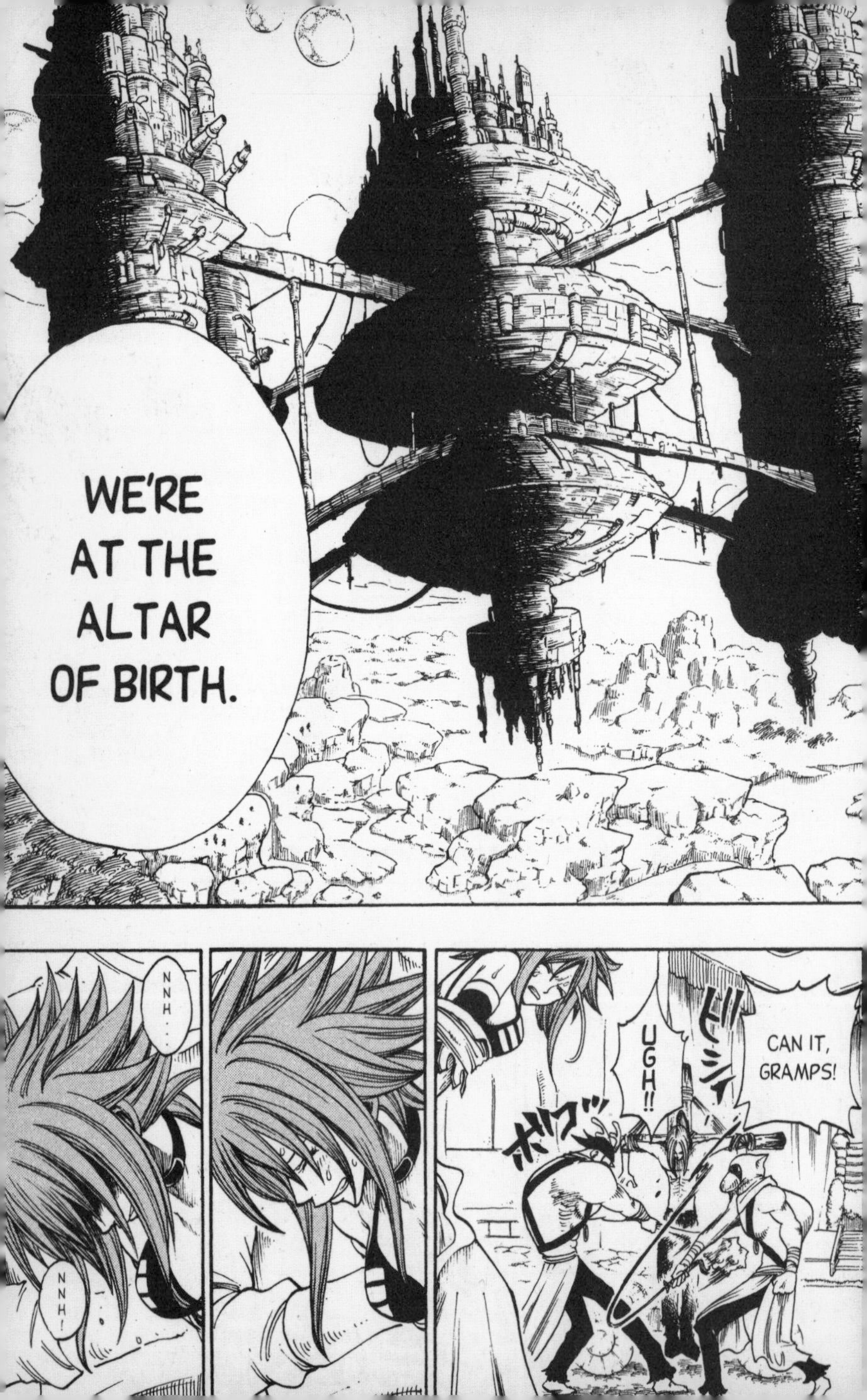
WE'RE AT THE ALTAR OF BIRTH.
CAN IT, GRAMPS!
UGH!!
NNH...
NNH!

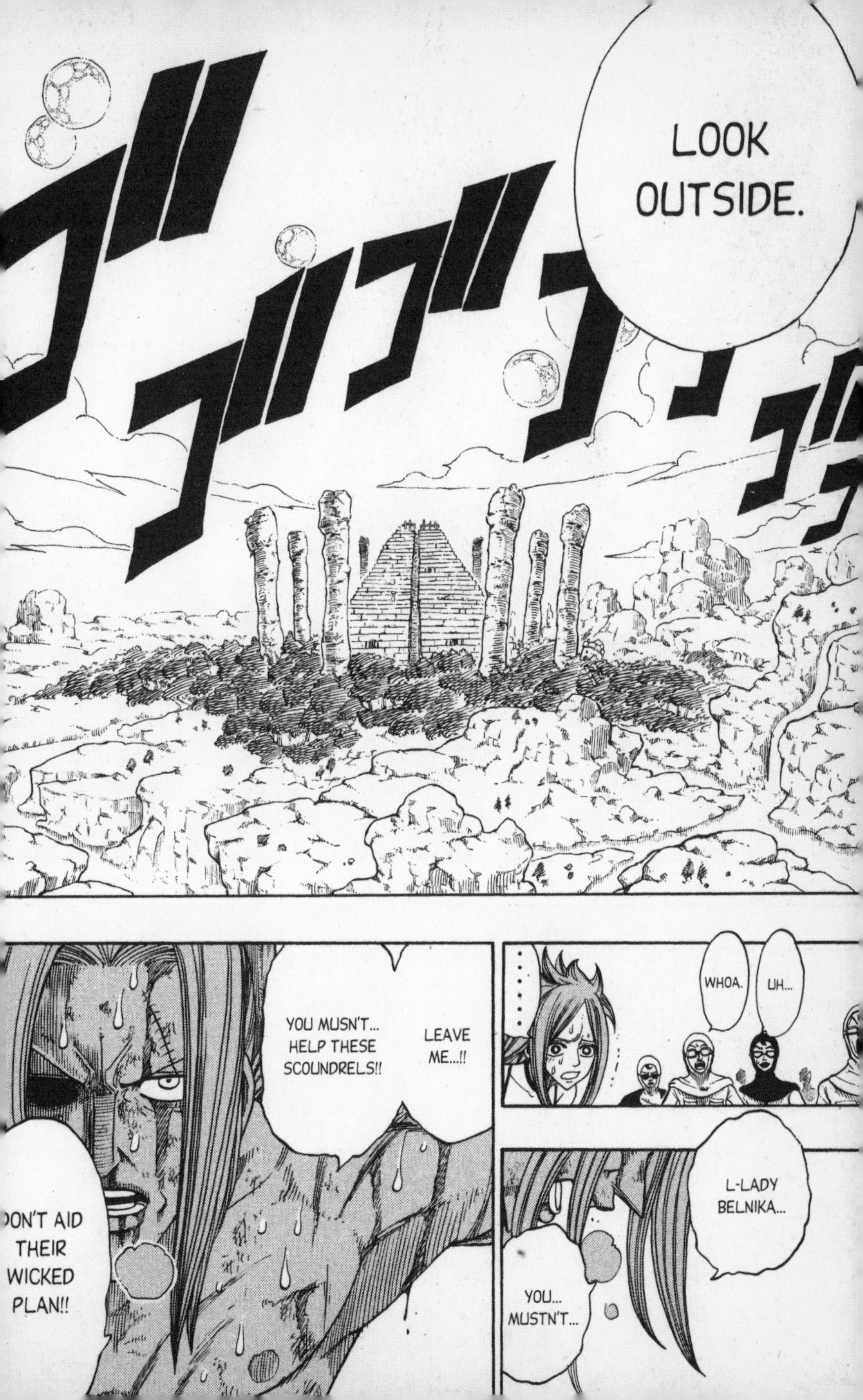
LOOK OUTSIDE.
UH...
WHOA.
......
L-LADY BELNIKA...
YOU... MUSTN'T...
LEAVE ME...!!
YOU MUSN'T... HELP THESE SCOUNDRELS!!
ON'T AID THEIR WICKED PLAN!!

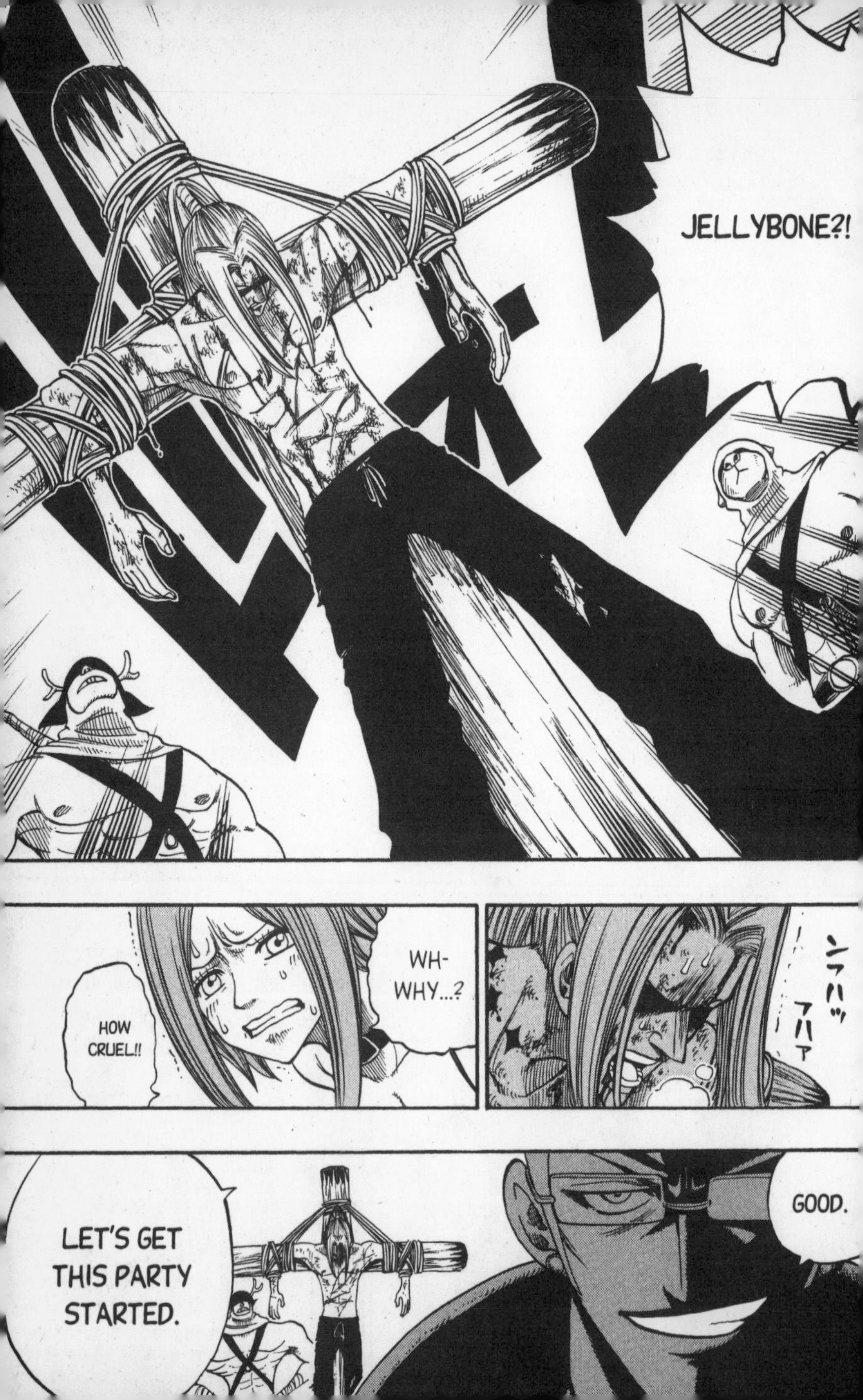
JELLYBONE?!
ンフハッ
アハァ
WH- WHY...?
HOW CRUEL!!
GOOD.
LET'S GET THIS PARTY STARTED.

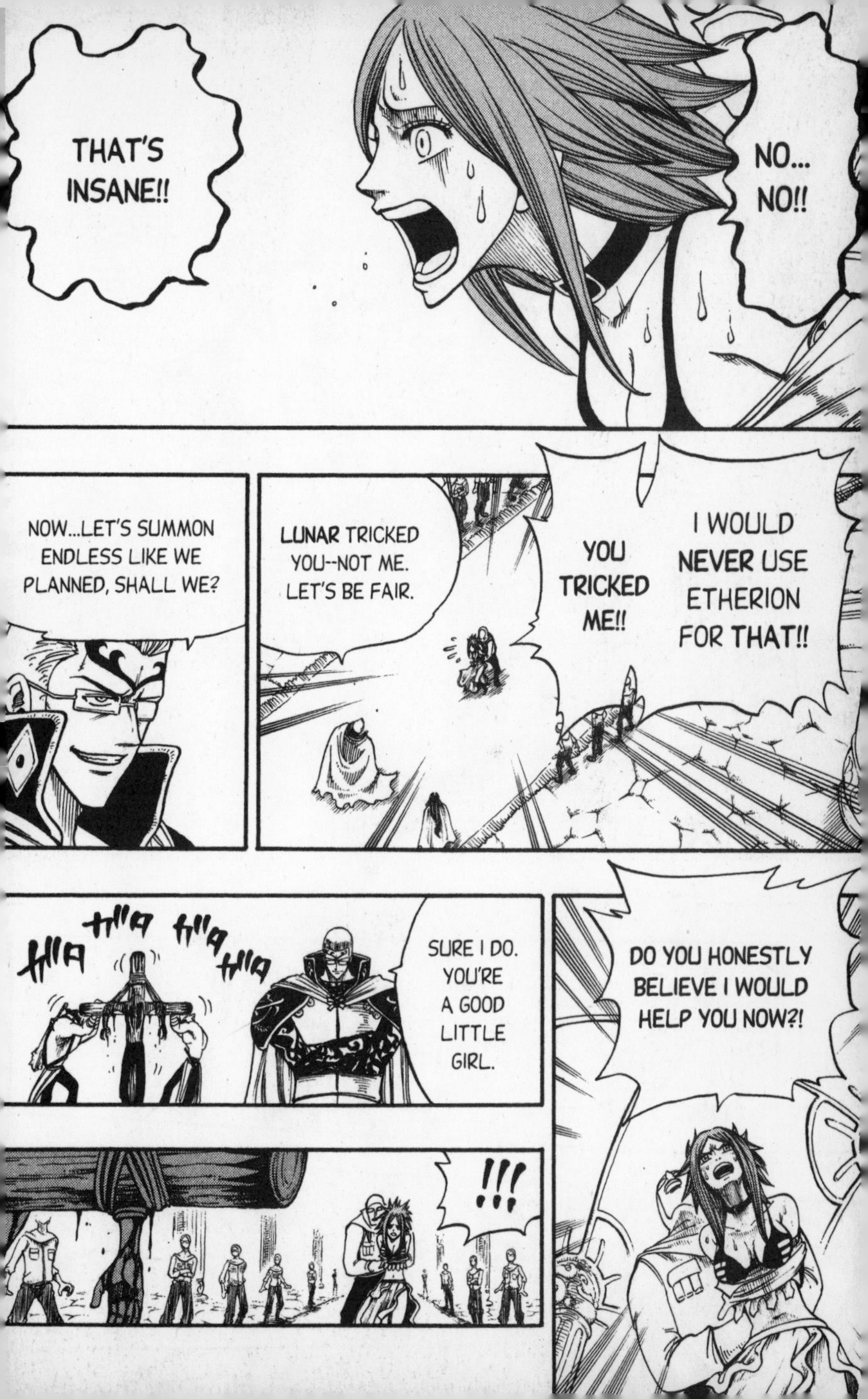
NO... NO!!
THAT'S INSANE!!
YOU TRICKED ME!!
I WOULD NEVER USE ETHERION FOR THAT!!
LUNAR TRICKED YOU--NOT ME. LET'S BE FAIR.
NOW...LET'S SUMMON ENDLESS LIKE WE PLANNED, SHALL WE?
DO YOU HONESTLY BELIEVE I WOULD HELP YOU NOW?!
SURE I DO. YOU'RE A GOOD LITTLE GIRL.
HA HA HA HA HA
!!!

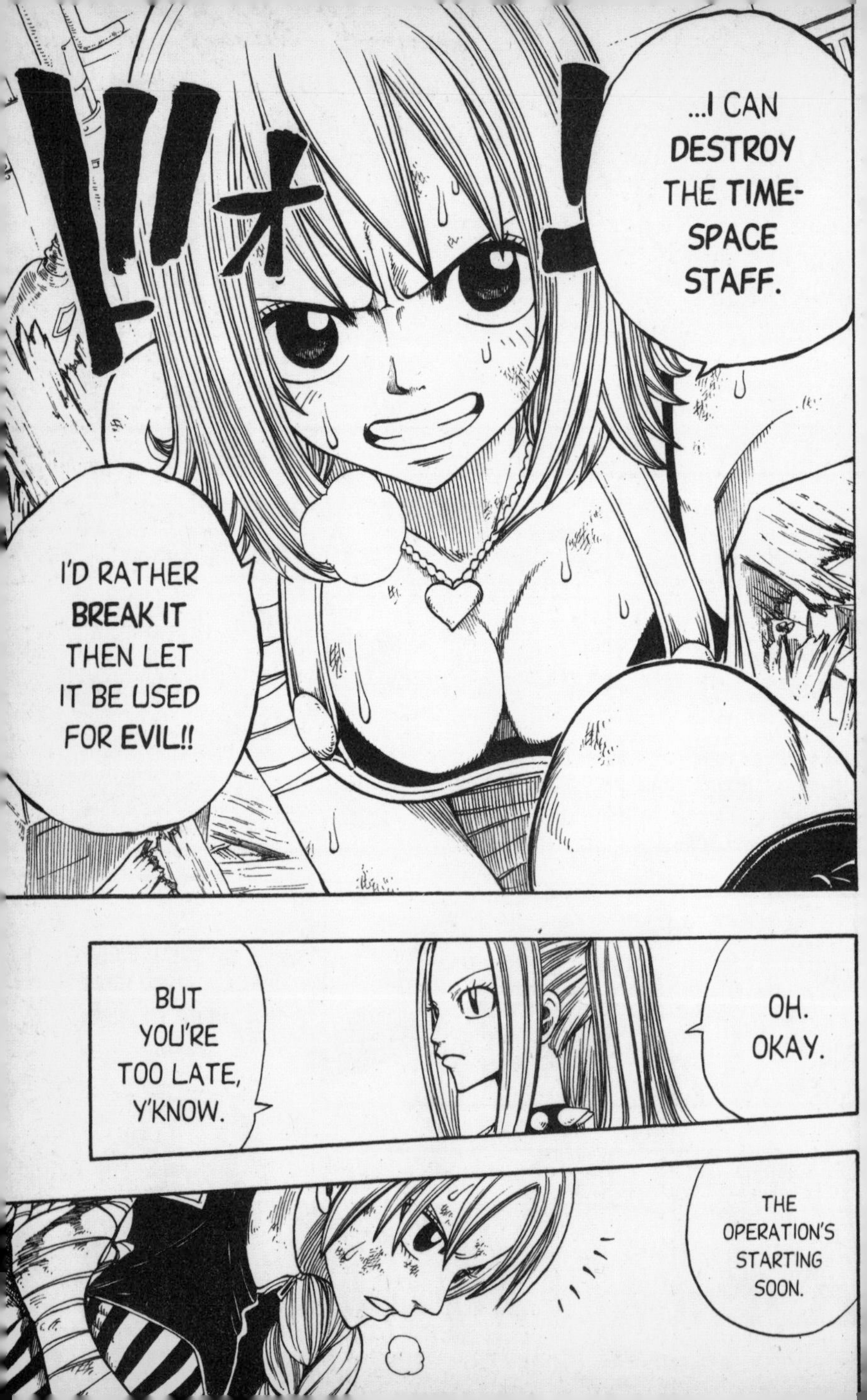
...I CAN DESTROY THE TIME-SPACE STAFF.
I'D RATHER BREAK IT THEN LET IT BE USED FOR EVIL!!
OH. OKAY.
BUT YOU'RE TOO LATE, Y'KNOW.
THE OPERATION'S STARTING SOON.

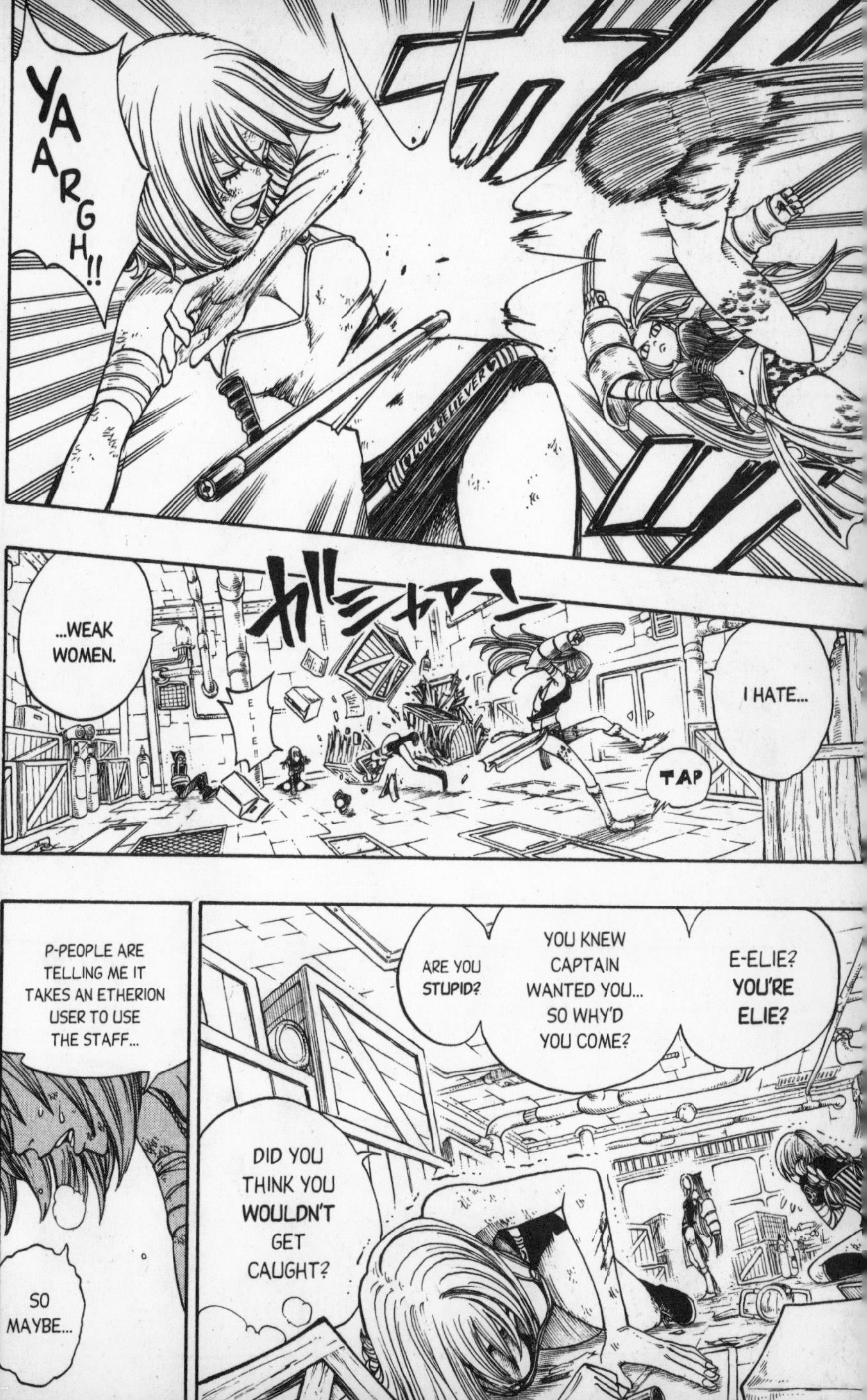
YAARGH!!
LOVE BELIEVER
I HATE...
TAP
...WEAK WOMEN.
ELIE!!
E-ELIE? YOU'RE ELIE?
YOU KNEW CAPTAIN WANTED YOU... SO WHY'D YOU COME?
ARE YOU STUPID?
DID YOU THINK YOU WOULDN'T GET CAUGHT?
P-PEOPLE ARE TELLING ME IT TAKES AN ETHERION USER TO USE THE STAFF...
SO MAYBE...

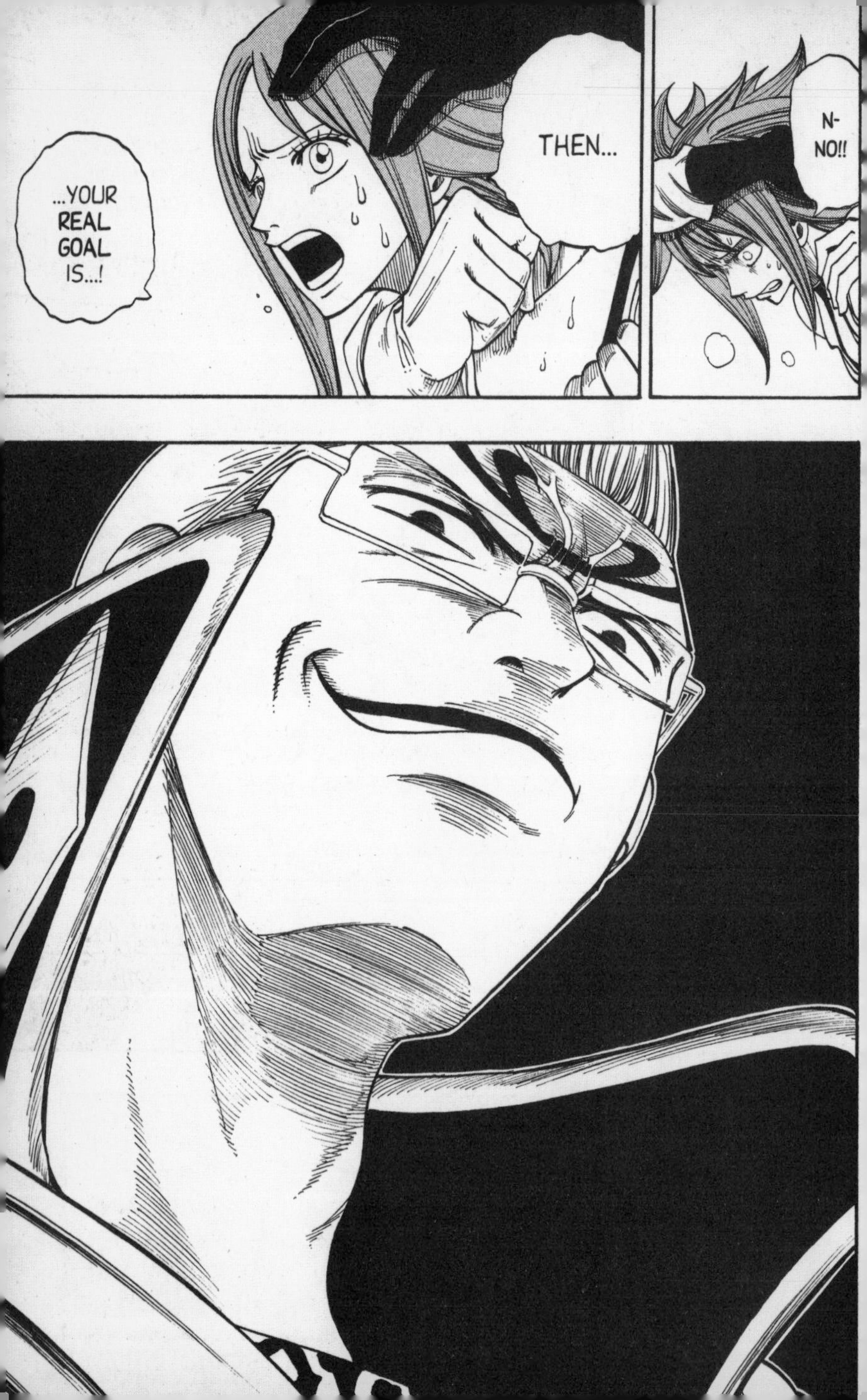
N-
NO!!
THEN...
...YOUR
REAL
GOAL
IS...!

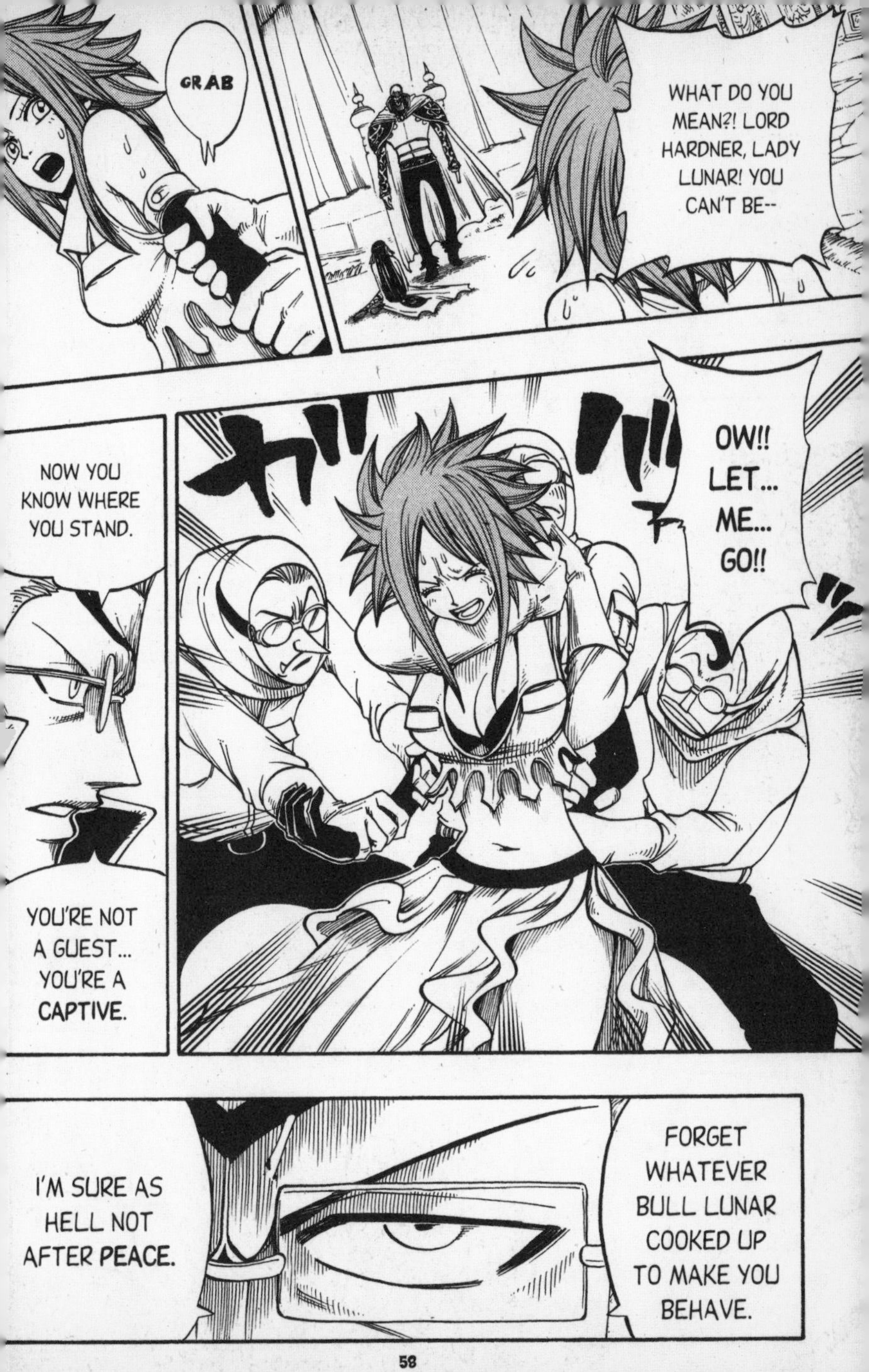
WHAT DO YOU MEAN?! LORD HARDNER, LADY LUNAR! YOU CAN'T BE--
GRAB
OW!! LET... ME... GO!!
NOW YOU KNOW WHERE YOU STAND.
YOU'RE NOT A GUEST... YOU'RE A CAPTIVE.
FORGET WHATEVER BULL LUNAR COOKED UP TO MAKE YOU BEHAVE.
I'M SURE AS HELL NOT AFTER PEACE.

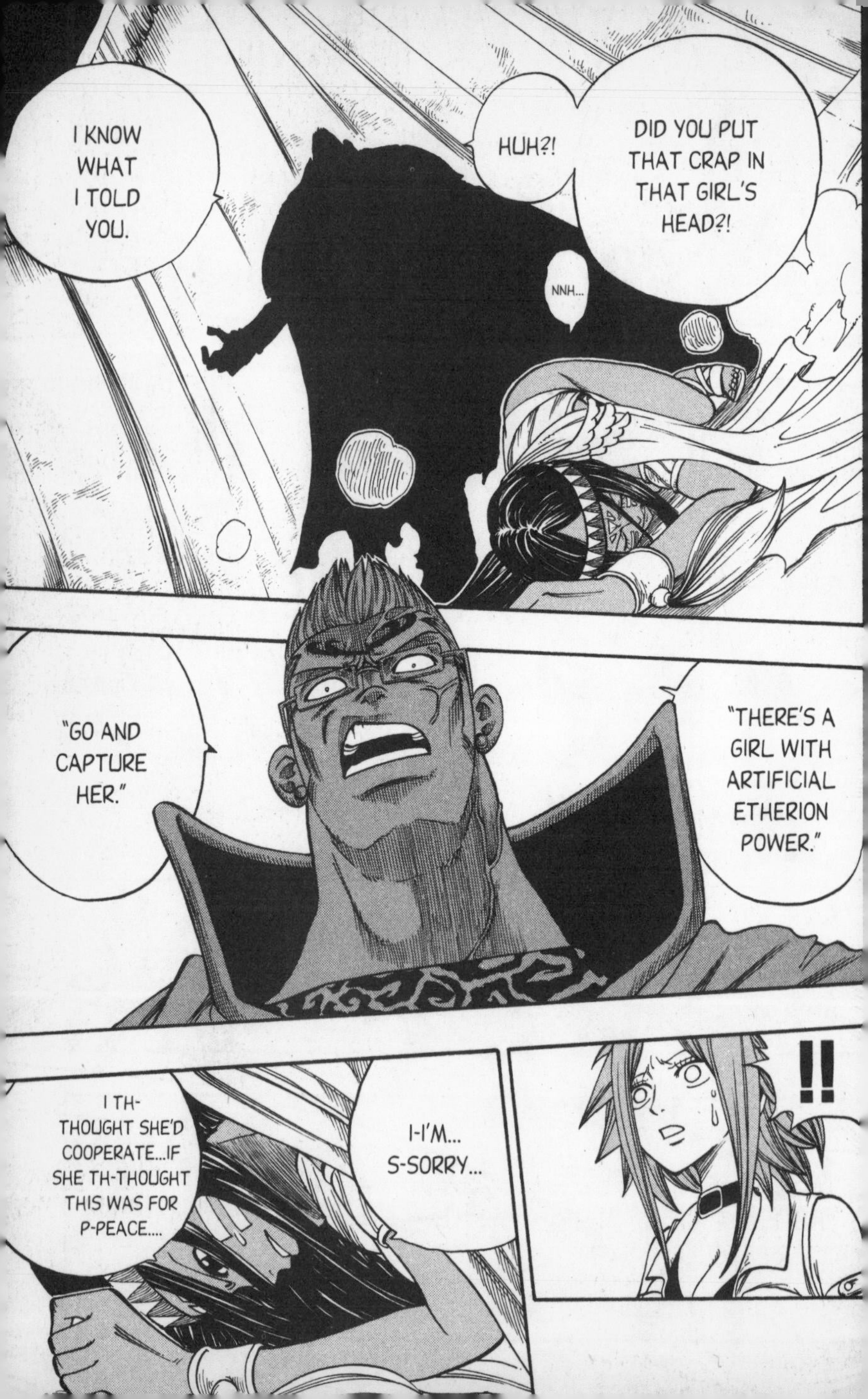
DID YOU PUT THAT CRAP IN THAT GIRL'S HEAD?!
HUH?!
NNH...
I KNOW WHAT I TOLD YOU.
"THERE'S A GIRL WITH ARTIFICIAL ETHERION POWER."
"GO AND CAPTURE HER."
!!
I-I'M... S-SORRY...
I TH-THOUGHT SHE'D COOPERATE...IF SHE TH-THOUGHT THIS WAS FOR P-PEACE....

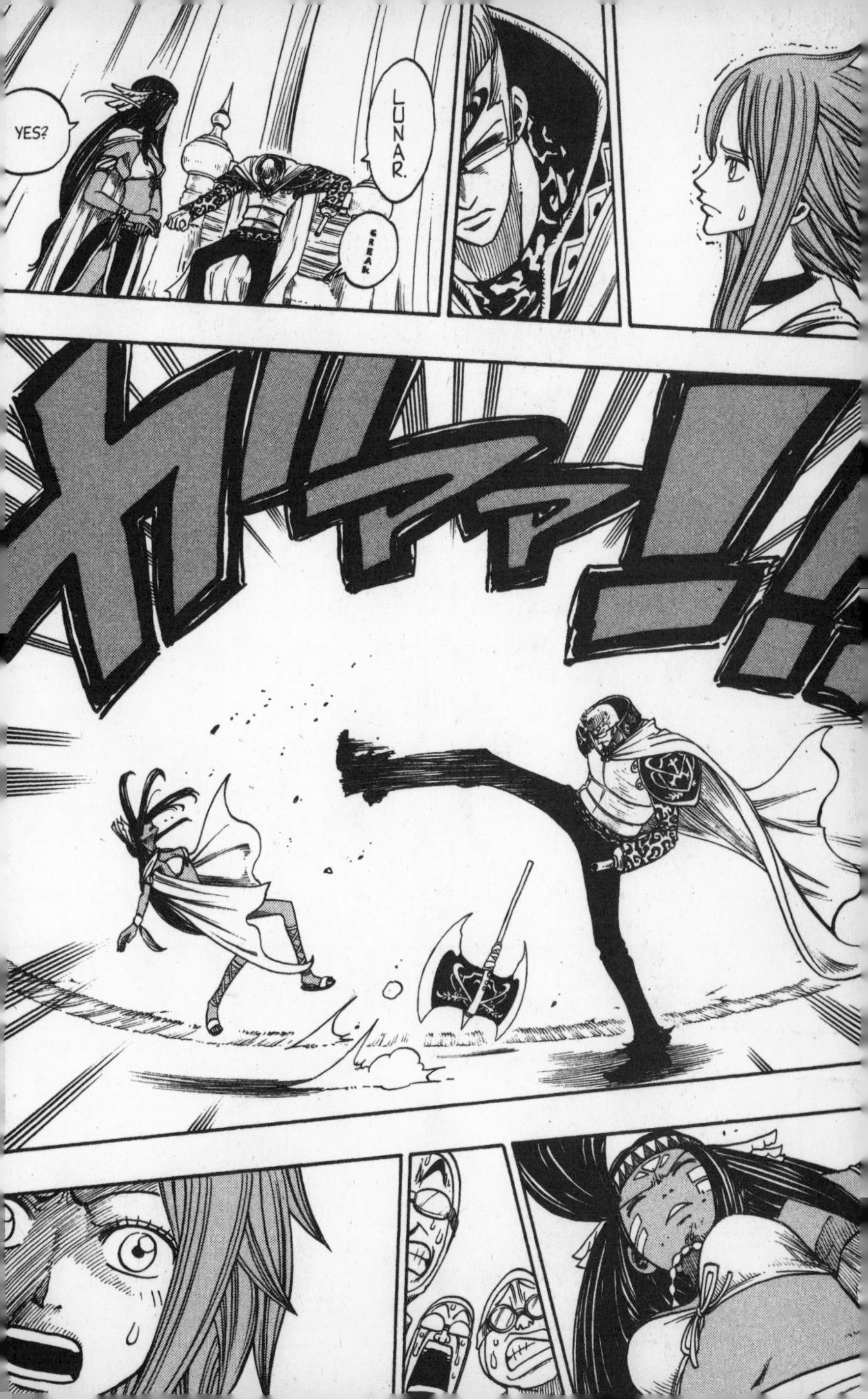
LUNAR.
CREAK
YES?

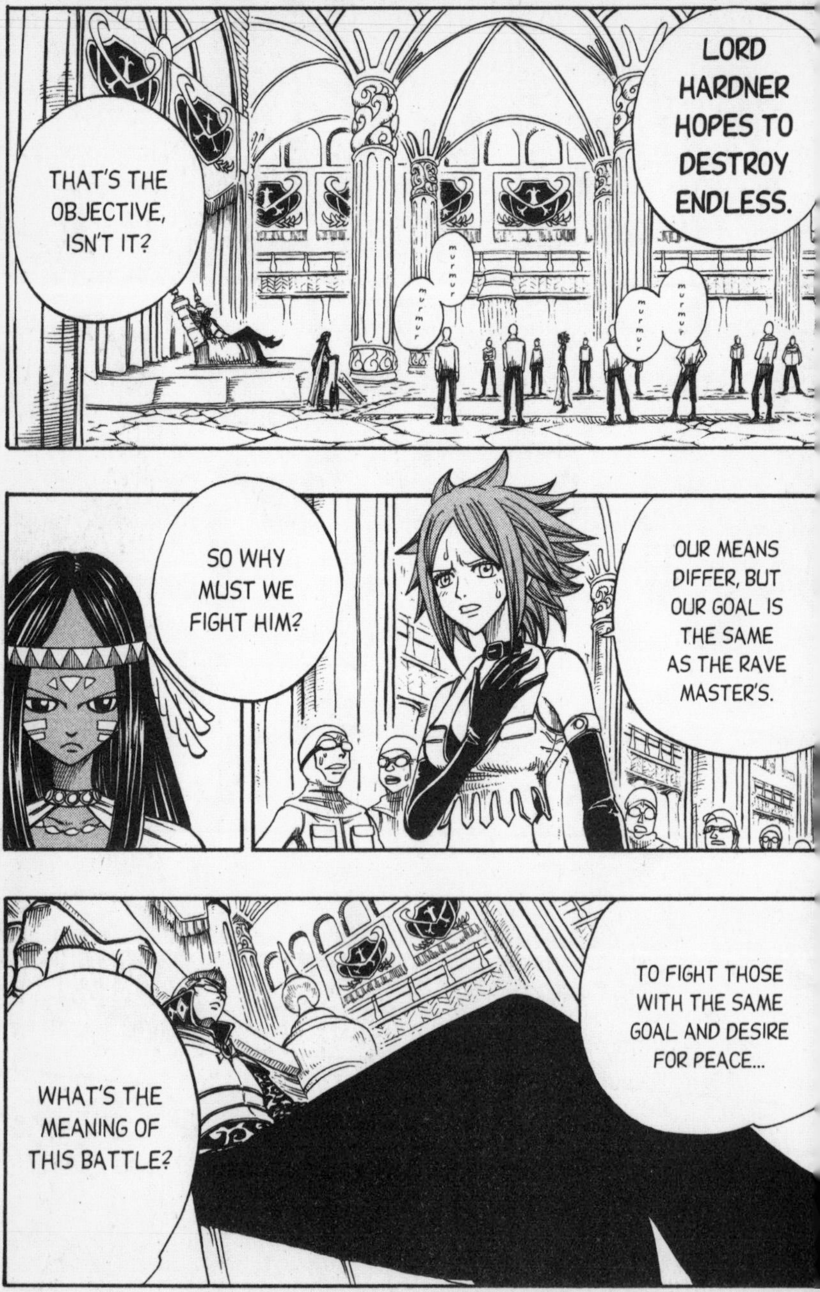

LORD HARDNER HOPES TO DESTROY ENDLESS.
murmur murmur
murmur murmur
THAT'S THE OBJECTIVE, ISN'T IT?
OUR MEANS DIFFER, BUT OUR GOAL IS THE SAME AS THE RAVE MASTER'S.
SO WHY MUST WE FIGHT HIM?
TO FIGHT THOSE WITH THE SAME GOAL AND DESIRE FOR PEACE...
WHAT'S THE MEANING OF THIS BATTLE?

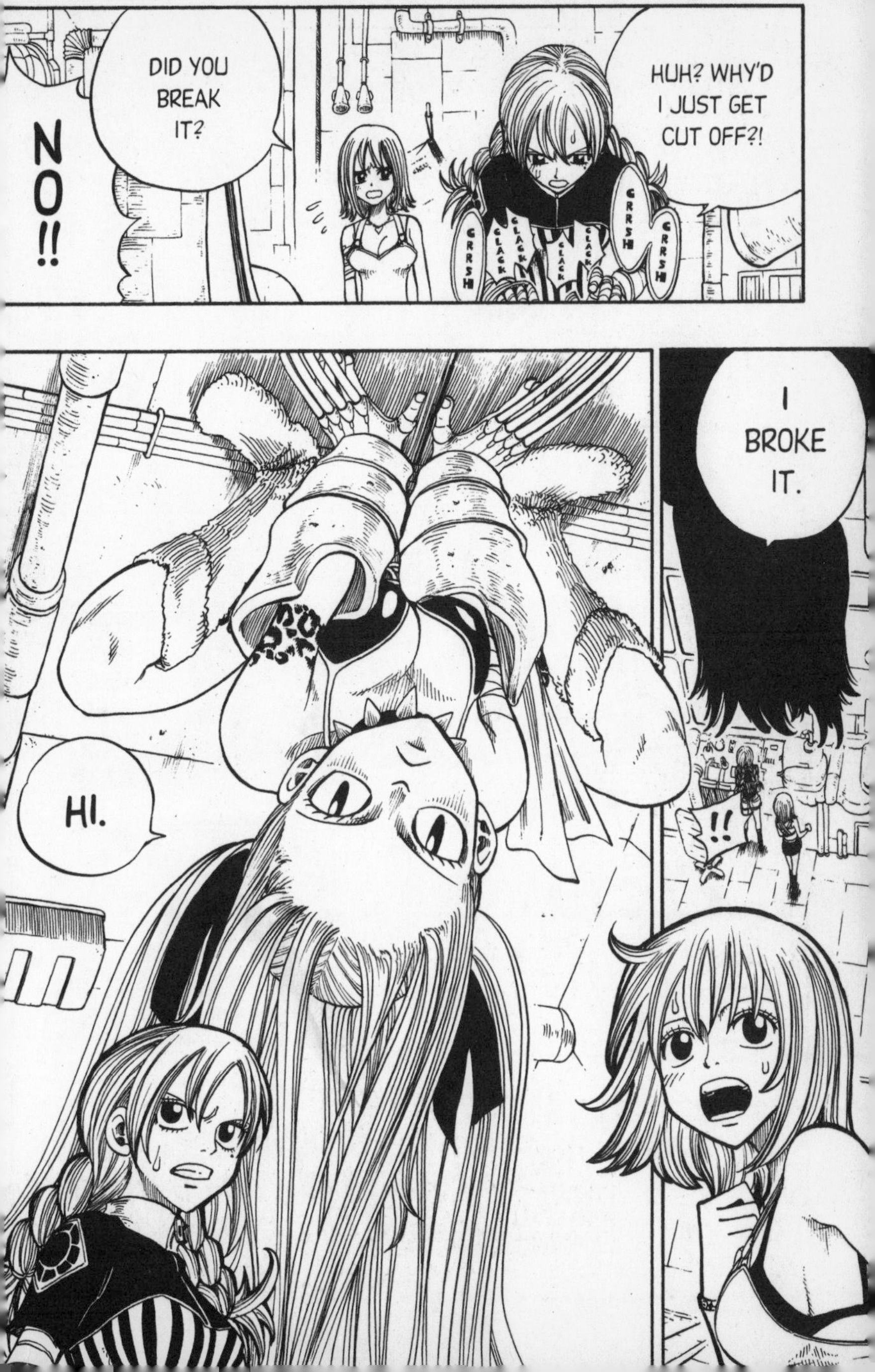
HUH? WHY'D I JUST GET CUT OFF?!
GRRSH
GRRSH
CLACK
CLACK
CLACK
CLACK
GRRSH
DID YOU BREAK IT?
NO!!
I BROKE IT.
!!
HI.

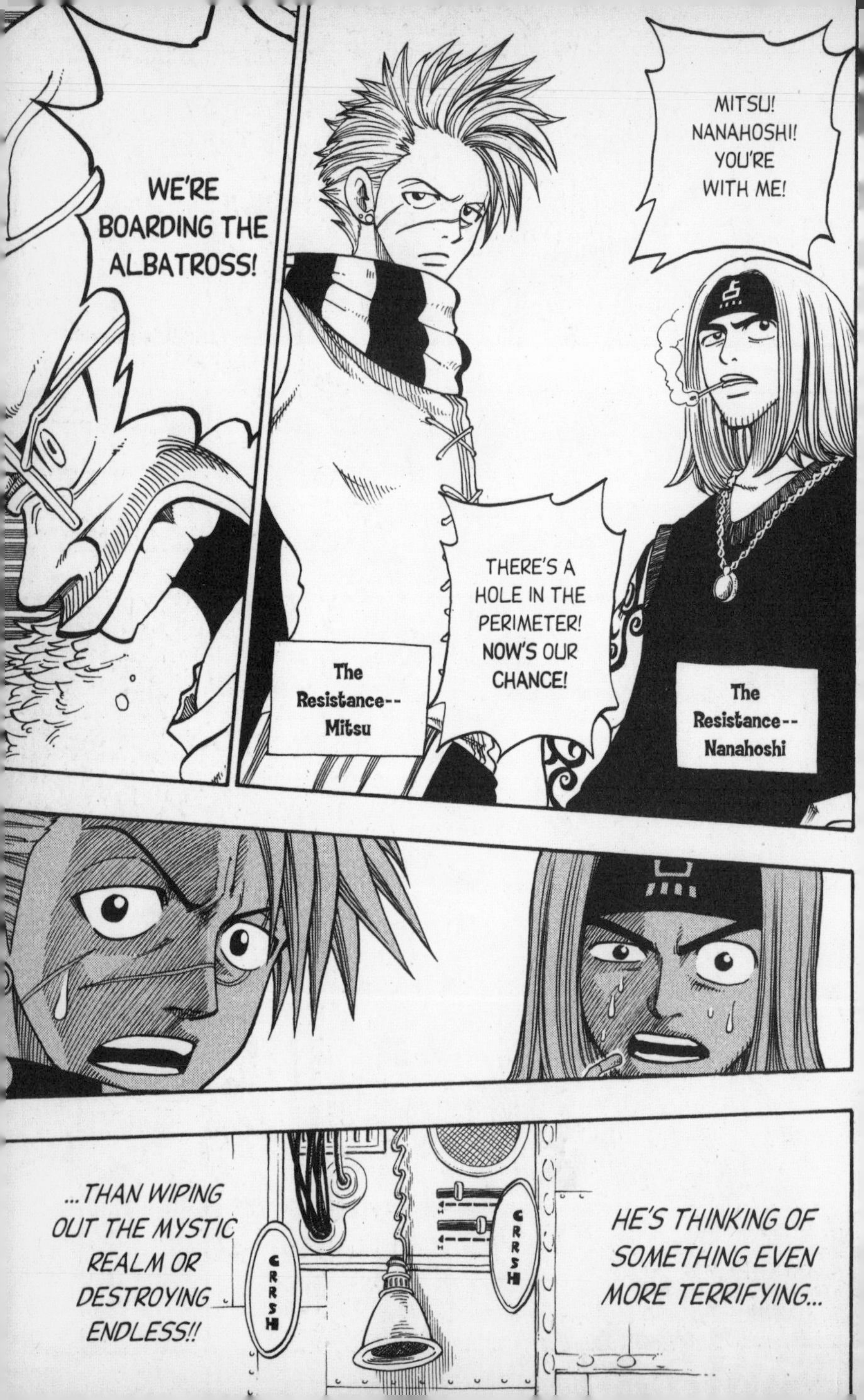
MITSU! NANAHOSHI! YOU'RE WITH ME!
The Resistance--Nanahoshi
THERE'S A HOLE IN THE PERIMETER! NOW'S OUR CHANCE!
The Resistance--Mitsu
WE'RE BOARDING THE ALBATROSS!
HE'S THINKING OF SOMETHING EVEN MORE TERRIFYING...
GRRSH
GRRSH
...THAN WIPING OUT THE MYSTIC REALM OR DESTROYING ENDLESS!!

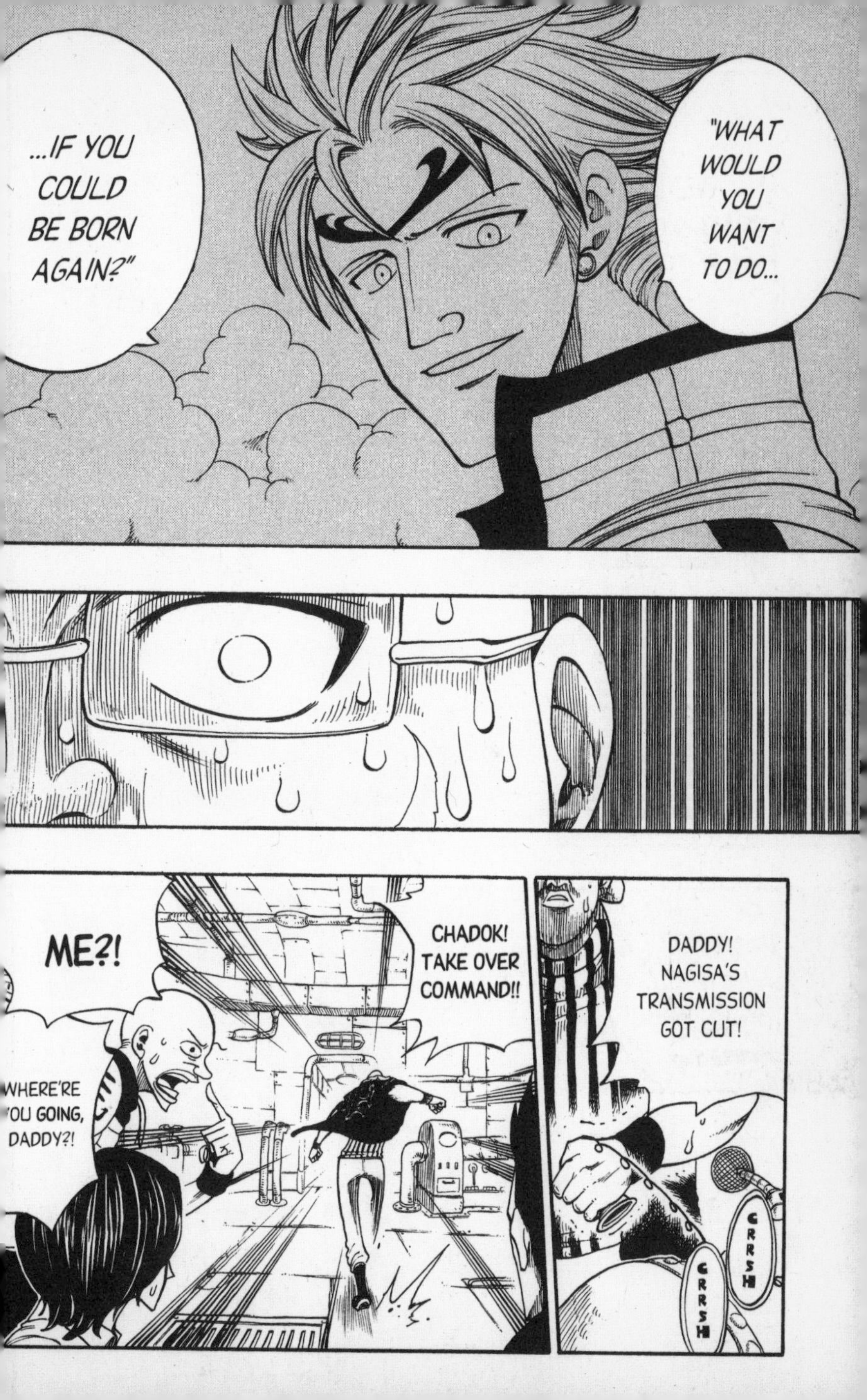
"WHAT WOULD YOU WANT TO DO...
...IF YOU COULD BE BORN AGAIN?"
DADDY! NAGISA'S TRANSMISSION GOT CUT!
GRRSH
GRRSH
CHADOK! TAKE OVER COMMAND!!
ME?!
WHERE'RE 'OU GOING, DADDY?!

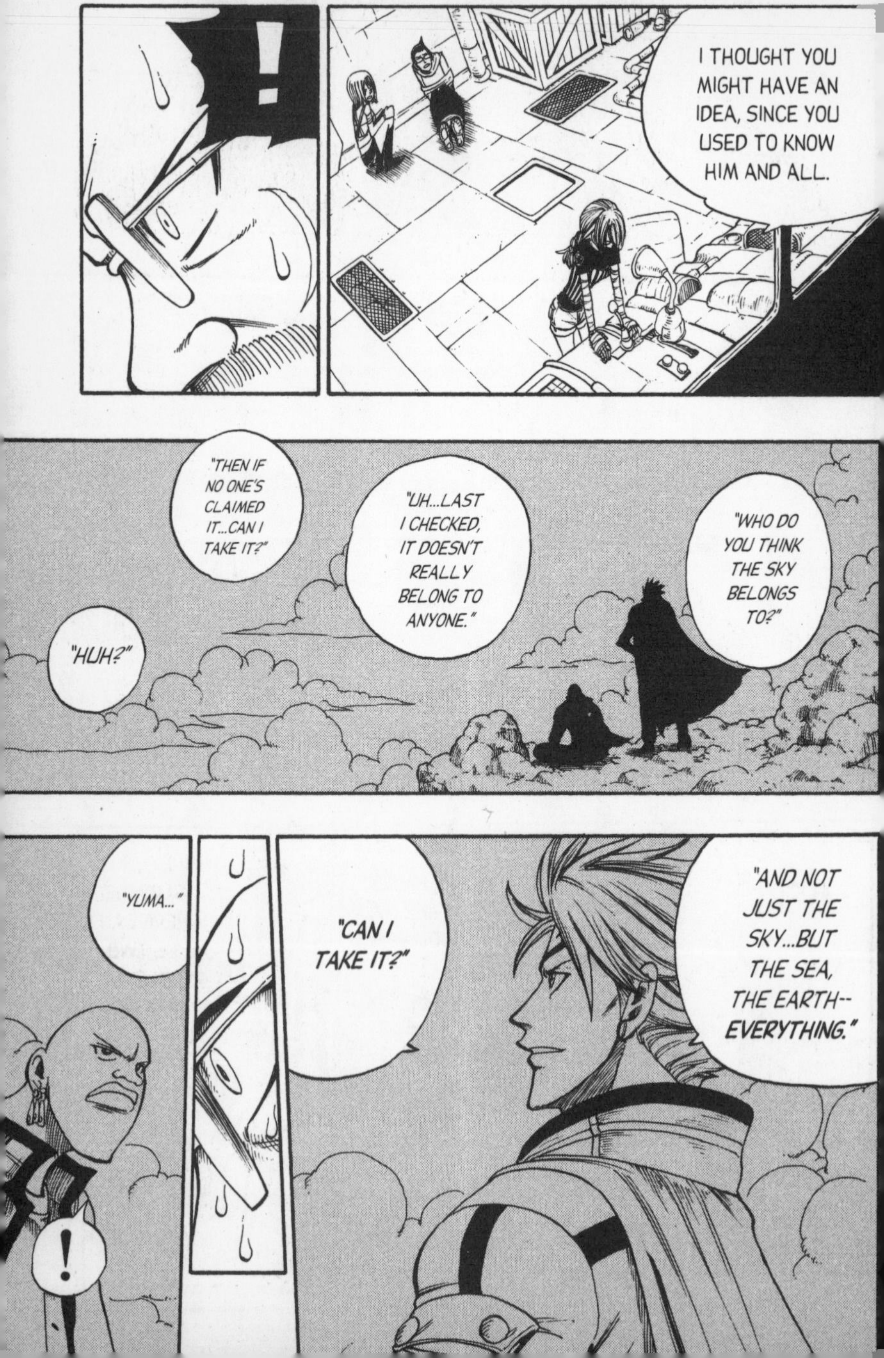
I THOUGHT YOU MIGHT HAVE AN IDEA, SINCE YOU USED TO KNOW HIM AND ALL.
!
"WHO DO YOU THINK THE SKY BELONGS TO?"
"UH...LAST I CHECKED, IT DOESN'T REALLY BELONG TO ANYONE."
"THEN IF NO ONE'S CLAIMED IT...CAN I TAKE IT?"
"HUH?"
"AND NOT JUST THE SKY...BUT THE SEA, THE EARTH--EVERYTHING."
"CAN I TAKE IT?"
"YUMA..."
!

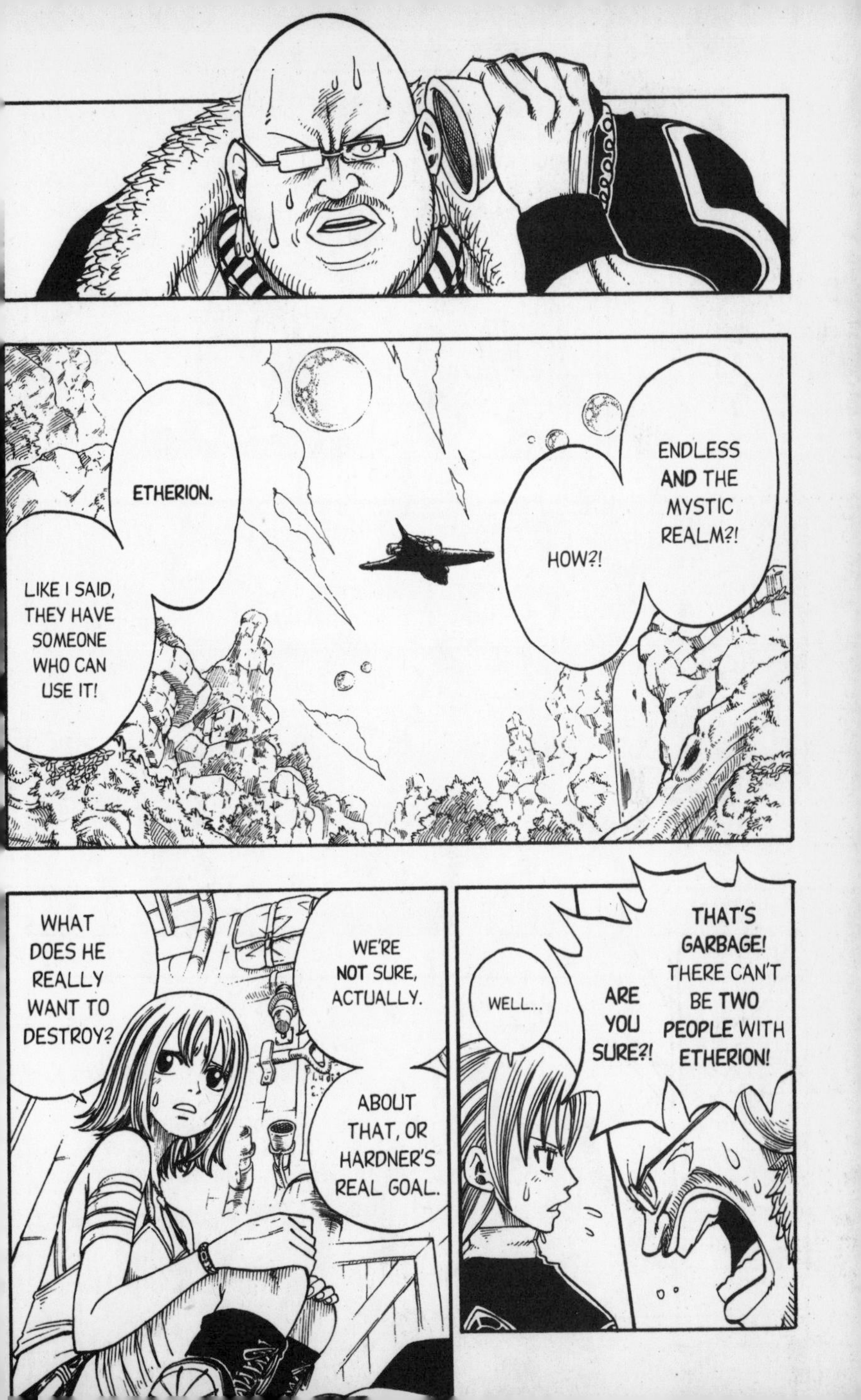
ENDLESS AND THE MYSTIC REALM?!
HOW?!
ETHERION.
LIKE I SAID, THEY HAVE SOMEONE WHO CAN USE IT!
THAT'S GARBAGE! THERE CAN'T BE TWO PEOPLE WITH ETHERION!
ARE YOU SURE?!
WELL...
WHAT DOES HE REALLY WANT TO DESTROY?
WE'RE NOT SURE, ACTUALLY.
ABOUT THAT, OR HARDNER'S REAL GOAL.

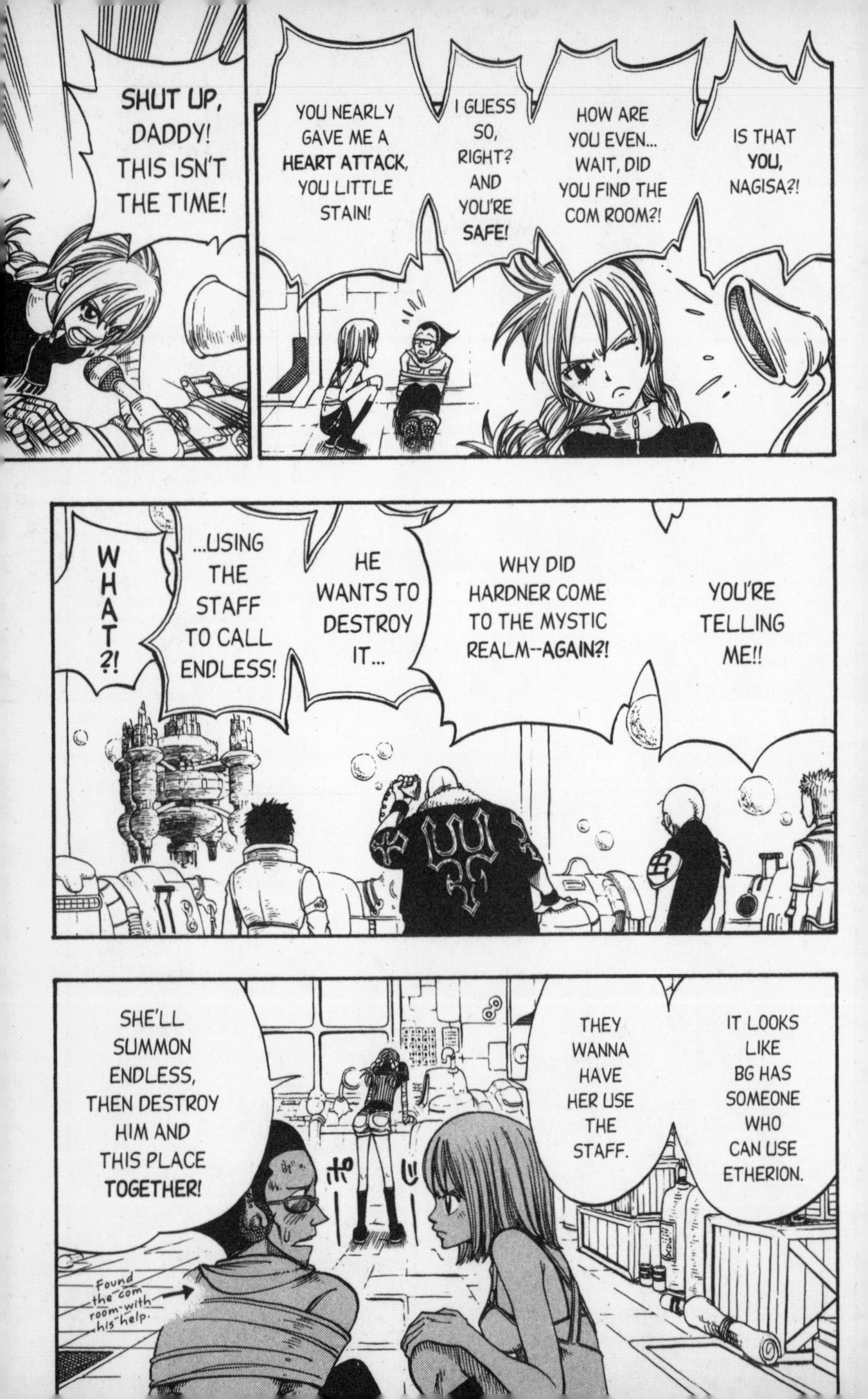
IS THAT YOU, NAGISA?!
HOW ARE YOU EVEN... WAIT, DID YOU FIND THE COM ROOM?!
I GUESS SO, RIGHT? AND YOU'RE SAFE!
YOU NEARLY GAVE ME A HEART ATTACK, YOU LITTLE STAIN!
SHUT UP, DADDY! THIS ISN'T THE TIME!
YOU'RE TELLING ME!!
WHY DID HARDNER COME TO THE MYSTIC REALM--AGAIN?!
HE WANTS TO DESTROY IT...
...USING THE STAFF TO CALL ENDLESS!
WHAT?!
IT LOOKS LIKE BG HAS SOMEONE WHO CAN USE ETHERION.
THEY WANNA HAVE HER USE THE STAFF.
SHE'LL SUMMON ENDLESS, THEN DESTROY HIM AND THIS PLACE TOGETHER!
Found the com room with his help.

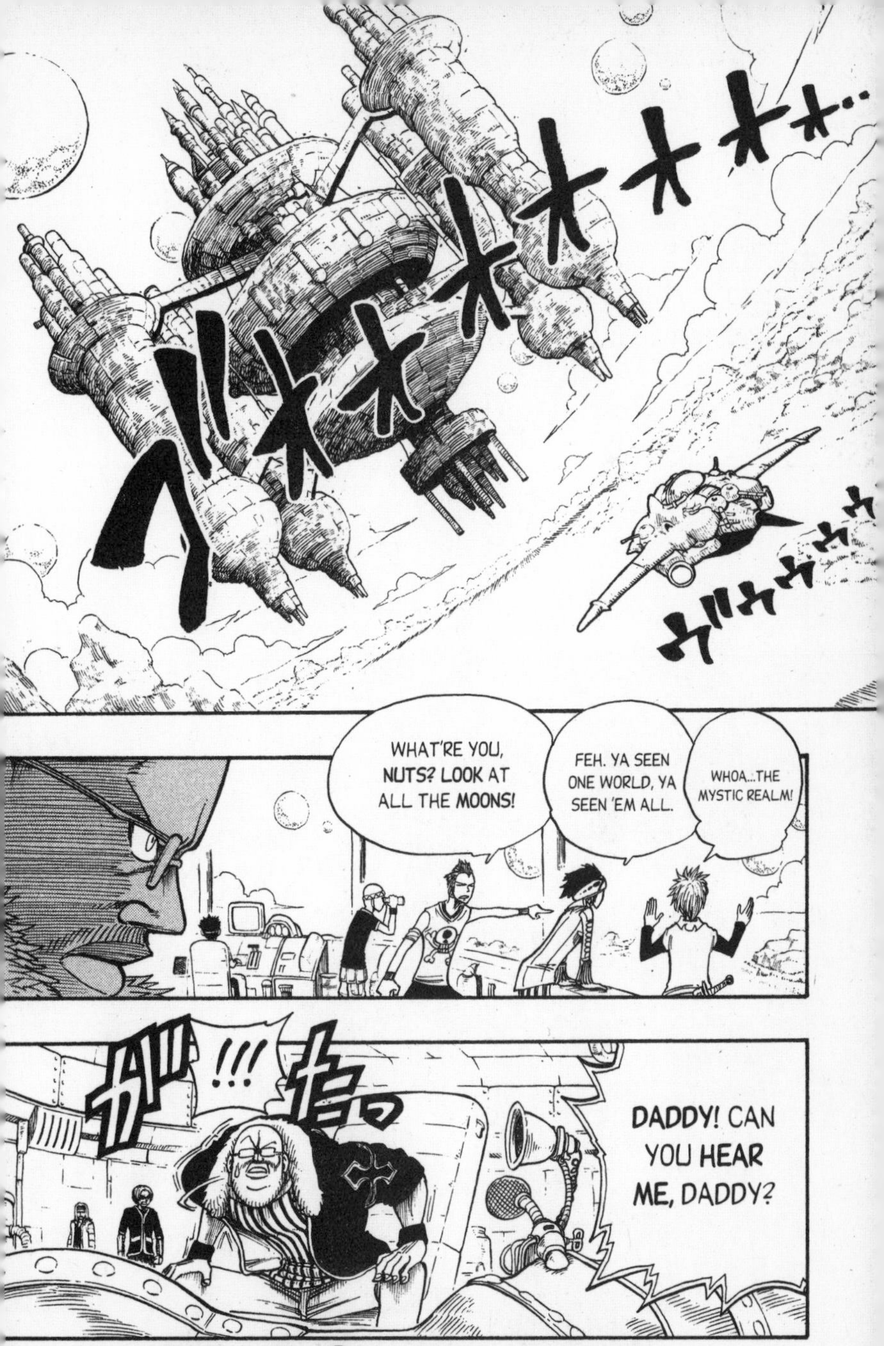
WHOA...THE MYSTIC REALM!
FEH. YA SEEN ONE WORLD, YA SEEN 'EM ALL.
WHAT'RE YOU, NUTS? LOOK AT ALL THE MOONS!
!!!
DADDY! CAN YOU HEAR ME, DADDY?

RAVE:212 ✠ BELNIKA'S TEARS

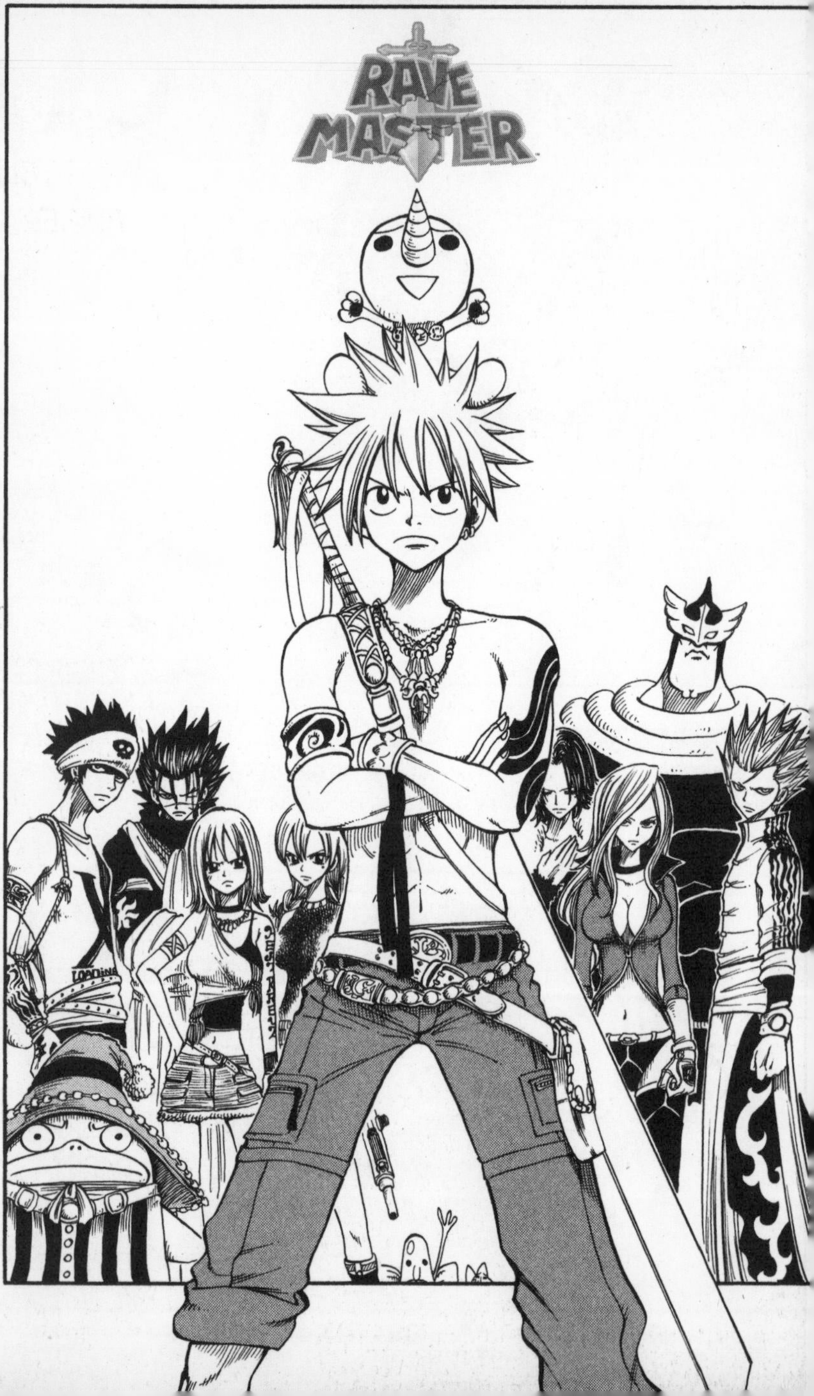
RAVE MASTER

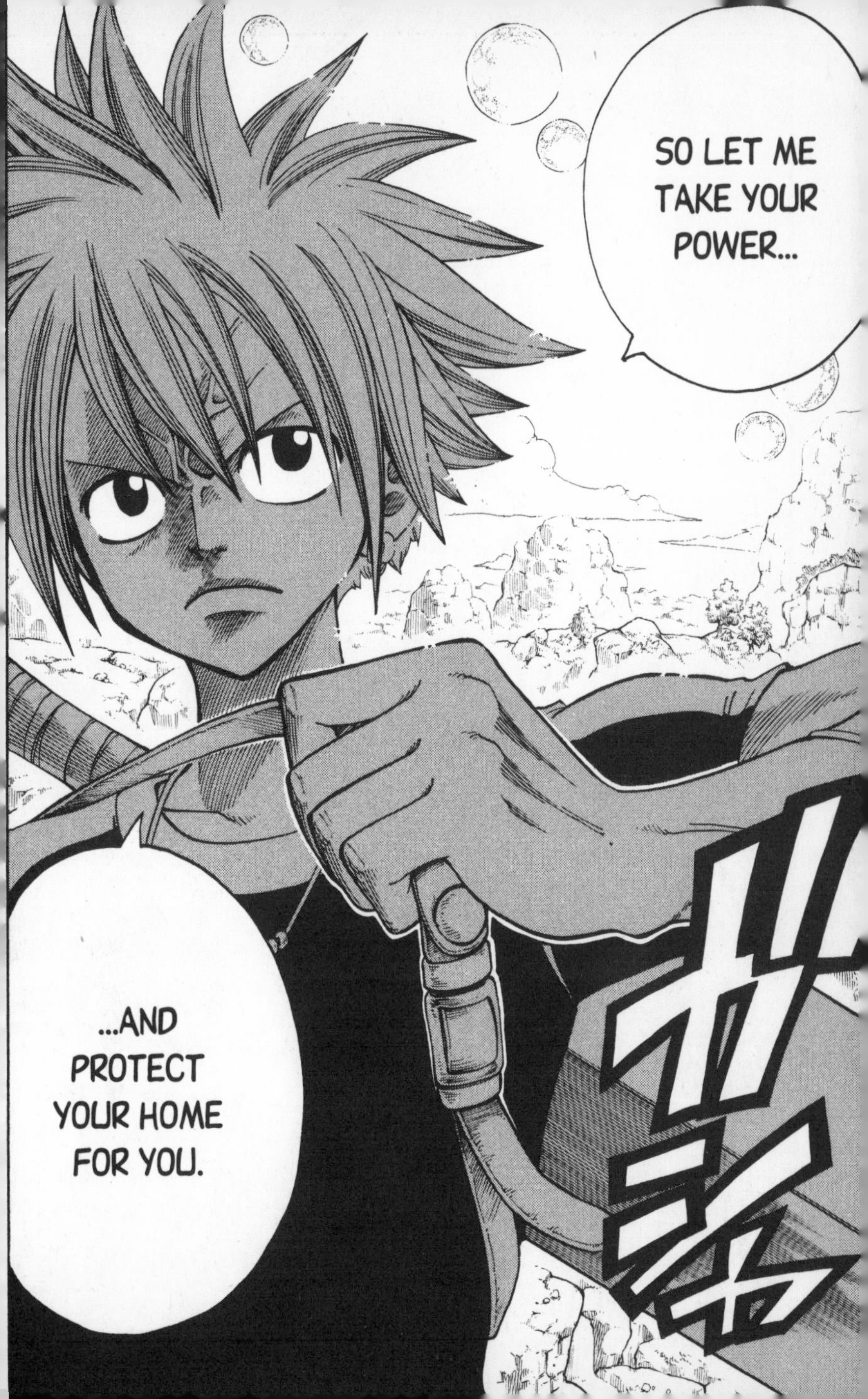
SO LET ME TAKE YOUR POWER...
...AND PROTECT YOUR HOME FOR YOU.

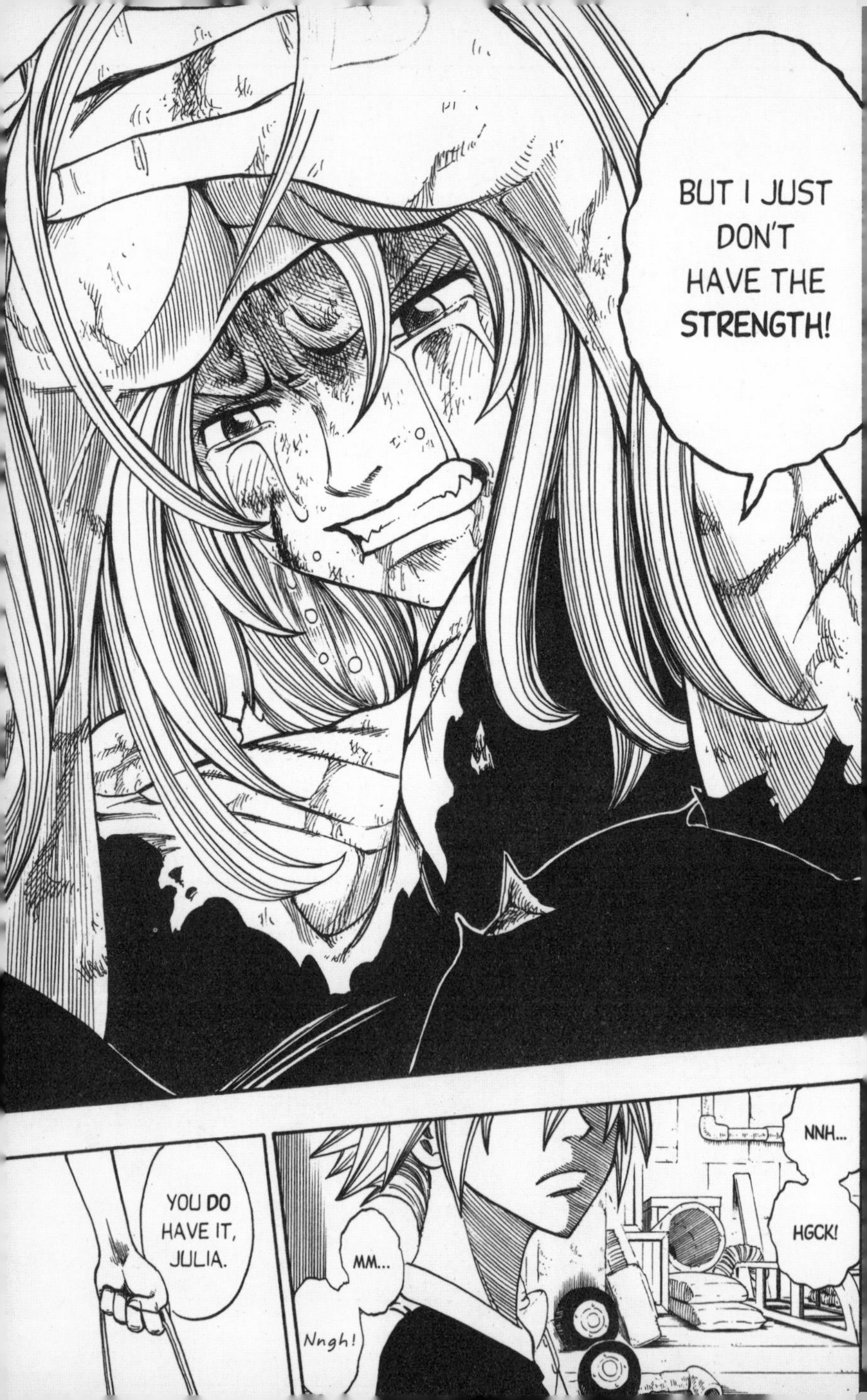
BUT I JUST DON'T HAVE THE STRENGTH!
NNH...
HGCK!
MM...
Nngh!
YOU DO HAVE IT, JULIA.

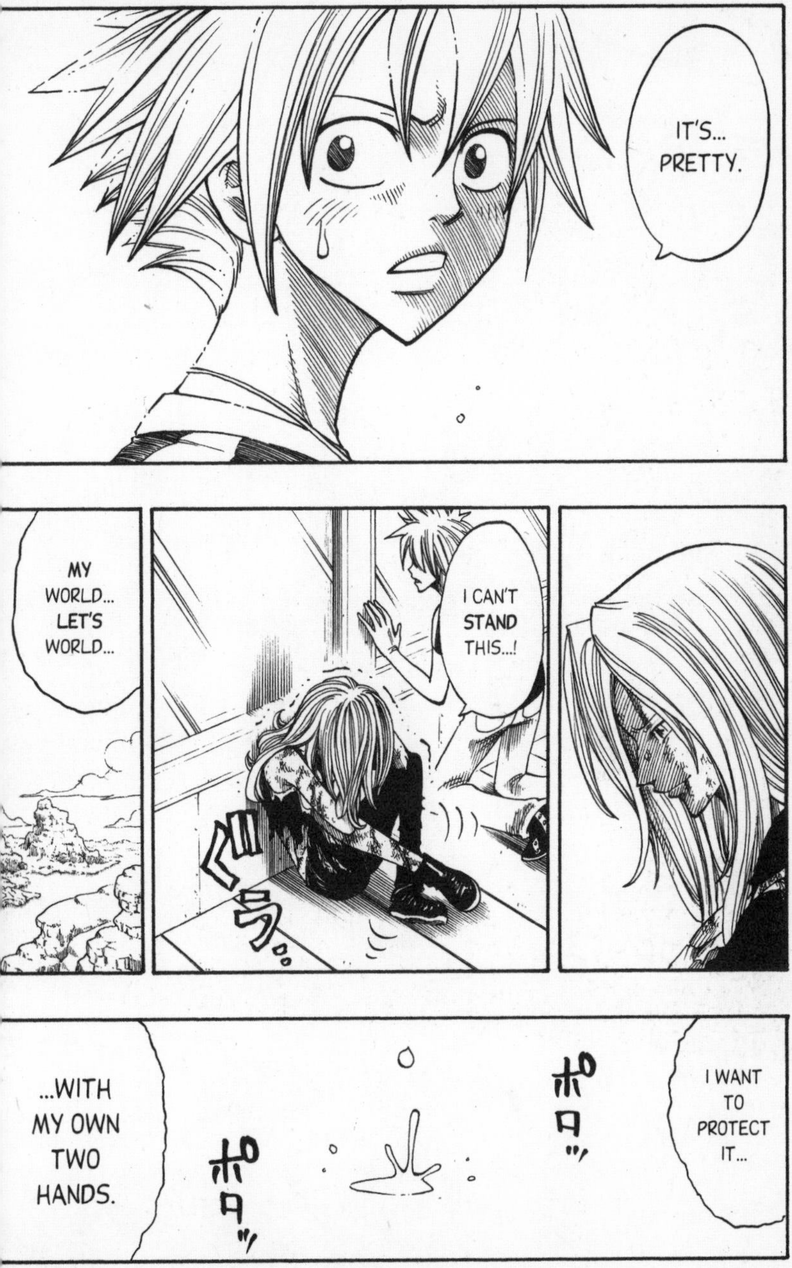
IT'S... PRETTY.
I CAN'T STAND THIS...!
ぐら
MY WORLD... LET'S WORLD...
I WANT TO PROTECT IT...
ポロッ
ポタッ
...WITH MY OWN TWO HANDS.

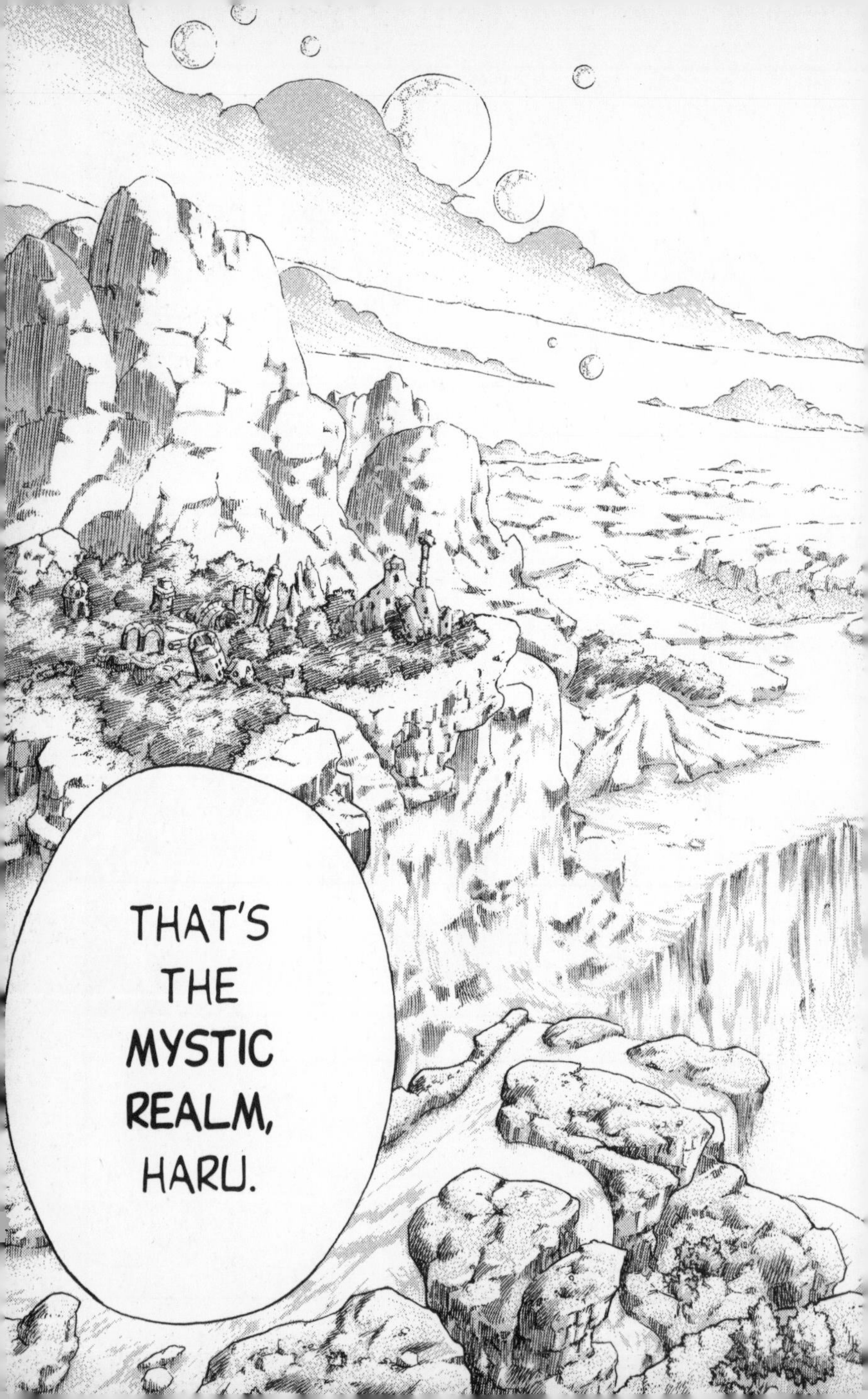
THAT'S THE MYSTIC REALM, HARU.

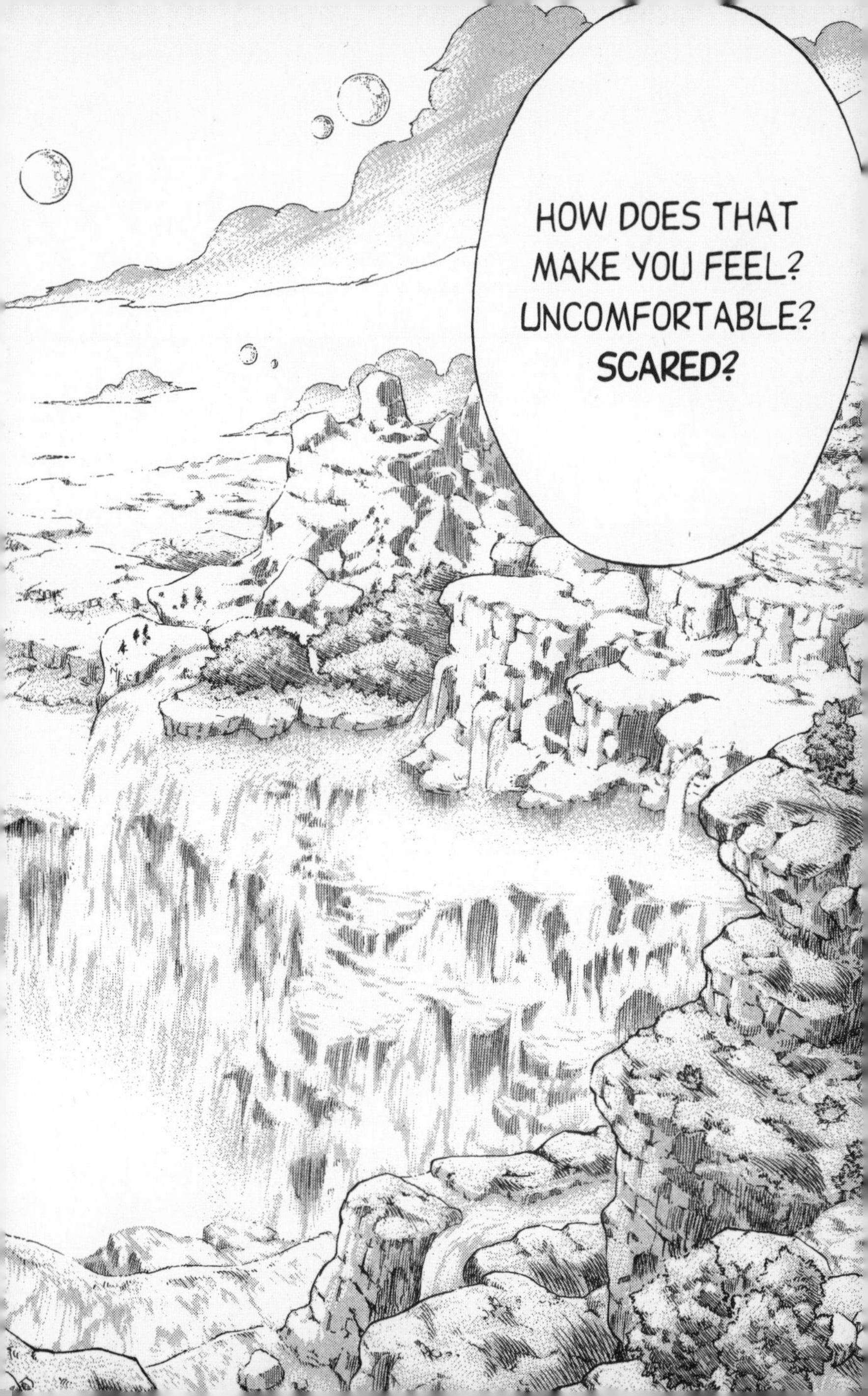
HOW DOES THAT MAKE YOU FEEL? UNCOMFORTABLE? **SCARED?**

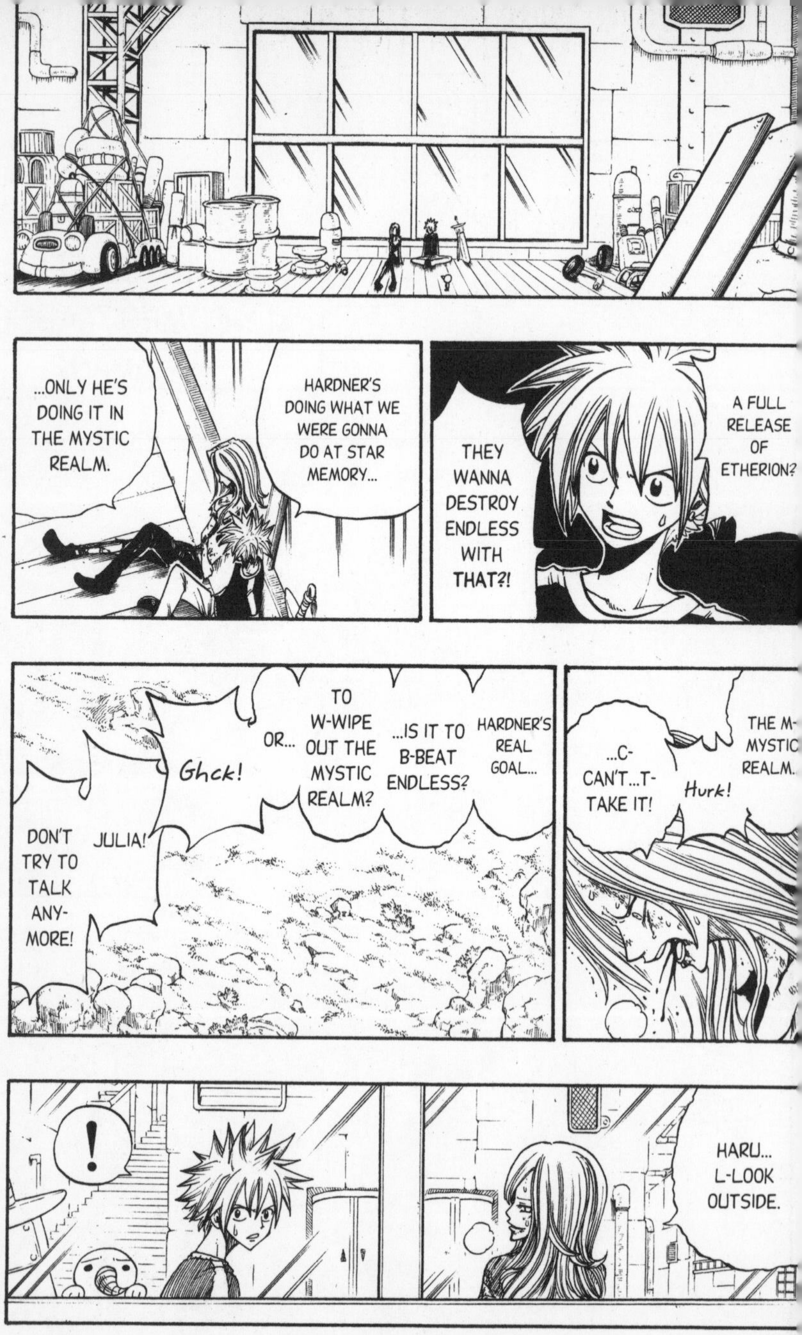
A FULL RELEASE OF ETHERION?
THEY WANNA DESTROY ENDLESS WITH THAT?!
HARDNER'S DOING WHAT WE WERE GONNA DO AT STAR MEMORY...
...ONLY HE'S DOING IT IN THE MYSTIC REALM.
THE M-MYSTIC REALM...
Hurk!
...C-CAN'T...T-TAKE IT!
HARDNER'S REAL GOAL...
...IS IT TO B-BEAT ENDLESS?
OR...
TO W-WIPE OUT THE MYSTIC REALM?
Ghck!
JULIA!
DON'T TRY TO TALK ANYMORE!
HARU... L-LOOK OUTSIDE.
!

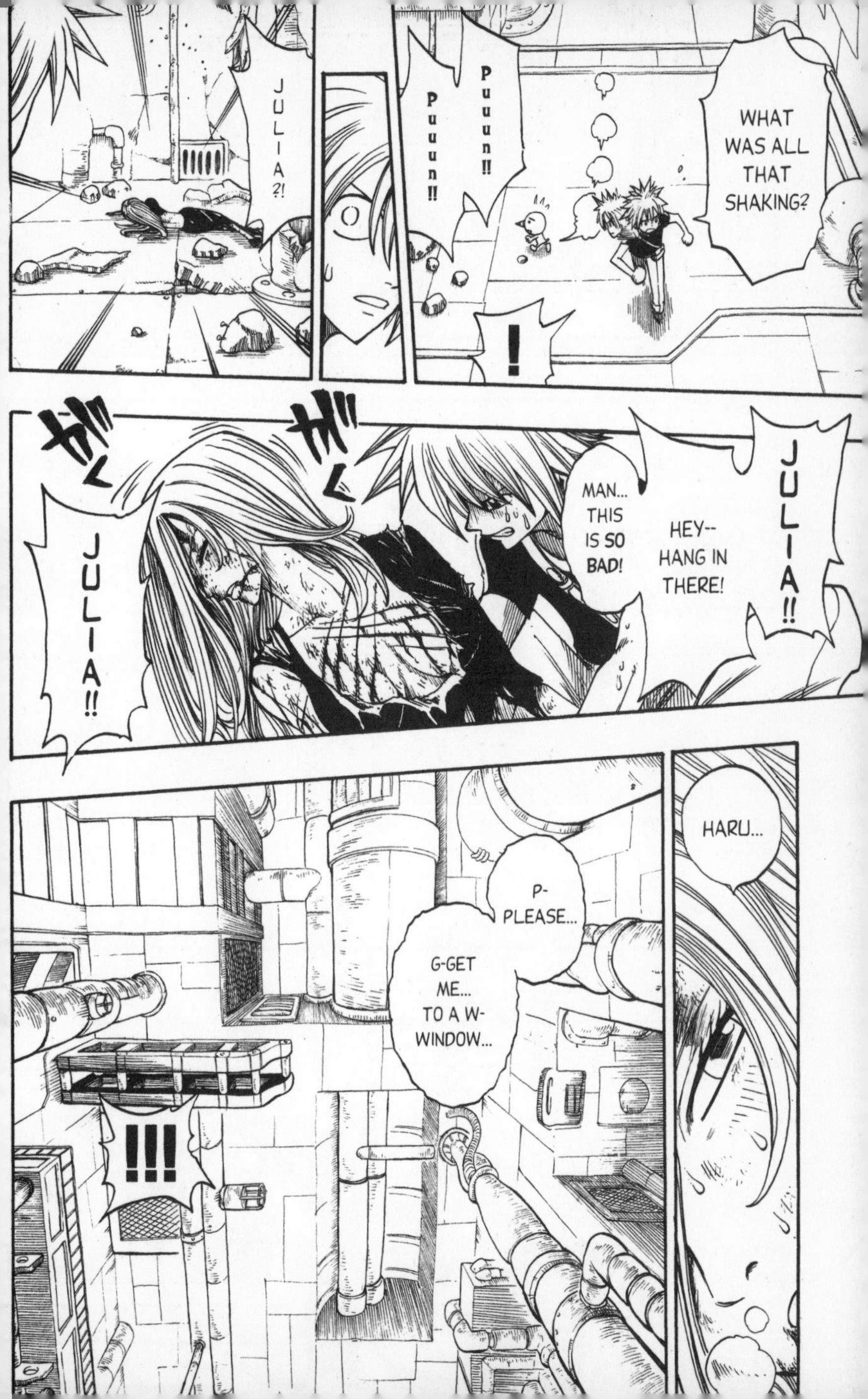
WHAT WAS ALL THAT SHAKING?
!
Puuun!!
Puuun!!
JULIA?!
JULIA!!
HEY-- HANG IN THERE!
MAN... THIS IS SO BAD!
JULIA!!
HARU...
P-PLEASE...
G-GET ME... TO A W-WINDOW...
!!!

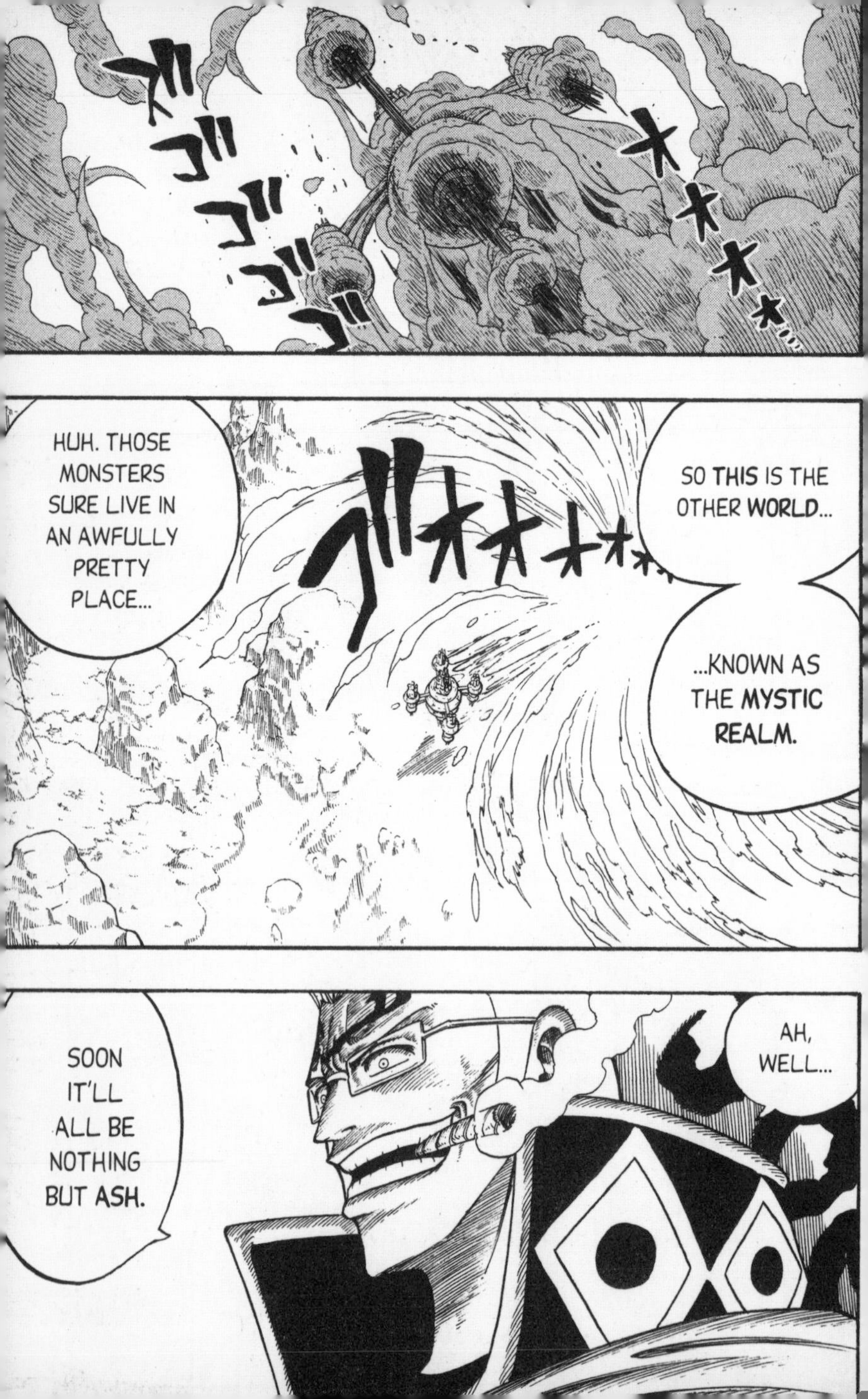
SO THIS IS THE OTHER WORLD...
...KNOWN AS THE MYSTIC REALM.
HUH. THOSE MONSTERS SURE LIVE IN AN AWFULLY PRETTY PLACE...
AH, WELL...
SOON IT'LL ALL BE NOTHING BUT ASH.

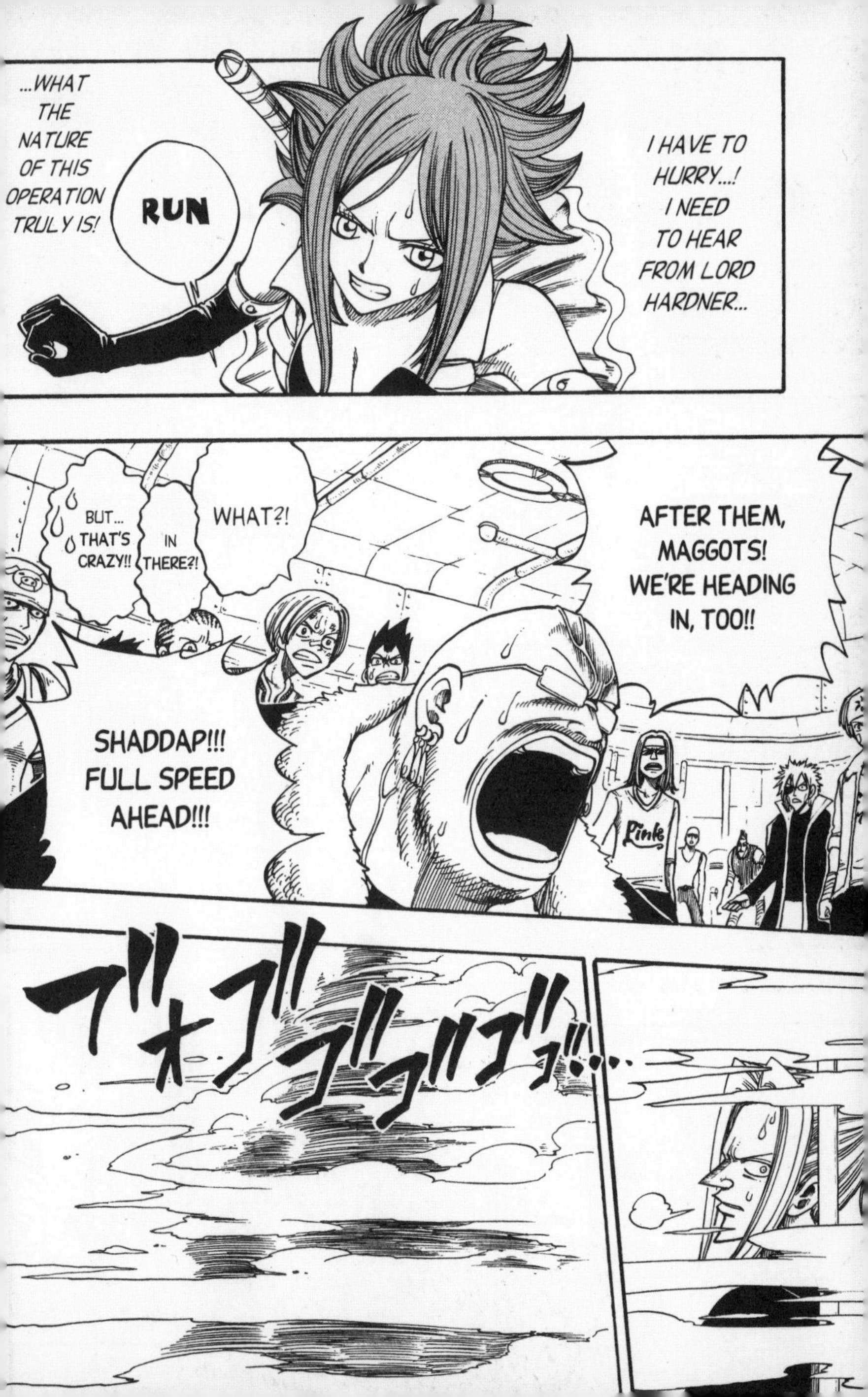
I HAVE TO HURRY...! I NEED TO HEAR FROM LORD HARDNER...
...WHAT THE NATURE OF THIS OPERATION TRULY IS!
RUN
AFTER THEM, MAGGOTS! WE'RE HEADING IN, TOO!!
WHAT?!
IN THERE?!
BUT... THAT'S CRAZY!!
SHADDAP!!! FULL SPEED AHEAD!!!
ブォブゴゴゴゴ‼…

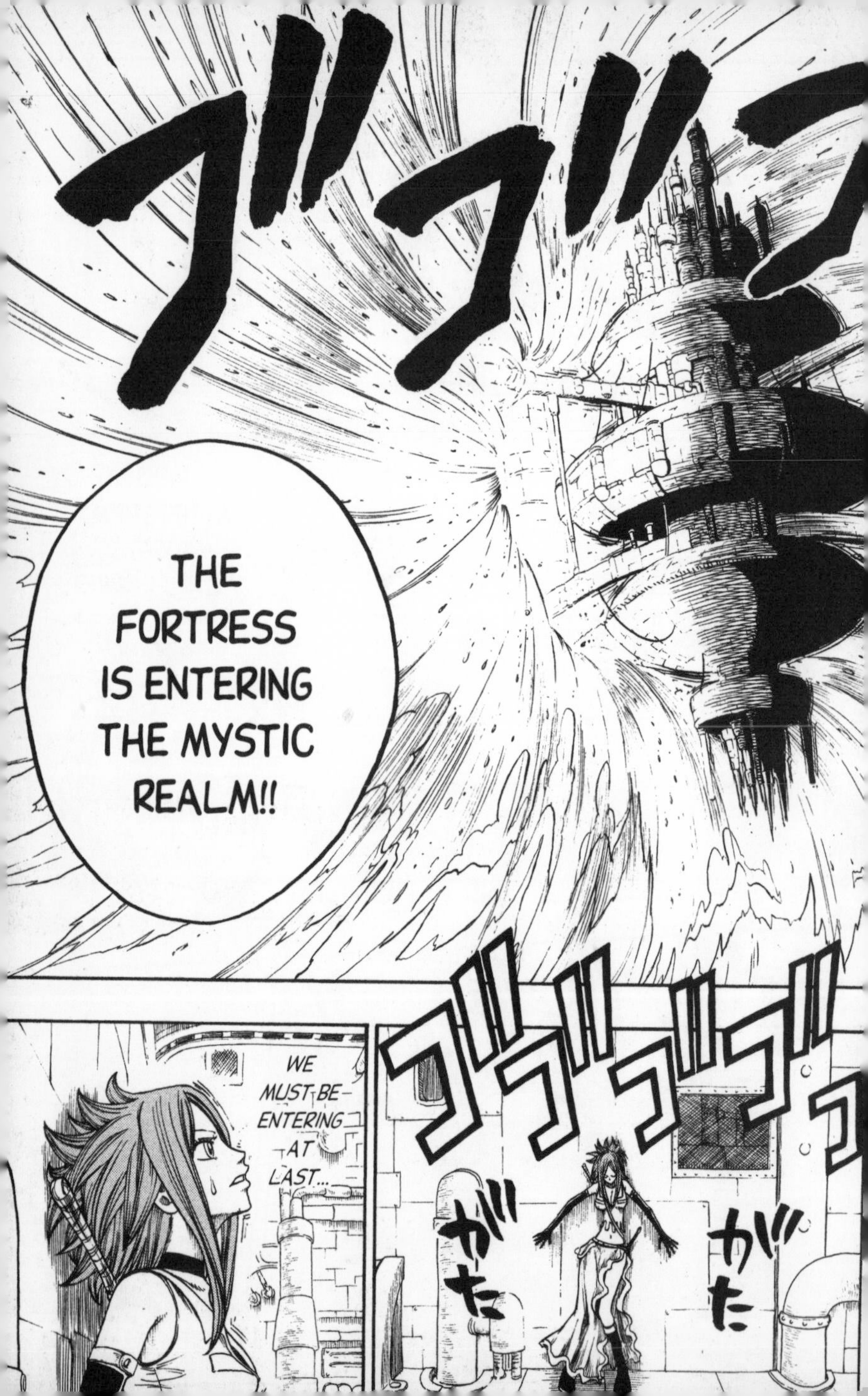

ゴゴゴゴ
THE FORTRESS IS ENTERING THE MYSTIC REALM!!
ゴゴゴゴ
がた
がた
WE MUST BE ENTERING AT LAST...

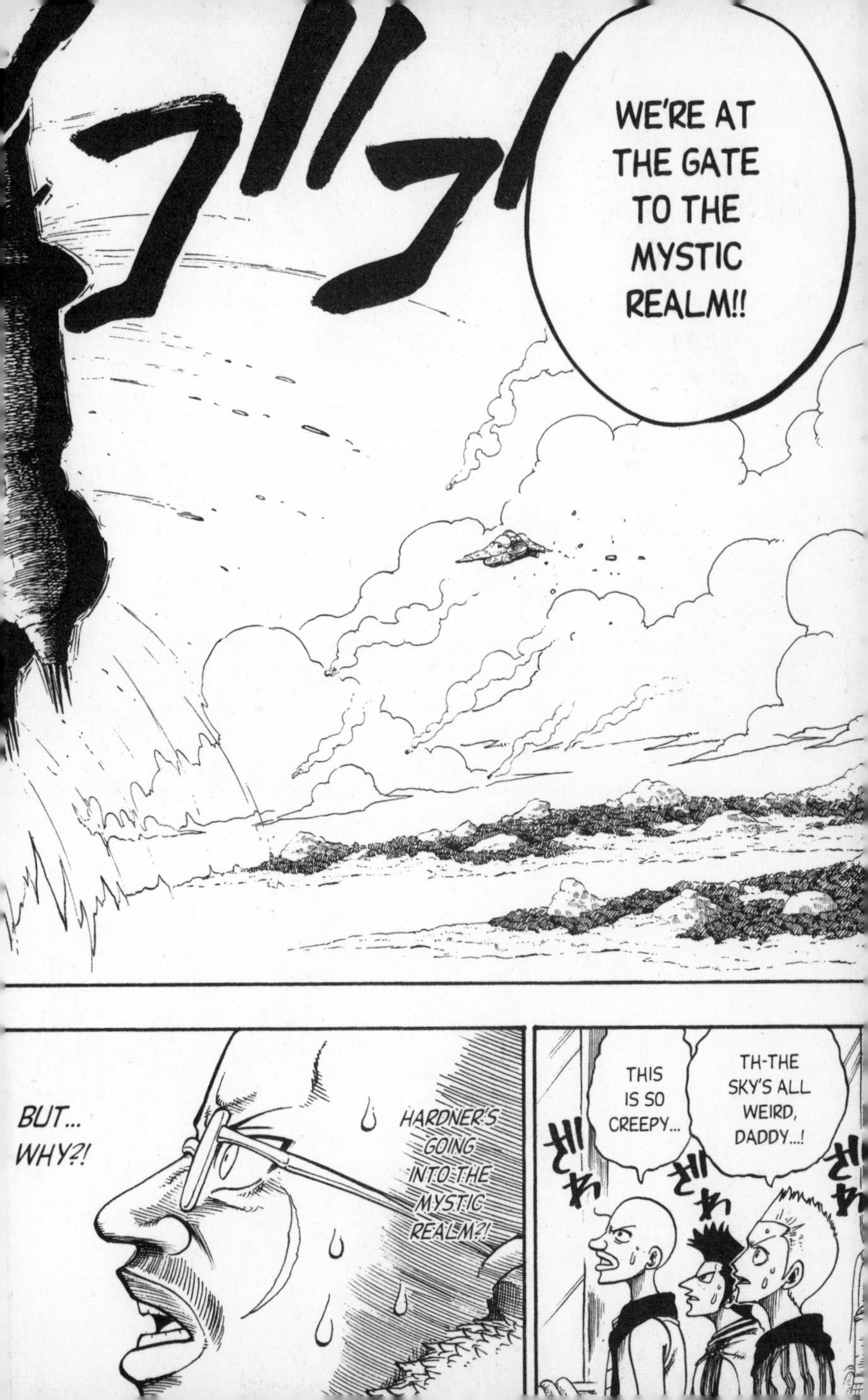
WE'RE AT THE GATE TO THE MYSTIC REALM!!
TH-THE SKY'S ALL WEIRD, DADDY...!
THIS IS SO CREEPY...
ざわ
ざわ
ざわ
HARDNER'S GOING INTO THE MYSTIC REALM?!
BUT... WHY?!

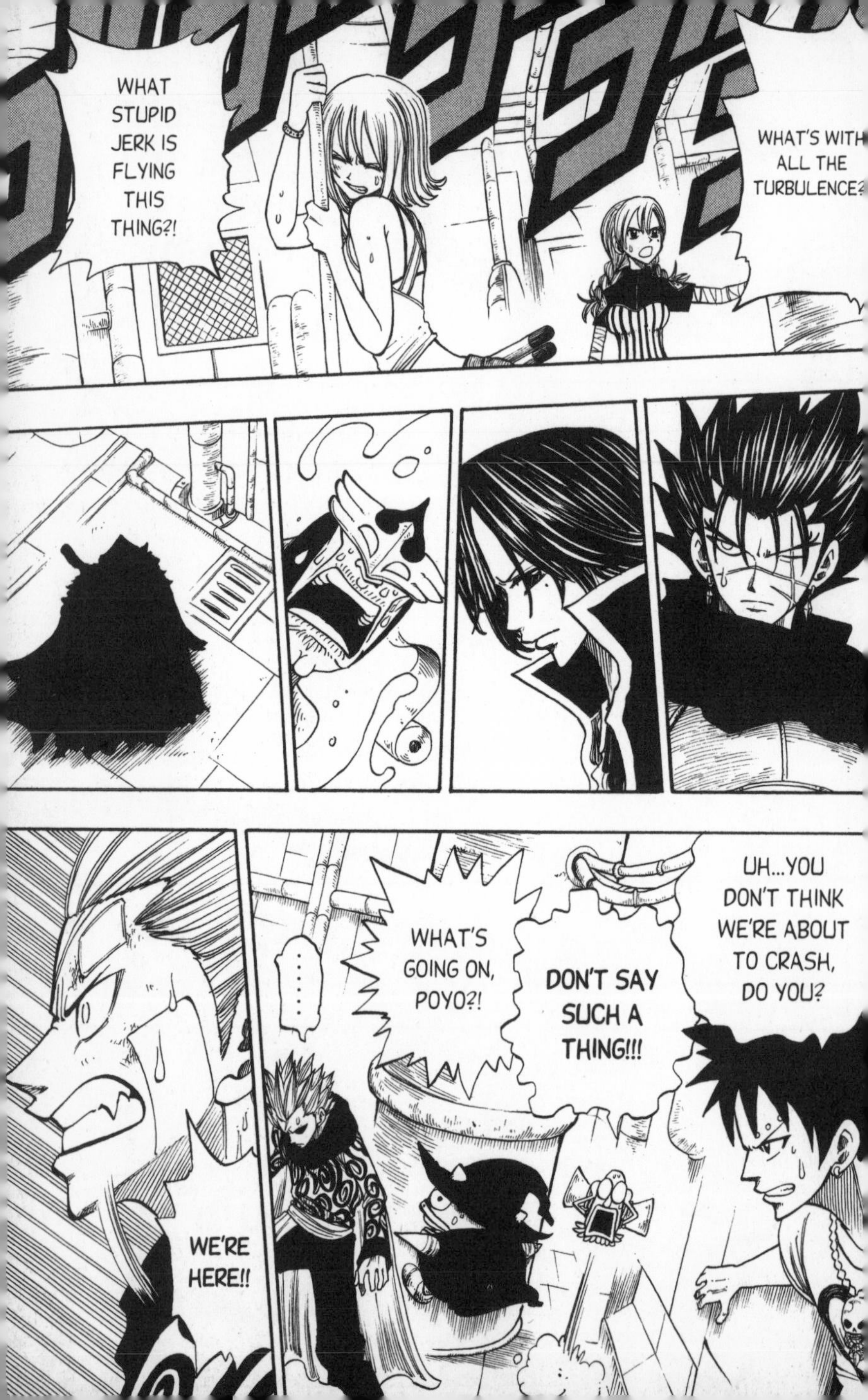
WHAT'S WITH ALL THE TURBULENCE?
WHAT STUPID JERK IS FLYING THIS THING?!
UH...YOU DON'T THINK WE'RE ABOUT TO CRASH, DO YOU?
DON'T SAY SUCH A THING!!!
WHAT'S GOING ON, POYO?!
......
WE'RE HERE!!

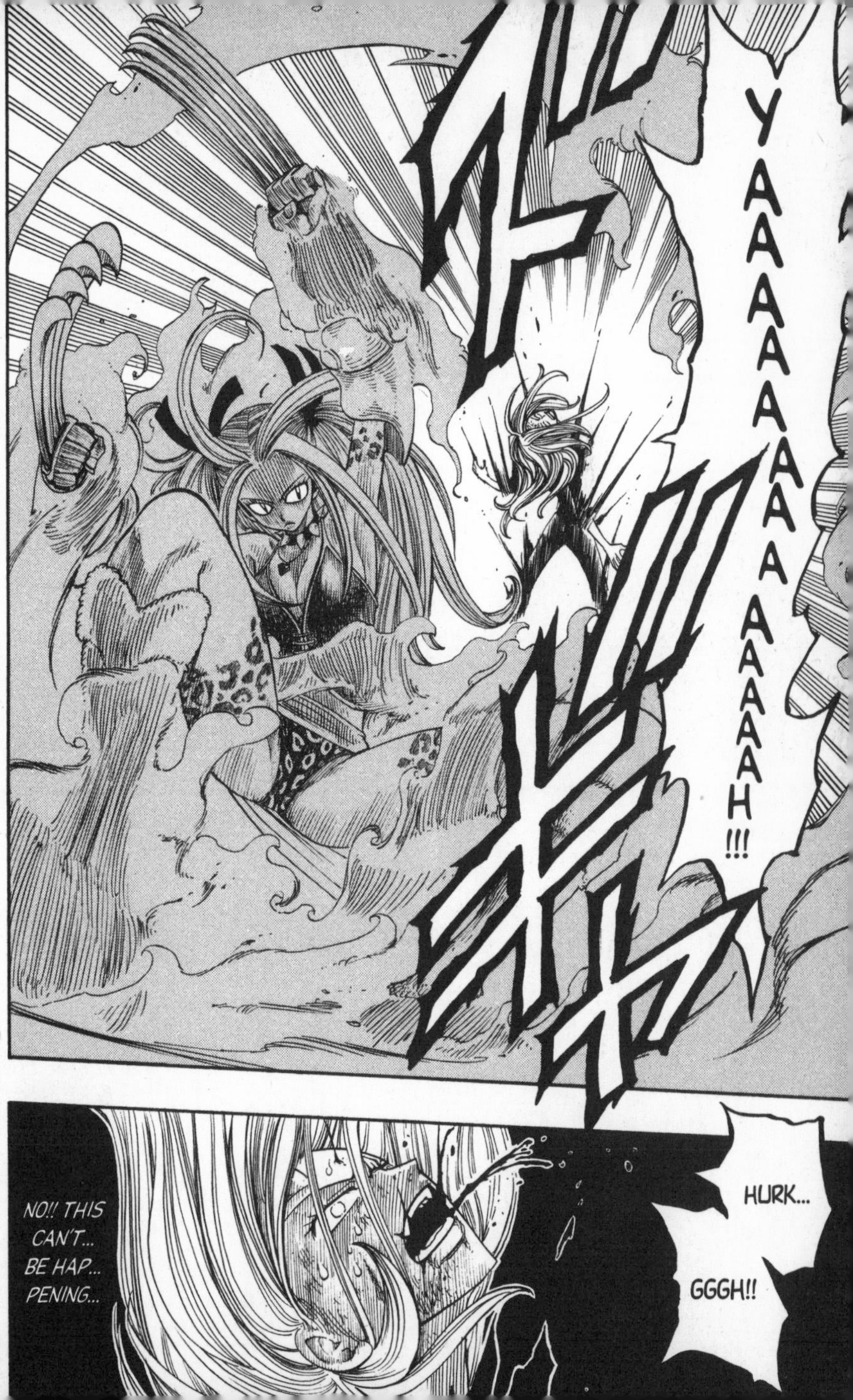
YAAAAAAAAAAAAH!!!
HURK...
GGGH!!
NO!! THIS CAN'T... BE HAP... PENING...

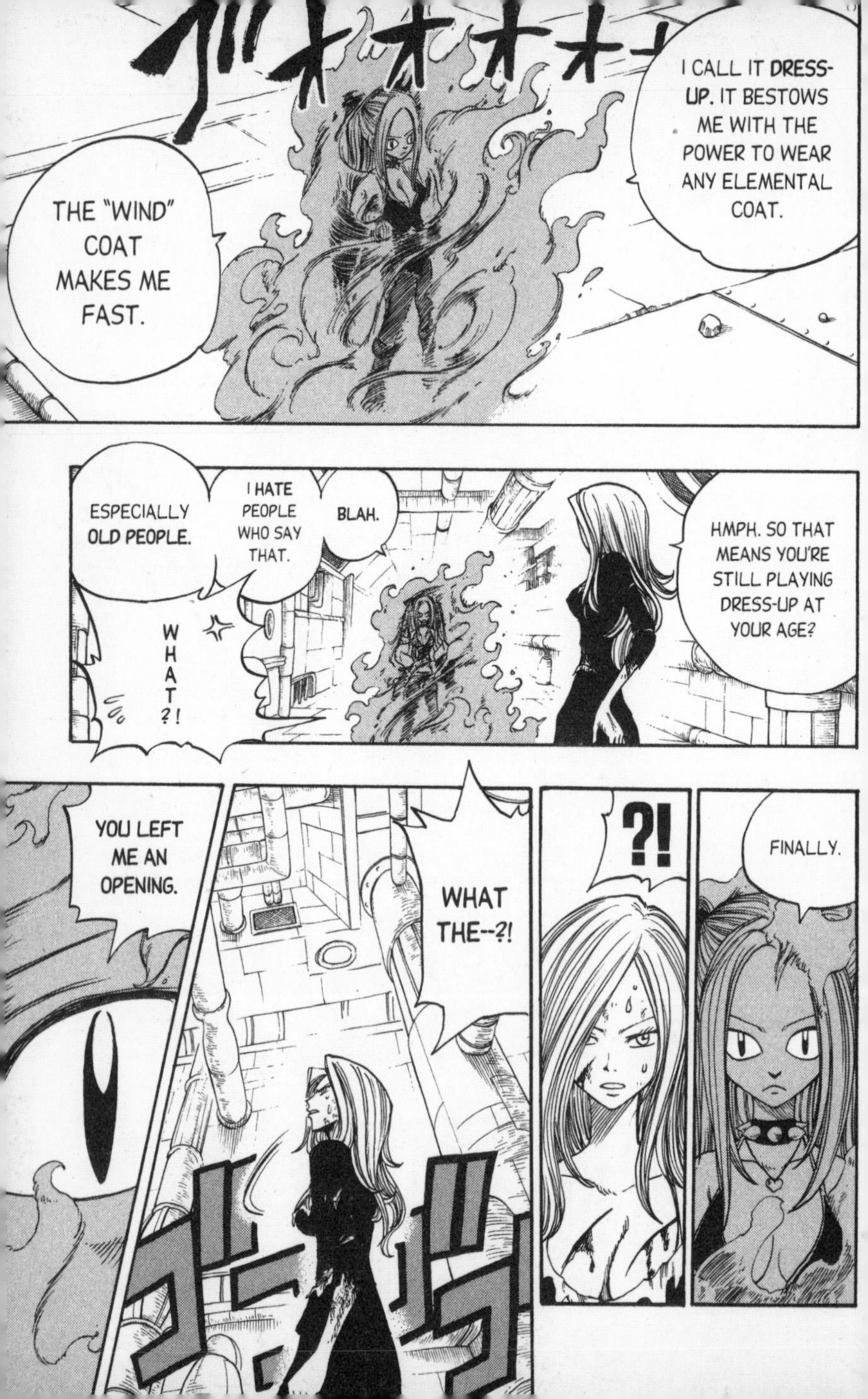
ブオオオオ
I CALL IT DRESS-UP. IT BESTOWS ME WITH THE POWER TO WEAR ANY ELEMENTAL COAT.
THE "WIND" COAT MAKES ME FAST.
HMPH. SO THAT MEANS YOU'RE STILL PLAYING DRESS-UP AT YOUR AGE?
BLAH.
I HATE PEOPLE WHO SAY THAT.
ESPECIALLY OLD PEOPLE.
WHAT?!
FINALLY.
?!
WHAT THE--?!
YOU LEFT ME AN OPENING.

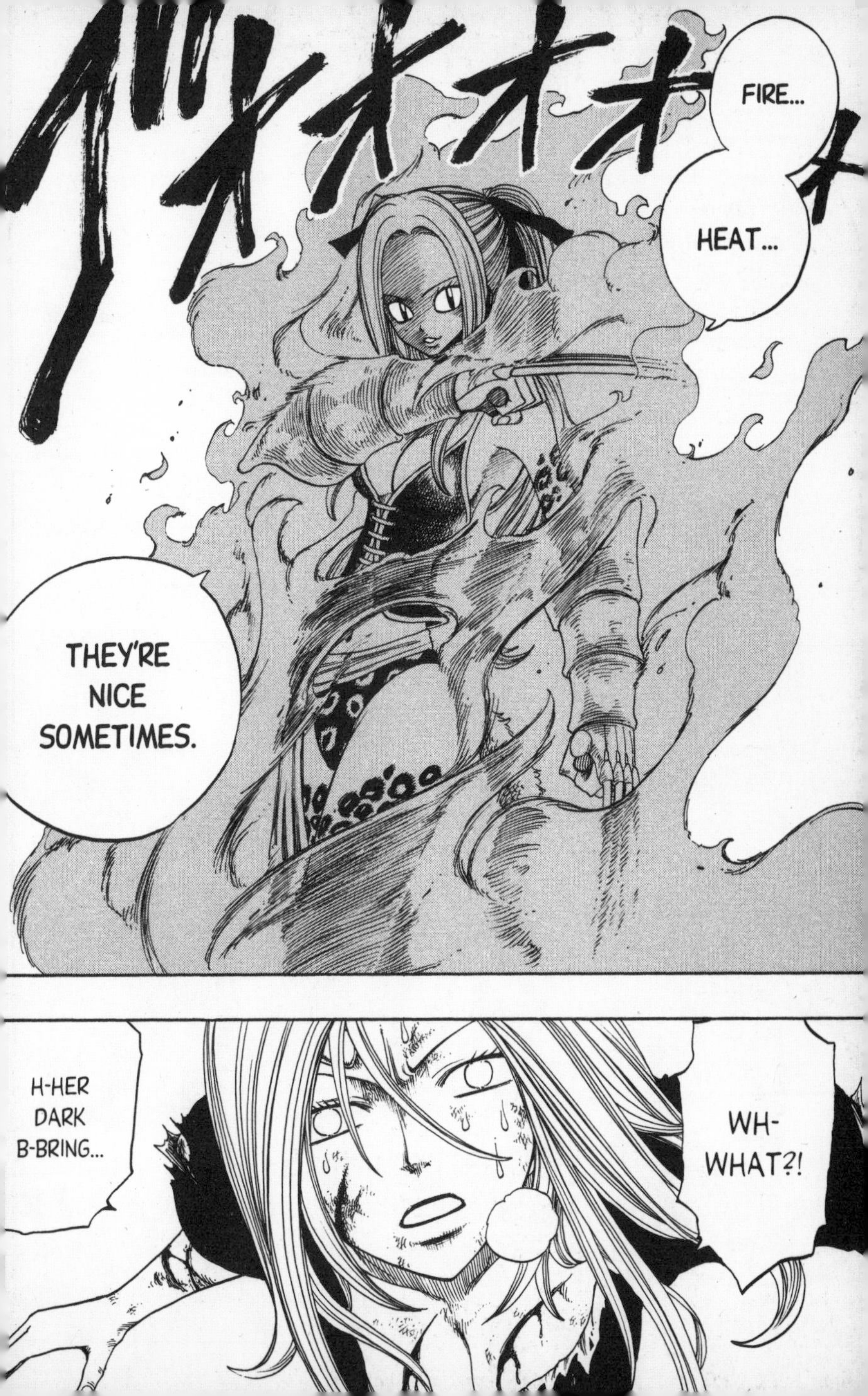
FIRE...
HEAT...
THEY'RE NICE SOMETIMES.
WH-WHAT?!
H-HER DARK B-BRING...

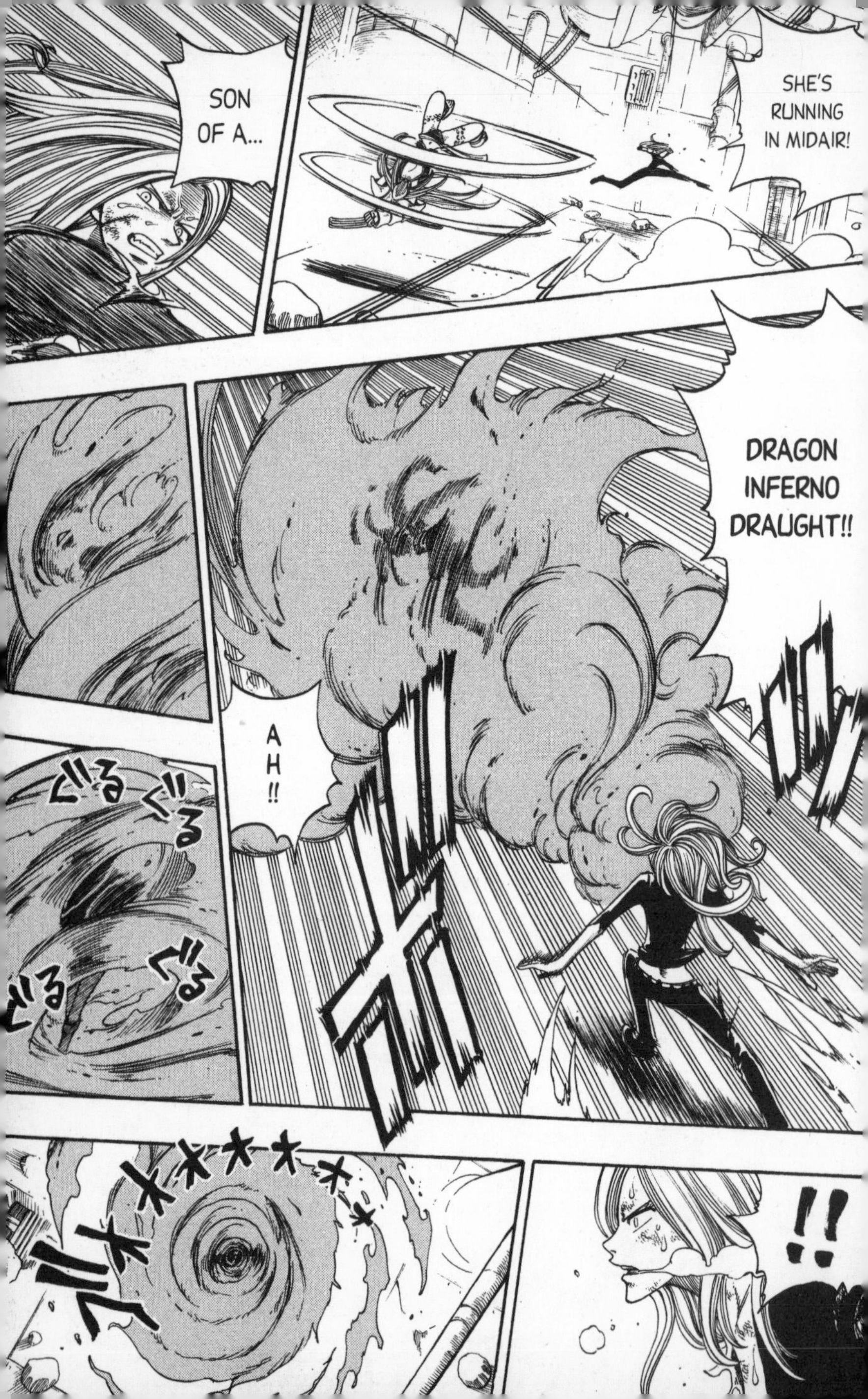
SHE'S RUNNING IN MIDAIR!
SON OF A...
DRAGON INFERNO DRAUGHT!!
AH!!
ぐるぐる
ぐるぐる
!!

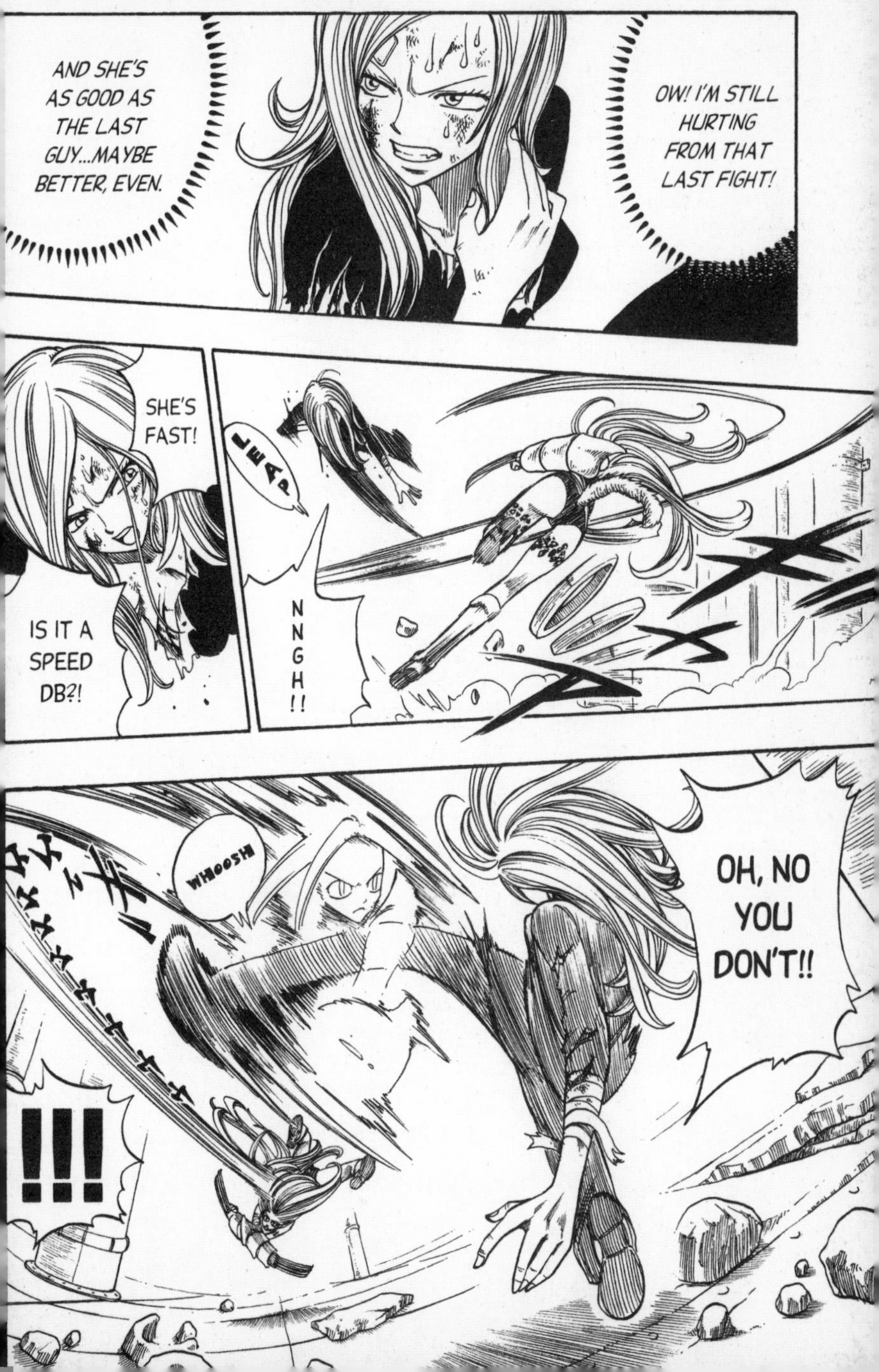
OW! I'M STILL HURTING FROM THAT LAST FIGHT!
AND SHE'S AS GOOD AS THE LAST GUY...MAYBE BETTER, EVEN.
LEAP
NNGH!!
SHE'S FAST!
IS IT A SPEED DB?!
OH, NO YOU DON'T!!
WHOOSH
!!!

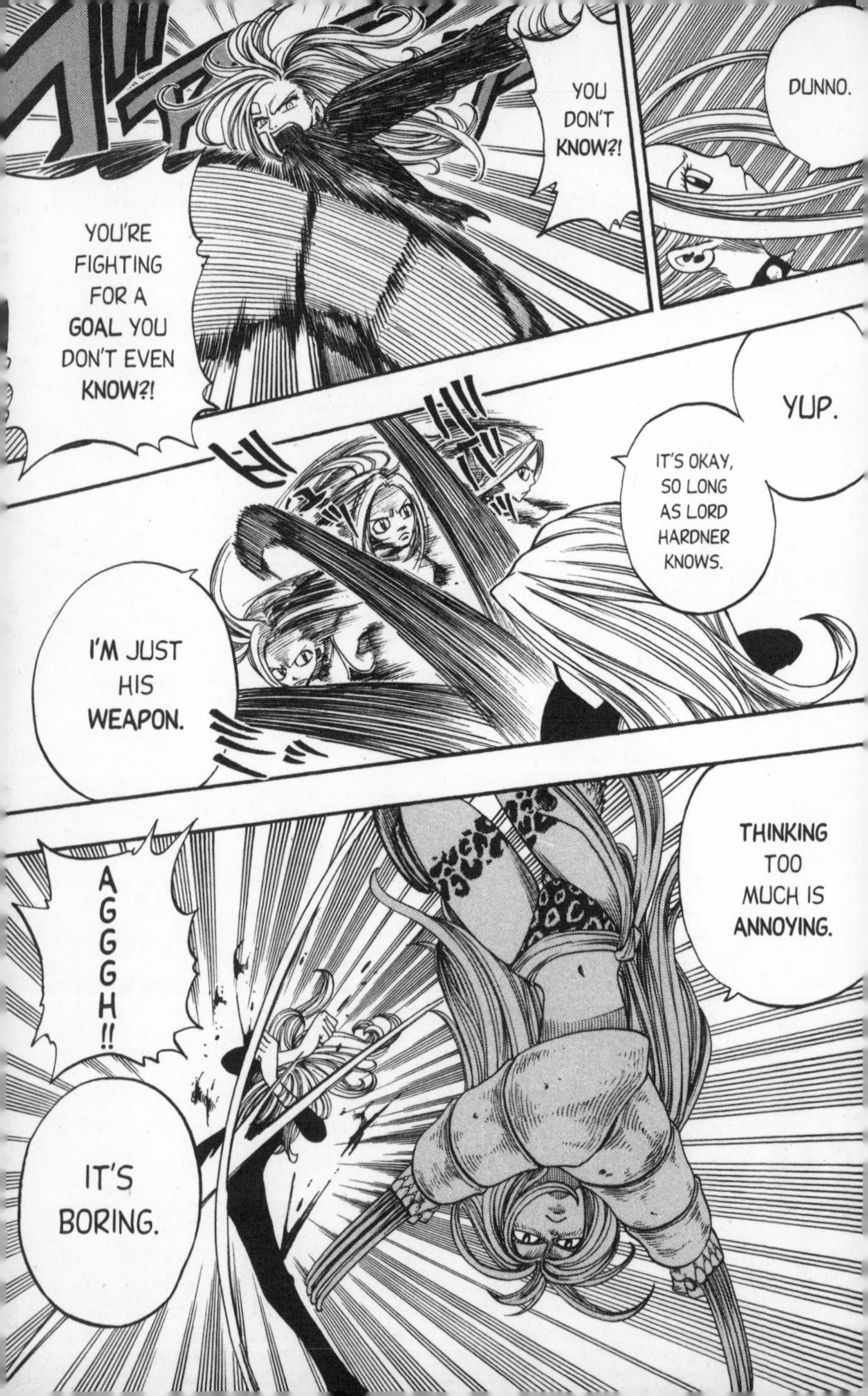
DUNNO.
YOU DON'T KNOW?!
YOU'RE FIGHTING FOR A GOAL YOU DON'T EVEN KNOW?!
YUP.
IT'S OKAY, SO LONG AS LORD HARDNER KNOWS.
I'M JUST HIS WEAPON.
THINKING TOO MUCH IS ANNOYING.
AGGGH!!
IT'S BORING.

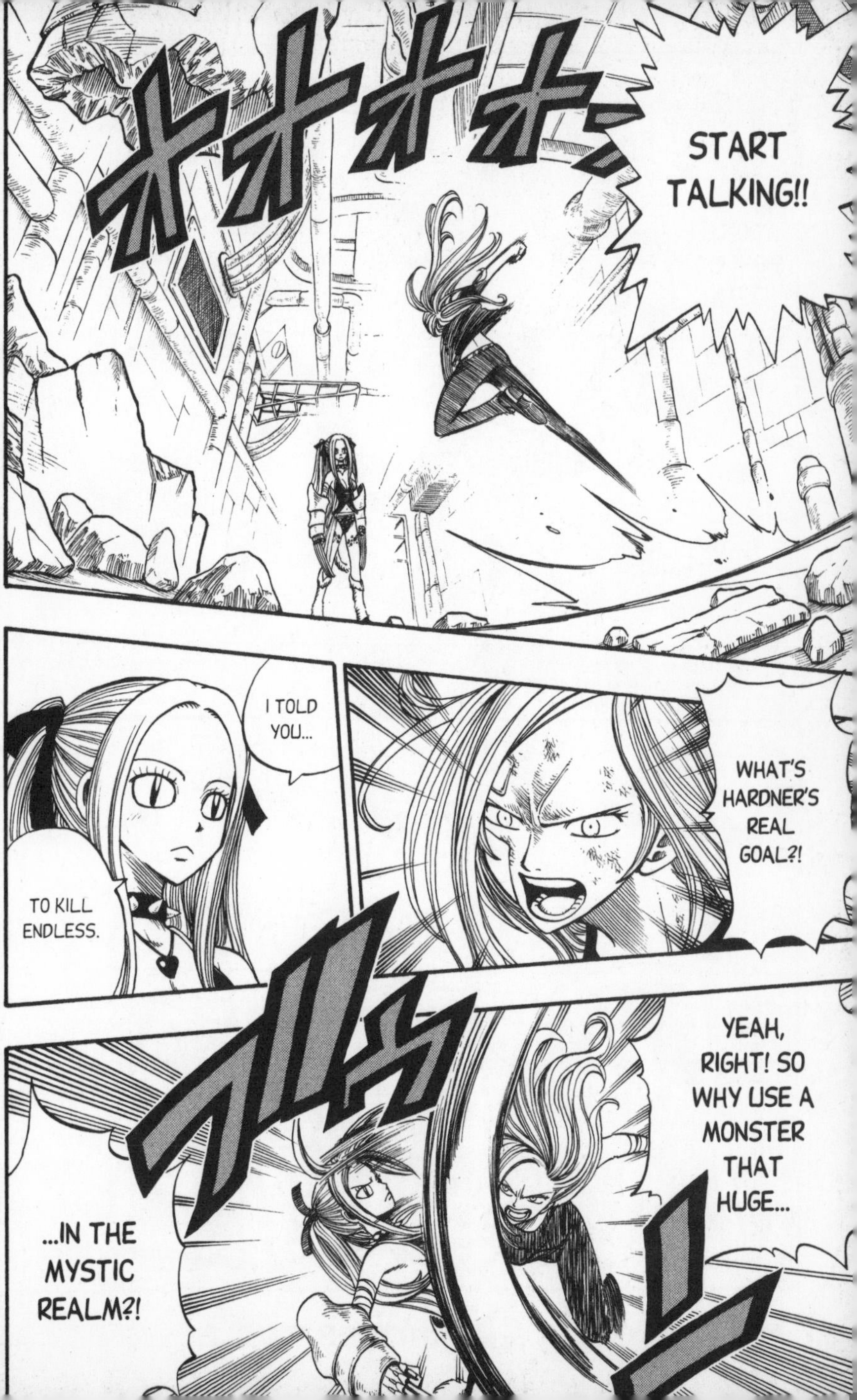
START TALKING!!
WHAT'S HARDNER'S REAL GOAL?!
I TOLD YOU...
TO KILL ENDLESS.
YEAH, RIGHT! SO WHY USE A MONSTER THAT HUGE...
...IN THE MYSTIC REALM?!

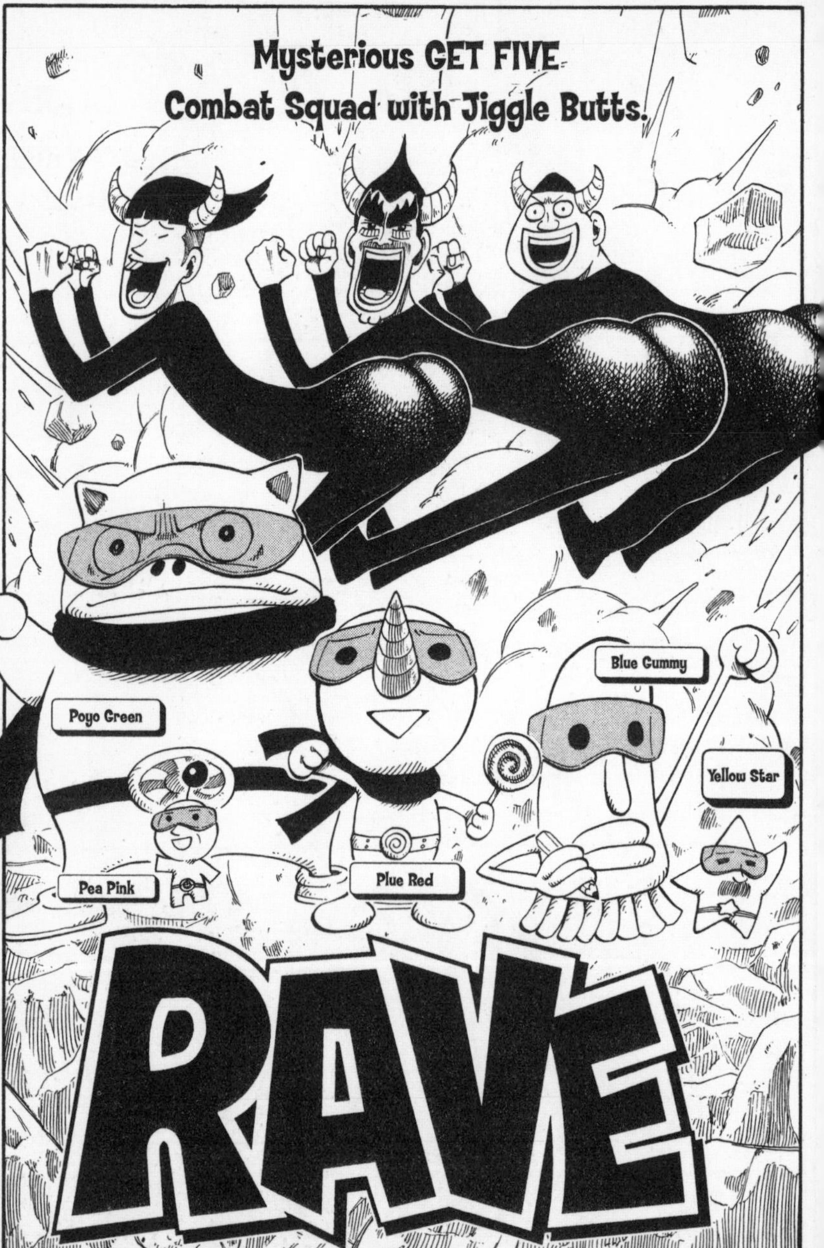

Mysterious GET FIVE
Combat Squad with Jiggle Butts.
Blue Gummy
Poyo Green
Yellow Star
Pea Pink
Plue Red
RAVE

RAVE:211 ✚ ANOTHER WORLD

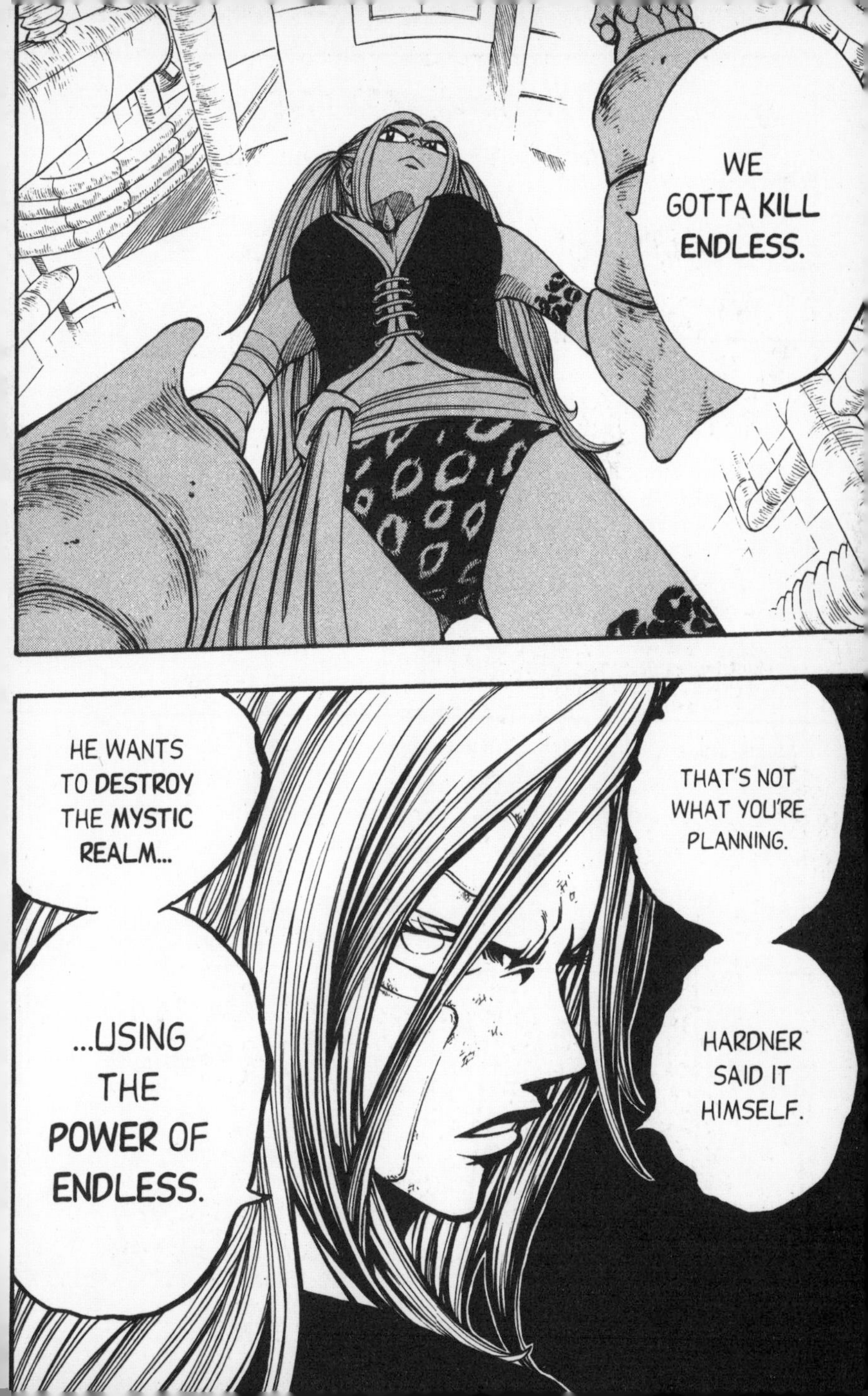
WE GOTTA KILL ENDLESS.
THAT'S NOT WHAT YOU'RE PLANNING.
HARDNER SAID IT HIMSELF.
HE WANTS TO DESTROY THE MYSTIC REALM...
...USING THE POWER OF ENDLESS.

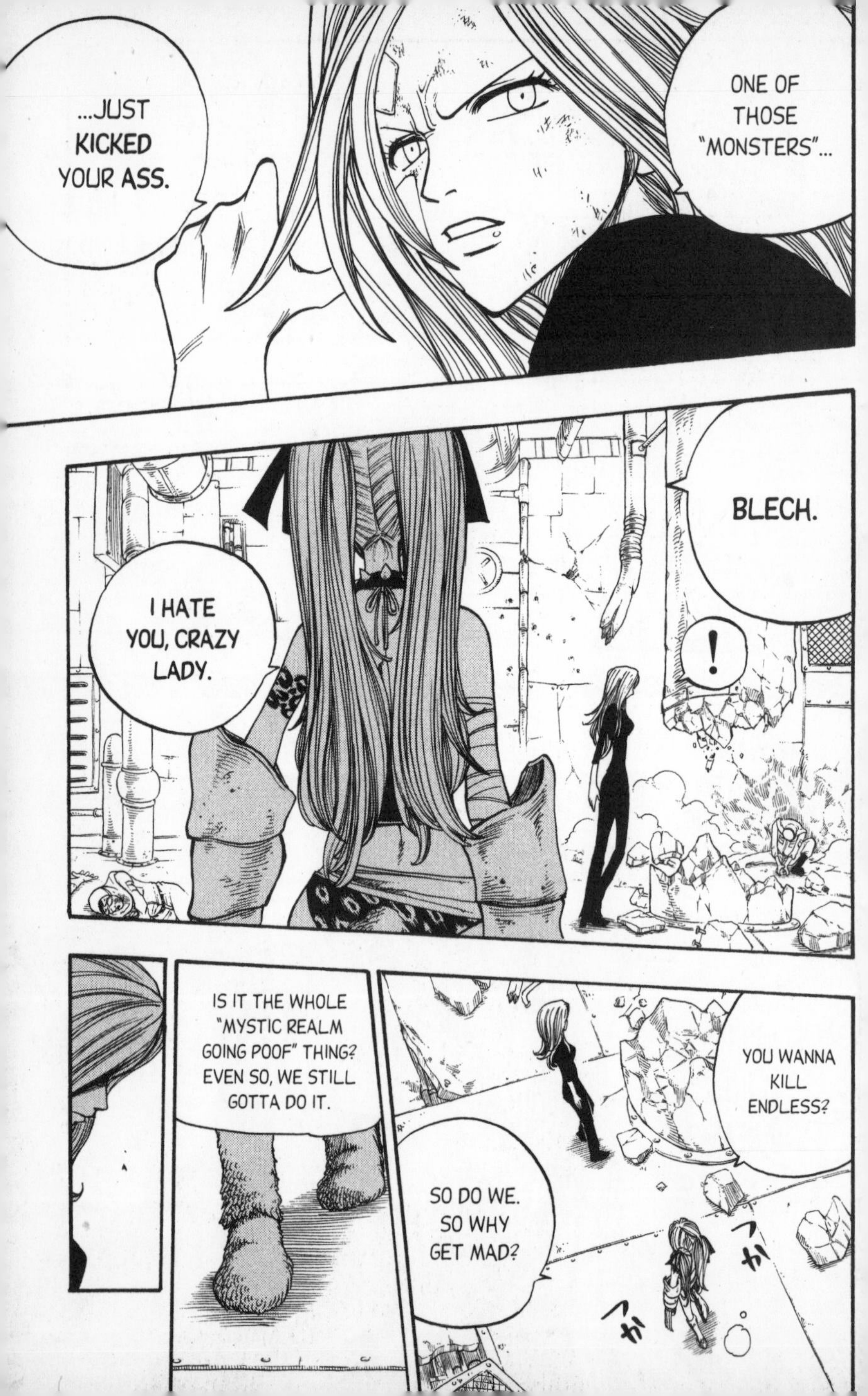
ONE OF THOSE "MONSTERS"...
...JUST KICKED YOUR ASS.
BLECH.
!
I HATE YOU, CRAZY LADY.
YOU WANNA KILL ENDLESS?
SO DO WE. SO WHY GET MAD?
つか
つか
IS IT THE WHOLE "MYSTIC REALM GOING POOF" THING? EVEN SO, WE STILL GOTTA DO IT.

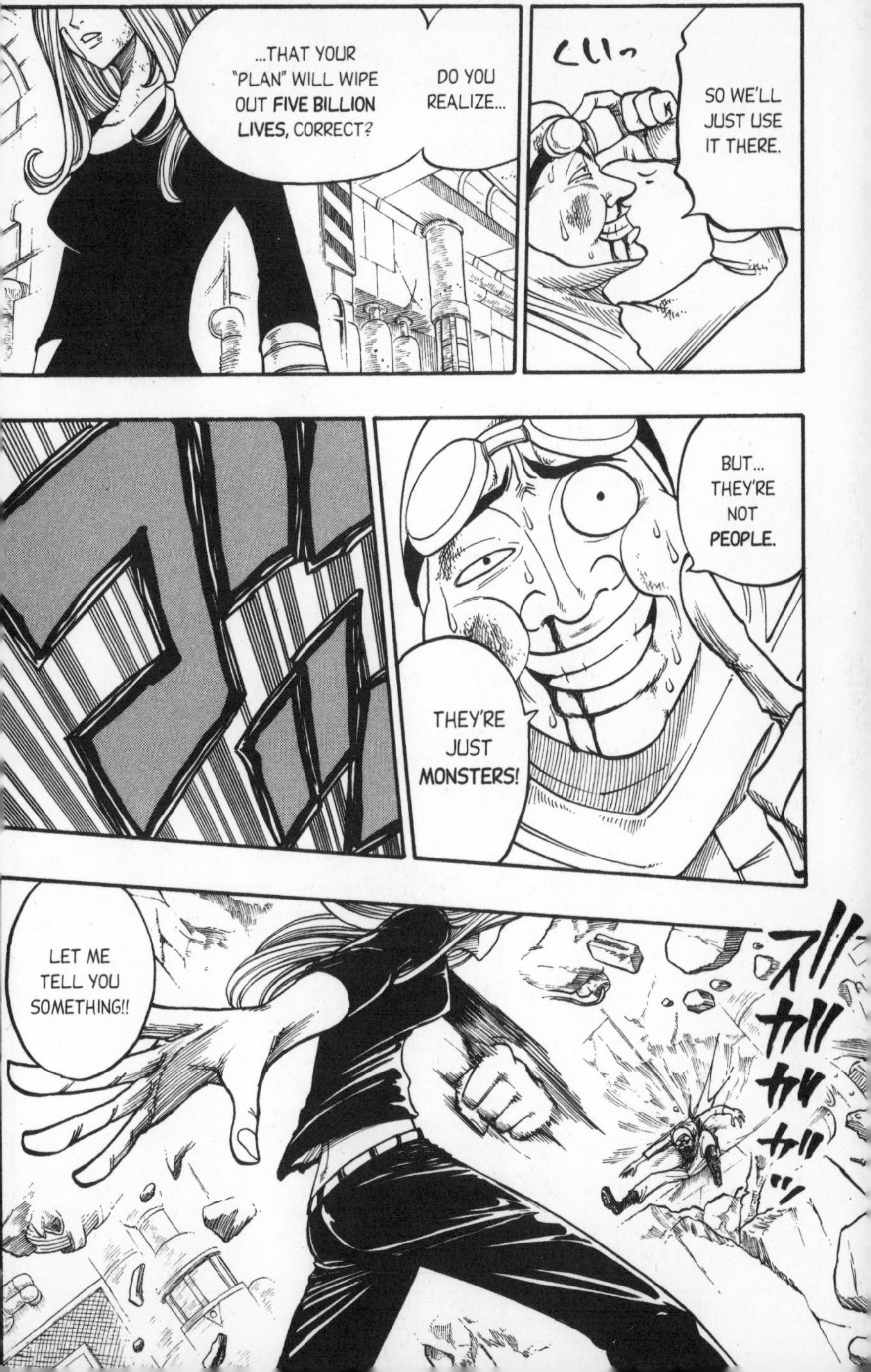
くいっ
SO WE'LL JUST USE IT THERE.
DO YOU REALIZE...
...THAT YOUR "PLAN" WILL WIPE OUT **FIVE BILLION LIVES**, CORRECT?
BUT... THEY'RE NOT **PEOPLE**.
THEY'RE JUST **MONSTERS!**
ズガガガガッ
LET ME TELL YOU SOMETHING!!

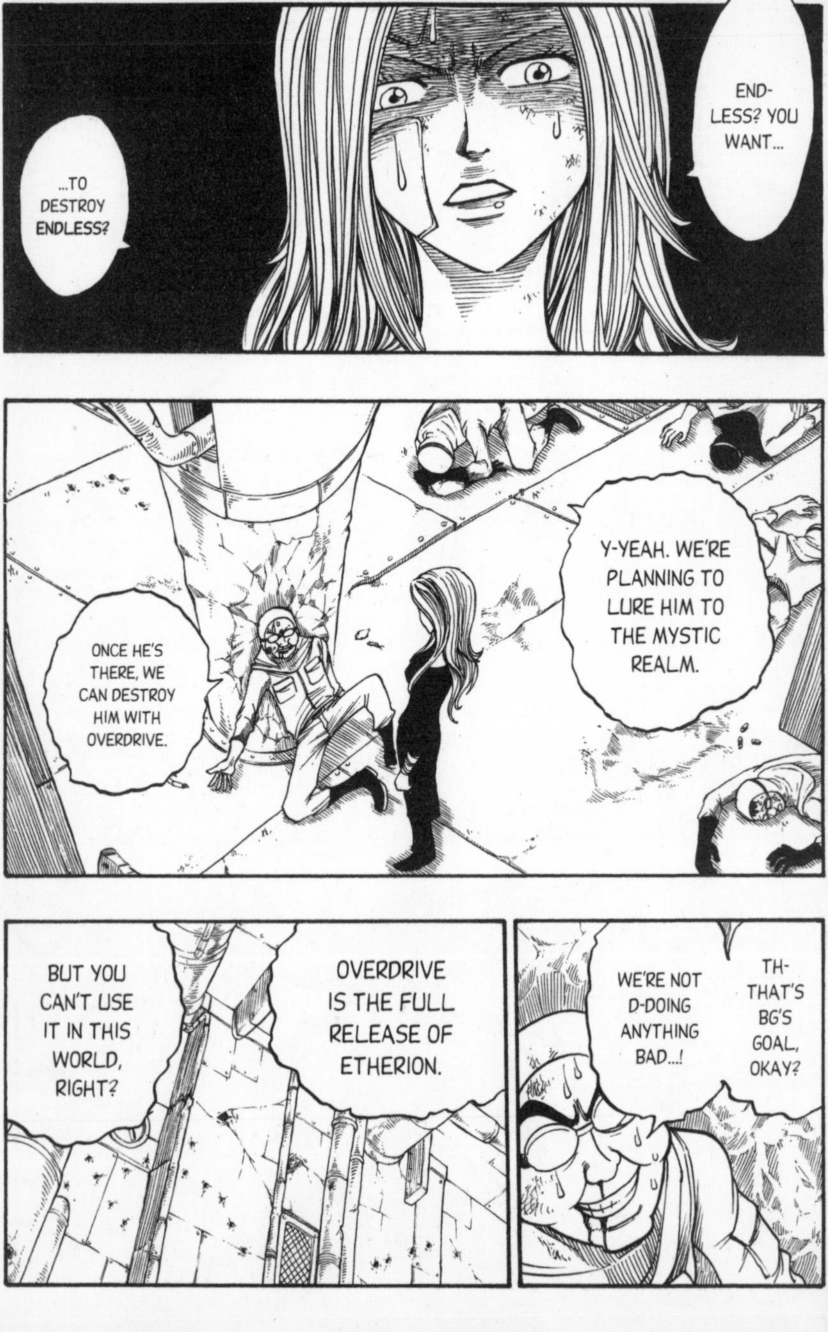
END-LESS? YOU WANT...
...TO DESTROY ENDLESS?
Y-YEAH. WE'RE PLANNING TO LURE HIM TO THE MYSTIC REALM.
ONCE HE'S THERE, WE CAN DESTROY HIM WITH OVERDRIVE.
TH-THAT'S BG'S GOAL, OKAY?
WE'RE NOT D-DOING ANYTHING BAD...!
OVERDRIVE IS THE FULL RELEASE OF ETHERION.
BUT YOU CAN'T USE IT IN THIS WORLD, RIGHT?

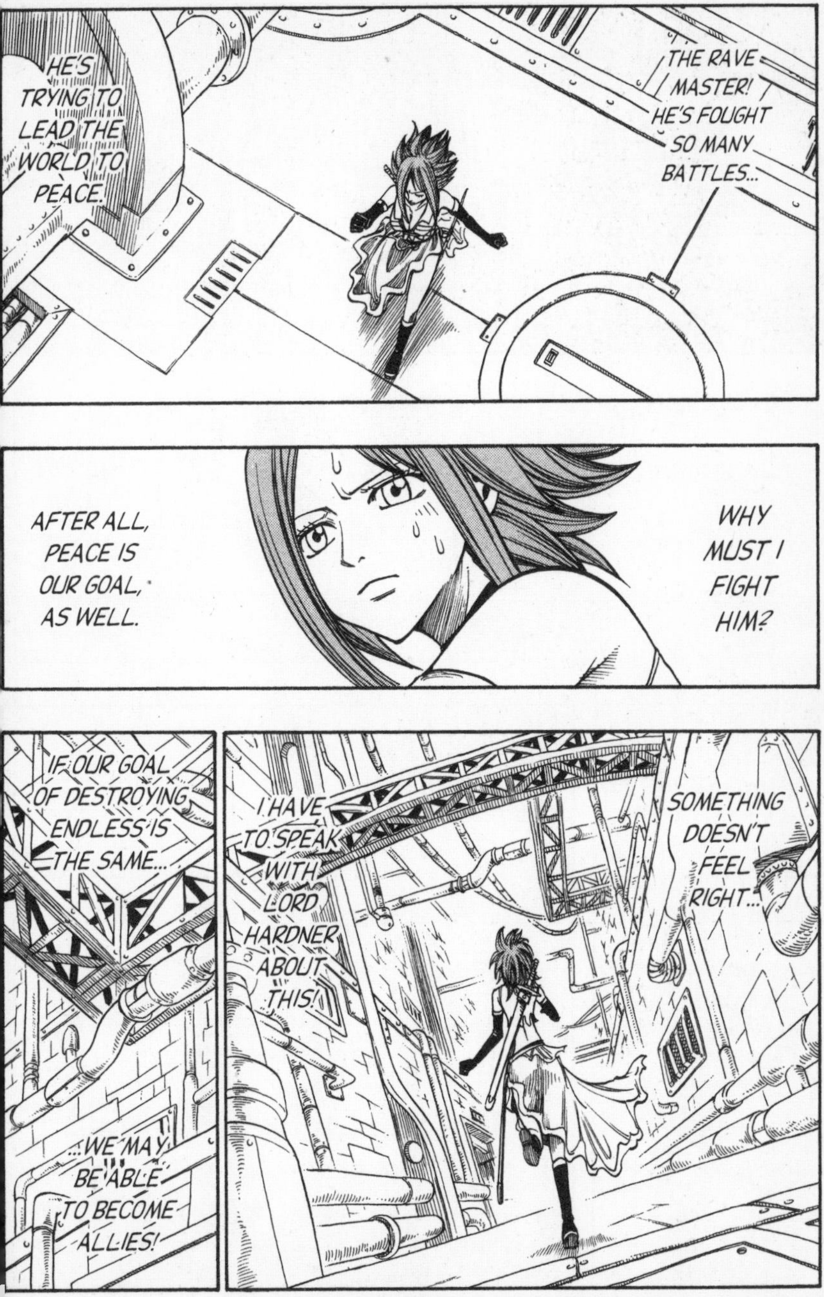
THE RAVE MASTER! HE'S FOUGHT SO MANY BATTLES...
HE'S TRYING TO LEAD THE WORLD TO PEACE.
WHY MUST I FIGHT HIM?
AFTER ALL, PEACE IS OUR GOAL, AS WELL.
SOMETHING DOESN'T FEEL RIGHT...
I HAVE TO SPEAK WITH LORD HARDNER ABOUT THIS!
IF OUR GOAL OF DESTROYING ENDLESS IS THE SAME...
...WE MAY BE ABLE TO BECOME ALLIES!

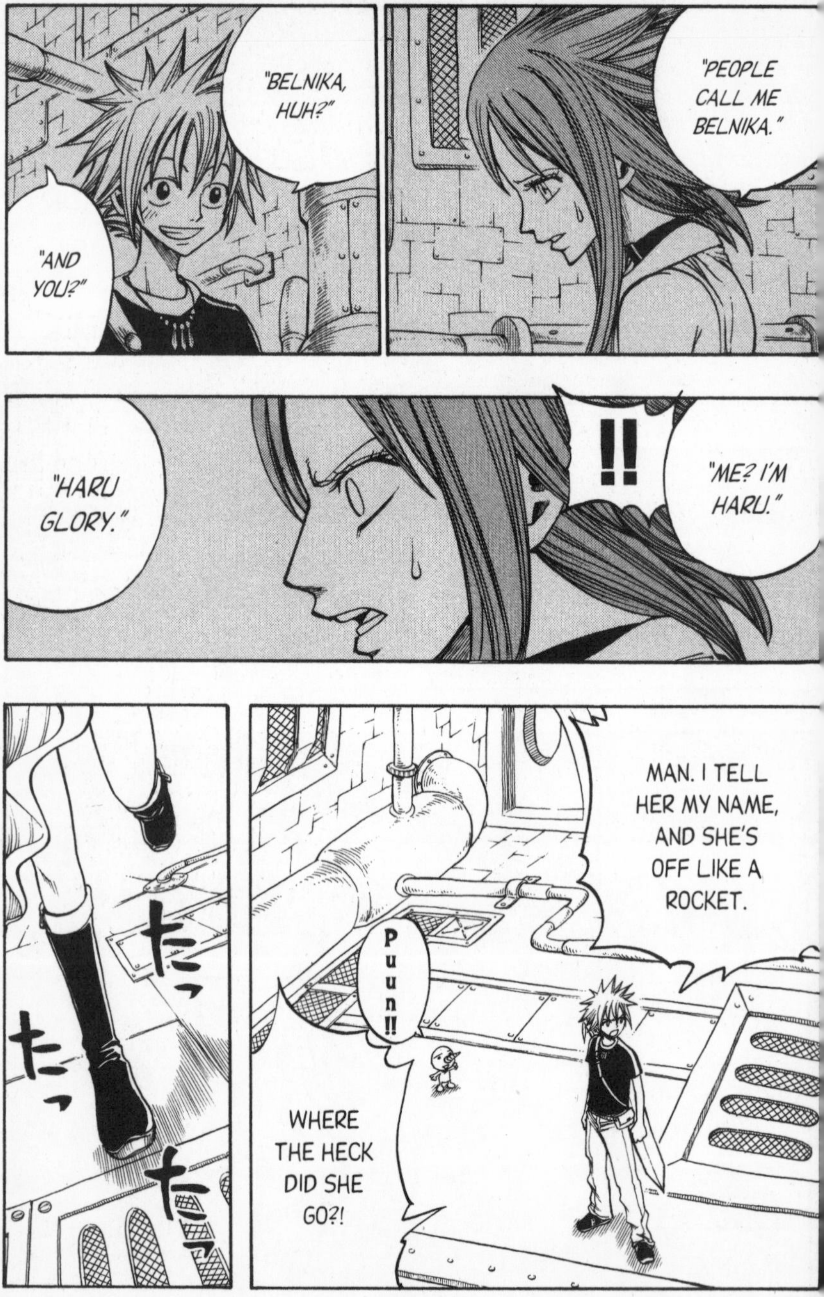
"PEOPLE CALL ME BELNIKA."
"BELNIKA, HUH?"
"AND YOU?"
!!
"ME? I'M HARU."
"HARU GLORY."
MAN. I TELL HER MY NAME, AND SHE'S OFF LIKE A ROCKET.
Puun!!
WHERE THE HECK DID SHE GO?!
たっ
たっ
たっ

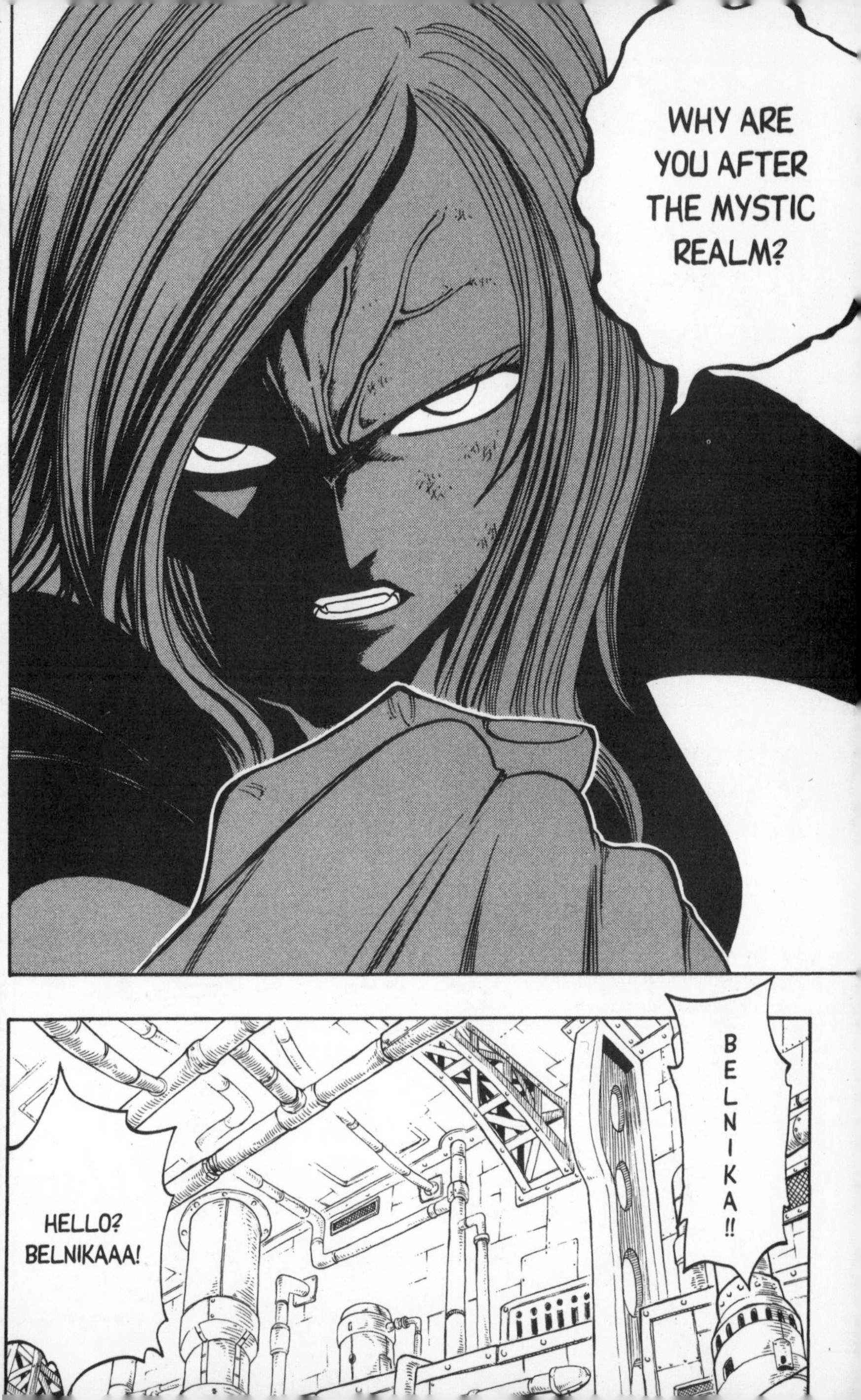
WHY ARE YOU AFTER THE MYSTIC REALM?
BELNIKA!!
HELLO? BELNIKAAA!

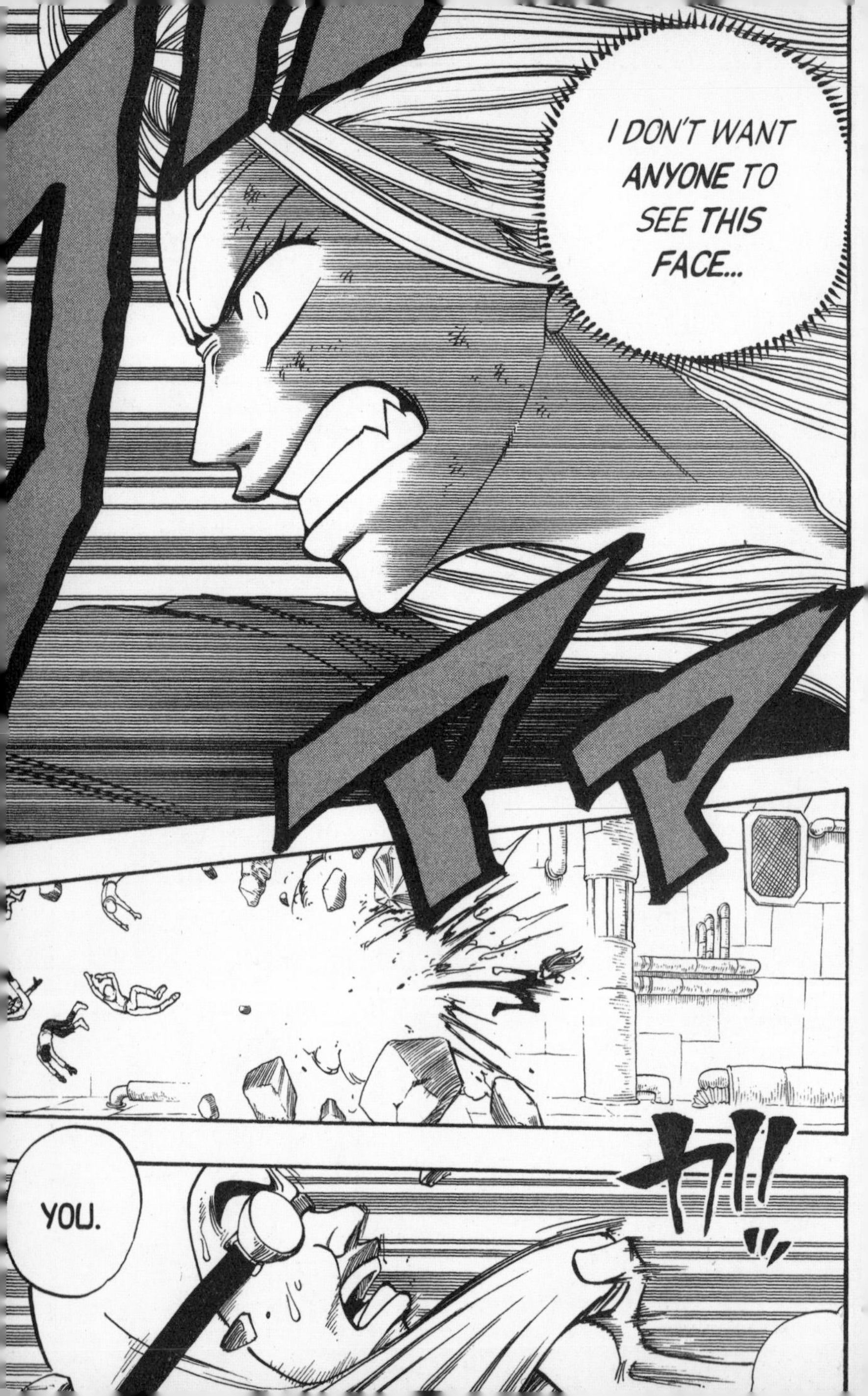
I DON'T WANT ANYONE TO SEE THIS FACE...
YOU.

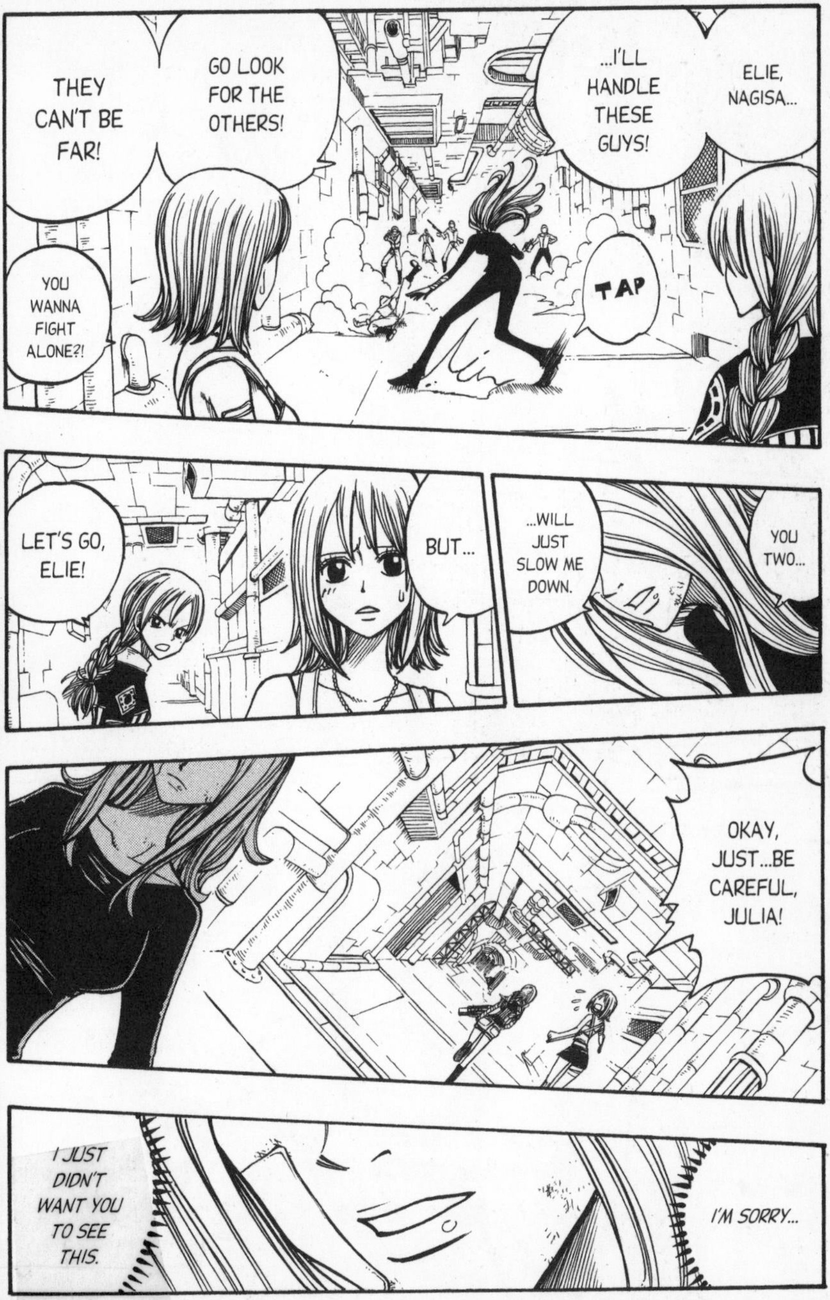
ELIE, NAGISA...
...I'LL HANDLE THESE GUYS!
TAP
GO LOOK FOR THE OTHERS!
THEY CAN'T BE FAR!
YOU WANNA FIGHT ALONE?!
YOU TWO...
...WILL JUST SLOW ME DOWN.
BUT...
LET'S GO, ELIE!
OKAY, JUST...BE CAREFUL, JULIA!
I'M SORRY...
I JUST DIDN'T WANT YOU TO SEE THIS.

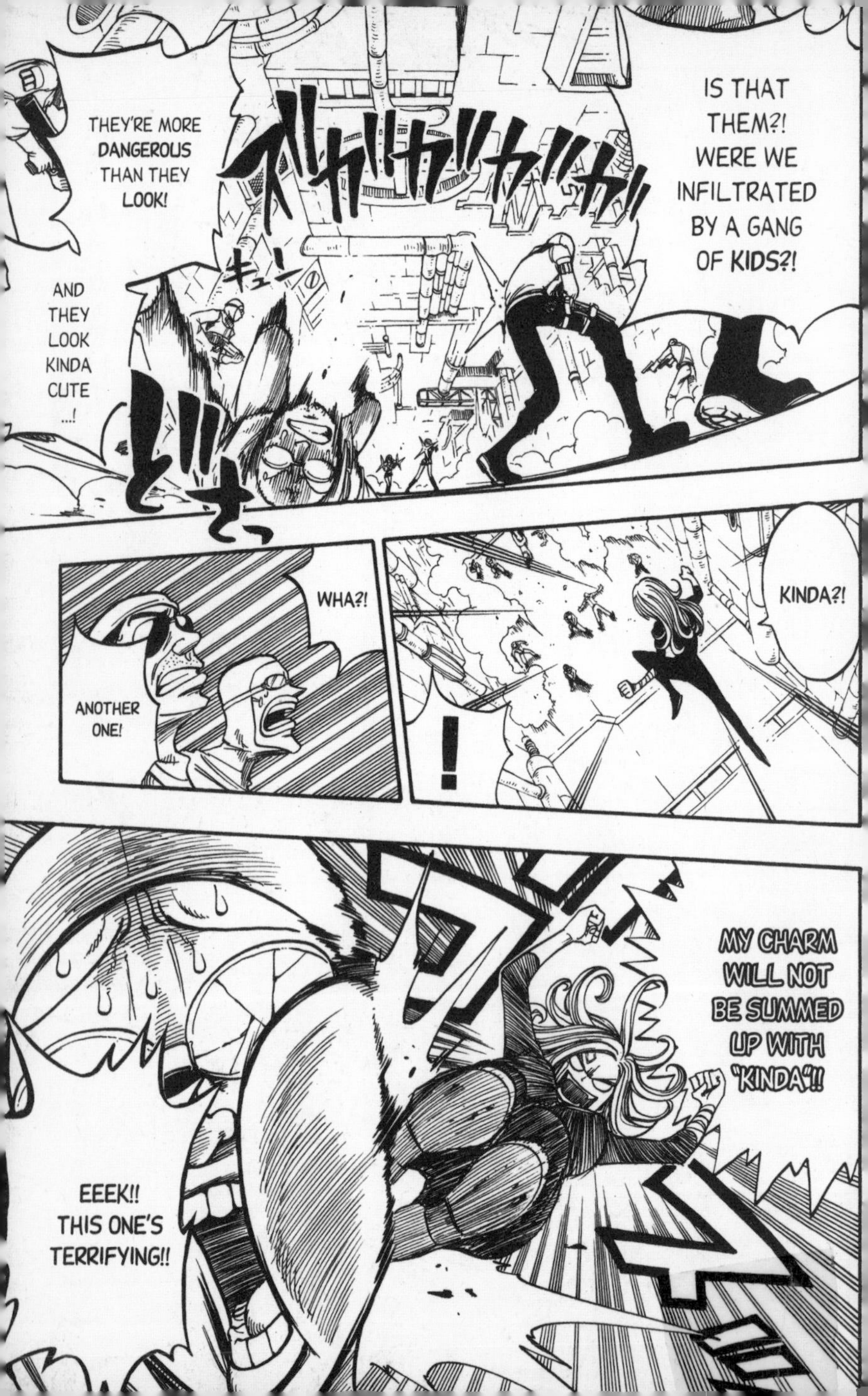
IS THAT THEM?! WERE WE INFILTRATED BY A GANG OF KIDS?!
THEY'RE MORE DANGEROUS THAN THEY LOOK!
AND THEY LOOK KINDA CUTE ...!
KINDA?!
!
WHA?!
ANOTHER ONE!
MY CHARM WILL NOT BE SUMMED UP WITH "KINDA"!!
EEEK!! THIS ONE'S TERRIFYING!!

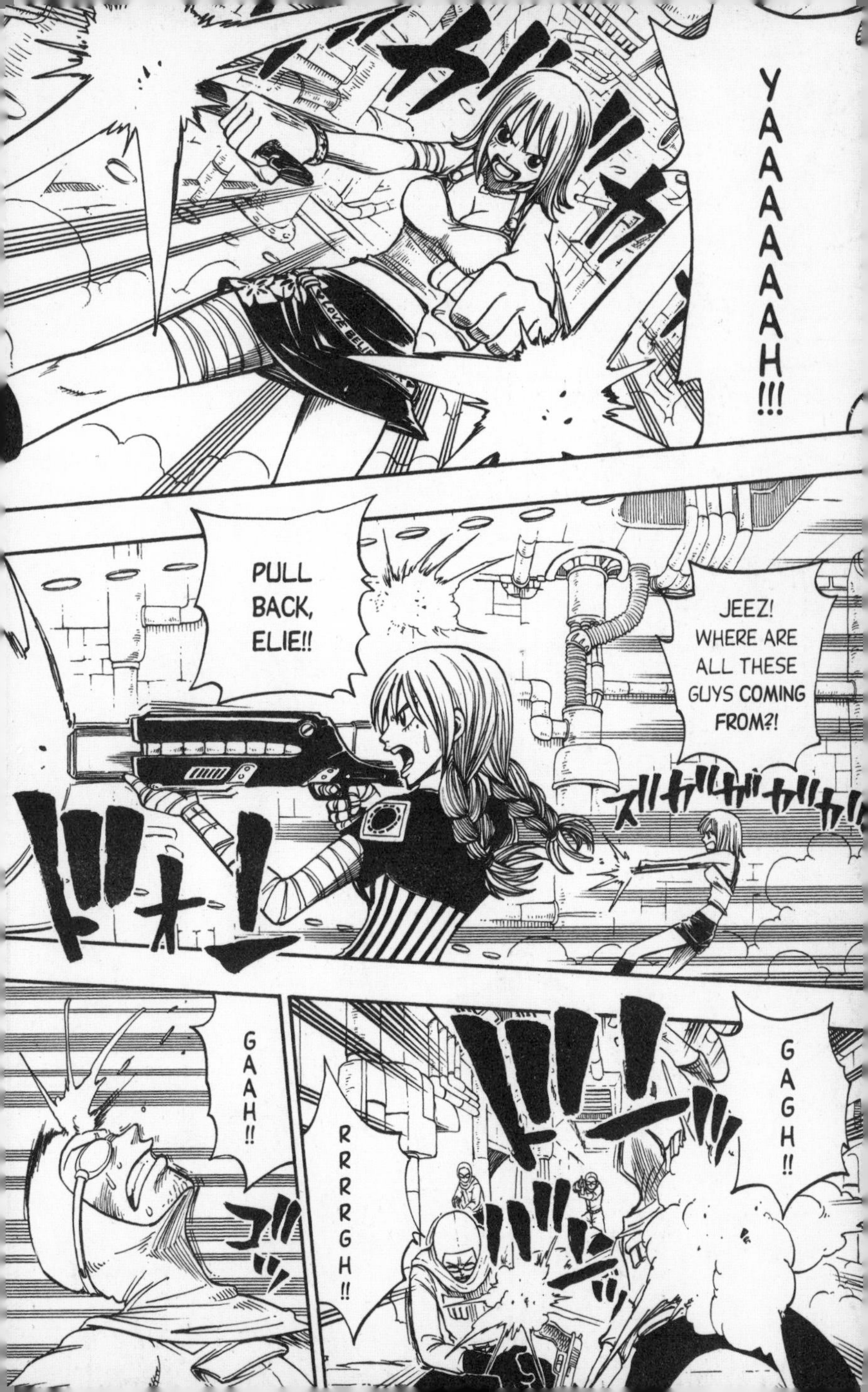
YAAAAAAH!!!
JEEZ! WHERE ARE ALL THESE GUYS COMING FROM?!
PULL BACK, ELIE!!
GAGH!!
RRRRGH!!
GAAH!!

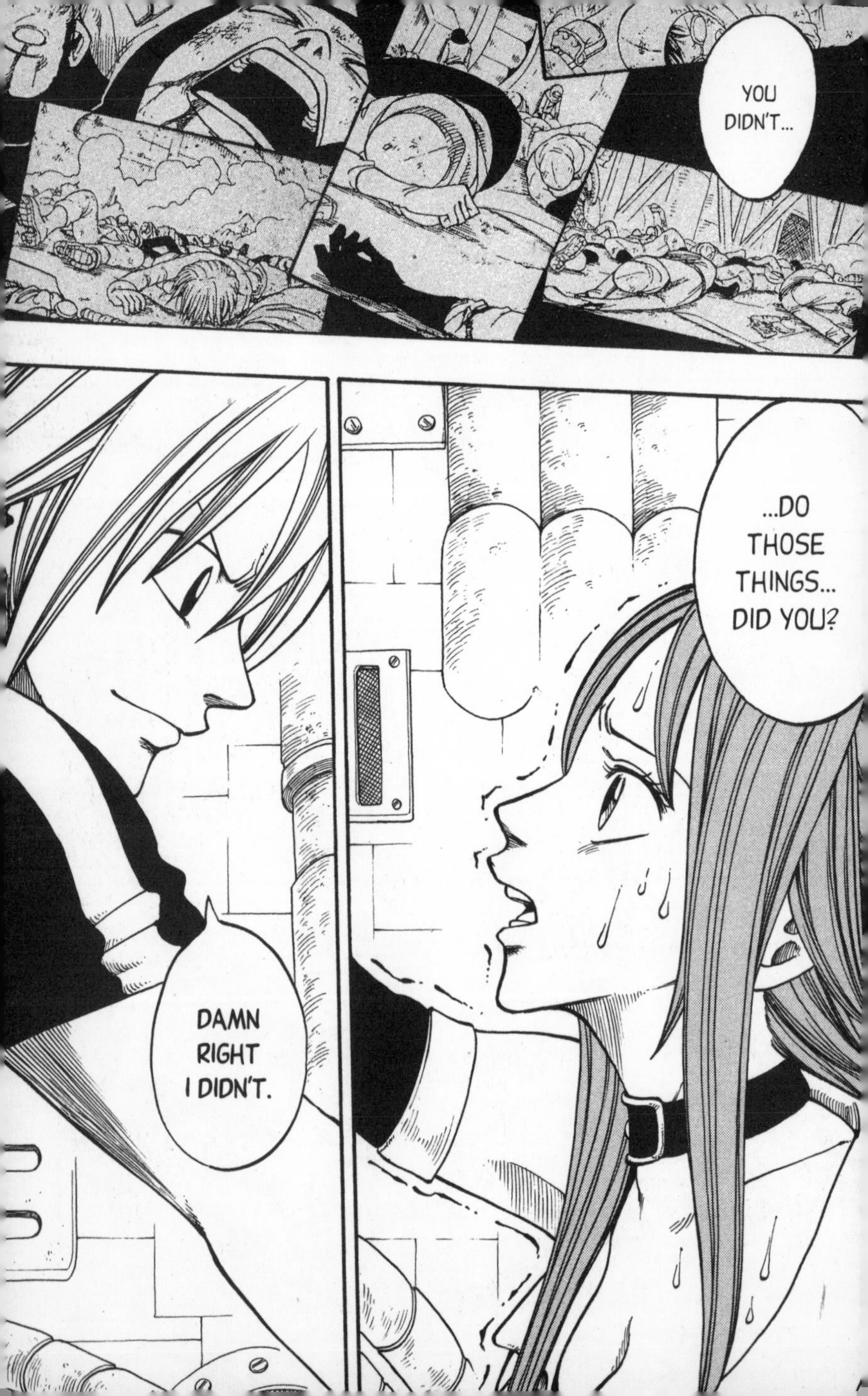
YOU DIDN'T...
...DO THOSE THINGS... DID YOU?
DAMN RIGHT I DIDN'T.

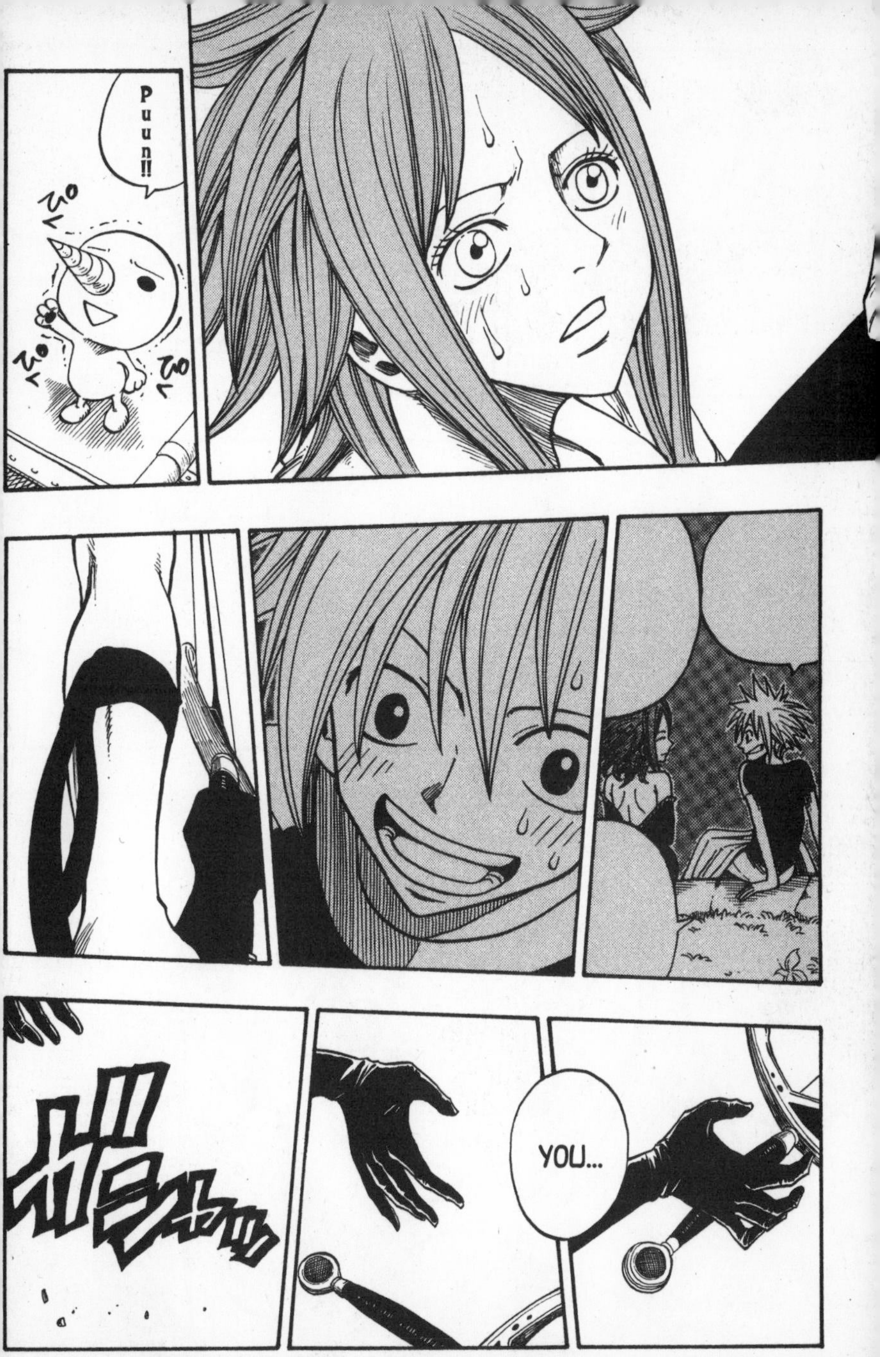
Puun!!
YOU...

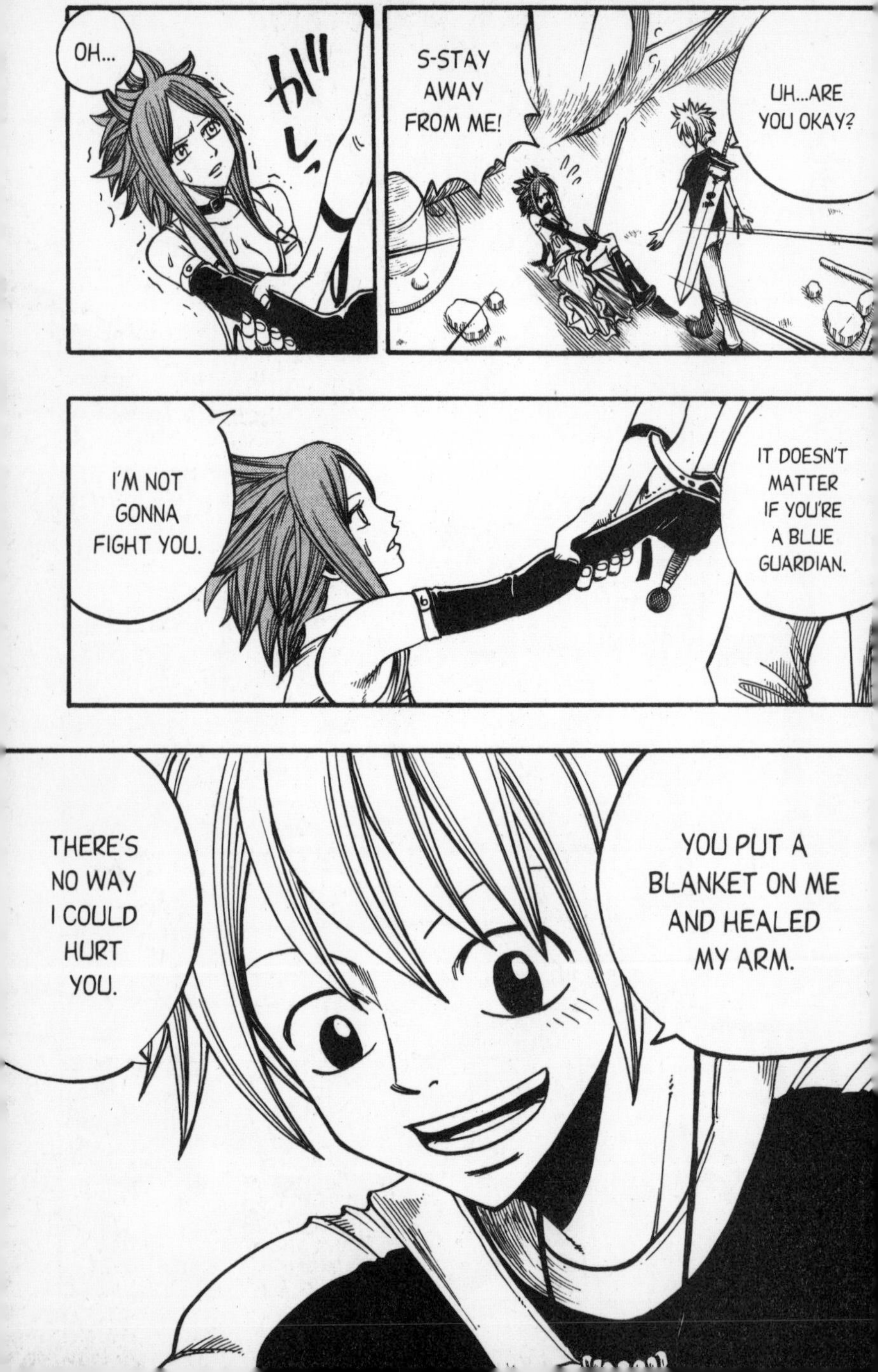
UH...ARE YOU OKAY?
S-STAY AWAY FROM ME!
OH...
IT DOESN'T MATTER IF YOU'RE A BLUE GUARDIAN.
I'M NOT GONNA FIGHT YOU.
YOU PUT A BLANKET ON ME AND HEALED MY ARM.
THERE'S NO WAY I COULD HURT YOU.

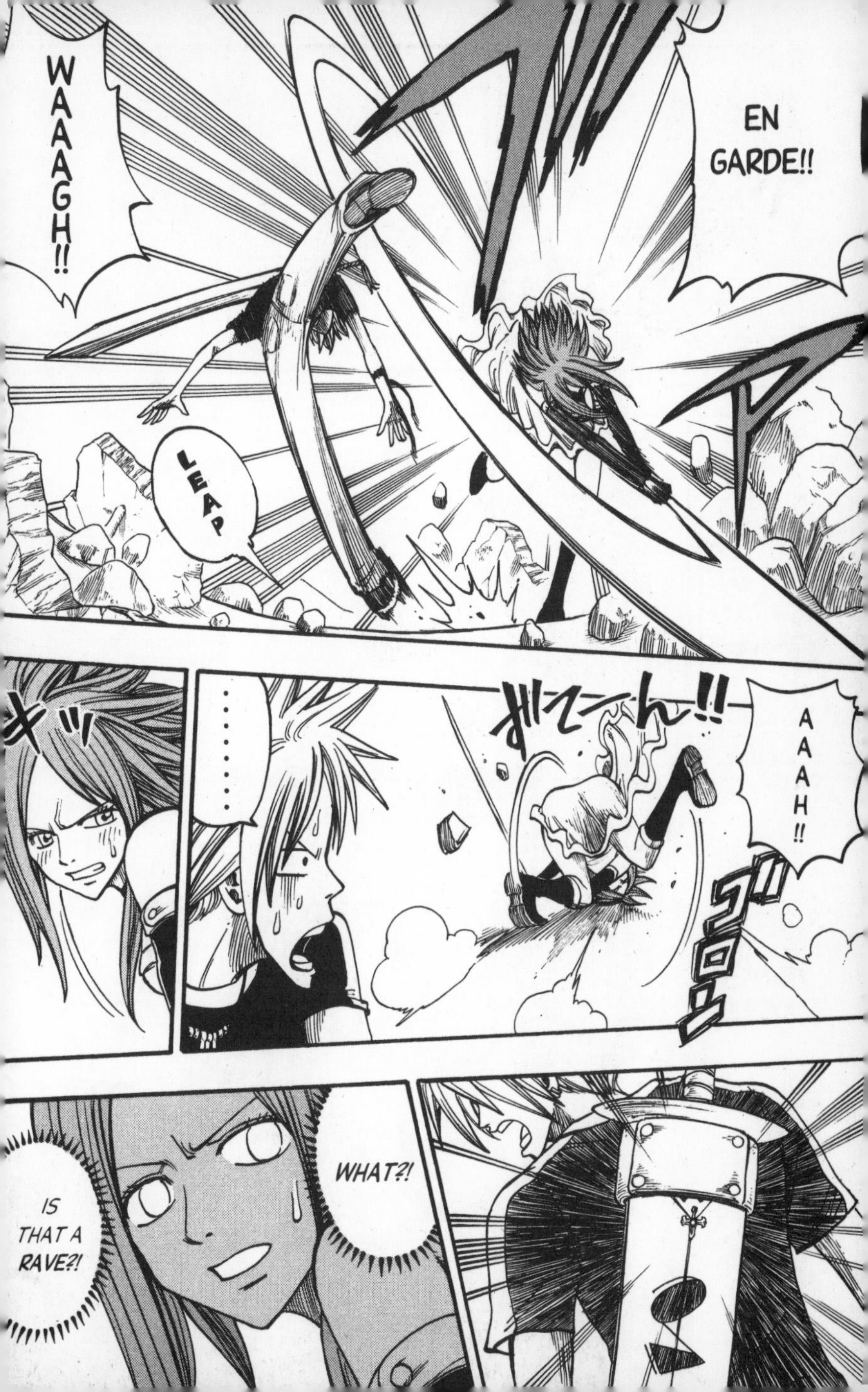

EN GARDE!!
WAAAAGH!!
LEAP
AAAAH!!
......
WHAT?!
IS THAT A RAVE?!

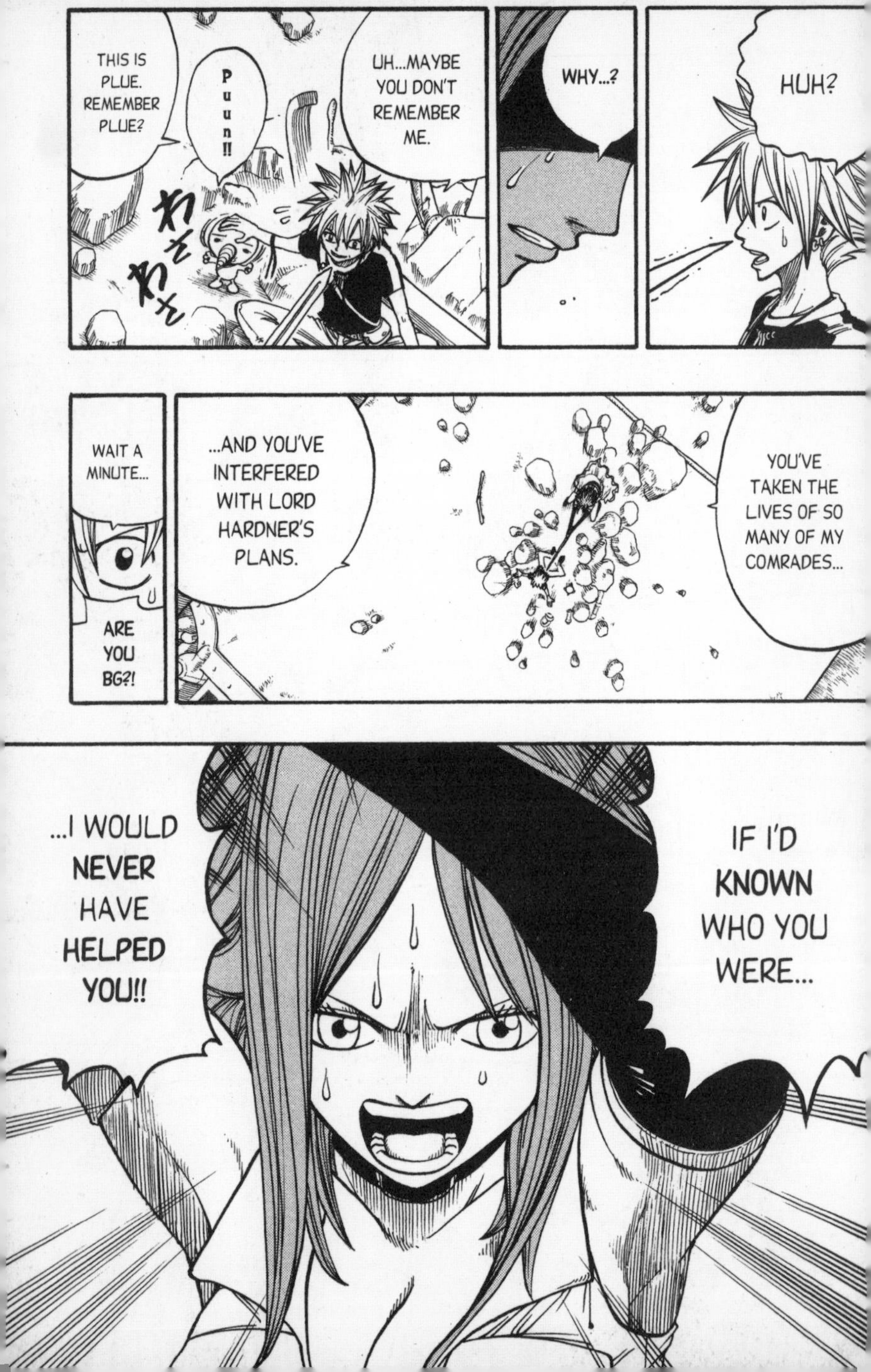
HUH?
WHY...?
UH...MAYBE YOU DON'T REMEMBER ME.
Puun!!
THIS IS PLUE. REMEMBER PLUE?
わさわさ
YOU'VE TAKEN THE LIVES OF SO MANY OF MY COMRADES...
...AND YOU'VE INTERFERED WITH LORD HARDNER'S PLANS.
WAIT A MINUTE...
ARE YOU BG?!
IF I'D KNOWN WHO YOU WERE...
...I WOULD NEVER HAVE HELPED YOU!!

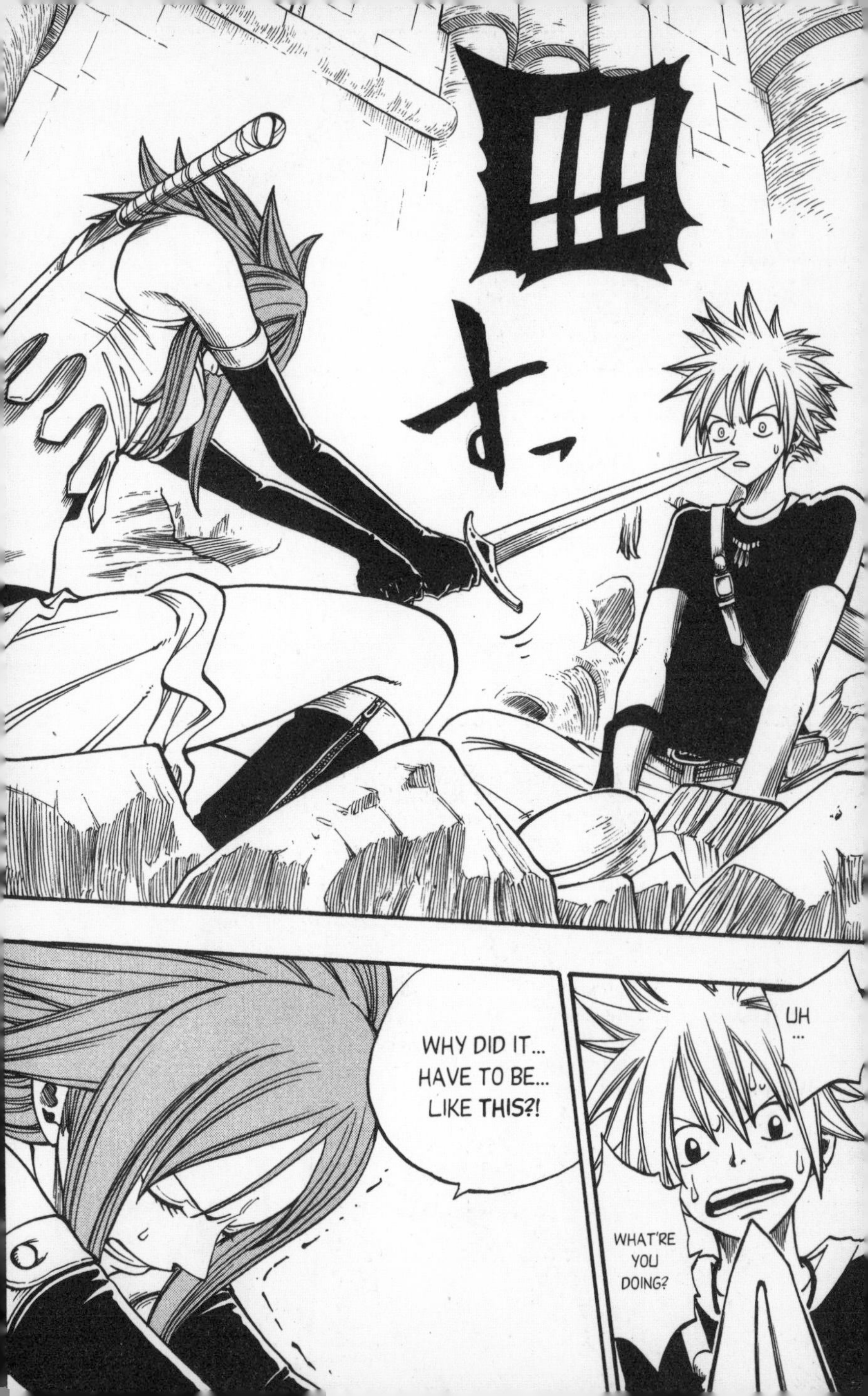
!!!
すっ
UH ...
WHAT'RE YOU DOING?
WHY DID IT... HAVE TO BE... LIKE THIS?!

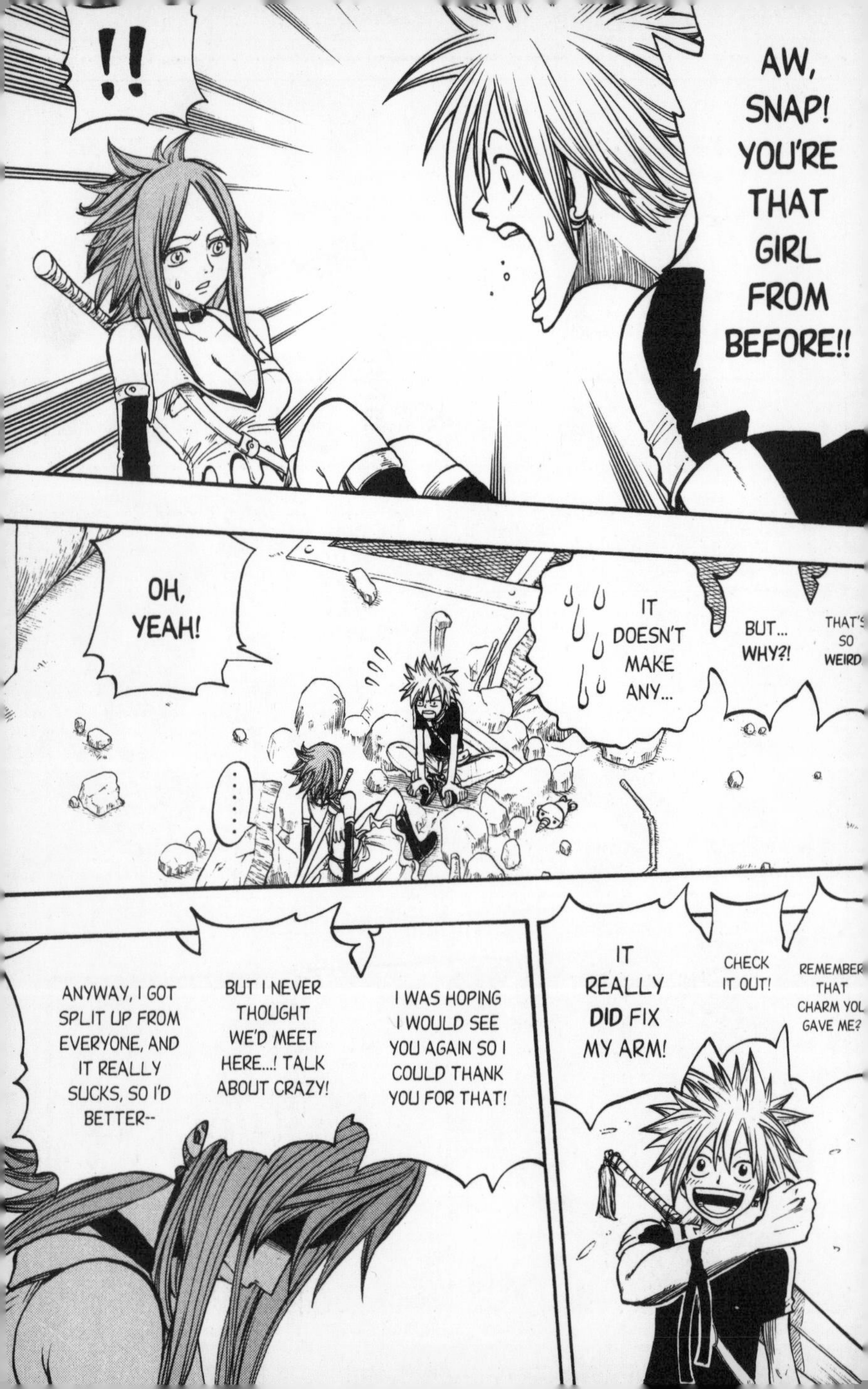
AW, SNAP! YOU'RE THAT GIRL FROM BEFORE!!
!!
THAT'S SO WEIRD
BUT... WHY?!
IT DOESN'T MAKE ANY...
OH, YEAH!
......
REMEMBER THAT CHARM YOU GAVE ME?
CHECK IT OUT!
IT REALLY DID FIX MY ARM!
I WAS HOPING I WOULD SEE YOU AGAIN SO I COULD THANK YOU FOR THAT!
BUT I NEVER THOUGHT WE'D MEET HERE...! TALK ABOUT CRAZY!
ANYWAY, I GOT SPLIT UP FROM EVERYONE, AND IT REALLY SUCKS, SO I'D BETTER--

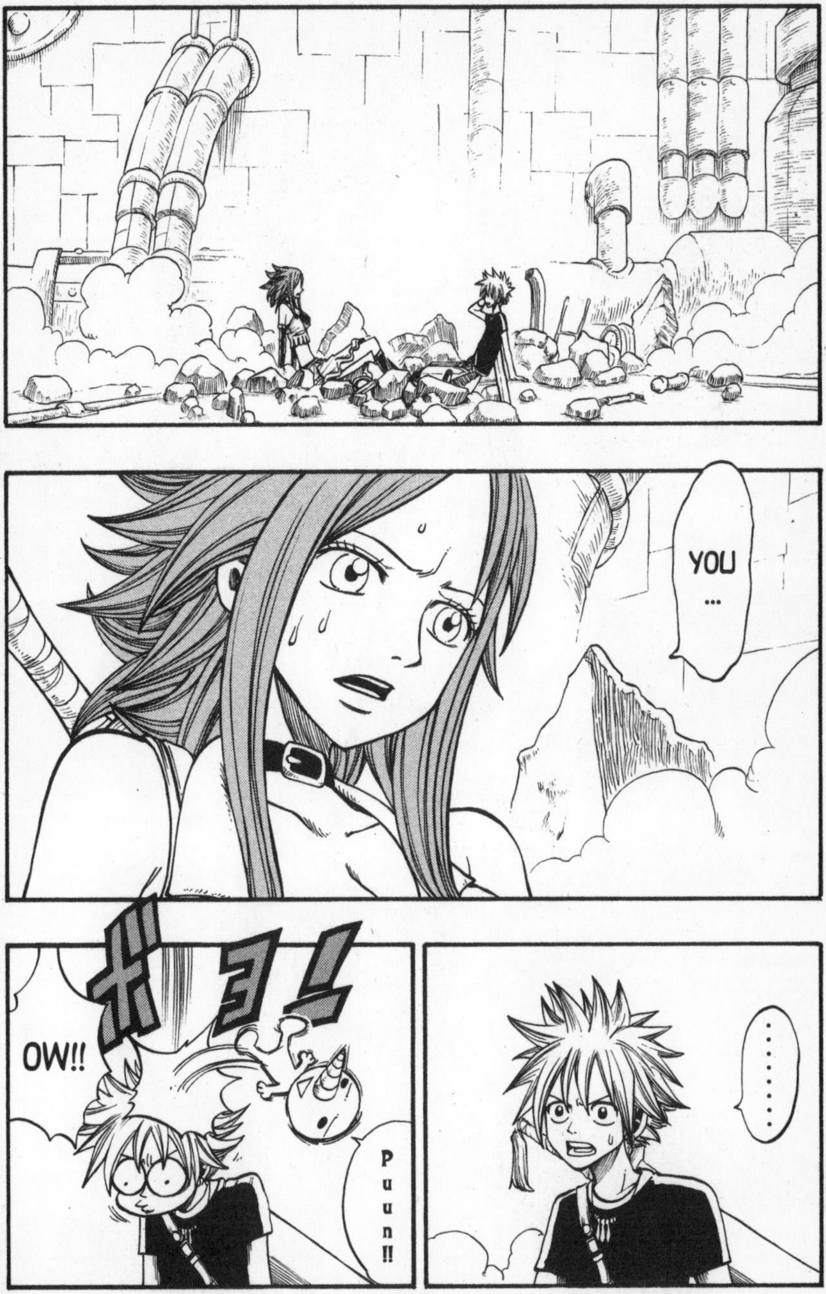
YOU ...
....
ボヨ!
OW!!
Puun!!

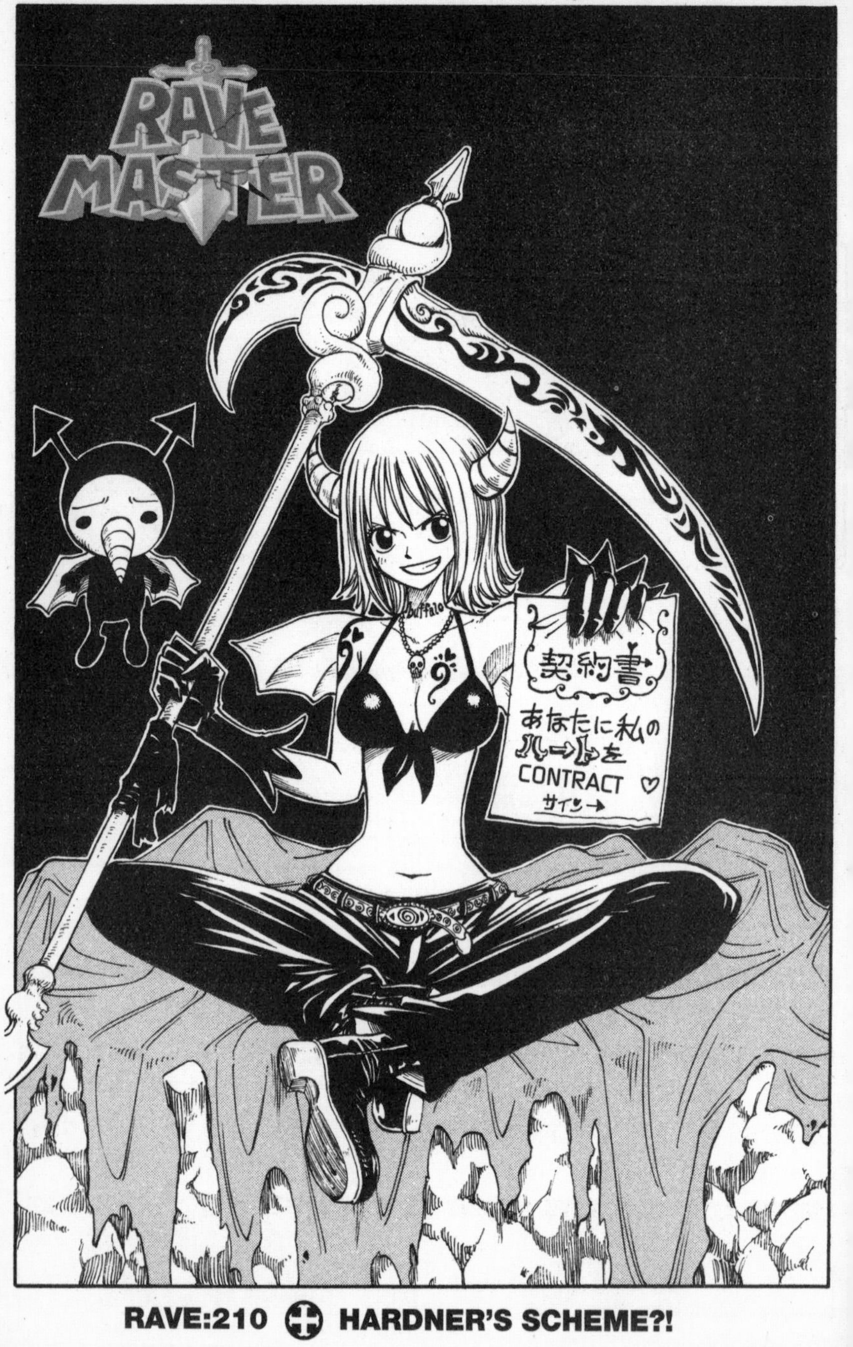
RAVE MASTER
buffalo
契約書
あなたに私の
ハートを
CONTRACT ♡
サイン→

RAVE:210 ✚ HARDNER'S SCHEME?!

I HATE... CONTENTS?

RAVE 26 CONTENTS

THE RAVE MASTER CREW

HARU GLORY

A small-town boy turned savior of the world. As the **Rave Master** (the only one capable of using the holy weapon RAVE), Haru set forth to find the missing Rave Stones and defeat Demon Card. He fights with the **Ten Powers Sword,** a weapon that takes on different forms at his command. With Demon Card seemingly out of the way, Haru now seeks the remaining two Rave Stones in order to open the way to Star Memory.

ELIE

The girl without memories. Elie joined Haru on his quest when he promised to help her find out about her past. She's cute, spunky and loves gambling and shopping in equal measures. Locked inside of her is the power of **Etherion.**

RUBY

A "penguin-type" senteniod, Ruby loves rare and unusual items. After Haru saved him from Pumpkin Doryu's gang, Ruby agreed to sponsor Haru's team in their search for the ultimate rare treasures: the Rave Stones!

GRIFFON KATO (GRIFF)

Griff is a loyal friend, even if he is a bit of a coward. His rubbery body can stretch and change shape as needed. Griff's two greatest pleasures in life are mapmaking and peeping on Elie.

MUSICA

A **"Silverclaimer"** (an alchemist who can shape silver at will) and a former street punk who made good. He joined Haru for the adventure, but now that Demon Card is defeated, does he have any reason to stick around?

LET

A member of the Dragon race, he was formerly a member of the Demon Card's Five Palace Guardians. He was so impressed by Haru's fighting skills and pureness of heart that he made a truce with the Rave Master.

PLUE

The **Rave Bearer,** Plue is the faithful companion to the Rave Master. In addition to being Haru's guide, Plue also has powers of his own. When he's not getting Haru into or out of trouble, Plue can be found enjoying a sucker, his favorite treat.

THE ORACION SIX

Demon Card's six generals. Haru defeated Shuda after finding the Rave of Wisdom. The other five generals were presumed dead after King destroyed Demon Card Headquarters.

THE STORY SO FAR...

Haru's battle against **BG** yields shocking results as he discovers his metallic foe is none other than **Branch.** After Branch is destroyed via a bomb planted inside him, Haru confronts Koala. But even though he is defeated, Koala still manages to steal **Elie's** Time-Space Staff. While the gang rests and heals, BG's pure-hearted but deluded Etherion user, **Belnika**, befriends Haru. Neither realizes who the other is, and Belnika helps to heal Haru's injuries. But later, when the gang launches an attack on a BG battleship, Haru and Belinka meet once more...only this time as enemies.

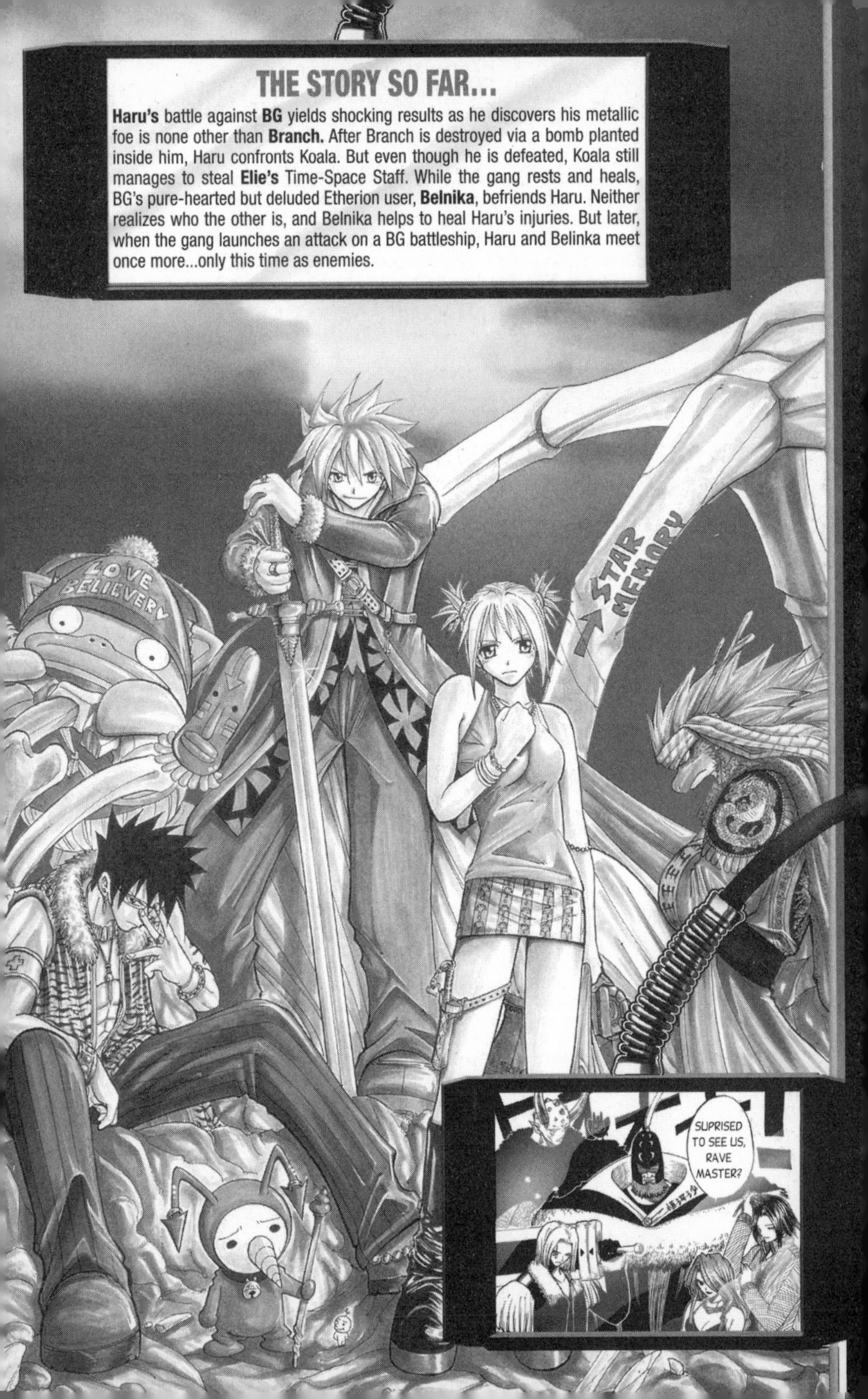

LOVE BELIEVER
STAR MEMORY
SUPRISED TO SEE US, RAVE MASTER?

VOLUME 26

Story and Art by

HIRO MASHIMA

HAMBURG // LONDON // LOS ANGELES // TOKYO

Rave Master Volume 26

Created by Hiro Mashima

Translation - Jeremiah Bourque
English Adaptation - Lianne Sentar
Copy Editor - Nikhil Burman
Retouch and Lettering - Star Print Brokers
Production Artist - Jessica Yurasek
Graphic Designer - Al-Insan Lashley

Editor - Troy Lewter
Digital Imaging Manager - Chris Buford
Pre-Production Supervisor - Erika Terriquez
Production Manager - Elisabeth Brizzi
Managing Editor - Vy Nguyen
Creative Director - Anne Marie Horne
Editor-in-Chief - Rob Tokar
Publisher - Mike Kiley
President and C.O.O. - John Parker
C.E.O. and Chief Creative Officer - Stuart Levy

A TOKYOPOP® Manga

TOKYOPOP and [logo] are trademarks or registered trademarks of TOKYOPOP Inc.

TOKYOPOP Inc.
5900 Wilshire Blvd. Suite 2000
Los Angeles, CA 90036

E-mail: info@TOKYOPOP.com
Come visit us online at www.TOKYOPOP.com

© 2004 Hiro Mashima. All Rights Reserved.
First published in Japan in 2004 by Kodansha Ltd., Tokyo
English publication rights arranged through Kodansha Ltd.

All rights reserved. No portion of this book may be reproduced or transmitted in any form or by any means without written permission from the copyright holders. This manga is a work of fiction. Any resemblance to actual events or locales or persons, living or dead, is entirely coincidental.

ISBN: 978-1-59532-630-0

First TOKYOPOP printing: December 2007

10 9 8 7 6 5 4 3 2 1

Printed in the USA

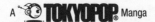

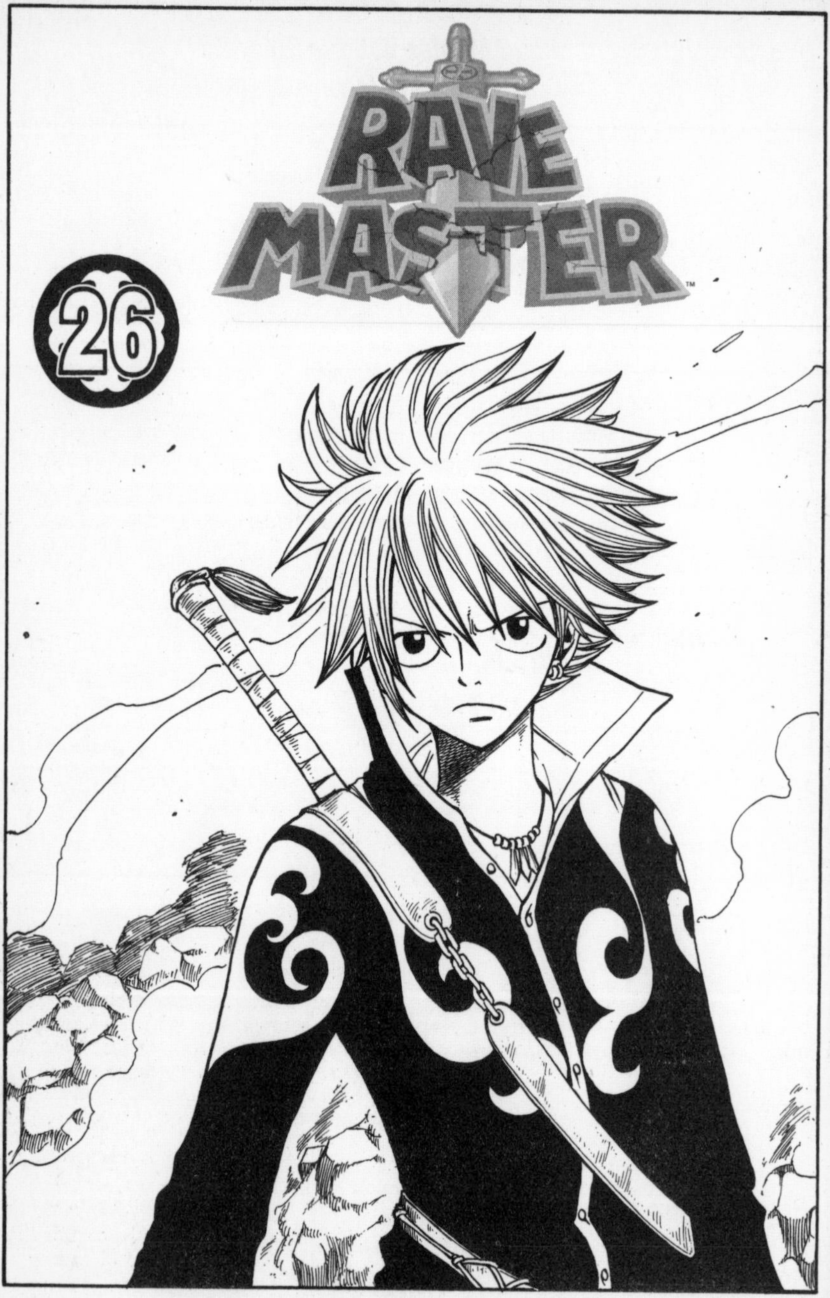
RAVE MASTER™
26

ましま
真島ヒロ